6/17/2000

To Barry and Arlene!
God Bless you as you rea

Benny Berquist
and
for
Berk

Posthumorously,
Berk

Maurice "Berk" Berquist

August 8, 1922 – February 8, 1993

Posthumorously, Berk

Life Story of a Man on Mission

Berny Berquist
a n d
Maxine McCall

C & M
ResourceS
Drexel, North Carolina

For Marty and Lori

Posthumorously, Berk
Copyright © 2000 by C & M Resources

Published by C & M Resources, Drexel, North Carolina 28619-0487

Book design by Maxine McCall

Printing by JostensGraphics, Charlotte, North Carolina, USA
        A Division of Jostens ®

Cover photograph by M.O. Braswell
        Berk on the Sea of Galilee, January, 1986.

Library of Congress Catalog Card Number: 97-77316

ISBN 1-891478-00-1

Contents

Foreword 5
Acknowledgements 6
Introduction   7

 1 Topeka 8

 2 Anderson College 24

 3 Early Ministry 32

 4 Berny 58

 5 California 80

 6 Daytona 92

 7 World Travels 128

 8 CBH 142

 9 Washington 156

10 Wichita 164

11 India 174

12 Requiem 182

A Berquist Sampler 204

Foreword

Maurice Berquist was an extraordinary man with a remarkable ministry. Millions around the world loved him for his caring heart and captivating sermons. His preaching had a powerful effect because he spent a lifetime probing the Bible, cover to cover, and perfecting his ability to preach the Word in a simple and engaging way, so that ordinary people could understand and, as a result, find from God the help they needed.

Countless people have been able to recall entire Berquist sermons twenty-five or thirty years later. And virtually everyone who heard him has remembered in detail some story Berk told and the point that went with it. At preaching, he was undeniably one of the best! His style was unique – disarming in its simplicity and humor, profound in its depth.

Preaching was his passion, his life.

Berk's life is the story of a boy, and then a man, sold out to God. When Maurice Berquist, as a senior in high school, answered God's call to preach, that call became his singular mission in life; everything else was secondary. Like the North Star, he never wavered from that mission; and, characteristically, he was on mission when God called him home.

We hope these pages will be a source of continued inspiration – a joyous reminder of this wonderful man whom Doug and Laura Lee Oldham once dubbed "an art treasure in the Kingdom of God."

Berny Berquist and Maxine McCall

Acknowledgements

We are indebted to many persons who have graciously shared memories, materials, and photographs. The book has been enriched by every contribution received. In addition, we extend special recognition to these, whose help was more extensive and invaluable for sections of the work listed here:

Topeka: Chester Edwards, Virginia Stage Chappell, Sada Kinch Scheibe, Wilma Reeder Hurst, and Bill Reeder. **Anderson College:** Robert and Dorothy Nicholson, Milton Buettner, Arthur Eikamp. **Early Ministry:** Milton Buettner, Arthur Eikamp, Wilbur and Evelyn Scaggs, Bob and Fran Clark, Kenneth Hall. **Daytona:** Walt and Mary Lou Sempsrott, Margie Van Ness. **CBH:** Gary Moore. **India:** Howard Baker. **Requiem:** Ray Cotton, Gerald Marvel, Jim Lyon, Howard Baker, David Boots, Helen Clarke (transcript of eulogy). **A Berquist Sampler:** Eldon Williams, Nancy Rohr, Walton Hooter. **Art work:** Saul Chaftez (posthumously), Dick Maloney, and Barry Sempsrott.

To Edna McCall we owe thanks beyond measure for countless hours of transcribing audio and video tapes of sermons and typing hundreds of pages of material from Berk's journals and folders into computer files for editing. (Some fragile and faded type-written sheets were more than fifty years old; many notes and journal entries had been hand-scrawled by Berk on yellow legal pads). Her years of experience as executive secretary were invaluable, not only in transcribing materials, but also in proof-reading. This project, in fact, simply would not have been "do-able" without her help.

To Don McCall, our deepest appreciation for his capable and efficient management of the business aspects of the project, for his assistance in acquiring and setting up the desk-top publishing equipment, for shuttling material to the printing company, for managing mailings and shipment of books, for his steadfast patience and encouragement from start to finish.

Many friends gave financially to make publication of this tribute to Berk and his ministry more than a dream. We especially acknowledge the exceptional generosity of those listed below, but for all gifts – our most profound THANKS.

Patrons
Howard and Elizabeth Baker
David Grubbs
Jon and Lorna Kardatzke
Norm, Rosalie, and Kelly Riley

Benefactors
Berrien Becks, Sr.
Bill and Gloria Gaither
N. Lee Hughes
Bob and Vida Pompelly
Jim and Maxine Sanders
Jack and Royetta Weir

Contributors
James and Norene Anthony
Herbert and Sylvia Bailey
M. O. and Ida Jean Braswell
Clinton and Charlotte Brown
Paul and Virginia Chappell
Mary Couch
Harvey A. Dodson
Frank Garmon
Reid Hughes
Robert and Wilma Hurst
Linda Kress
Gerald and Rena Marvel
Joe and Mary Minkler
Gary Moore
Robert and Dorothy Nicholson
Barry and Norma Lou Richardson
Greg Sempsrott
Lewis and Thera Sigmon
Dale and Marilyn Warman

Introduction

The tilt of the head.
   The mischief in his eyes.
      The wry smile that became
         an irresistible grin.

   You knew at once it was Berk: the Kansas-born son-of-Sweden
      who reached for the stars and brought the Gospel down to earth.

   When he spoke you laughed – and sometimes you cried.

   *"There are only two moments when people are completely open,
      without pretense, without prejudice," he would often tell me,
   "when they laugh and when they cry. Open that door and then
      you can walk into their hearts with the Gospel."*

   When he spoke, you were entertained and provoked;
      you could at once be drawn into an impossible yarn and then be forced
         to face the truth.

   When he spoke you could never avoid the Word and the voice of God.
      You might resist the truth, but you could not ignore it.

   Berk's sense of humor was the mark of his great mind.
      His ability to face the world with a smile was evidence of his deep faith.

   He inspired generations;
      he touched continents;
         he was an instrument upon which the Lord played everywhere, oh-so-sweetly.

   Few men have influenced me more;
      few in the Church of God have left a more profound legacy.

   In the end, it was not his grin,
      not his stories,
         not his incomparable gift for extemporaneous preaching,
            not even his tender heart that endeared him to us –
               it was the way the living Christ lived in him.

   It was the company of Christ that he kept so well that made Maurice Berquist
      one-of-a-kind.

   To catch a glimpse of his mind was to see the mind of Christ,
      to see the world from Heaven's view.

   And for that glimpse of a lifetime, I will be forever grateful.

                  Jim Lyon,
                  Pastor, North Anderson Church of God, Anderson, IN
                  Speaker, CBH - *ViewPoint*

On the back of this photo of himself in cap and gown, Berk wrote: "Taken in back of my home in Topeka, Kansas – June 1, 1940. There were 597 in my graduating class."

1
Topeka

The air was electric in the little white frame church on the corner of Seventh and College as Junior Bergquist rose from his seat down front and stepped onto the platform to preach his first sermon.

Behind him people in dark-stained pews leaned forward or to the side for a better view and waited expectantly. They had heard him speak before. For years now he had regularly stood on Sunday nights or Wednesday nights to share a testimony, usually embellished with an interesting story. But today marked his first time to stand before them on the platform to preach.

As Junior turned to look out over the sea of expectant faces, neither posture nor countenance betrayed any feeling of anxiety. The voice was strong; the manner at ease. With energy and animation, he moved confidently about the stage as he spoke, punctuating points with strong gestures and vocal emphasis. He held young and old in rapt attention.

One person present would years later describe the event as simply "amazing!"

Junior Bergquist was eleven years old.

The Boy Preacher

After that, folks around the neighborhood called him "the boy preacher," but little did they realize the far-reaching influence this blond-headed son of Swedish immigrants would have over the next fifty-nine years upon places and lives far distant from Topeka, Kansas.

Neither could they imagine that Topeka would be the only place in the world where he would be known as "Junior" Bergquist.

He was born Mathew Maurice Bergquist, Jr. But early in his career as preacher and world evangelist, persons unfamiliar with Swedish spelling would, more often than not, drop the "g" in Bergquist when using his name in printed programs or newspaper articles. And in conversation the difficult-to-pronounce last name was affectionately shortened to "Berk." The young preacher was not offended by these adaptations and, eventually, adopted them himself. Thus, he became known world-wide as Maurice "Berk" Berquist.

Berk always said that his mother wanted him to be a preacher, for she named him after two of them – Matthew the Gospel writer and his father, Mathew Maurice, Sr. By trade, Berk's father was a brakeman for the Atcheson, Topeka, and Santa Fe Railroad. But he also served as a lay preacher for the Church of God in Topeka, where he and his family were faithful attenders.

The Bergquist family, including four-year-old Junior, came as visitors to the church on the corner of Seventh and College on June 19, 1927. Celebrating what today might be called a "Super Sunday," the congregation was bidding a sad farewell to their second pastor, the Rev. L.E. Neal, and his family, while simultaneously welcoming to the pastorate the Rev. B.C.C. Fansler, with his wife and daughter. Pastor Neal, much loved by the congregation, had led them in erecting their new church building, an almost miraculous accomplishment on the eve of the Depression. Before the Neals came, the newly organized church, led by Rev. Irwin L. Sadler, had met in a basement at Eighth and College.

First Church of God in Topeka, Kansas
Church of Berk's childhood

From their home just one block east of the church, the Bergquist family had daily passed by the construction project. Curiosity, as much as anything, sparked their acceptance of an invitation to the special service.

Mathew Bergquist came from Swedish Baptist stock. But that day he found himself instantly captivated by the Church of God message of unity. Later he said of the experience: "The first time I came into the Church of God, I was a Baptist. But when I went out, I was a member of the Church of God!"

From that day, he and his family became enthusiastic participants in the life of the Topeka congregation.

Topeka congregation, 1922. **(From left by number)** *(1) Chester Edwards, Berk's mentor; (2) Berk's mother, Ellen Bergquist, holding baby Paul; sisters (3) Catherine and (4) Helen; (5) brother Carl;* **(6) Berk, seven years old;** *(7) his father, Mathew Bergquist; (8) Josephine Dawson, Berk's Sunday school teacher; (9) Rev. I.K. Dawson, pastor.*

Family Background

Born September 21, 1886, in Linchoping, Sweden, the senior Bergquist had come to the United States in 1903. A dozen years later, on August 10, 1915, he married his cousin, Tillie E. Johnson. They had two daughters, Catherine and Helen.

After Tillie's untimely death, he married Ellen Sophia Anderson, from Boston, Massachusetts.

Just how this widower from Kansas with two young daughters discovered a shy Swedish housemaid in Boston and persuaded her to trade comfort, even luxury, for the humble life he could offer her in Topeka is not known. With a free railroad pass, he may have visited friends in Boston who introduced them. Perhaps a mutual acquaintance wrote him about her, and their romance blossomed through letters. However they were introduced, in February of 1920, she came to Kansas as his bride.

Later Ellen would tell her children about growing up in Sweden and how her life was changed one day by a letter from the United States. A wealthy family in Boston wanted her to come work for them. Accepting their invitation meant free passage to America. It also meant, most likely, never seeing her family again. The decision was agonizing. Such opportunity might come only once in a lifetime. Her family urged her to go. So, in 1914, as a young woman of twenty-four years, she bade farewell to family and friends in Kalmar, Sweden, and sailed across the Atlantic to seek her destiny.

The picture she painted for the children of her early years in the States presented a sharp contrast to the meagerness of their life in Topeka. The Boston family lived in a fine mansion, a castle compared to the small clapboard structure that was home to the Bergquists. The children's eyes grew wide as she told how every summer in Boston they closed the Beacon Hill house and went to Nantucket. She spoke of picnics there and the fun of picking blueberries and cranberries, and making muffins. The family stayed on the island all summer, savoring the cool Atlantic breezes before returning to Boston for the winter. She described a wonderful life.

When Mathew Maurice, Jr., her first-born, arrived on August 8, 1922, Ellen's former employer in Boston, Lillie E. Seeley, sent a gift of money and good wishes.

The Bergquists' rented home at 701 Morris Avenue (later renamed Mulvane) was a modest stained house with asphalt roof and small stoops rather than porches. As the family grew – three more boys joining Berk and the two girls – the house became more and more crowded. Berk and brother Carl shared a bed set up in the living room. A large wood-and-coal-burning stove in the kitchen provided heat for cooking and doing laundry.

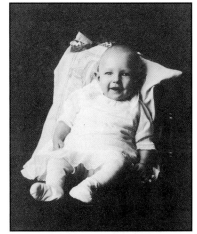

Mathew Maurice Bergquist, Jr., known in Topeka as "Junior."

Mathew Maurice Bergquist, Sr.

Persons who knew Mathew Bergquist have described him as "nice looking," with small facial features and "hair so blond it sometimes had to be touched up in pictures so it would show." He was small-boned, of medium height, with slightly stooped posture. When Berk grew to his full stature of six feet one and a half inches, his father came only to his shoulders. Apparently, Berk's bone structure, including his prominent nose, came from his mother's side of the family.

Mathew or "Father Bergquist," as he was called by many in the church family, was a hard worker with a generous heart. A kind of neighborhood handyman, he kept in a storage building behind his house a quantity of leftover lumber, plumbing and electrical supplies, and the like, to do odd jobs for himself and neighbors.

The name Bergquist means "mountain twig," more evident from its old Swedish spelling, Berg kvist: berg (mountain), kvist (twig).

Berk remembered a graciousness and courtesy his parents showed to everyone. When meeting people, his father always gave a gentlemanly bow and his mother always curtseyed.

Though mannerly and polite, Mathew Bergquist was not one to show public emotion or express affection openly to his family. He was a stoic Swede, who taught his sons that displaying emotion was a sign of weakness in men. The Bergquist boys seldom received hugs or kisses from their dad. They knew he loved them and that he worked hard for them, but their emotional support came from their mother or others outside the family who took an interest in them.

Also a firm disciplinarian, Father Bergquist held his children to a strict curfew. Sada Kinch Scheibe, once Berk's Sunday School teacher, recalls this incident:

"One night we had a young people's party, and Junior's dad rode a bike to our house about 8:45 p.m. wanting his girls taken home immediately by someone who drove a car

Mathew Bergquist
Berk's father

so they could be in bed by nine or shortly after."

He spoke English, but with a heavy Swedish accent. "J's" became "Y's" in characteristic Swedish fashion. Thus, he always addressed his oldest son as "Yunior" or "Yunie."

Virginia Stage Chappell, who as a girl attended the Topeka church with the Bergquists, remembers not only the accent, but also that Father Bergquist was a man of considerable intellect, as evidenced by his testimonies in church. Always he was ready to testify, and as he did so he preached a mini-sermon in effect, with a well-appointed story to illustrate his point. On occasion he preached from the pulpit as well.

"We church folks," Chappel goes on to say, "loved and respected him."

From all indications, Berk's first role model for the story-telling preaching style he spent a lifetime perfecting was his dad.

Ellen Sophia Bergquist

As is often true of foreign-born people in America, the Bergquists were more comfortable and fluent in their native language and used it when praying, singing, or conversing among themselves at home. Berk remembered his mother's kneeling by each child's bed at night, praying and then singing in Swedish, "Will There Be Any Stars in My Crown?"

Although she was a devout Christian, Ellen Bergquist did not often attend church services. Either she did not understand or speak English well enough to follow the services or she was extremely shy. Nevertheless, the congregation knew her to be a sincere, sweet, warm-hearted person and a gracious hostess.

Ellen Bergquist
Berk's mother

Affectionately known as "Mother Bergquist," she always had cookies, cake, or other scrumptious delicacies whenever anyone came to the Bergquist home. Her exceptional culinary skills were much touted throughout the neighborhood. A deft Swedish cook, she knew how to flavor foods with seasonings she grew herself – like mint, for instance. Everything she cooked was delicious! Even in Berk's adulthood, his favorite Swedish dishes were ones his mother had prepared so well: Swedish meatballs, cabbage rolls and brown beans, boiled potatoes and sill salad (herring and sour cream). He was also partial to one or two non-Swedish delicacies she had mastered back East: cream puffs and Boston cream pie!

Berk's family: *(L to R) His father holding David, Paul (on stool), Berk, his mother, Carl, Helen, and Catherine.*

In particular, she was known for her baking – homemade doughnuts, Swedish limpa (bread), and bulla (cinnamon rolls). Berk didn't know what it was to go to the store for bread until after his mother's death. Visitors to the Bergquist home all loved her baked goods and asked her to bake for them whenever she made bread. Thus, selling home-made loaves of bread became one way of supplementing the family's income.

Father Bergquist's job with the railroad provided scant pay with few benefits. With six children there simply was not enough to live on, no matter how frugal she was. Thus, she also took in washing and ironing, which in those days meant scrubbing clothes on a scrub board! On wash days she heated water in huge boilers on the big stove in their kitchen.

Berk had a little red wagon he used for laundry and bakery deliveries. Much as other boys might have paper routes, he had a bread and laundry route. His mother would fold the freshly ironed clothes and put them on the wagon with the rolls and other baked goods, which Berk then delivered to their customers.

Berk often said that "they were the poor people the poor people thought were poor."

Out of their poverty came a wealth of "poor stories" Berk effectively cultivated to give humor and pathos to future sermons. One noted example:

"The only time we had running water at our house when I was growing up was when somebody got in a hurry with a bucket!"

And though she never knew it, his mother planted the seeds of his ambition to traverse the globe. As Berk told it, in an effort to teach him good table manners, more than once her soft Swedish accent cajoled: "Yunie, take your elbows off the table! Only those who have traveled around the world may put elbows on the table."

Even as he complied with her wishes, Berk's young mind savored the thought of one day earning that privilege.

Early Involvement in the Church

Berk was saved during a revival meeting at the church. Chester Edwards, youth pastor at the time, remembers it well: "When they gave the plan of salvation and talked about sin, Berk said he felt that he was the worst sinner that walked the streets and that he just had to get saved. He was only seven, but God spoke to him so surely that he had to respond."

Shortly after the revival Berk overheard a conversation that later found its way into some of his sermons. Two men were talking:

"How did the meeting go over at the Church of God."

"Not much activity. Just one little kid got saved."

Surely, no one who knew Berk could ever again underestimate the significance of a child's conversion.

Berk's Sunday School teacher at that time was Josephine Dawson, the pastor's wife. She and her husband, I.K. Dawson, both had a great influence on the young convert. Berk always remembered them fondly and spoke of lessons learned from them.

After he was saved, seven-year-old "Junior" always had a testimony at church; and in a quite grown-up fashion, following his dad's example, he generally added an appropriate story for illustration.

A Lesson from Poverty

I do know who first made me think about money. My father.

On my eighth birthday someone gave me a quarter – which in those days was a great deal of money for a young man to have. After pondering where I should spend this vast amount of money, I decided to buy a bottle of Nehi orange soda.

The walk to the Sugar Bowl Restaurant in Topeka, Kansas, was a happy walk as I thought about getting this extravagant purchase. The walk home was a happy walk as I drank the soft drink, without having to share it with anyone. Finally, as I came into the yard of our home, I met my father.

"Where did you get that?" he asked.

"I got it with my birthday money. It cost a nickel."

"How do you ever expect to have anything in this world if you spend your money for foolishness?"

I owe a lot to my father. He managed to survive the Depression years and leave to me a heritage of values that even poor people could afford.

Virginia Stage Chappell remembers Berk at age seven:

My family moved to Topeka in 1929. The "Little Church with a Big Welcome" became our church home. Maurice was seven at the time. I was eleven. My sister Ruth was seven, also. Maurice's two sisters, Helen and Catherine, were about my age. We became close friends, and our friendship lasted throughout the years. Both are now deceased.

I remember that in those days we were all impressed with Maurice, astounded really by this young man who was only seven years old. During testimony times in church this little guy would stand and really "preach" a sermon. He would do this every chance they gave him. We would sit and listen in awe and amazement.

We were also impressed with his alto singing. He really sang a good alto. In fact, one could hear his alto singing above the rest of the congregation half way into the next block. Of course, in the summer the windows were wide open because air-conditioning did not exist.

From an early age, Berk loved the church. Chester Edwards, youth leader and Sunday School Superintendent, attests to that fact: "From the time he became a Christian at seven years old, Maurice was so eager that he was always early to church and late to leave. He helped open up and close. Always he was faithful to the church and participated in every way, including his turn at janitor work. We had what we called the 'Dirt Chasers League,' with a picture of the old Dutch Cleanser woman chasing dirt with a stick."

Cleaning was a challenge. The building was never finished in the basement. Edwards describes classrooms "divided by studs on which we tacked corrugated paper from cardboard boxes."

Early on, Chester Edwards saw the extraordinary potential in the Bergquist boy and took the youngster under wing. In 1932 Edwards and his wife invited Berk as a young teen to attend one of the first Church of God International Youth Conventions held outside of Anderson, Indiana. The experience was significant.

"No delegation," Edwards explains, "just the four of us, including our new baby boy. Junior was thrilled to go and did a lot of maturing."

The year after that Youth Convention, it was Edwards who prompted Junior Bergquist to step forward to preach his first sermon from the platform of the church. Sada Kinch Scheibe was in the audience:

C.L. Edwards and his wife, Verle, were pastors at the time Junior preached his first sermon when he was eleven years old. It was only a ten-or-fifteen-minute sermon . . . but we all enjoyed it, coming from a little fellow like him.

> *We were all impressed with Maurice, astounded really by this young man who was only seven years old. During testimony times in church this little guy would stand and really "preach" a sermon. He would do this every chance they gave him. We would sit and listen in awe and amazement.*
>
> – Virginia Stage Chappell

At age eleven, Berk preached his first sermon from this pulpit in Topeka, Kansas.

Lessons Learned from Tragedy

Only hushed whispers broke the stillness of the darkened bedroom. Anxious faces looked for signs of hope. The doctor removed his stethoscope and shook his head. Black bag in hand, he descended creaking stairs and paused at the front door just long enough to lay a comforting hand on the shoulder of Father Bergquist before stepping out into the cold December night.

Wearily, Bergquist closed the door and turned back into the room. The kitchen was silent. No aroma of fresh bread baking wafted through the house. His shoulders bent more than usual, he climbed the stairs to where the children were waiting. It would be a long night.

When Berk was twelve, the unthinkable happened. Ellen Anderson Bergquist died of pneumonia at age forty-four.

The family was devastated. None, perhaps, more than Berk. Her death had a profound impact on his life – and his ministry. Questions that plagued him as a child regarding the tragic circumstances of her death later triggered his passion to learn more of what the Bible says about healing. Divine healing became one of his most enduring preaching themes. In 1982, in a book entitled *When You Seek Healing*, he wrote about his mother's death and its effect on him:

While I had been raised in a Christian family and attended every single service our little evangelical church had, I cannot remember hearing about healing as a part of the church's ministry.

When I was twelve years old my mother died of pneumonia.

While she was sick, friends came to bring hot soup and sympathy. Dr. Harrison came with his little black bag of medicines and talked somberly to my father.

I do not remember anyone talking to me about the possibility of God's healing my mother.

After a few days of illness, she died and left behind her six children and a sorrowing husband. Why?

When the funeral services were finished and the long black Pierce-Arrow of Penwell Mortuary returned our family to our little wooden house, I remember my father going to the library table in the middle of the front room, and then picking up the black Swedish Bible. He opened it to the front fly-leaf and began to write.

To write in English was not easy for my Swedish immigrant father. He wrote slowly, almost painfully. Then he blew on the page to dry the ink and closed the book. He walked away. He walked down the creaking back stairs and out into the yard to be alone with his thoughts.

What thoughts?

It was a long time before I could summon courage to look in the Swedish Bible to see what my father had written in this moment of sorrow. Finally I did. The angular black writing was hard to read. But it was impossible to forget:

> *To Ellen —*
> *The one we loved is gone.*
> *The voice we loved is stilled.*
> *Her place remaineth vacant.*
> *It never shall be filled.*

I closed the worn leather book and asked simply, "Why?"

Death I do not question. It is the other side of the coin of life. But sickness . . . sickness makes me think.

I am forced to think about healing.

In another book, *When You Lose a Loved One (1983)*, Berk wrote again of the pain of losing his Mother:

When my mother died, I was twelve; and so, I imagine I was in the sixth grade. As I look back on the experience I try to remember how I felt, how I understood the lessons of sorrow. The following lines give me the freedom to tell the story:

The Vacant Place

The day was bright with winter sun
As cold as it was bright,
But the day was like no other day,
Nor the night like any night.

Hour on hour the gusty wind
Had rattled window panes,
It whistled sadly through the trees
Its melancholy strains.

I hear it now, I heard it then,
The voice of childhood past
Reminding me, reminding me
That sorrow cannot last.

For sorrow came on stealthy feet
Like the first faint light of day,
On that bleak December night
My mother passed away.

Yes, sorrow comes to everyone
Unwelcome and unsought,
The rich, the poor, the young, the old
In sorrow's school are taught.

Long years have passed as years will do
Since I heard that numbing word,
A neighbor kind relayed the news,
"Your mother's with the Lord."

She's with the Lord," this cannot be
We need her, oh, so much,
How much we children, six in all,
Long for a mother's touch.

I heard the words, "Your mother's gone"
I heard as in a dream,
For dreams like darkness vanish
At the dawning's early gleam.

But day by day I came to know
The truth that sorrow brings,
I missed my mother, hour by hour
Remembering certain things.

The heavenly smell of new baked bread
The clothes hung out to dry,
The songs she sang around the house,
The Swedish lullaby.

The creaking of the wooden stairs,
As late she came to bed,
The well-worn Swedish Bible,
My mother nightly read.

A thousand memories flood my mind,
Of years that used to be,
A thousand lessons I have learned,
Since sorrow walked with me.

Ellen's illness stemmed from a lung infection caused by hanging wet clothes to dry in the house during winter time. "Labor pneumonia," the coroner's report said. Berk always believed his mother worked herself to death. She died on December 16, 1934, a date Berk would mark every year thereafter.

Christmas was awkward that year. The only gift the children each received was a bag of treats the Church gave out: a small paper sack of hard candy and an orange. Their father had nothing to give them. The kitchen, once a haven of hugs and warm spicy smells, was empty and cold. And little was done to celebrate Christmases after that, even after Ethel came into their lives.

A Childhood Memory

On a vacant lot next to their house in Topeka, the neighborhood children would gather to play ball – football, volleyball, dodge ball – whatever game they could play with whatever ball anyone had. Usually baseball.

As the afternoon waned, one by one each child would be called in for supper or to do chores. And always when the names were called, the children would beg to stay a little longer, depending on where they were in the game – at third base, next up to bat, one more inning, and so on.

The spring after his mother's death, Berk was playing with all the other children in the vacant lot. As shadows lengthened, one by one the children were called home – until finally only he was left, standing all alone on the ball field.

In that moment, a sudden wave of sadness washed over him. In later sermons he told the story. Never before had he felt such an overwhelming sense of grief, because he had been taught that "big boys don't cry."

All the children had been called – all but him.

16

Since his mother's death, his father let him come in whenever he wanted. And when he did go home, no tantalizing aroma of fresh baked bread or donuts awaited him. On the table for supper would be pork and beans or salmon cakes – whatever the sisters could open a can to serve.

Standing alone in the field holding onto his homemade oil-cloth glove, Junior Bergquist suddenly realized that no one had called him home – and never would again.

A smothering anguish enveloped him as the enormity of his loss loomed before him. Never again would his mother call him home.

"O God," he prayed, "if my mother could just come back one more time and call for me – if I could just hear her voice calling, 'Yunie,'– how fast I would run to go home."

Ethel Swanson

Mathew Bergquist was left with six children: four boys by Berk's mother – Berk (12), Carl (9), Paul (6), John David (3) – and two daughters, Catherine and Helen, by his first wife. The girls, five and seven years older, helped raise the boys and also helped out financially by getting jobs as housemaids.

After Ellen's death, Mathew told in church of praying for a new Swedish wife and how the Lord answered his prayer by sending Ethel Swanson, a piano teacher from Chanute. He married her in December of 1935.

Ethel came from a Nazarene background, but she affiliated herself with the Topeka church. Virginia Chappel recalls her dedication to the church and to her new family:

Berk (left), with brother Carl and Papa Bergquist, about the time of his mother's death.

Not only did she take up the duties of being mother to her six new children, but she started teaching a Sunday School class at our church. She was also an excellent pianist and played for the church for many years.

Though loving and talented in many ways, Ethel did not have the culinary gifts of Berk's mother. He once commented that Ethel's cooking tasted like "sticking your tongue out the window."

Becoming a Church Leader

After his mother's death, Berk threw himself even more fully into the life of the church. Chester and Verle Edwards and members of the Youth group became like an extended family and helped fill the aching void left by the loss of his mother.

A roster of officers and committees elected by the Topeka church on January 3, 1936, shows thirteen-year-old Junior Bergquist as Vice-President. Church stationery of that vintage also lists Junior Bergquist as youth leader.

In Sunday School that same year Berk started teaching the youth, ages twelve to eighteen. Class members rated him as an exceptionally good teacher, involving class members in lively discussions.

Also in 1936 Geraldine Hurst (later married to Robert Reardon, future President of Anderson College) held a revival at the church. She was an acclaimed "child evangelist," but when she came to Topeka, Geraldine was the same age as some members of the youth group, eighteen. After church each evening, some of the young people rode the church "bus" with Chester Edwards to take people home. Actually the "bus" was a home-made trailer that Chester pulled behind his car to transport people to and from church. With sides built up on a trailer bed and topped by a slanted roof and a small belfry, the contraption looked like a small church. Inside the trailer, passengers sat on benches attached along each side. Afterwards, Geraldine declared the trailer "very rickety and perhaps unsafe," but it made for a memorable ride!

As Virginia Chappell remembers it:

Maurice, Chester, and Geraldine were hilarious, trying to out do each other in jokes and using "big words." Maurice had taken all the Latin courses he could at his young age, so he knew lots of "big words" and could use them correctly in sentences.

Berk always attributed to Chester Edwards his initial fascination with words, saying that it was Edwards who introduced him to gems like *halloalphacabilitudinitodamus.* One of the first to sense the boy's keen intellect, Edwards was both a spiritual and intellectual mentor.

Berk once said of Chester and Verle Edwards, that they helped him "to look at life with creative humor and enthusiasm."

On September 11, 1936 the youth group staged Walter Ben Hare's *"An Old-Fashioned Mother."* This elaborate dramatic production, housed in a large tent erected behind the church, involved all twelve members of the youth group and some young married couples. The lead roles of the wayward son and his mother were played by Pastor David Lighty and his wife, Alta Mae. But from all accounts, the scene stealer was "Jerry Gosling, a comical country boy," hilariously portrayed by Junior Bergquist. As cast members recall, his being tall and lanky made him look the part, and that in itself was funny. But his line delivery was a riot! At age fourteen, his voice was changing; and every time he spoke, it cracked at the all the right places. Natural-born talent!

*In 1936 Berk "stole the show" in the church's production of **"An Old Fashioned Mother"** with his rib-tickling rendering of country boy Jerry Gosling.* **Cast: (L to R)** *Dorothy McFerren, Winston Johnson, Ellen Kinch, Homer Kinch, Earl Martindale,* **Junior Bergquist,** *Chester Edwards, Helen Bergquist, Rev. David Lighty, Alta Mae Lighty (seated), Catherine Bergquist, Ruth Stage, Genevieve Martindale, Audry Snook, Juanita Snook, Sada Kinch, Virginia Stage, Alberta Shaner, Beth Lighty (little girl), Dorothy Shaner, Verle Edwards, Bessie Adsit, Hurshel Adsit.*

Partial cast of "An Old Fashioned Mother":
(L to R) **Junior Bergquist**, *Alberta Shaner,*
Dorothy McFerren, Catherine Bergquist,
Ruth Stage, Virginia Stage.

After a week's run in September, the cast gave a reprise performance October 16 at Loman Methodist Church for their Fiftieth Anniversary celebration.

Old church bulletins reveal Berk's involvement in other church events. For instance, on December 19, 1937, Junior Bergquist was the "Prophet" in *Come Ye Unto Bethlehem,* a Sunday night Christmas pageant." An advertisement inviting the community to *Revival: Different* shows Maurice Bergquist, Jr. preaching on Friday, March 31, 1939, as part of a two-week revival series at the church. His father, listed as M.M. Bergquist, Sr., preached in that same revival on Wednesday, April 5.

Acting, preaching, teaching, leading as an elected officer of the church and youth president, janitor – from seven years old to the day he died, Maurice Berquist was totally devoted to God and immersed in the church. And all his life, wherever he was, being in church was important. Come Sunday morning, Sunday night, Wednesday night – Berk expected to be "in church."

From all indications, the little church in Topeka was fertile training ground for future leaders. Virginia Chappell paid tribute to those who made it so:

> Under the leadership of Pastor David C. Lighty and his wife, Alta Mae, we youth had to take our turn at directing youth meetings and leading prayer meetings. We learned to do our part fearlessly. Under the leadership of our pastor, Youth sponsor Chester Edwards, and Youth president, Maurice Bergquist, Jr., we received the training that helped us in later years to be church workers. Our little church with only a dozen youth did produce many devout church workers and Anderson College students.

Education

A scrawny kid, Berk described himself as "a rag of bone and a hank of hair." His clothes, though worn, were impeccably neat and clean; but his pants and shirts always looked too small because he grew so fast. One ear stuck out from his head more than the other, and his nose was of generous proportions. But he never worried about his looks. He had a good self-image because of his intellect. Always a diligent student, he made excellent grades.

He went to Clay Elementary, Roosevelt Junior High, and graduated from Topeka High School. He was valedictorian of his graduating class of 597.

His brothers and close friends called him "Doc," a name Berk chose, but not because he considered himself smart. Among his friends were Marne Coats, Hurshel Adsit, Leslie Shaner, and Bill Reeder. Bill recalls his friendship with "Doc":

> My twin sister, Wilma Hurst, and I joined the First Church of God in Topeka, Kansas, in our junior year of high school in 1939. Meeting Maurice was a pleasant experience from the first day. He was easy to talk with and always had a ready smile.

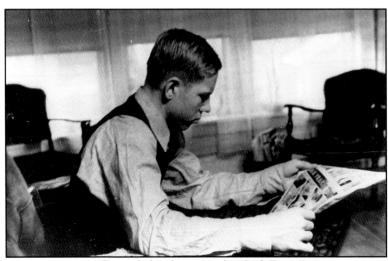

Even scholars have time for "Dick Tracy."

19

He and I spent many hours talking about Bible verses and how they applied to our everyday lives. I remember sitting with him on his front porch one summer morning when his step-mother brought out some biscuits she had just made. She encouraged us to exchange information about the Bible and anything else that seemed important at the time.

We had code names for one another, and the one Maurice picked for himself was "Doc," because of his keen interest in the doctrines of the church. He felt that doctrine was the most important thing in his life.

Maurice, it seemed to me, had adopted as his slogan, "For me to live is Christ." He was always focused on that quote.

Berk (left) with friends from the Topeka youth group. (From left, next to Berk) Bill Reeder and his twin sister, Wilma (who later married Bob Hurst, brother of Geraldine Hurst Reardon). (Far right) Virginia Stage (now Chappell). Others unidentified.

When his mother died, Berk lost his greatest fan; and he missed her for the rest of his life. His father, overburdened by work and not given to praise or sentiment, demonstrated little interest in "Yunior's" accomplishments in school.

But Berk's intellectual promise did not go unnoted by his teachers. One teacher, for instance, insisted that he learn how to type.

"I didn't want to," Berk said, "but she said someday people might want to read what I wrote and unless it was typed they couldn't."

Anyone who has tried to read one of Berk's hand-scrawled letters can appreciate Mrs. Fuller.

Perhaps it was the same Mrs. Fuller, or another teacher, who was grooming Berk for a career in law because of his eloquence as a speaker. He was on the debate team and showed all the makings of a good lawyer. Law, in fact, had been his choice of career since junior high school. But in his senior year, another call beckoned.

Scholarship offers came from Yale and Harvard. The teacher was elated and pressed him to accept one of those opportunities to study law. When he told her he was not going to accept either of those scholarships – was not, in fact, going to be a lawyer, but was going to a small church college with very little funds to study to be a preacher – she was furious.

"No! . . . No! You can't do that!," she screamed at him, her words punctuated by the sharp snap of her pencil on the wall across the room.

Berk was valedictorian of the Class of 1940 at Topeka High School.

20

"We have worked so hard, Junior, to get you those scholarships. You cannot pass up this opportunity to go to one of the nation's most prestigious schools and prepare yourself to become somebody. You have a brilliant mind. You have so much to offer. How can you throw it all away to go to some no-name, unaccredited church school in the mid-west to become a . . . a common preacher? You're a fool . . . an absolute fool!"

Though stunned by her rage, Berk understood the depth of her disappointment. She knew he was poor and had many strikes against him. She had been his greatest advocate, cheering him on in all his high school accomplishments, giving him the encouragement his mother was not there to give. She was livid with anger because her "golden boy" was passing up this once-in-a-lifetime opportunity to become "somebody," a person of influence and power, choosing instead to become just an ordinary preacher.

"I'm sorry to let you down," Berk said to her, "but please try to understand. God has called me to preach. I cannot say 'No' to Him."

> *Maurice, it seemed to me, had adopted the slogan, "For me to live is Christ." He was always focused on that quote.*
> **– Bill Reeder**

Wearing the second-hand suit his father bought for him at the goodwill store for graduation, Berk walked to his commencement exercises. His father came later on the bicycle.

At 7:00 p.m. a huge crowd was gathered in Moore Bowl at Washburn College when the seniors marched in between rows of junior girls forming the traditional "daisy chain." Berk and three other students addressed the program theme: *The American Way Is Our Way.*

*Topeka High School Commencement speakers: (L to R) John McBride, **Maurice Bergquist**, Martha Page, and Barton Bayly. Theme: "The American Way is Our Way."*

Berk's friend Bill Reeder was there:

"Doc" gave the valedictory speech at his graduation day festivities on June 1, 1940. That same month the German army took over Paris from the Allies. It was a somber time for everyone, but that speech gave us all a hope for better days ahead.

After the ceremonies, Berk walked outside and found his father. Mathew Bergquist put his arm around his son's shoulders and said, "Not bad, Yunie, Not bad."

No other family member was there.

At seventeen, with $65.00 in his pocket, Berk left Topeka to go to college in Anderson, Indiana. With rare exceptions – the death of his father, his step-mother, a sister – he never went "home" again.

Reflections on Topeka

Berk rarely talked about his childhood. Occasional glimpses from sermons and books give only a sketchy picture of the foundational forces at work in his life in those formative years. Among his papers were found two reflective pieces he wrote about his life then. One is unfinished. Both give insight into what growing up in Topeka meant to him.

* * *

Flashback

By Maurice Berquist

It wasn't in my plans, but as I look at life I realize that many good things that happen to us are not in our plans. Sometimes God, in His wisdom, superimposes His plans on ours., although we tend to call those happenings "accidents."

The backdrop for this story was the fantastically beautiful countryside of northern California. My responsibilities of speaking and traveling had crowded my date book and my capabilities. There wasn't room for anything else. Or so I thought.

"There's a lady who would like to see you before you go back east."

My response to Pastor Judson Sealey was a typical executive evasion.

"Let me see when I can find time before my flight back."

"It would mean a lot to her for you to spend a few moments. She is one of your old Sunday School Teachers."

Now, on a scale of one to ten, Sunday School teachers rate about eleven in my book. Any Sunday School teacher. Especially mine. There must have been hundreds of times in my youth when my concern for spiritual things lay in the hands of some Sunday School teacher. I owe them all a great deal.

As Pastor Sealey observed my shifting priorities, he continued, "You remember Josephine Dawson, don't you?"

Of course, I remembered. But I didn't call her "Josephine." She was not only the teacher of the Junior Class in Topeka, Kansas, but she was also the pastor's wife. I called her – and I still call her – "Sister Dawson."

I remembered that only a few months ago her husband, I. K. Dawson, had died. I didn't need any more reasons to try to visit her, but the chance to express my concern in her time of sorrow was certainly one more good reason to change my plans.

An extra hundred miles of driving in California doesn't seem like much. The rugged grandeur of the mountains and the exhilarating clearness of the air would have made the trip worthwhile. But there was more.

The little cottage nestled among the trees and flowers. Inside was a little lady, who now must be in her late seventies – a lady who held my soul in her hands when I was seven.

It was only seconds after Pastor Sealey's knock on the door that Sister Dawson came out.

"Junior Berquist of the Busy Bees Sunday School Class," she exclaimed. "I am so glad you could come to see me."

For an hour and a half we reminisced. Faded photographs passed from hand to hand. Stories of "old times" triggered more stories of older times. Things that had for years hung undisturbed in the closet of memory were brought out into the light of our conversation.

Josephine Dawson and Berk in 1929, when Berk was seven and she was his Sunday school teacher.

"I remember how your father used to walk across the street to the parsonage and say, 'Ellen has just baked some cinnamon rolls – why don't you come over and have coffee with us." Your mother was a wonderful cook," Sister Dawson said. "Those Swedish pastries were unforgettable."

Strange, isn't it?, I thought to myself, that no one remembers the cracks in the linoleum or the cups without handles. No one seemed to care that milk had to be kept cool by hanging it down in the well. We had an ice box, of course, but no money to buy ice.

Then I said to her, "I remember when you inherited some money from somewhere and bought a new car -- a 1929 Model A Sedan. It was blue. I can almost feel the scratchy mohair of the seats against my bare legs as I got to ride with you. That was an event."

The event was made more impressive by the fact that my own family didn't have a car of any kind. My father had a bicycle. And it didn't have mohair seats.

Every now and then I would sneak a glance at my watch as we talked. There was a jet plane to catch at 10:32. Since I fly so much, the airlines and I have worked out an agreement: If I don't arrive on time, the plane can go without me. Time does not stand still . . . even for nostalgia.

As I sat there remembering the 1929 Ford, the blue one with the mohair seats, I suddenly calculated my own age. I was born in 1922. That would mean that I was seven years old. That was when I was in Sister Dawson's "Busy Bees Sunday School Class."

And that was the year I was saved.

Seven years old I was when the Dawsons pastored our church in Topeka. The night I made my decision for Christ, C.H. Featherstone preached. We were having a revival meeting. That was the night when my mind had been made ready. But who made my mind ready? Why had I thought about giving my life to the Lord? Surely this lady who gave me a star to paste on my Sunday School attendance record – she must have said something. Whatever she did, I thank God for it.

"Would you like a cup of coffee before you go," Sister Dawson asked. "I had many cups in your house a long time ago."

Would it be irreverent to say that drinking coffee out of china cups (with handles) in a little cottage in California was a sort of a Communion service? A Eucharist?

Eucharist means "a service of thanks." I was, and am, thankful for this couple. They were my pastors when I was a boy. They held my soul in their hands. And they were faithful.

Fifty years have passed since I was Junior Bergquist in the Busy Bees Sunday School Class. Fifty years from now, will someone thank God that I "held their soul in my hands and was faithful?"

The Book I Wrote in the Kansas City Airport

By Maurice Berquist

Did you ever wonder what it might be like to crawl back in the womb, and then, with your eyes open, to see what happened there to make you what you are?

I did. I did that today. This is November 19, 1975.

For anyone who is interested, I made my appearance on this planet August 8, 1922. That's 53 years and some months and days ago. The place was 701 Morris Avenue in Topeka, Kansas.

There was no primal scream or anything like that. Even though Topeka itself is well-known in the psychiatric world because of the outstanding work of the Menninger Brothers, Karl and Will, that fact has no real importance for this event.

There was no particular plan to my journey into the past. Saturday I received word of the sudden death of my sister Catherine in Topeka. Today I am in Kansas to attend her funeral.

With a green Plymouth car borrowed from Al, my brother-in-law, I drove to the place of my birth.

It is perhaps necessary to say that I am not accustomed to going back to my past. Since leaving my home town in 1940, I have returned briefly less than a half dozen times, including visits home from college.

Today I walked around the old home place.

The street is now called Mulvane. Seventh Street is still the same. My old home is gone. The house next door has been made into an apartment. The third house down seems unchanged.

I stood at the hill that sloped down beside where our house used to be. We used to roll down that hill in our home-made racer. The yellow barn is gone, of course – with nothing but memories to mark its place.

Who would ever guess that right in the middle of someone's apartment-sized living room stands the memory of a huge old tree. Below it, maybe in the area of someone else's postage-stamp kitchen, is the memory of a cherry tree. Between these two, a long, long clothes line wire – which was our aerial ride. If you've never had such a ride, you can't possibly imagine the memories that flooded my mind.

Brooks Street, two streets west, was a good street, with a special kind of people. When Carl and I would collect old newspapers and magazines to sell, the people on Brooks always had some. Magazines brought higher prices in the scrap drives, and the people on Brooks always seemed to subscribe.

Today I even walked down the alley where Carl and I used to go to collect whatever it was people threw away.

"Dibs on that!" I'd say. Or Carl, if he saw it first.

I can't recall now what valuable things we collected, but it was interesting. Nehi bottles were worth 2¢ a piece. When money for five of them went into the sugar bowl, we could both purchase Nehi's for ourselves. Cream soda I liked. Carl was loyal to orange.

I broke my credit card trying to get into our old church. It was still there on the corner –7th and College. It wasn't any smaller than I had remembered it. And it was still decently white, as though it had been spruced up for my coming.

It is still a church. Newly varnished doors resisted my efforts to pick the lock.

What would happen, I thought if my lock picking were successful? Suppose the people who lived in the Jones' old house across the Street were to report me? What would I say if they had found me?

Of course, had they found me, I would have been kneeling at the altar – and I doubt they would have advanced with guns drawn. I would have risked it to go back.

I tried to enter by a back door; but it, too, was locked. So I just walked around the building.

It's strange. How many churches have I seen during these years past? I have stood in St. Peter's in Rome, the Blue Mosque in Istanbul, the Church of the Holy Sepulchre in Jerusalem, temples in India and Japan. But the ground on which stood this "little white church" seemed holy beyond words.

Here is where I learned to kneel.

And here is where I learned to dream.

Is it true that the little lot in back of the church was really where we put a tent for "outdoor services"? We only knew how to put up the walls of the tent. Chester Edwards, our leader, called it "our sky-dome cathedral." Today at that spot, I saw a grey compressor for an air conditioner.

An air conditioner. Of course, we didn't have one of those. When the windows were open during the stifling heat of Kansas summers, the locusts used to come in the open windows and buzz like airplanes as they attacked the lights.

Why is it I am so strongly moved as I walk slowly around this humble place? I don't feel this way when I drive by Clay School. It seemed deserted, too. It's made of brick and seems still strong and sure. The thousands of skinned knees have not worn away the graveled play grounds. But I do not weep over it.

And I do weep.

Not for sorrow. But for joy?

No. For a reason I do not know.

Does it seem strange to the people working in the construction yard next door that a tall man should walk slowly around a greying spinster of a building and weep?

I stoop and pluck a dandelion. I put it in the button hole of my jacket and smile at myself. Who cares? If people could know what I am thinking about as I stand there, a dandelion boutonniere would seem perfectly proper.

It was here that I was born. I was born of the Spirit. The sky was the dome. It was infinite.

How small was my world –

Something great is going to happen with me – the events of the past months are fermenting in my mind. Some days I feel that it will be only months until the world will listen.

Do all these feelings come in focus for a reason? Do we reassure ourselves by looking at our roots as we –

* * *

And there the manuscript abruptly ends – flight call, perhaps – leaving the conclusion of The Book I Wrote in the Kansas City Airport (1975) *to be written in the living manuscript of Berk's life over the next seventeen years.*

MAURICE BERGQUIST. *President Senior Class; President Junior Class; President Sophomore Class; Secretary Freshman Class; President Sachem Club,'43,'44, Secretary,'41,'42; President Student Council, '41, '42, '44; Social Committee,'42; Secretary Deputation Committee,'43; Dramatics Club, '41;* Who's Who Among Students in American Colleges and Universities, '43, '44; *Minister of Youth, Church of God, Bedford, Indiana,'42, '43; Associate Editor* Orange and Black, 40, '41; Debate, '41; The Confessional, '42; Magnificent Obsession, '42; *Associate Editor* Echoes, '43; *Editor* Echoes, '44.

2
Anderson College

My first recollection of seeing Berk was memorable, if not awe-inspiring. Early in our freshman year (1940-41), the only year we did not room together, I would see him coming down the hall at odd hours, somewhat covered in coal dust, dragging himself to his room on the same hall where I lived. Like many of us, Berk had to earn virtually all of his tuition, room and board. Thus, he began the year firing the boiler in what we called the "old barnitory" – the upstairs of the old camp ground dining hall, and a pretty sad place to live.

The speaker is Robert A. Nicholson, who one day would become president of the school where he and Berk started out as freshmen in the fall of 1940. In their four years together as students at Anderson College, "Nick," as he was known to his friends, and "Berk" developed an affinity that was warm and deep and forged a friendship that lasted a lifetime.

The two men were quite different in style, but both were razor-sharp wits with a zany zest for life and were intellectually stimulating to each other. In Nick's words:

I was a math major, and Berk a man of literature, philosophy, and ideas. During our freshman year, we were both taken into social clubs. Berk was a Sachem; I, a Booster. Most of Berk's friends were Boosters, and we tormented him regularly about that.

I recall one class we took together – "Principles of Education," taught by Carl Kardatzke. For economic purposes we used the same textbook, which I still have and treasure. I was an under-liner and margin note-maker; Berk also wrote in the margins. Generally, I would read and underline first; Berk would get there later, and would carry on a written dialogue with me. Recently, I have looked at that book again, and quote three notations in his rambling hand: "College of Mounds Baptist" (where I led a church choir for five dollars a week); "Last minute Bergquist"(comment upon his needing a plan for learning); and (after I had written "But this emphasizes subject matter for its own sake") he wrote, "Sam Hill, Nick, what do you go to school for?" A treasure!

Living conditions improved a bit during their sophomore and junior years(1941-42 and 1942-43). Berk and Nick lived in a two-room arrangement for four men in East Hall, the former "Old People's Home," (on the site of the present Executive Office Building). Originally the building had housed retired workers of the *Gospel Trumpet Company* who could no longer care for themselves; but most of those elderly folks had died, so male students were permitted to move in.

For both years Art Eikamp joined Berk and Nick as a third roommate. Art said of the place, "We called it 'La Cucaracha' for obvious reasons. Berk said he didn't mind riding the cockroaches down the hall to the bathroom, but he resented it when they lined up to use his toothbrush."

> *So much of Berk's humor came spontaneously out of the situation of the moment. That, of course, was the unique thing about it.*
> **– Arthur EiKamp**

All three roommates were, in Nick's words, "poor and working." During part of that time, Thurman Hall was the fourth man in their "suite." Thurman worked a night shift at General Motors, came and went at odd hours, and, in the view of the other three, was "very rich." Nick, Art, and Berk tried to organize a sort of Christian-socialist "share what the Lord has given us" system, but for some odd reason could never get Thurman interested.

However, the three others put the system to good use, at least to a modest degree – most evident in their suits. Since the three friends were about the same size, they could wear each other's clothes. Nick explains:

> *Berk had a snazzy striped suit with pockets in rare places which we called the "zoot suit." I had a solemn dark suit we called the "preaching suit." So when one of us had an important date, he wore the zoot suit; when anyone went out for a one-night preaching stand (as Art and Berk often did), the preaching suit was worn. The "zoot suit" was easily recognized -- no other like it on the campus.*

Art still wonders what the girls they dated thought when they compared notes and found that they were all dating "the same suit."

Berk had much in common with Art, both being sons of the prairie – Berk from Kansas; Art, from South Dakota. In Art's words, "We both felt a call to the ministry, shared an eagerness to learn and a love of the ironic in life."

Art has always held great appreciation for Berk's sense of humor. He says:

> *So much of Berk's humor came spontaneously out of the situation of the moment. That, of course, was the unique thing about it. His humor was not a matter of just telling jokes – though he could do that very well, too. Berk loved to tell jokes, but the delightful thing about being with him was the humor that he saw and expressed in the everyday affairs of life. He had a humorous view of life. People have said, "Cleanliness is next to godliness." I think Berk would have said, not that "humor is next to godliness," but that "humor is an essential part of godliness."*

Others in East Hall with whom lasting friendships developed were Gerald Erickson, Franny Lowe, Bob Hurst, Bob Clark, Milton Buettner, Ron Joiner, and Pete Meyer.

Milton Buettner has fond memories of those years. As there were few young men his age in his youth group back home in Milwaukee, Wisconsin, he said, "I was elated upon arrival at Anderson College to find myself in a paradise of male companions who were committed, as I was, to Christ and the life he set as our example."

He goes on to say, "What measure of wit I possessed before enrolling had lain dormant, because it is futile to cast one's wit to those who cannot toss back a witticism of their own. All at once there were these friends whose wit and humor were infectious. Berk especially had a creative mind, and his thoughts were expressed with a vocabulary all his own."

Buettner recalls a typical escapade involving the East Hall wits.

> *Val Clear had an old Ford nicknamed "Abie," and we often piled in and drove to Shadyside Park by the river and roasted franks and other digestibles on a fire of sticks. One time the jibes and jokes were ricocheting fast and sparklingly, when Bob Clark pulled a pun so outrageous that we had to do something appropriate to the outrage.*
>
> *Bob had been catching mosquitoes in a quart bottle, when someone looked in and asked, "What are they doing in there?"*

Berk's leadership emerged early on campus. Elected Secretary-Treasurer of the Freshman Class, he stands (at right) with other class officers: Edwin ("Bus") Upshaw, Vice-President, and Marie Esper, President.

During freshman and sophomore years, Bergquist wrote editorials as a staff member of the Orange and Black, *the campus newspaper. (L to R) Berk, in a familiar pose at the typewriter, Evelyn Clark, Jean Reynolds, Fred Richardson, Libby Ramsey, and Duane Windemiller.*

(L to R) Bergquist, Sophomore Class President, with Secretary-Treasurer Naomi Hunter and Vice-President William Baxter.

Developing Leadership at Anderson College

Freshman Bergquist with sophomore Carl Olson comprised the affirmative team of the school's intercollegeate debate club.

Maurice Bergquist   Robert Nicholson

College Roommates and Life-long Friends

Arthur Eikamp

Berk, the Sachem . . .

LEFT: Berk is "holding forth" – either delivering an entertaining speech or presiding as auctioneer for a Sachem fund-raiser. ABOVE: Berk (second row, second from right) led the Sachems as President for two years.

Berk, the Editor . . .

ABOVE LEFT: Berk (standing center) was in his element as Associate Editor of the Echoes in his junior year. It was said of him: "Maurice Bergquist contributed some vital, punch-full copy . . . so when a line hits you right between the eyes – oh, there is no mistaking a Bergquist witticism!"

ABOVE: In his senior year, Berk (seated at typewriter) took over the Editor's position. As the country was still heavily engaged in World War II, the book reflects a patriotic theme.

LEFT: Berk visits with E.A. Reardon, to whom the 1944 Echoes was dedicated. The yearbook lauds Reardon, pastor of Park Place Church, for his "seasoned sense of spiritual values," for his "spontaneous humor and sharp wit," for his friendly interest in the students and his "ability to call each student by name" – all traits Berk admired and would later reflect in his own ministry.

Quick as lightning Bob replied, "Perhaps they're quart-in."
Berk, as I remember it, called out: "That's it, lads. Let's give him a ducking in the brink."
We gladly pitched in and soon Bob came out dripping wet."

Studies, work, extra-curricular activities, and preaching engagements made for a full schedule, but whenever there was time for it, the fellows enjoyed a fast game of ping-pong.

"All of us," Nick says, "put a lot of 'English' on the ball, and stood way back from the table. Berk was not as good as I was, and I was not as good as Carl Fortner. But no one could rival the facial expressions of Berk when he would 'cut' the ball; his mobile, facile face was unbelievable!"

Berk bought a new car (a Hudson with wooden bumpers) near the end of his sojourn at Anderson, but he didn't know how to drive. Art had, after a fashion, learned to drive in the alfalfa field at home. Berk always said that Art taught him to drive, but Art says, "I don't remember doing much except showing him what to do to go forward and backward. I think we both thought that was all one had to know. We didn't yet need a driver's license." Berk later got his license through the mail.

Berk's was a double major: Bible and English. He was a good student, brilliant in class; but it was obvious to both his friends and his professors that he was interested in and loved doing so many things that he viewed term papers and the like, in Art's words, "as irritations that were way down on his list of necessary things to do."

Berk had been preaching since he was eleven years old. Once challenged to accept God's call to devote his life to preaching, he became consumed by a burning desire to "get at it." Consequently, he booked himself out for preaching engagements on weekends, often arriving back on campus barely in time for class. His school work suffered as a result, much to the chagrin of his professors, who could see evidence of Berk's genius in class, but were frustrated by his wanton lack of attention to detail and polish in papers turned in. [Several of those papers Berk kept in his files and were found there after his death.] Comments on the papers showed appreciation for his intellect, but disappointment in the lack of attention to revision and polish.

> One thing Berk left behind in Topeka was the moniker "Junior." His college friends knew him as "Maurice" or "Berk."
>
> Virginia Stage (Chappell) from Topeka, also a student at the college, tells that once when Berk was standing with a group of other students in the lobby of "Old Main," he was greeted by his former Sunday school teacher, Mrs. I.K. Dawson, with a "Hello, Junior."
>
> "Everyone in the lobby but me," Virginia recalls," had a surprised look on their faces at that greeting."

A look at the yearbook listing of the various roles Berk assumed in college, leaves no doubt of his leadership ability. Many of the gifts he developed as a youth in Topeka were put to good use at Anderson. He continued, for a couple of years at least, his involvement with debate and drama. He served as a class officer all four years, the last three as president. He also served three of the four years as president of the Student Council. Because of his academic excellence and demonstrated leadership, he was selected in his junior and senior years for inclusion in *Who's Who in American Universities and Colleges.*

While Berk was at the college, his youth pastor and mentor from Topeka, Chester Edwards, moved to Anderson to serve on staff at the school. ["The Edwards Room" in the Student Center is, in fact, named for him.] Chester remembers Berk as an outstanding student. He also recalls that Berk served as Master of Ceremonies at a particular banquet and "dazzled" everyone with his wit and stories.

Two activities on campus, however, seemed to have claimed a lion's share of Berk's attention and dedication – the Sachems and the Echoes staff.

During his first year on campus, Berk became a loyal member of the Sachem Club, captivated by its commitment to leadership and service. "Sachem," of course, is an Indian word, meaning "leader" or "chief." As president of the club and associate editor of the college yearbook his junior year, he may well have written these words describing the driving motivation of the Sachems:

> *There is something thrilling about a group of men bound together by a common loyalty. This is especially true of a brotherhood that is united to serve and increase its capacity for service. The Sachems, leaders in service activities and in school spirit, incorporate the finest aspirations of manhood in their motto: God first, others second, and ourselves last.*

Certainly, the "Sachem code" fit well with the phrase from Scripture that Berk took for his personal motto as a youth in Topeka: "For me to live is Christ."

Top-ranking scholastic in the Senor Class, Bob Nicholson and Dorothy Jane.

Nick Nicholson tells a great story about Berk as editor of *the Echoes:*

> *Just the two of us were rooming together, Art having graduated and gone to seminary at Yale. During the long winter months, Berk said to me one day, "Nick, why don't you try to get your mother to send us a box of those wonderful cookies. If she does, I'll put a big picture of you and Dorothy in the Echoes."*
>
> *Mother did send a box of her wonderful cherry and nut cookies from Minnesota; and Berk kept his part of the bargain, putting in a full-page picture of Dorothy and me sitting on the old bridge in the ravine, with the caption: "Top ranking scholastic in the Senior Class, Bob Nicholson and Dorothy Jane."*
>
> *When the Echoes went to print, Berk knew we were engaged; but it had not been announced. (With engagement rings not used in those days, you had to have a party; ours was at Carl Kardatzke's home). So he risked that caption (without our knowing about it.) He enjoyed the cookies; we enjoyed the picture."*

Berk graduated a bachelor, and remained one for a number of years – "the most eligible bachelor in the Church of God," everyone said.

"During our senior year," Nick says,"Berk was an enthusiast for Dorothy and my romance. He believed in the 'holy estate,' but just couldn't slow down enough for it."

Berk was best man for the Nicholsons' wedding. And after college, he stayed at their house regularly whenever he was in Anderson. When Dorothy first gave him directions to the Nicholsons' tiny house on Ellynhurst Drive, she unwittingly furnished Berk with a sermon illustration he used many times: "Go east on 10th Street," she told him, "and when you come to a yard with a wagon-wheel out front, you will know you have gone a block too far!"

As further testimony to their friendship, when the Nicholson's first son was born several years later, Dorothy said they named him "for the Apostle Paul and for our contemporary apostle Maurice: Paul Maurice Nicholson. Good name!"

Against the backdrop of World War II, the 1944 *Echoes* presented that school year using a patriotic theme: "Ye Shall Know the Truth and the Truth Shall Make You Free." Berk, as editor likely wrote the introduction for the book, which echoes the spirit of the address he delivered at his Commencement exercises in Topeka four years before, when the United States had just entered the War. While the vocabulary is typical of Berk the scholar, the words ring as true today as they did then.

> *These days of clamant opinions give no higher challenge than that expressed by Christ: "Know the truth." So in Anderson College we are trying through work-crammed days to find among the debris of proposed panaceas and discarded theories the principles upon which our lives shall be built. Whether it is the perplexed freshman grimacing over a particularly difficult assignment or the sedate professor in brow-furrowing conference, we have a single aim . . . the truth. Not always is our search confined to the cloistered precincts of the library or classroom – frequently we are led by our quest for truth to informal conversations with our professors, to long meditative walks, to vigorous conclaves in the dormitory room, to the lecture room, or to one of the many friendly churches. Whatever our path, our goal is common . . . to know the truth.*
>
> *A college is not a parasite upon freedom; it is its guardian. It is the arsenal of democracy. Men are free as their minds are free and at liberty only as their spirits are unfettered. Therefore, though not so dramatic in their service as our valiant men and women who must crawl through the smoke and hell of war or those who toil tirelessly in hospitals or rehabilitation centers, the teachers and students of our school guarantee, through their propagation of the truth, those five freedoms whose price is that of blood – freedom of worship, service, learning, friendship, and expression. We must work assiduously that these shall not be lost.*

Berk especially had a creative mind, and his thoughts were expressed with a vocabulary all his own.

– Milton Buettner

Berk's studies took a sharp downward turn, in one department at least, during his senior year. For two years he had driven every weekend to Bedford, where he was youth pastor. He returned late Sunday nights, desperately tired. And he was often sick, the harsh winters of Anderson plaguing the weak lungs he had inherited from his mother. Those were contributing factors in the fact that he did not pass physics. He needed an additional science course and, consequently, did not graduate with his class in 1944. But, stubborn Swede that he was, the next year he took physics again. And failed it again. He took it another time and finally passed.

Berk did graduate – in 1946. But in those two additional years he was busy doing the two things he loved best: preaching and traveling.

As for Berk's delayed graduation, Chester Edwards – Berk's first mentor, the man who saw "the preacher" in a scrawny little Kansas boy, who nurtured him and gifted him with a love of words and a humorous outlook on life – remembers Berk's tongue-in-cheek explanation:

"He was just waiting for accreditation, so that he could graduate from an accredited college."

Chester Edwards

"What is the most interesting city in the world?"

I am walking down the table-level highway with my esteemed friend and brother, Dr. C.E. Brown. The country is Denmark and I am in the early stages of my "hoboeing."

Not more than two steps lapsed between my question and his answer.

"Rome," he said.

"Then, by all means, I must practice up on my spaghetti twirling and visit the land of the Caesars." I responded.

"Listen to the words of the Scripture," continued my companion; "I was a stranger and they took me in."

Then he went on to explain that in that land of Augustan glory, the stranger one is, the more they "take him in."

Maurice Bergquist
World Traveler and Evangelist

3
Early Ministry

The lanky traveler stood on deck, watching the land recede as the freighter plowed out to sea. A wave of excitement swept over him as he pulled from his pocket once again the small blue booklet – a passport. His first.

"My key to the world," he thought.

Just then from the deep recesses of memory came a familiar voice:

"Take your elbows off the table, Yunie. Only those who have traveled around the world may put elbows on the table."

The traveler smiled to remember his Swedish mother's oft-spoken words to him at their supper table when he was just a lad. Her "Yunie" was about to earn the right to put his elbows on any table anywhere in the world.

Maurice Bergquist launched his ministerial career as an evangelist – preaching for revivals, camp meetings, and youth conventions all across the United States and at churches and mission stations around the world.

During a five-year period in the late '40's and early '50's, his world travels included an eight-month preaching tour through Europe, the Middle East, and Africa (June, 1947 - February, 1948); a thirteen-months' trip with Ralph Starr, preaching in mission stations around the world (December, 1948 - January, 1950); a missions tour of South America with Everett Minkler (1951); and a five-months' tour of mission stations around the world with Everett Minkler and C.E. Byers (September, 1952 - January, 1953). Between journeys, he heavily booked preaching engagements in the States until he could save enough money to travel again.

In a letter written after Berk's death, Dorothy Nicholson noted:

Berk was the first person I knew who traveled to Europe after World War II. Traveling overseas was not a thing ordinary people did in those days. He came back with vivid word pictures of the devastation and misery prevalent throughout Europe. He brought word of how the church and the Christians had survived. It was in those days that our keen interest in the world-wide church had its beginning.

After graduation from Anderson College, Berk aligned himself with the national Youth Fellowship Office (YFO) in Anderson, IN, using that as his "home" address. His global interest in the church was sparked in part by his personal acquaintance with some of the missionaries (former schoolmates at Anderson College) and in part because of the promise he had made to himself that one day he would see the world his mother hinted of in her gentle admonition, the world that stood as a globe on top of the bookcase in their living room. But his prime motivation was wanting to see for himself the full extent of the church's ministry in winning the lost. In answering God's call to preach, Berk took literally Christ's command to "Go therefore and make disciples of all nations . . . ." He saw himself as a catalyst, energizer, encourager to those out there on the field, whether it was waking up an old established church in Pennsylvania to needs on the mission field or preaching to a little group of believers huddled around a kerosene stove in China. All of Berk's abilities and all his worldly goods were at God's disposal, whenever and wherever God wanted him to go.

His alliance with YFO provided a workable center from which to schedule preaching assignments around the country and abroad. YFO Director Tom A. Smith was a great help to him, as was another special benefactor, Ida Byrd Rowe, editor of the national youth paper, *Young People's Friend*.

Ida Byrd Rowe

1947 – Missions Tour of Europe, Middle East, Africa

In 1947 Berk traveled as a representative to the International Youth Convention in Oslo, Norway, with the assignment to mail reports of the convention to Mrs. Rowe for publication in *YPF.* From all indications, this was Berk's first trans-Atlantic journey. He sailed on a Norwegian freighter, working out some, if not all, of his fare by doing menial chores on the ship. His daily journal of thoughts and experiences suggests that he was traveling, not on a shoestring, but on a thread! Leisure time on board was spent reading and trying to break the "Norse code" (learning to speak Norwegian). The journal also reflects Melville-like moments of meditation and introspection, inner revelations about Berk himself at this point in his life:

[Getting on board] *This traveling by boat has certainly disillusioned me. . . . Always I had imagined that leaving America on a boat would be one of the most dramatic events in one's life – walking up the gang plank while tearful relatives and friends stand on the dock, heaving the throaty "bon voyage," watching the waving handkerchiefs till the boat pulls out of sight.*

Perhaps my days of travel are not over yet. So I may yet have a chance at this dramatic experience. But this trip wasn't like that – not by a bucketful of barnacles! It was atop a load of acetylene drums that I rode out to the battered freighter. And with a suitcase in either hand I struggled up the swaying ladder which was alongside the ship.

And so the story begins with my being bewildered again – this time among a ship load of sweating deck hands and nervous passengers – all of whom appear to talk Norwegian.

[Second day] *Was it I who hoped there would be someone aboard who would talk Norwegian to me? That was a mistake! Now, I find myself wishing for somebody who would talk English. But I shall learn. Witness last night. After supper I had a sudden fleeting inspiration to write a letter. But the desk in our cabin was of no value without a chair, so I promenaded around the ship in an unsuccessful attempt to find a chair. My search brought me to the dining room where the mess boy was working.*

"Can I write a letter here?" I asked.

No response.

I repeated the question.

No answer.

Concluding that he did not understand English, I ventured my first word of Norwegian. "Skrivet," I mumbled.

This worked. He nodded and replied, "Ja."

The door of opportunity was creaking open. Perhaps, thought I, with the help of Hugo's Norwegian Self Taught I can carry on a conversation. So I flicked through the book to the "useful conversational phrases." But, alas, I could find no way to use such sparkling repartee as "How many umbrellas have you?" or "How far is it to the railroad station?" I returned to my writing.

Tuesday, June 10: *In spite of all my ardent prayers that we would have a really worthwhile storm today, the sea remained about the same as last night. Even at that, it was the roughest day we have had this trip. As Mrs. Natwig (who is quite a wit) commented: "This is the cheapest and longest drunk I have ever been on." That* *describes it. The floor recedes from you as you walk, or rises to intercept your step. But I am fascinated with it all – in fact, I spent most of my free time today watching the water.*

There is endless variety in the seething foaming water. With boyish delight I stand on the second afterdeck and await almost breathlessly to see the blue waters dash over the deck below. Or kneeling on the bench in the lounge, I gaze out the porthole to watch the prow of the boat rise and dip. I did some creative thinking as I scrubbed the walls in the downstairs corridor this morning. . . .

Friday, June 11: *. . . I am about the happiest of the passengers. With my daily stint of work I am hungry enough to eat ravenously, tired enough to sleep blissfully, disciplined enough to enjoy my leisure, and occupied enough to have no trouble with sea sickness. Selah! . . . On the gastronomic side: We had "silta" (herring in sour cream and onions) for supper – hadn't had it since my boyhood in Kansas.*

Thursday, June 12: *I managed enough decks to swab to keep the morning from dragging. Now, however, my sweater is stretched till it approximately fits me – and I inadvertently contracted to give it to Lindy at the end of the trip. My sailor hat I contracted to sell to the shipowner's son-in-law, so I shall be solvent to the extent of 85 cents when we land on the bonny shores of Stavanger, Norway.*

Read Sea of Grass; *plugged through 100 pages of Thomas Paine, and enjoyed about 50 pages of* The Challenge of Our Culture.

Tonight afforded me a wonderful opportunity to soliloquize. Standing at the prow of the ship all alone, listening to the waves break periodically against the side, seeing ahead the almost interminable expanse of grey water, I felt a strange pensiveness. And, too, I felt a strange reckless courage. Here am I – I, who love company and must pry myself loose from friends, am all alone. All alone and the world is in front of me. Behind me are thousands of friends, countless happy hours and many hours that I would like for a kind heaven to forget. But everything is behind. Ahead are great tasks to humble me, friends to stimulate me, and adventures to challenge me. Somehow I feel I am becoming the person I have always wanted to be – an independent rover – a man of many experiences (many of them painful), but a man whose faith in himself is only exceeded by his inward sense of inadequacy, an inadequacy which no one senses. An inadequacy that drives him on like a relentless scourge.

Maybe this is not the man I really would like to be, but somehow it is dawning upon me that one's dreams form the mold in which his life is shaped. And this description is of the man I dreamed of becoming.

[The effect of dreams in shaping character and destiny became a life-long study for Berk, a recurring theme in sermons, in a conference series he called *Nite Life*, and in his last book, *The Secret of Immunity*.]

Friday, June 13: [He notes graduation from Anderson College *"one year ago today,"* and that while he is on the rolling seas headed for Europe, *"the faithful are gathering for the Feast of the Passover"* in Anderson, Indiana.]

This, I think, will be the greatest expense of the trip – remembering that at this hour I might have been sauntering down the concrete "midway" [in Anderson,] *with a bag of popcorn in my hand greeting friends from all over the country. . . . Most of all I will miss Arthur and Norma's wedding in New York a week from Sunday. . . .*

Tonight I have the rather unusual (for me) feeling that I may be something of a bore. It is a little strange, I know, for swash-buckling Bergquist to admit this, but I fear it is true nonetheless. Maybe it is because I am developing a sense of smugness that is becoming repugnant to everyone – including myself. Maybe I am a little deflated because the Norwegian language is still as baffling as ever. In fact, I begin to have grave doubts of my learning it at all – although I studied quite religiously today.

[Nine days later Berk was in Norway, on a train headed for Oslo.]

Monday, June 22: *I am sitting on one of the hard third class compartment seats – just like they do in the movies. And for more excitement I was met by a newspaper reporter who interviewed me about my trip This, too, is just like in the movies. So, in a flurry of activity and attention I have left the wonderful village of Stavanger.*

One Christ Is Lord
By Maurice Bergquist
(Excerpts)

The conference at Oslo was more than a conference – it was a testimony. Bearing as its motto, "Jesus is Lord," it set out to prove that Christ Jesus really is Lord, that He is greater than all the cleavages which separate, that He is greater than our inadequacy and bewilderment, that He is greater than all our own efforts; that He indeed is Lord and beside Him there is no other. One could not forget this theme, for it was written with huge characters at the front of the auditorium in French, German, English and Norwegian; it was inscribed in all the literature we received.

But more than this, one could see it in operation in the lives of the delegates. How, for example, were the delegates from Indonesia to feel when they first met the Dutch delegates knowing their countries were at that moment at war with one another? How were the French to feel when they met the German delegates, or the Indians when they met the English, or the French and Africans?

Between national groups there were high walls of loyalty or great chasms of misunderstanding. How were these people to react when they met? There was only one response they could make – the response stated in the theme of the conference, that Jesus Christ is Lord. Their loyalty to Him must transcend their loyalty to their own state.

Not only were there nationalistic cleavages, but there were ecclesiastical barriers between delegates – there were state church members and free church members, Anglicans and Quakers, Orthodox and Evangelical. All these must worship and work together; they must learn that above all our words and thoughts about Jesus is Jesus Himself, and in drawing near to Him we are brought near to each other.

Yet we did become one in Christ Jesus. I felt it as I, with twelve hundred other young persons took Communion in Vor Frelsers Kirke on Sunday morning; and I felt it every time we said the Lord's Prayer together – each in his own tongue – and I felt it with poignancy as on the last night of the conference I walked down the steps of the cathedral with a multitude of others, others whom I had not known ten days earlier, but whom I had come to regard as brothers and sisters in God's family. Someone began to sing, "Blest Be the Tie That Binds." A thousand voices took up the strain. The streets of Oslo rang with the testimony that Jesus, indeed, is Lord.

Leaving the train, he rode a ferry across the North Sea to Oslo, where he was met by the General Secretary of the Youth Conference and taken to the conference headquarters. There the work began for which he had been sent. His report of the convention was published in the October 26, 1947, issue of *Young People's Friend*.

At the convention he caught up with C.E. Brown, editor of *The Gospel Trumpet*, and traveled a bit with him in Europe.

Round Robin

Near the end of spring semester at Anderson College in 1944, Berk and nine of his Sachem and Booster buddies made a pact to keep in touch with one another through a round-robin letter. Sitting together in Milton and Eleanor Buettner's living room, they devised this plan: Their cumulative missive would circulate in alphabetical sequence – Maurice Bergquist, Milton Buettner, Bob Clark, Arthur Eikamp, Gerald Erickson, Bob Hurst, Ron Joiner, Franny Lowe, Pete Meyer, Bob Nicholson. As the letter completed its circuit, each would remove his own letter, insert a new one and, after having read the other nine letters, send the pack to the next in line. Milton Buettner made copies of the letters and still reads them occasionally. He notes:

Most round-robin letters last only one or two years before petering out, but this circuit of ours lasted almost five years. Each time, "the Bird" flew thousands of miles because Clark was in Pakistan, Erickson in Grand Cayman, Eikamp was in Japan, and the Buettners were in West China. In these letters Berk's refreshing style, along with all the other letters I thought were worth preserving, gave me the idea to type all nine letters, at the time I received them, on butcher paper in an endless roll which at the conclusion could be rolled up into a scroll and kept with a rubber band around it. The wear and tear have slightly damaged the scrolls, but I still reread a set every few months and revel in nostalgia while doing so.

The letters show a deep friendship and camaraderie among these men, each of whom have made significant contributions to the work of the church at home and abroad. Berk kept several of his RR letters. Each of them carried not only news of his whereabouts, but also words of appreciation and encouragement to the other men. They also provided a forum for testing new perceptions about life, world events, and spiritual insights evolving from his travels.

Experiencing the World Youth Conference and seeing the effects of World War II in Europe gave Berk much to digest about man's inhumanity to man. From Tvarskog, Sweden, on August 8, 1947, he wrote:

Dear Brothers,

May I begin . . .with the notation that both my mail and I have been trailing around Scandinavia like the children of Israel. Unfortunately, our paths haven't crossed very often.

. . . I speak this morning with the background of the youth conference in Oslo – a meeting of Christian leaders from all over the world. . . . I have come to feel that all the humanly engineered systems for improving the lives of other men are doomed to disaster. The world is not made smaller just because a man can fly from New York to Shannon, Ireland, in thirteen hours nor made more compact because of the radio. Men are not bound to each other by proximity, but by charity, by love. And this is something . . . that can never be engineered into existence; it can never be legislated. I note with despair that man's vaunted internationalism soon becomes a guise for imperialism; I see that men can as easily sell their souls for silver in times of peace as they can be sold for glory in the time of war. . . . And so all the organizations of men, righteous as they are in their inception, soon fall prey to the power of evil . . . because theirs is a righteousness of desperation – an international "fox hole" religion.

If the world is to be saved, it must be saved, in Milton Buettner's words, "by people who are incorruptible." People who do not despair in adversity nor become self-righteous in the moment of victory. They must be ones whose righteousness is not of themselves, but is a reflection of the purity of God. . . . These last few weeks have been times of perplexity, but not of despair, for I have come to feel that there is salvation, a salvation not of our own works, but of God.

Perhaps I can make this a little clearer by telling an experience of the Oslo confer-

BELOW:
Round Robin Conspirators

ence. When the conference convened, the war between the Dutch and Indonesians was reaching a crisis so the delegates from both these countries felt revengeful and self-righteous. The walls of nationalism are strong and high. Said one nationalist

Maurice Bergquist	*Robert Clark*	*Gerald Erickson*	*Ron Joiner*	*Pete Meyer*
Milton Buettner	*Arthur EiKamp*	*Robert Hurst*	*Franny Lowe*	*Robert Nicholson*

NOW TRY GOD!!

M. R. RIMMER
PASTOR

The County Line Church of God

State Road 135 — South Meridian Street — Bus Stop 11

INDIANAPOLIS, INDIANA

Invites you to hear ...

Reverend Maurice Bergquist

Youth Evangelist

Each Evening at 7:30 O'clock

Jan. 27 to Feb. 10

1946

Bergquist, the Evangelist

His was a "world view" of the Church's mission — **to carry the gospel to all nations.** *Between travels abroad, Berk traversed the width and breadth of the United States, and even into Canada, preaching the gospel and sounding a wake-up call to the Church for the cause of missions around the world. Then, as soon as he had enough money for passage, he was off again to do what he could to assist and encourage churches around the world and missionaries on the field.*

MAURICE BERGQUIST

COMING TO PORTLAND
October 1st to 15th

HOLLADAY PARK CHURCH of GOD
N. E. 8th and Wasco

A GREAT EVANGELIST
PREACHED CHRIST AROUND THE WORLD!

PLAN TO HEAR HIM . . .
. . . TELL YOUR FRIENDS

Rev. Maurice Bergquist

from South India whose sympathy for the Indonesians was not only strong, but aggressive: "On the opening day, we were in this hall with the news of the Dutch-Indonesian war disturbing us. I knew where my political decision lay, and I came to that meeting full of righteousness for myself and for my political decision, and full of anger against the Dutch. But when Vissar t'Hooft (Dutchman) confessed the guilt of his nation and extended his hand of Christian fellowship to the Indonesians, my righteousness . . . and the justification of my politics had broken down into a sense of common guilt before God in Christ."

*This kind of experience can never be legislated. This bond can never be woven on the looms of men. This is the miracle of the gospel; not the gospel **about** Jesus, but the gospel **of** Jesus Christ – of God in Christ reconciling men unto himself. . . . So as I said, these months of travel are leaving me perplexed . . . about the way out of our morass. But like a cool breeze from the Father's house upon the heated and furious questioning came your letters, reminding me that the love of God is at work in the world. And it will redeem the world. . . .*   *Bergquist*

From Oslo, Berk traveled to Denmark, Holland, and across Europe to Switzerland, Italy, and Greece, with stops in Rome and Athens. Then, aboard the *Aksu*, he sailed to Turkey, Syria, and across the Mediterranean to spend several weeks in Egypt before sailing home in late December on the *S.S. Marine Carp*. All along the route, he recorded impressions of what he saw, noted ideas for sermons, and mailed dispatches to Ida Byrd Rowe for publication in *Young People's Friend*.

That the young journalist already had a gift for words is obvious from Berk's travel diary and carbons kept of reports mailed to Mrs. Rowe. His verbal pictures reflect sharp observation skills and a flair for imagery that carried over into his preaching. In one place he speaks of "prices so high that merchants use kites for price tags." He describes a couple of accordion players as "push-pull troubadours." In Asuit, Egypt, he describes a village of mud-brick houses where "donkeys, chickens, and children swarm in front of us." And from Istanbul come these vivid images:

. . . Little ragged children putting flowers in your buttonhole – children whose clothes were so patched they resembled a tattered quilt. . . . Riding in a dining car of an Ankara-bound Toros Express, we were left in the dark as the lights went out. The tinkle of glass and silverware stopped as we could see outside, the squatty stone huts in which the peasants lived, silhouetted against the sky. Maybe that is the function of suffering – our lights go out so that we can enter into the sufferings of others. But even with the lights on, we can still see, if we will put our faces to the glass.

Early he learned the value of latching onto sensual detail if a story is to be retold. He notes in his journal: "I am coming to realize that unless one records his impressions and experiences, he is very apt to lose them or at least lose the luster from them. For somehow the memory retains the silhouettes, but never the colors and characteristics that incited the interest. Thus, in telling the experiences to someone else, one presents only the skeleton and is met with cold unresponse."

Berk's prose rose to the challenge of conveying to people back home in America the heart-wrenching realities of life in war-torn Europe. From the Oslo Convention and from Brother and Sister Donohew in Switzerland, he learned about conditions in Germany after the war and recorded them in this report for *YPF*:

Everywhere in Germany is hunger. And cold. You will have read of it elsewhere, but one Sunday morning after a church service the minister and his wife invited the Donohews home with them for dinner. There was only rhubarb soup, consisting of very little rhubarb and a great deal of water; potatoes cooked with yard greens. No more . . . no shortening or fat or any kind of seasoning. While this is not a very robust Sunday dinner, it is much more than many others had the same day. Multitudes of children have not so much as seen milk or fruit since the beginning of the war. Even though one would have the money to buy, there is nothing to be bought. It is easy to understand why people would lose the ambition to work when they find that the money they earn will not purchase anything. It is easy, too, to understand why a system of barter has been instituted in which food or clothing are the articles of exchange.

I remember the lady, typical of many, who had nothing out of which to make clothes for her child last winter. Through some stroke of providence she was able to get a ten-pound sugar sack which she unraveled thread by thread to knit again into a pair of stockings for her child. The situation is even more grave now than during the war, for the few clothes that were left have been worn to threads, patched and worn longer, until there is nothing to patch and nothing to patch with.

We know the Germans are enterprising people. They will work as long as there is anything to work with. But what can be done even by the most industrious housewife when there is no needle, no thread, and no cloth of any kind to be had. What of the thousands of mothers who had not the sugar sack to unravel?

He describes students on starvation diets of 850 calories a day and other people too malnourished to ward off sickness. *"Tuberculosis is silently killing thousands; influenza and pneumonia are not being spoken of in the headlines, but they are stealthily murdering thousands more."*

He quotes a speaker at the Oslo conference who described German suffering in terms of the one thing worse than hunger – the cold. Imagine what it is like, he said, *"night and day, sleeping or waking, to be constantly blue and shivering with the knife-like cold; to have to put your plate on the little stove on which your food was cooked so that your fingers would not be too numb to hold the fork."*

Berk concludes by saying:

After hours of listening to the Donohews' descriptions of the heart-wrenching conditions in Germany, I did as you would have done. I went to my suitcase and counted out just how many clothes I would need to get back to America, down to the last razor blade, and left the rest to be shared with my German brothers.

Those who need are our brothers, no less so because we have not seen them. They are not strangers merely because we do not know their names.

Those were the words Dorothy Nicholson spoke of – words that moved people to respond with money and C.A.R.E. packages for war-torn Europe after reading Berk's articles or hearing him speak passionately about those conditions in sermons back home.

Heard Any Good Hymns Lately?

Apparently Berk met up with another traveler from the States in Switzerland, for his journal speaks of Brother Donohew asking "if Maurice Caldwell and I would like to visit some of the tourist attractions of the country." In writing about their return trip from one such excursion, Berk reveals an interesting penchant of his – a pattern of behavior, that echoes throughout his life's journey:

Even a young man becomes nostalgic and retrospective at times. Anyway, I do. I want to browse through old books and sing old songs. In a mood like this I always take off my tie, unbutton my collar, and burrow around and find a copy of the Melodies of Zion. *The old blue-backed hymnal has a place in the life of this lad. For ten years I sang out of it – Sunday morning, Sunday evening, Wednesday evening, and in between times when I cleaned the church. I like it. Oh, I know it is not a great hymnal, but then we do not like books because they are great, but because they hold a great place in our lives, because they hold not only words and black and white notes, but volumes of tinkling memories that chime away the pleasant hour of reverie.*

I want to tell you about riding home to Zurich. [Maurice Caldwell and I] having shoehorned ourselves into the little blue Opel [with the Donahews], we started down the winding mountain road, past the cascading streams, the angling hillside farms, and the picturesque Swiss chalets. Well, as we started back, we started to sing Number 7 in Melodies of Zion, *"Once Again We Come." No sooner had we warbled through all three verses than someone asked, "Do you know Number 157?" So we sang "On to the Goal." For more than an hour we sang without stopping. When we couldn't think of all the words, we la-la-ed our way along to the chorus. As we sang we all grew a little homesick to be back in a camp meeting in the States when a great congregation would lift the old songs until the uncovered rafters would vibrate in the old tabernacle. And, as for me, I was just a little homesick for the time when in that everlasting city of God, I can stumble onto a little group gathered around an old blue-backed copy of the Melodies of Zion, singing the songs of my boyhood. I want to mingle my rasping baritone with their voices as they sing "The River of Pleasure," Number 124.*

By January of 1948, Berk was back in the states; but his journey to Europe and the Middle East had further ignited his passion for and life-long commitment to the world-wide ministry of the church. Wherever there were lost souls, confused perhaps by faithless creeds; wherever there was human suffering; wherever God's workers needed help and encouragement – the church needed to respond. Berk pledged himself to be one person committed to doing everything he could to minister in that arena and to awaken the church to her global responsibility. That purpose became a driving, personal mission that would undergird the whole of his life's work.

Missionaries for Japan

Just how much difference can one person make?

Not long after the close of World War II, Berk heard Dr. Adam Miller give a speech in which he quoted General Douglas MacArthur, who had said he could use 1,000 Missionaries in Japan. In response to MacArthur's challenge, Dr. Miller went on to say, "We have young people willing to go, but we have no money."

After the meeting Berk approached Dr. Miller and asked, "How much do you need?"

"$10,000.00."

"I'll get it," Berk said.

And he did.

For at least a year, he dedicated his preaching ministry to that cause. He made a preaching circuit through several states, pleading the cause of missions in Japan and challenging the church to respond. He sent Dr. Miller all the money he collected in those meetings, including his honorariums (save for what he could get by on for travel and food). After some months he called Dr. Miller.

"How much do we have?" he asked.

"About $9,500 or so – close to $10,000."

"Well, let's get cracking." Berk said. "Who do you have in mind?"

Dr. Miller answered, "Art and Norma Eikamp."

What a thrill that was for Berk! Art had been his roommate at Anderson College. They had shared many things in those days, including that basic black preaching suit. They had kept in touch after graduation. Berk had visited Art and Norma a couple of times in New England when Art was in seminary and, in Art's words, they "always talked far into the night."

The Eikamps had applied to the Missions Board for an assignment in India, but the Board had no openings there. Thus, they were serving in home missions among immigrant workers from Texas to the Canadian border when the Board made contact to see if they would consider going to Japan.

Berk secured the required funds by October of 1948, but another year passed before arrangements were finalized. The Eikamps sailed for Japan in November of 1949.

[Found among Berk's papers after his death were diary entries of donations for the Japan project and a file folder holding additional records of donations and correspondence with the Missions Board. This project meant a great deal to him.]

1948 – Tour of Mission Stations Around the World

October 7, 1948, found Berk in San Francisco waiting impatiently for a longshoreman strike to end so he could embark on another 'round the world preaching tour of mission stations. Traveling with him was Ralph Starr, friend and former classmate at Anderson University. Their itinerary included stops in Japan, China, India, Africa, and Europe.

Finally, by December 16, 1948, they were at sea on board the *General Meigs*. They anticipated learning something about missions in many lands as they crossed the Pacific, for Berk notes in his journal that their ship had "more missionaries in it than a cannibal stew." Compared with other ships he had sailed on, he found it refreshing that "the ratio of Bibles to poker decks is about three to one . . . ."

Among the passengers was Paul Sweet, producer of several short films on home missions. Berk and Ralph hoped to do some filming on this trip, but knew little about it. Meeting Sweet, they felt, was providential; and they picked up many pointers.

Conversations with Rev. George Belle, of the Chinese Inland Mission, were also stimulating and informative. "The purpose of the missionary sent out from the States," Belle said, " is to raise up as many native leaders as possible so that he can give his time to the erection of new works." And on the subject of ecumenicity, they were in agreement that "the church universal becomes much more apparent on the mission field than on the home front."

Particularly moving was the testimony of a Mr. Bartell, whom Berk identified in his journal as "the old gentleman with the goatee." Bartell told of leaving his home church in Hillsboro, Kansas, as a young man to rear his family in China. "Now," he said, "I have returned to America for six months just to say goodbye. I will die in China."

Berk wrote: "There is something heroic about the old gentleman's simple statement of the opportunities and of his obligations to the Chinese. The years have brushed away the illusions of youth, but they have brought to him a somber sense of responsibility."

"There is still so much to be done," Bartell said simply, "and I can do something."

Berk noted the absence of December 22 from his journal, the day lost in crossing the International Dateline. He described the ship's festive Christmas celebration: reading the Christmas story, singing carols, Santa's arrival for the children, opening presents. In California the Minklers had given Berk and Ralph each a present, and Sylvia Wood had given them a card – all with instructions not to open until Christmas. Ralph's surprise was a pair of socks and a tie; Berk's, cuff links and a scarf.

Recounting the Christmas Eve moment for *YPF*, Berk said:

> *It would be difficult to find a more heterogeneous group than that assembled Christmas evening in the lounge of the* General Meigs. *Almost every denomination was represented . . . for the most part, leaders of their respective groups, who take their religion seriously. Yet in this Christmas service we sang together and felt the glow of the spirit of the season. At no other time of the year would it have happened. No other time but Christmas. Catholics and Protestants. Evangelical churches and liturgical churches. Episcopalians and Methodists; Presbyterians and Congregationalists. Together. And our rallying point was the cradle of Bethlehem.*

Into China – Shanghai

As it turned out, their visas allowed Berk and Ralph only a one-day tour of Yokohama and Tokyo. Then it was on to their point of disembarkment – Shanghai, China – for a brief stay with Mr. and Mrs. Edgar Williams, Daisy Maiden, and Henry Jones before pressing inland to find Milton and Eleanor Buettner.

Arriving on January 1, 1949, they found Shanghai in the death-grip of a cold wave. Headlines on January 3 read: "4727 die from cold, hunger since November." Temperatures were actually dipping only a few degrees below zero Centigrade (not so bad), but humidity ranging between 65 and 90 percent made the cold, according to Berk, "as penetrating as a bed of spikes."

His article for *YPF* gave more of "the cold facts about Shanghai."

The Church in China
(The Rest of the Family series – excerpts)

. . . Mr. Henry Jones of the Presbyterian mission in Shanghai rated an entry in my little black book on the morning of January 3, 1949. Said he: "There is one thing you can be sure of in China and that is that you cannot be sure of anything. Only uncertainty is certain." . . . Jones is right. The only thing to expect in China is the unexpected. Consider the first Sunday morning in Shanghai, for example.

The Rest of the Family was the series Berk wrote about this journey for *Young People's Friend*. In this article, Berk dramatically captures in a single image the power of sending missionaries to the field.

Today Is Tomorrow in Japan

Dawn slid silently in through the porthole. In the dimly lit precincts of Cabin 201 stirred two or three pajama-clad passengers. Occasionally one would steal over to the porthole and scan the horizon for a sign of land. But the mists of morning were so heavy that for all he could see he might just as well have been in the middle of the Pacific. Suddenly one of the vigilantes wheeled and beckoned to a fellow traveler who was at the moment trying to shave in the half light. The shaver joined the watchful one at the little round window. Then he blubbered through the lather, "We're approaching land."

The declaration called for action. Decisive action. I rolled over. Then running my fingers through my slumber-tousled locks, I concluded that we had at last reached Japan. Japan – the land that had claimed tons of headline ink in the stateside newspapers during the past few years. Japan – the name about which were woven stories of wonder and romance, and of brightly tinted pictures of paper parasols and tiny gardens with midget bridges since the days of Miss Carnahan's fifth-grade geography class. Japan – one time target for annihilation bombings. And now Japan – the newest frontier for Christian missions. The declaration did indeed call for action. I planted my feet on the cold steel floor and made valiant efforts in the direction of rising. This would indeed be a momentous day.

The springs in the bunk just above mine had, for the preceding fourteen days, sagged under the weight of John Schwabb. Mr. Schwabb is a congenial young minister with a lean and intent face. He, with his wife and two small children, Phil and Stevie, is a missionary to Japan for the Scandinavian Alliance Mission. Many times during the voyage I had talked with Mr. Schwabb about the country to which they were going for their first term as missionaries. In a sense, I felt a vicarious victory in their getting to Japan at this time, for my own interest during the past year has been focused on these historic islands, and my most fervent prayers have been that our church could send a missionary couple to this most strategic of all mission fields. And now, for them, if not for us, the day had come. Years of praying and seeking the mind of God. Years of undramatic study and preparation. Finally the decision. Then the feverish ordeal of packing all the things that would be needed during the next five years. Finally the tearful "bon voyages" from the shore and the ship pulled out of the harbor. And after the ship had put safely to sea, the writing of letters to be mailed to mother and dad when the ship would dock at Honolulu. All these were done and now came the day of adventure, the beginning of five years in a strange land under the hardships of a recovering economy.

Sensing the quiet thoughtfulness of my friend Schwabb, who was preparing to go up on deck to get his first glance at his new parish, I fumbled for some thread of thought out of which to weave a conversation.

"Well, it looks as though this is D-Day," I ventured.

Schwabb is not one to banter words.

"I would rather call it V-J Day," he said meaningfully as he slipped his little testament into the pocket in his vest and headed for the promenade deck.

I am not so speedy as my missionary friend. So as he sped up to the "A Deck," I was just in the shoe-string-tying stage of operation wardrobe. I still had a little time to sit on the edge of my bunk and let my mind bend itself around the words of Mr. Schwabb.

"I would rather think of it as V-J Day."

Twenty minutes later I was still sitting on the edge of my bunk, still in the shoe-string-tying stage. If anyone had thought it important to observe my unchanged position, they would have concluded that I had not moved. But I had. In those twenty minutes my sleep-clogged mind had managed to skim half way around the world. It was 1946, and I was standing on the deck of the battleship on which the surrender pact which ended World Two was signed. As I stood on the bronze plaque that marked the spot on the deck of the "Mighty Mo" where the Japanese officers signed the terms of surrender, I had, tourist-like, had my picture taken so that future generations would have no cause to doubt.

Then I tried to recall the two-inch headlines that had screamed to a nervous world, "Japan Surrenders!" What a contrast! The V-J Day the world knows about was the triumph of the unleashed hell of the atomic bomb, the *coup de grace* of years of military strategy. But V-J Day Number Two . . . is heralded by a young father slipping a New Testament into his pocket and walking up to "A Deck" to see the dim outlines of his new parish, Japan.

I would not detract from the orotund phrase of General MacArthur as he speaks of the need of a "spiritual recrudescence," but would call attention to the analysis of the Holy Scripture: *"This is the victory that overcomes the world, even your faith."* . . . The church has sent hundreds of young men to Japan in order that they might read in the newspapers the headlines of the military victory over Japan. Can we not now make it possible for many other young men to watch with thoughtful eyes the dim outlines of a new field of work as the ship brings them to the shore of Yokohama in order that they can share their faith with this devastated country? It may be that the history books will tell us that the Allies were victorious over Japan, but I cannot believe that it is so. Perhaps, although I cannot be certain, the earth-shaking and heart-melting horror of the war was truly a "softening up operation." I cannot say. It may be that the "Beachhead" is indeed established. Who can know? But not the most rabid militarist would say that the victory is complete and final. Some of the more thoughtful observers feel that the exclamation point at the end of the declaration, "Japan Surrenders!" is beginning to look strangely like a question mark. If there is a victory it must be a victory of the spirit of love, the spirit of the Son of God – it must be a victory of faith, the victory that overcomes the world.

The day was cold. It, like the days before it, made you upholster yourself with all the clothes in the suitcase. Including red flannel pajamas in my case. Ralph and I had timidly inquired about in the stores until we each found a pair of fleece lined "long handled" underwear in our size. This we found to be no small undertaking for most of the Chinese men are smaller both horizontally and vertically than Ralph and I. Also, we had not sported such sartorial insulation since grade-school days. And then only by parental constraint. But China in wintertime exercises a powerful logic that makes even the most arctic-tempered soul happy to adorn himself like an animated pin cushion and then venturing out in this seven-layer veneer only to find that even with all the double order of every article of clothing in the wardrobe, he shivers like the leaf of a neurasthenic aspen.

On the subject of heating houses in China, Milton Buettner has been heard to explode, "Central heating! China doesn't even have peripheral heating."

The Church in Shanghai qualifies under this description. . . . Ralph and I expected the church not to be heated and we were not disappointed, but we were a little surprised to find that the only "pews" were the midget chairs of the primary department. To jack-knife our manly frames into the dollhouse furniture would, if accompanied by a one-two-three count, qualify as setting up exercises. And resting our chins on our knees was an excellent method of keeping our teeth from chattering. As for the hands, the best way to keep them warm was to keep them in the pockets. But that made it difficult to hold the hymn book. Of course, in a moment I found that I could understand the Chinese hymns quite as well with the book closed in my lap.. . .

When the time came for the sermon, I was called upon to speak. In one way, this was one of the most remarkable sermons I ever preached – I had to keep my hands in my pockets!

Apart from the dwarf-size chairs, the refrigerated atmosphere, and the remains of Friday's lessons on the blackboard, the room might have been any one of a number of churches at home. The songs were the same, "Stand Up, Stand Up for Jesus" and "Love Divine All Loves Excelling." The people, apart from their dress and language, were the same. And the Word of God spoke to the same needs in each life. To use a phrase common a few years ago, "There is one Word for one world."

When the sermon was finished, we took communion. As we ate the unleavened bread and drank the fruit of the vine from the crooked little Chinese glasses with these newly met brothers in China, I found myself getting new meanings from a very old song, "The Church's One Foundation."

> *Elect from every nation, Yet one o'er all the earth,*
> *Her charter of Salvation, One Lord, one faith, one birth;*
> *One holy name she blesses, Partakes one holy food,*
> *And to one hope she presses, with every grace endued.*
> *Yet She on earth hath union with God, the Three in One,*
> *And mystic sweet communion with those whose rest is won.*

On this particular morning, . . . [the experience] made us consider again the true nature of the church, the family of the one God . . . the wonder of it all seems never to fade. . . . It is as though one could suddenly transcend the barriers of time and space and simultaneously be in conversation with every member of God's church that he has ever met. A thousand names and faces. A thousand church buildings, from the majestic cathedral whose spires clasp hands with the sky to the smoke-smudged store-front chapel by the street car tracks. All of these, and more, the faces of those whose worship is no longer in Gothic halls or clapboard chapels, but who ever live in the presence of God, all of these speed swiftly through my mind. I see them all. Not as vague elusive memories, but as contemporary as now and as near as breath.

As I sit at my typewriter, I fumble over the keys trying to find some figure of speech that will tell what I mean. To say that one suddenly sees the whole world through the telescope of infinity as does God, who is "above us all," is not accurate, for [this new insight bears] no feeling of distance. Only nearness. The nearness of the hand to the wrist, the arm to the body. When I remember this relationship, I see what men have seen since the days of the Great Apostle, "We are the body of Christ." And for this body there can be no separation as long as there is life. We are members of one another.

Into China – To Tengchung

On January 19, 1948, in a letter to Mrs. Rowe (whom he addresses as "Dear Mom"), Berk described dickering for transportation from Kunming to Tengchung [China] to visit the mission outpost served by Milton and Eleanor Buettner. He told her that "the vehicle which the company graciously calls a 'truck' will begin to St.Vitus its way over the road to Paoshan tomorrow morning," meaning that he and Ralph Starr would be virtually out of circulation for three or four weeks.

He had talked to Milton by phone the day before. And although most of their three minutes consisted of shouting, "Hello! Can you hear me?" and similar expressions, Berk was able to confirm that Milton would come down to Paoshan to meet them. The schedule, then, would be to leave January 20 and arrive, with luck, four or five days later in Paoshan. Horses would then carry them fifty miles inland, a journey of several more days. Having been warned about bandits on the road, they were leaving half their clothes in Kunming to pick up on their return. Then he went on to say:

> Here in Kunming, the weather is perfect. Shanghai, of course, made us feel that anything other than absolutely freezing weather would be heavenly. It is probably a good thing that the weather is so salubrious because the poor people here are about the raggedest I have ever seen. The tatters that pass for clothing, look like a poor and very dirty grade of Belgian lace. The beggars are more hideous and malformed than anything that the most morbid imagination could conjure up – eyes swollen shut, mouths twisted to show one or two fang-like yellow teeth, hair that is matted and snarled. All of this partially covered by an accumulation of rags that could not be graced by the title "clothing." But this is part of China – China where the life expectancy is thirty-six and where most of the peasants look with sad or suspicious eyes upon their brothers in this fraternity of desperation.

> God is working miracles for us almost as regularly as the sun climbs above the edge of the pagoda. Please pray that during these next few days we shall be able to be an inspiration to the Tengchung folks.

He concluded with this note: "We have a lead on a fairly respectable jeep for the hospital . . . . The convention, you may remember raised almost a thousand dollars to buy a jeep for the P.M. hospital. It will be called *the A.W. Miller Jeep*."

He signed the letter, "Your wandering boy, Maurice."

Later letters to Mrs. Rowe carried vivid descriptions of this journey made just shortly before the Communists dropped the Bamboo Curtain and ousted the missionaries. Mission work is not for the faint-hearted. Just getting from place to place can be torturous business, as illustrated by this story:

From Under Crumbling Walls
(Excerpt from *The Rest of the Family* series)

"A journey of a thousand miles begins with a single step," says a proverb generally attributed to the Chinese. While there is wisdom in this thought, I have some amendments to make to this time-honored epithet. Namely and to wit: There is much more to a journey of a thousand miles than the first brave step. I remember well enough the first steps of our journey to Lun-Ling, the first city to which we would come after departing from Tengchung.

"It's only forty-five miles," Dave had assured us; "you should be able to make it in two days."

So saying he wished us well and we strode off – down the long dusty road. Our faces-to-the-dawn attitude was strictly something to make the heart of Horatio Alger rejoice. In fact, I feel almost heroic just writing about it.

But the single jaunty step with which we started was not all the journey. In the first place, there were three days of weary trudging up and down the rocky hills of west China. The sun burned down and there was no water to drink – only the dirty water in the streams and rice paddies on either side of the road. We remembered the "Water, water everywhere" quatrain from Coleridge and knew that he would have understood, but lamented his not being in a position to sympathize at the

45

time. Just at the moment when I felt that I would drink some of the water in the little streams at the side of the road just so long as the microbes were not too big to swallow, Eleanor remembered something her professor in language school had told her about all of these streams being full of cholera germs and liver flukes.

"And," she added sagely, "there is no cure for liver flukes."

So, though we were dry as mummies, we trudged on without water.

One of the great gifts Berk brought to those faithful laborers in foreign fields was laughter. Milton Buettner recalls a rollicking episode with Berk on a later visit he made to their mission station in China:

Eleanor, Berk, and I were walking on the winding mountain road toward the Burma Road in China. Our only companions were the porters carrying our luggage. It was early morning, only shortly after sunup. Rounding a curve in the road we saw a short distance ahead, standing in front of a pair of huts, two teen-aged girls. They had apparently just risen from sleep, for their hair stood at all angles from their head and were in a tangle that no comb could easily cope with.

Not long before this time a company manufacturing a kit for giving a home permanent was advertised on television. They would show two women, one having had a professional perm, the other having had the Toni brand they were advertising.

Now, back to our story. Right after we walked past the two girls, Berk said to us, "Which one has the Toni?"

We could not help laughing until our knees threatened to give way under us.

The girls, of course, did not understand the words, but nevertheless it was all too obvious that the laughter had to do with them. It goes without saying that we felt sorry we had not been able to control our mirth for another minute or two.

The Buettners had been in China about one and a half years when Berk made his first visit with Ralph. "What a lift their brief stay brought to us," Milton recalls.

While there, Berk and Ralph did use their movie camera to film activities in and around the the temple (used as a hospital) and in the streets outside. Years later, those films became very precious to the Buettners. Milton explains:

When China turned Communist and we had to leave our beloved fellow Christians, we tried to see how the pictures turned out, but nobody seemed to know where they were. A few years ago, however, Ralph's widow wrote that she had found in their attic the films, which she took to a professional technician who salvaged what had not been damaged by heat and mold. This footage is now a prized treasure . . . .

Berk and Ralph had purchased a truck from a Swedish missionary couple. While they were with the Buettners, word came of the Communist take-over in China. Thus, they decided that Ralph and the truck would stay with the Buettners, should it become necessary for them to escape to Burma. Besides that, Ralph wanted to make some mechanical and electrical repairs at the mission station while he was there. Berk would go on to India and rondezvous with Ralph at a later point in their itinerary.

To India with Love

From China, Berk flew to Calcutta; then caught a train to the mission station at Lalmanirhat (Pakistan), served by his friends Bob and Fran Clark. From the start, Berk was captivated by India, possibly because their great need is exceeded only by their appreciation for any help given, no matter how small. He captured some of his wonder in this report for Mrs. Rowe, "From Under Crumbling Walls."

Calcutta presents an interesting and perplexing sight to the stranger. Boasting a population second only to that of London in the British Commonwealth [in1949], it preserves many of the insignia of the large cities and yet a great many characteristics of the smallest English village.

Brown skinned natives still drink fresh cocoanut milk from the green fruit as the streetcars rattle past. Streamlined American-made taxis honk for the rickshaws

46

and gharries to make way. The crowds that throng the ancient and, for the most part, dirty streets are a strange aggregation of Europeans wearing pith-lined sun helmets, Indian women in beautiful saris, Indians wearing buisness suits or dhotis (a thin garment worn somewhat after the manner of under-slung diapers), turbanned Sikhs with their uncut hair tied in a knot on top of their heads, cowherds that look after the sacred cattle that wander along in the busy traffic and lounge in front of the Clive Building and the Indian National Bank. Little children follow like one's very shadow, whispering softly and persistently, "Baksheesh, Sahib, baksheesh. No mamma, no poppa, no money. Baksheesh, Sahib, baksheesh." Along the sidewalk in front of Cook's Travel Service, a little old lady, with skin as wrinkled as an old prune, squats selling betel nut. Little boys, almost totally naked, call out, "Shoe shine, Mister; two annas (about four cents). Only two annas – good shine. One anna, Mister. No good, no pay. Shoeshine, Mister."

Around the railway station at Calcutta, I got my first glimpse into one of the most interesting phases of Indian life – the Indian railway platforms. They swarm with life at almost any hour of the day or night. At times one can scarcely see the bricks for the layer of humanity that covers them. With boxes, baskets, and children piled around them, people sleep on the platforms. Their polished brass water jars stand by their side. Occasionally they stir to buy a packet of betel nut wrapped in a green leaf, or perhaps to spit the red juice out on the brick platform.

When morning comes, they board the trains, crowding into the third-class coaches until they veritably bulge the sides. If there is no room for one more passenger, then those on the platform push until . . . the victim . . . contracts to make room for one more fare.

As Berk's train "chuffed into Lalmanirhat junction" at some pre-dawn hour, Bob Clark stood there in the drizzling rain to meet him. "Then," Berk says, "in the only car in town, down the only paved road in town, we drove the half mile to the mission house." He described the days spent with the Clarks as filled with both joy and sorrow; but " all of them," he wrote, "were filled with importance to me."

Berk noted the vastness of the mission field in India and Pakistan: one Christian to six hundred non-Christians in the Bengal region; one to seven thousand in Rangpur. Bob and Fran Clark, who had come to east Pakistan to pick up the work begun by the F.W. Heinlys thirty years before, were not merely the only Church of God missionaries there; they were the only Christian missionaries of any kind in the region. The significance of their presence in so vast an area, in Berk's words, "seems pitiably small" in view of the numbers to be reached; but the light of Christ shone brightly in the lives of those they had touched. He tried to capture that spirit on film to show back home. Of a particular Sunday morning (March 20, 1949) he wrote:

During the closing song of the morning service, I slipped out of the chapel and ran across the yard to the misson house. Going upstairs and stationing myself by the window of the Heinly's back porch, I prepared to take some moving pictures of the congregation coming out of the church. There was the beautiful brick chapel with the flower-lined walk leading to it. Outside the door stood the sandals of the worshippers.

After a moment, the service ended and the people came out into the blazing sunlight. From my vantage point, I took pictures of Brother and Sister Heinly as they walked together to the house. There was Fran carrying little Eric Scott. Pammy [the Clarks' daughter] was playing tag with one of the little Indian boys. Were it not for the saris which the women wore and the dhoti's of the men, one might have thought it to be an ordinary American congregation leaving the church after the regular Sunday morning service.

After spending some time with the Clarks and the Heinlys in Lalminirhat, Berk left with Bob for Calcutta to make a circuit of churches in Cuttack before Berk would travel on to Travencore in south India. The Clark's baby boy, six-months-old Eric, had a cold when they left. Four days later he died. Word reached Bob and Berk by wire in Calcutta; and Berk made the long train journey back with Bob, thankful that he was there to offer these dear friends what comfort he could.

In his travel diary, on April 4, 1949, Berk jotted down images and experiences from his time in Pakistan to include in articles to Mrs. Rowe or in speaking engagements back in the States. He also listed photos he had made of the Clarks, including daughter Pam and little Eric; the church at Lalmanirpal, Aurellious Seige (editor of *Khasi Gospel Trumpet*), the gate with its "Welcome" sign, the Mission House, workers' cottages, students reciting and singing, site of new school building.

On April 15, 1949, Berk resumed his journey, spending a week or so in south India before sailing for Africa. His next article to Mrs. Rowe, anticipated questions from folks back home:

"So you have been to India," they will say and then ask (without pausing for breath), "what kind of country is it?"

In my best evasive answer: India is really a great many countries all in the same part of the world. There is every kind of climate, from the torrid wastelands of central India to the lush tropical valleys of south India and then up to the cold of the Himalayas in the north. There are all kinds of religions: the Hindus, who burn their dead; the Moslems, who bury them; and the Parsees, who feed them to the vultures. There were all kinds of governments; in the day before the partitioning of India, there were 601 native states with a separate Maharaja for each. Now, of course, most of these are absorbed into the New Government and the Rajahs are put on a pension.

What is India like? The answer requires a lifetime of study and at the end of it, one would be wise enough not to attempt an answer.

There are many doors by which one can enter a discussion of India in the present day, but each of these doors leads only to another door and it, in turn to another door. Some of these doors are locked, and others of them contain a window of frosted glass through which one can see but dimly, if at all.

> Fran Clark recalls funny moments from Berk's visits to their mission in Pakistan:
>
> *...His wiring Bob from a normally inaccessible train station in east Pakistan — Bob went looking for him as soon as possible on a moonless night, asking in Bengali if anyone had seen a tall American, and Berk calling out of the black dark, "I'm over here!"*
>
> *...His sleeping in thick red flannel pajamas in the stifling heat of the downstairs of the Lalmanirhat house, after suffering pneumonia in China or somewhere.*

Berk's experience in India was profound. Judging from the articles he wrote and the notes he prepared for talks back home, India was for him a fascinating land of intrigue and mystery. But more than than that, this sub-continent of Asia held the greatest concentration of Earth's population — teeming millions who needed to hear about Jesus. That was the call of India that would beckon Berk again and again.

On to Africa

Berk's journal places him in Kenya, British East Africa, on July 11, 1949. He spoke in Chapel on "Growth after Birth," based on John 1:15 ff and Ephesians 4:12 ff; then spent most of the afternoon writing for *YPF*. He preached that night on Ephesians 2:1-6, and made a note that "three came to the altar."

On Wednesday, July 13, 1949, he wrote: "Brother Schweiger bought me a walking stick – the knob is not supposed to be larger than a person can put in his mouth. The man from whom he bought it for 20 African cents said that it had raised knots on many a man's head."

That he was deeply moved by the labors of Ruben and Nora Schweiger is evident from this story he recorded in a book (*When You Need Healing*) more than thirty years after he visited them:

The African sun scorched the barren ground around my feet. I stepped under the welcoming shade of a scrubby tree and looked up at its meager branches. Then Nora spoke.

"This tree was our first hospital."

Nora Schweiger, with her lean and energetic husband, had left Oklahoma where they were teachers in the public school system and had come to Africa to teach. Nora's field was home economics. Reuben's was woodworking. Their desire to help people and their sense of a divine calling had made them sell their possessions, leave their friends and come to Kenya – to Ingotse, a tiny village made up of grass thatched mud huts and needy people.

Nora continued, "We had no idea of getting into the medical field. We simply looked out the door of our cottage the first morning after our arrival and saw a small army of sick people. They wanted help. We couldn't turn them away."

"I moved the kitchen table out under the shade of this tree and began to bandage their wounds. I had only the medicines we had brought for ourselves and I didn't feel competent to give them. But the people came. As many as a hundred would be waiting for us each morning as we looked out the back door of our cottage."

"For two years the only hospital we had was this tree."

"Finally we built a clinic and continued our training and the development of a staff. We didn't choose to be healers. We had no choice."

Up-staged in Kenya

One of the funniest things that ever happened to Berk, took place on one of his visits to Kenya. When traveling in other parts of the world, Berk learned early to expect the unexpected. But nothing could have prepared him for the surprising turn of events one fine Sunday in Kenya. Berk loved telling the story. Berny recalls that he told it something like this:

Some of Berk's friends in Kenya were the Herman Smiths and the Frank LaFonts. Herman was an icon to the natives – at over 6 feet and weighing 300 pounds.

Berk was especially impressed with the eagerness of the African people to hear the gospel. Church meetings were always packed out with those wanting to hear the Word.

He was preaching in a Sunday service. The LaFonts were out of town. Herman Smith was chairman for the service. A native interpreter, Jocko, was translating into Swahili. Berk was preaching away. Jocko, repeating and gesturing.

After a sudden hustle-bustle at a side door, in scampers a baboon – escaped from his chain. It was N-Gogi, the LaFonts' pet.

The natives were stoic, although their eyes registered fear. Herman rose and tried to grab her, but the agility of the monkey versus Herman's girth was no match.

"She" jumped on stage and turned cart-wheels. Berk kept on preaching. And the audience remained quiet. Not a grin or a giggle.

N-Gogi kept racing, swinging, and picking at people and objects. Herman kept pursuit.

N-Gogi came up to Berk. As he would bring his hand up to gesture, N-Gogi pulled it down. Jocko was wearing khaki shorts. N-Gogi reached up, grabbed the bottom cuff and pulled them down past the knees – then scampered away.

Offering baskets were sitting on the altar. Some of the natives had given ears of corn as their offering. N-Gogi ate the corn, twirling as she ate, dumped the money on the floor, and put the basket on her head for a hat. The meeting continued.

She next went over to a flower arrangement, pushed the flowers aside and drank the water. At that, Herman captured her. And as "they" were leaving the church, N-Gogi reached out and grabbed a lady's Bible for an encore.

Berk said he was able to finish the sermon without collapsing in laughter. But the mirth was side-splitting when he and others returned to the mission house.

Later he told the LaFonts, "I knew you were out of town, but I didn't know you were sending a member of the family to represent you."

Sweeping Through Europe

By August 19, 1949, Berk had booked passage from Kenya to England by way of the Suez Canal and the Mediterranean Sea. On August 24, he met Wilbur Skaggs briefly at Port Said, receiving from him a Round Robin letter and other mail. He would return in December, after a preaching circuit through Europe to hold a series of revival meetings in Egypt before heading back to the States.

Upon arrival in England, he had planned to spend ten days touring England and Scotland before moving on to Scandinavia. His journal entry for September 8, however, showed an abrupt change in plans:

> *Among other things one can learn from life is the fact that one never wants to plan too heavily that he will do one thing or another. At the moment, instead of poking around in Westminster Abbey as I had planned to do, I am being shaken to atoms at the stern of the S.S. Saga en route to Gothenburg [Sweden]. How this came about is a "saga" in itself . . . .*
>
> *We did arrive in Tilbury yesterday , . . . however . . . because I had only £8 with which to pay my board in England and my passage to Sweden . . . they said that unless I produced evidence of some more worldly wealth they would not let me into the country – in which case the Union Castle Company would have to take me [back to where I came from] free. But, of course, without any money I could not get back into Kenya and so would have to travel round and round. Which, you must admit, is pretty pointless in view of having some other work to do in the world.*
>
> *Well, finally though, I did convince the authorities that I would wire for money and that I would stay no longer than two weeks. So they reluctantly stamped my passport. Then customs – in spite of all my protestations – would not let me through without payment of duty. And that amounted to 80 percent of the value. Of course, it is not difficult to see that with £8, I would not manage anything so grand. So after a little work on the part of the passenger agent – I decided to catch the ship for Gothenburg. That meant that all of my plans had to be changed – and immediately.*
>
> *The English lady who sat at the end of our table [for meals during the voyage] very generously offered to lend me as much as £40. In fact, she insisted! After all of our fights, religious and political, this was no small thing. Miss Stone, the lady who, I think, became a Christian in the course of the voyage, seemed most upset. But once the decision was made, there could be no recanting. I don't know why, but as I left the train – it was pulling out for London – I was as near to tears of frustration as I have been in my adult life. But so it goes!*
>
> *There were several surprises upon coming to the ship last night – one, that almost everyone talked Swedish. Usually I have talked Swedish only when there was something I wanted to say in that language – or when there was something I knew I could say. But now everyone talks Swedish.*
>
> *Then, one more thing strikes my attention – all the girls look like Ingrid Bergman.*

Once in Sweden, Berk's initial disappointment at missing Great Britain quickly faded, replaced by his enthusiasm for learning to speak Swedish, the language of his ancestry.

> *Attended church twice today again and had an almost irresistible desire to learn Swedish properly. It is a natural language for preaching – and the people really seem quite eager to hear. I am confident that a great work can be done in this land, and I hope I can have some small part. Tonight the church, which seats 1000, was almost filled. Tomorrow the prediction is that it will be.*

Judging from his journal, he did achieve some fluency in the language, for Swedish phrases began to appear in his text, with some entries written entirely in Swedish.

By 1949 the tentacles of Communism were already stretching across Russian borders in Europe. It was a matter of grave concern. In Sweden Berk met a German girl who was going to live in the Russian Zone to "better understand the problems of the Russians." His journal entry for September 16, 1949, records her thoughts on the only way to fight Communism :

"We must not rely on our background of culture, for we in Germany have seen how quickly a whole nation can be changed. And we must not rely only on the level of food, but on the level of belief. The real issue is this: Is the most important thing in the world God or is it man? This is the only 'front' on which we can meet Communism and conquer it."

Wherever he traveled, Berk's antenna was always alert for sermon illustrations, noting them in his little black diary/address book or typing them out on sheets of onion skin paper. While lying in bed one evening in a hotel in Sweden, reading the Swedish edition of *The War Cry*, he chanced to look up from his reading and saw something so unusual he entered it into his journal:

What I saw I could scarcely believe. On the dresser there was a paper bag with two apples in it. The person who left the room before I came today apparently left them. But as I looked at the top of the crumpled sack, it looked to be a white stone statue of the face of Jesus. The amazing thing is that for some moments I looked at it and wondered how such a thing came to be in the room. Then, of course, I remembered that it was a paper sack. I thought to get up and look at it more closely because I wanted to study the play of light and shadow on the face; but I did not for fear that once I started examining it, the illusion would be gone. That, I add homiletically, is due to its being a creation of a person. Some folks are afraid to examine their concept of Christ because if they look at it closely it will prove to be only a human fabrication.

We do not need to fear. The real Jesus will stand close scrutiny.

Berk spent a month in Denmark and Holland, holding meetings in homes and revival services in churches. He stayed with various parishioners and spent time with the missionaries there: the Lars Olsens (Denmark) and Aletta Van der Breggen (Holland).

Out walking one afternoon, he happened upon a classic sermon illustration, duly noted in his diary on October 6, 1949:

"The wind bloweth where it listeth – thou hearest the sound thereof but cannot tell where it comes from or whither it goeth."

Today I am sitting on a mile stone to write. I have just come from dinner at Sorensons and am out for a walk in the autumn sunshine. I am noticing the big windmills that stand in the farms on both sides of the road. Some stand picturesque and still while only one is turning. The wind blows upon them all. But only one has its blades turned to catch the wind.

> **A Funny Thing Happened While Preaching in Denmark . . .**
> *(from Berk's little black travel diary)*
>
> *On the night of October 19, 1949, I was preaching in the church at Hjoring, Denmark. It was the fourth sermon I had preached in Danish and the effort was proving far greater than the results.*
>
> *I looked pleadingly at the clock: 8:50. Ten minutes to go.*
>
> *Words wouldn't come to my mind. The clock leered at me. I was desperate. One good brother was already taking refuge in sleep, and others were joining him. Time not only stood still – so did my mind.*
>
> *At length I decided to look at my watch. 9:20! The clock had been stopped for half an hour!*

Germany was the final segment of Berk's sweep through Europe before returning to Egypt. He spent much of November there, visiting churches and holding meetings. This time he saw for himself the devastating effects of war that he had only heard about from others on his trip in 1947. An undated journal entry records this observation:

When one sees the ruins of a city like Hamburg, there is nothing particularly remarkable in the fact that there are miles of rubble and brick – weeds climb in and out among the debris. There is nothing remarkable, that is, unless one remembers the buildings that stood there.

So with life – there is nothing particularly remarkable in the animal-level on which people live, unless one remembers that man was made in the image of God. To see from what heights man has fallen.

51

Berk and Ralph Starr with the Skaggs family in Egypt. (L to R) Berk with Mary Margaret, Evelyn, Wilbur (back), Russell, Ralph.

Return to Egypt

December found Berk back in Egypt and reunited with his traveling buddy, Ralph Starr.

Wilbur and Evelyn Scaggs agree with other missionaries who have said that the greatest gift Berk brought them, other than the encouragement of his presence and his preaching, was his humor. Laughter means survival on the mission field. And Berk's particular brand of spontaneous humor was infectious and refreshing. Berk loved languages, of course, and came up with rib-cracking "Bergquist versions" of Arabic phrases. Wilbur and Evelyn still remember some of them:

"Apples in a sack" was his way of saying the greeting *ahlan we sahlen.*

"Spinach with a cold" was his description of the popular Egyptian dish *mullakheya.*

"Cut the carrot" was his version of the Egyptian phrase for "thank you": *katar kharak.*

His heavy red flannel underwear was another source of amusement. Having been in colder climes before coming to Egypt, he decided take advantage of Egypt's warmer weather to wash his flannels. Took three days in the Egyptian sun to dry them out!

Berk often told that when Wilbur drove him places around Cairo, every so often Wilbur had to get out of his car and scrape people off the bumper. Berk noted only two kinds of pedestrians in Egyptian traffic – the quick and the dead!

Funniest of all their shenanigans, however, must have been the Bergquist/Starr rendition of "Where Can I Go but to the Board?" sung in "harmony" – Berk singing the melody with a twang and Ralph harmonizing with a "whiskey tenor."

But Berk's greatest pleasure came from the preaching he was able to do for them. From December 4 through December 25, he preached in 28 services Wilbur had arranged in Cairo and Alexandria. One series of meetings was held in cooperation with other Christian groups in Cairo, another series with Arabic Churches of God, and a third series in cooperation with the Egypt Inter-Mission Council. His travel diary contained the schedule with titles of sermons he preached in each service. He spoke to Greek, Armenian, French, and Arabic-speaking church groups.

In a Round Robin letter written not long after he and Ralph left Egypt, Berk explained that mission work is particularly difficult there because (today as it was in 1949) it is illegal to try to convert any Muslim to Christianity. Thus, Christian missions in Egypt concentrate primarily on witnessing to the Coptic church (which through the centuries has become a rather dormant and mechanical organization), on strengthening other Christian churches already in existence, and on maintaining a Christian presence in this Muslim-dominated part of the world.

Berk also related in the letter an unusual experience that occurred after one of the services on his preaching tour in Egypt:

A number of students in the University came to the meeting and made decisions for Christ. A teacher in the girls' college came several times and brought her mother. One night when the service was over, and I was walking to the back of the tent (for the services were held in a tent out in the yard because there was not room for the crowds in the building), a man stopped me and asked me if I would talk to a certain lady whom, he thought, was interested in becoming a Christian. He introduced me to her. (It was the teacher's mother.) We began to talk and in the course of the conversation, I asked her if she were a Christian. She was a Jew. Then I asked if she would like to become a Christian. I tried to explain to her that Salvation came not with understanding, but with the surrender of one's will to the will of God and through the mystic indwelling of Christ's Spirit. After a time she said she whould like to pray, and so we walked back to the front of the tent and knelt down to ask God's forgiveness and to make a personal commitment.

I asked the daughter to come down and pray with her mother. As we were praying together, I could not help thinking what an "international" group we were. Here was a Jewish lady, praying in the French language; the man who introduced her to me was an Armenian and pastor of the Armenian church; praying with us was Panayoti, a Greek pastor; we were praying together in the Arabic church, and I, who was praying, too, am an American of Swedish descent.

When the prayer was finished, the mother rose with joy upon her face. Her daughter reached to embrace her and said, "Welcome into the family, Mother." Here was an interesting phenomenon – a daughter welcoming her mother into the family. But it was a meaningful sentence, for it tells of the kind of strong family ties which unite us. Even though we are oceans apart much of the time . . . we are a family.

That scene made a fitting close for this trek around the world and the magazine series Berk wrote about it, *The Rest of the Family.*

With one footnote: The journey ended as it began – with a longshoremen's strike, this one in Paris. The plan was to sail home on the *Queen Mary*, but all the places were taken because of a dock strike that kept the *Ile de France* from sailing. So January 19, 1950, found Berk "sitting in the lobby of the Atlantic Hotel trying to figure a way to get across the piece of water it is named after" – illustrating once again two of the most essential qualities for world travel: patience and flexibility!

Champion for Missions

When Berk finally returned to the States in February of 1950, he brought films, photographs, and hundreds of stories – giving testimony to what God was doing to penetrate spiritual darkness around the world. In revival meetings all across the country, he took it as part of his preaching mission to rally the Church in America to meet the challenges and opportunities of taking the gospel to all nations. His experiences in China, India, Kenya, Europe, and Egypt found their way into sermons he preached for years to come.

1951 – Missions Tour of South America

In the fall of 1950 Everett Minkler, a California businessman with a heart for missions, persuaded Berk to go with him on a missions tour of South America. They made the journey in 1951, to produce a promotional film about South American missions entitled *Missions Crossroads*. Berk also wrote a series of articles for *Youth* magazine, giving readers, as *Youth* editor Kenneth Hall put it, "a Bergquist-eye-view" of the people and missions in that part of the world. Berk's gift with words was again evident in the writing.

After driving from California to Miami, they caught a DC-3 that flew them to Panama, just as a hurricane was moving up the east coast of Florida. Flying over Cuba, Berk was trying to type, with little success. "This skygoing windmill," he wrote, " is bouncing up and down like an elevator with hiccups."

In **Panama** they were guests of the A.E. Rathers and the Ernie LaFonts (Ernie being the brother of Frank LaFont, Berk's friend in Kenya.) The work in Panama at that time consisted of five congregations, primarily ministering to English-speaking immigrants from the West Indies. On Sunday they visited three of them —Abajo, the Canal Zone, and Colon — where Everett sang and Berk preached, the last service being an Assembly of all the churches. Berk's article spoke to the need of expanding the ministry there to Spanish-speaking people as well.

One of Berk's favorite quotes in later years was "Life is what happens to you while you are making other plans." Those words certainly fit the next sequence of events in their journey. They were en route to **Quito, Ecuador,** hoping to speak with someone at radio station HCJB (Heralding Christ Jesus' Blessings) about getting CBH on the air. Early in the flight, however, Ernie got sick . . . really sick. So sick that the flight attendant urged them to

> **MISSION CROSSROADS:**
> *Maurice Bergquist's Latin-American Travel Diary*
>
> *(from Chapter IX Rio de Janeiro, Brazil)*
> **Thursday:** *Through the open windows of room 504 in the Ambassador Hotel pours a symphony of sounds. All kinds. The whispering song of trolley lines. An imperious auto horn. Loudspeakers turned to hysteria volume blaring out on the pulsating night air the qualities of political candidates. A muted trumpet of a dance band somewhere. Again the whisper of a trolley and the incessant whir of automobiles . . . When other sounds hush for a moment, even the sound of shuffling feet – thousands of them – comes up from the street five stories below us.*
>
> *The sidewalks of Rio are wide as prairie skies. They are made of marble mosaic, and each block has a different motif in black and white. And buildings, new as tomorrow's sunrise and almost as beautiful, reach so high that while I stopped to count the number of stories, Everett, my companion, had walked a block ahead.*
>
> *There are enough lights to make the Milky Way blush modestly. Through the center of town automobiles may cruise at forty miles an hour on parkways such as one sees elsewhere only on engineers' drawing boards*
>
> **Friday:** *Did I write all that jargon about the "music of streetcars and the symphny of sounds?" If I am guilty, at least let me add a postscript. At two o'clock in the morning these same sounds are far less musical. I tried ignoring them, forgetting them. Then in desperation I tried to drown them out by playing my harmonica. I played about half way through the* Melodies of Zion *before sleep finally brought relief. Don't these South Americans go to bed at all?*
>
> *For all my lack of sleep, however, I still believe this is the most beautiful city in the world. It is not only a pretty place to make pictures; two and a half million people live here. Here one of the world's most perfect harbors welcomes seagoing steamers. Here the door to an undeveloped future is wide open. Will the church enter this door?*

alter their plans and fly instead to **Lima, Peru**, where Ernie underwent emergency surgery. Berk did not specify in his writing the nature of the operation, but Ernie recovered fully and their journey continued without further mishap. Not counting the fact that while Ernie was in the hospital Berk was arrested on the streets of Lima by secret service police, who confiscated his camera and took him to police headquarters seated in the back seat of a squad car between two soldiers, one holding a rifle and the other a submachine gun. Innocently, Berk had snapped a photograph of a girl carrying a flower basket on her head, unaware that the building in the background was the Columbian Embassy, which housed a political prisoner who would lead an uprising against the government if he were to escape. Thus the embassy was guarded around the clock by secret police. "People are shot for what you did," Berk's hotel keeper told him.

Berk (right) and Everett Minkler with cameras ready for action in South America.

From the Missions Crossroads Series, Chapter IV
A Bell for Rio Abajo
By Maurice Bergquist

I was overjoyed that Everett suggested we travel together. As far as South America was concerned, I knew absolutely nothing, and very little of that! But I had the haunting suspicion that something is happening there of which the church in the United States ought to be made aware. So Explorer Minkler and your gangling correspondent, Bergquist, followed the path of their dreams and their wild ideas to South America.

Across the hills with their rash of unpainted houses comes the velvet voice of a church bell. From where I sit I can see it rhythmically swinging in the church steeple – back of it a lacery of palm fronds. I wonder what thoughts would ring in the mind of the bell if it could talk as it rings out across the miles from the hillsides of Rio Abajo. For it was not always there. This is its adopted home. And thereon hangs a story.

On a windswept hill in Ohio stood a forsaken country church. The paint had long since worn off in the wind and weather. Blackened shingles curled on the aging roof. A melancholy bell rusted in the steeple. Doubtless it longed for someone to pull the frayed rope that would set its warm tones calling to the people who rushed by it to the city. But there was no one to care, none to release the voice of praise. And who knows that anyone so much as saw the gray building that blended into the landscape of an Ohio countryside.

One day an automobile rolled by. It was no different from the scores of cars that swished by day after day. But wait. It stopped. Perhaps, thought the lonely bell, there is a flat tire. Or car trouble. Nothing more.

The driver climbed out of the vehicle, ascended the hill, and stood looking at the bell. He made some notes on an old envelope and walked away. Life went on as before.

What the mute bell could not know was that the man who stood looking was not thinking of the deserted church; his mind and heart were full of other things: fields of cane and palm trees scarcely moving in a lazy tropic breeze; a church on a hill in Panama; how much the little church needed the voice of a bell to call the people in a land that time forgets.

In a matter of hours Brother Rather had met with representatives of the abandoned church. He told the needs of the church in a land where poor people do not have clocks or watches. Apparently his sincere enthusiasm for Panama was contagious. It was agreed that the bell could accept the call for missionary service.

Now the bell hangs in the steeple of the Church of God in Rio Abajo. As I listen to it this moment, I try to imagine the joy that must have been unmistakable in the first notes that pealed out over the neighborhood, notes that meant "Welcome to Church." This time, welcome to a white chapel on a hill in the tropics.

Flying over **the Andes** in an unpressurized DC-3 that was "going up and down like a synchopated yo-yo," and where the air was "thinner than boarding-house soup," the passengers had to wear oxygen masks to breathe. Everett went up to see if he could meet the pilot. Sometime later he returned with the stunning news that he had been flying the plane for the past twenty minutes! Turned out, the pilot lived just a little way from Everett's house in Pasadena. Had Everett ever flown a plane before? NO!

In **Sao Paulo, Brazil**, Berk and Everett visited the David Meier family and learned about their work among German immigrants. Having no church building in Sao Paulo, the people met in a make-do tabernacle made of old lumber and canvas. But they had purchased land on a hilltop and dreamed of building a church there. Berk preached at their prayer meeting. In addition to the church in Sao Paula, German immigrants had established 25 other Church of God congregations in Brazil and Argentina, a training school for workers, and an annual camp meeting drawing 1000 persons – a moving work "through the persistent sacrifice of people like the Meiers." For at that time the Missionary Board had no fully funded missionaries in Brazil.

Also impressive was the work of missionaries Clair and Retha Shultz and Ralph and Ruth Coolidge in **Port-of-Spain, Trinidad**. Their dream had been to establish a training school for church workers. With 23 churches on Trinidad, 19 on Barbados, and more on neighboring islands, the need for leaders was great. And the missionaries saw scores of young people on the islands eager to work for God and to invest their lives in His service. So they stepped out with little more than faith, ingenuity, and hard work to start a school. The West Indies Bible Insititue opened its doors the day after Berk and Everett arrived. Using the church building for classrooms and dining hall, little lean-tos were built for boys' dormitories; girls were housed in homes around the community. Teaching was added to the already full load carried by the Shultzes and Coolidges. To provide money for students, a small factory had been built for making household novelties and tourist souvenirs. "Coat hangers, salt and pepper shakers, dish covers, sweeping compound, and . . . other things are being sold," Berk wrote, "to pay for the education of the students. Not only will the young people be able to pay their expenses . . .but they will learn trades and crafts they can pass on to others. . . . Sometimes, I guess, the kingdom of God is built with hammers and saws."

What Berk witnessed in Trinidad enhanced his own faith for building schools with minimal resources (a seed that would produce fruit more than once in the future ministry of the young evangelist).

On the last stop of their tour, Berk preached in four of the eighty-four churches in **Jamaica**. A story he heard in Kingston also had a lasting effect on his ministry. Thinking of the significance of the work there, he wrote:

> *Tonight I realize once more that churches are made up of people. Not only are they made up of the people who sit in front of me as I preach, but also of all who have dreamed to make the church possible, of all who have worked to make it grow.*
>
> *In the large church in Kingston, I think of the dreams of Nellie Olson. One day she walked by a corner on which a tavern was being built. "Here," she thought, "should be a church." And from that moment she bombarded heaven and anyone else who would listen to her petition. Now because of God's blessing upon her and her husband, George Olson – and upon numbers of other workers, including daughter Mary, Edith Young, Charles and Florence Struthers, and the Cohens – a church is here. When you think of it, you must think of it in terms of God's grace and of human endeavor. So the large church on Highholborn Street stands as testimony to an adventurous faith.*

Everett's wife, Ruth, had flown to Jamaica to join them for the last leg of the journey. On the road, back in Florida, Everett and Berk relived for her great moments of their expedition. Then they each drifted into their own thoughts as the station wagon sped through the night, mile after mile. Eventually, Berk pulled his battered harmonica from a pocket and began to play softly, the melody of one old hymn blending into another. "It comes almost as a surprise," he wrote in the closing lines of his travel diary, "when Ruth and Everett join in singing the words. As I listen, my heart beats high with joy: 'Where cross the crowded ways of life,/ Where sound the cries of race and clan,/ Above the noise of selfish strife,/ We hear thy voice, O Son of Man.' This indeed is Missions Crossroads – the intersection of our hearts with God."

1952 – World Tour of Mission Stations Around the World

Everett was so thrilled with the trip to South America that Berk had little trouble convincing him to come along for an around-the-world tour of mission stations in 1952. C.E. Byers, long-time pastor in Springfield, Ohio, would accompany them.

In giving Brother Byers pointers for traveling abroad, Berk told him to take along one of those new nylon shirts and to be sure to try washing it before they went. When Brother Byers handed the shirt to his wife to wash, Berk said, "No, **you** try to wash it; **you** will have to wash it in Europe." For Brother Byers, doing his own laundry was one of the first shocks of traveling.

This expedition followed much the same pattern as the 1948 trek with Ralph Starr,

(L to R) Berk, C.E. Byers, and Everett Minkler – travelers of the world together.

56

except that the 1952 itinerary moved from west to east, starting with Europe and ending in Japan.

Wilbur and Evelyn Scaggs looked forward to the trio's stop in Egypt. In a letter to Berny after Berk's death, they summed up the joy of that visit:

> When Berk and Everett Minkler and C.E. Byers came to see us they kept telling jokes, funny stories, and making up crazy song titles until we were laughing so hard we were crying. What a tonic they were for us!

In Japan, Art and Norma Eikamp were also excited. This was Berk's first opportunity to visit them since he had raised the money to send them there.

Berk kept in his files a letter from Art dated December 31, 1949 – quite likely the first correspondence he received from them after their arrival in Japan. Getting mail to Berk during these years proved to be something of a challenge. Letters, Art said, often came back marked "Whereabouts Unknown." In this particular letter, Art told about their ministry in Japan and their first Christmas there. "Bergquist is a kind of legend around our house as in many other places in the church," he said. Then he urged him to come some time so the Japanese could see that he was for real.

It was winter when Berk arrived in 1952. He had stayed behind in India and then came on to Tokyo after Everett and Brother Byers had already left for the States to get home for Christmas. Art remembers well the visit:

> It was cold in Tokyo. Our house had no central heating, but we had obtained a primitive oil stove. The kerosene just dripped down into the bottom of the stove and there it burned. Norma and I were getting used to the cold somewhat, but poor Berk, newly arrived from India, sat and shivered. He kept his pajamas on, put on the two pairs of trousers he had brought with him, and sat by the stove and shivered. I remember saying to him, "Shades of Shadrack, Berk, I don't know what else we can do for you unless it is to have you crawl inside." I finally unearthed a pair of long handled, all wool, bullet-proof underwear for him. From then on he scratched instead of shivered.

> We had a special evangelistic meeting for three days and had Berk preach while Pastor Shimizu interpreted. We hadn't been there long enough to know the language yet. In one sermon Berk had a long illustration involving Mohammed's beard. He told how the faithful expected to walk to safety on the Prophet's beard which was stretched between two mountains. This illustration mentioned the beard several times. Pastor Shimizu translated without missing a beat. After the sermon was finished and we were drinking tea, Mr. Shimizu said to me, "By the way, what does 'beard' mean?" I wish I could have understood that sermon as it was heard in Japanese!

During these early years of ministry, Berk, in his global travels and preaching marathons, was defining himself and his place in God's great scheme of Kingdom work. To his Round Robin colleagues, he wrote:

> I am jubilant when I think of you fellows who are . . . working on the fields. . . . Your lives are challenging the Christians in this country to live sacrificially and intensely. . . . The church will not let you down. At this point I think of the others of our fellowshp who are working to keep alive the spiritual perception and devotion it will take here in America. Pete expresses it well in the words, "I feel called to the pastoral mission." Those words have been jostling together in my mind for the past couple of weeks – the word mission seems to be taking on new meaning – mittere – "to send." Each of us must find the sense of being apostles, of being commissioned to a definite place where we may work most effectively for God. My heart rejoices as I think of the way you fellows are doing this, and I pray that I may be worthy of your fellowship.

Evangelist, world traveler, journalist, champion of world missions – this was Maurice Bergquist, on mission, at the start of his career. But when he returned home in January of 1953, his life would take another unexpected, but most delightful, turn.

Rev. and Mrs. Maurice Bergquist
June 13, 1953

4
Berny

When I graduated from high school in 1947, I was only sixteen. Schools in Saltville, Virginia, had only eleven grades back then. Small for my age, weighing in at about ninety pounds, I was naive and immature to boot. Job opportunities were nil. I was too young for college and totally without funds. With my younger brother and sister, ages six and eight, still at home, as well as my older brother who had cerebral palsy, my folks had all they could manage financially.

My older sister, Lois, had moved with her husband, Verne Troutman, to Winside, Nebraska, where they had a large farm and raised wheat. They had three toddlers and another on the way. Lois was concerned about my lack of opportunities. She knew I would have to stay home and that I probably would marry young, as so many of my friends did, without ever getting to see what was on the other side of the mountain. Besides that, she was weary from child-rearing and farm responsibilities and needed help. So, she wrote our parents, asking if I could come to her. She would send train fare with the understanding that I would commit to stay a year. The next summer she and Verne would bring me back to Virginia.

In August Daddy took me to Bluefield, West Virginia, and put me on a "Pullman" bound for Omaha, Nebraska. He stayed on board until the porter made up my bed. Then he bade me farewell, and I was bound for the Midwest. Verne picked me up in Omaha a few days later.

What a change from the Blue Ridge Mountains of Virginia to the plains of Nebraska! I had never seen so much sky. I loved the animals on the farm, especially a pony-horse named Midge. I learned to ride her right away – barebacked – sometimes with a bridle and sometimes just holding on to her mane.

I earned $1.00 per day, plus my room and board. Lois was a great home-economics teacher, for she had learned cooking skills from the Midwest farm wives. I had never seen so much meat – huge slabs of ham, homemade sausage, T-bone steaks for breakfast – and potatoes twice a day. I had never eaten a whole steak in my life until I went there. We had pure cream to make pies, cakes, and ice cream. It was "cholesterol city" before we knew better. I learned to make loaves of bread and cinnamon rolls, mostly on wintry days when we were snowed in.

Lois and Verne attended the Methodist church, but they introduced me to the Lutheran minister's daughter, Janice Hilpert.

Janice became my best friend; consequently, I was knighted a Lutheran and became part of their youth group. What freedom they had, compared to my upbringing! They had skating parties, bowling leagues, dancing (whoopee!), and card parties with a real deck of cards. I had only played Old Maid and Authors. So here was "Sin City."

I dated occasionally, but not seriously, except for one young man from Laurel, Nebraska. We dated steadily for about three months. When it became apparent that "we" were serious, Lois and Verne broke us up, refusing to let us date.

My beau, Pat, was a devout Catholic and bent on "converting" me. And I, at seventeen, starry-eyed and naive, was wavering that way. Lois was not about to have Mother's wrath come down on her for letting me turn Catholic!

Return to Saltville

Winter passed all too quickly; and in the summer of 1948, Lois and Verne drove me home to Virginia. I had grown up in that year – literally – for the cream had added twenty pounds! Mother was hugging a rosy cheeked, robust young lady instead of the scrawny teen-child who had gone away.

While I was away, Mother's sister-in-law from Alabama had died, leaving four children. Mother had "taken in" Susie and Martha, ages eleven and thirteen, until Uncle Mack could "get on his feet again." So when I arrived back home, our family had increased.

Nothing had improved financially – still no jobs and certainly no college funds. I hired on at the "Star Dust" slip factory in Marion, Virginia, about thirty miles away. Every morning the ritual was the same: I got up at 4:30 and walked in the dark from our house to the bottom of the hill to catch a bus that transported me with all the other ladies to the factory. Along the winding road en route we picked up other employees. My job – "piece work" they called it – was to attach lace to the hem of petticoats. I stitched away at a sewing machine with an oversized wheel. Some challenge! I got home at 6:00 p.m. It was literally dawn-to-dusk. Take-home pay was $17 per week. Of that fortune, I gave Mother $5 for room and board. The rest I squandered.

After two months I had had it. A crowded house, a tiny town – it was smaller than I remembered! – and no future.

After the "freedom" of Nebraska, this was jail.

Moving to Roanoke – Luck Or Destiny?

One day while visiting Joan Woodie, our pastor's daughter and my best friend, her mother said, "Berny, we have just accepted the pastorate in Roanoke. We'll be leaving in a month. Why don't you move with us? There's nothing for you here. You could get a job there, live with us, and pay room and board. Joanie would love it."

I literally ran home to ask my parents. I was still under eighteen, and a "nice" young girl did not just leave home without consent. They agreed.

So when the Woodies pulled out for Roanoke, I was along.

Once there, I immediately landed a job with the City Department of Parks and Recreation as secretary to the Athletic Director.

I loved Roanoke. And I loved the Woodies. I lived in their delightful home for nearly three years.

Mrs. Woodie was a wonderful cook and housekeeper, qualities surpassed only by her rollicking sense of humor. Whereas Joan was more serious and scholarly, Mrs. Woodie and I had some memorable times together – laughing and playing practical jokes on each other.

"Brother Woodie," as he was affectionately known, was both serious and humorous. This dedicated man of God had no formal ministerial education, but was called and enabled to preach while serving in World War II. He was also a good singer, his trademark song being "Victory in Jesus." He had that victory and helped many others find it, too.

Both Joan and I were involved in the church. Joan was an excellent pianist, and I helped with the youth group.

In January of 1950, I began dating H. L. Hungate. A handsome blond fellow, H. L. was gentlemanly, had a good job as an engineer, a nice car, and was a Christian. He was also an excellent singer – a paid soloist, in fact, at the Baptist Church – and a troop leader of the Boy Scouts. On Sunday evenings he came to our church.

In the spring of 1950, Brother Woodie, Joan, and several from the youth group were making plans to attend the Virginia State Youth Convention during the weekend of May 5 - 7. They were pressing me to go, but I didn't want to leave my boy friend behind. However, when I voiced my reticence to H.L., he said, "I'll be out of town that weekend on a Scout outing. Why don't you go?"

It was settled then.

My friend, Dorcas Preston, from nearby Lynchburg came up to accompany us.

The Convention speaker was a twenty-eight-year-old youth evangelist with an odd name. But he was getting rave reviews as an evangelist-missionary, already a world traveler and a recruiter of students for Anderson College.

When we arrived Friday night, I ran into my best buddy from Saltville – Dick Wassum. Eager for news from home, I sat talking with Dick in his car for the entire evening service – only half listening to the speaker inside.

It rained all day Saturday. Nothing else to do but attend the services. The speaker was good, but neither Dorcas nor I were shaken out of our seats.

Then on Sunday morning he preached on "Dreams" and what we do about them. Taking his text from Genesis 37:5, "And Joseph dreamed a dream," he challenged us to pursue the dreams we then had or once had for ourselves.

Sitting there, I thought about my safe, lukewarm experience of salvation – sheltered under an umbrella of protection all my life. No earth-shattering sins: a vanilla coke, a Gene Autry movie, maybe a cornsilk smoke behind the outhouse – all these before I went to Nebraska and was corrupted by the Lutherans! And no earth-shattering salvation!

Never had I had a real challenge. Suddenly, desperately, I wanted a change. In that moment I knew that I wanted to go to college to study for a Christian career. I knew I had to leave Roanoke.

Dorcus and I, both weeping, walked down the aisle together to rededicate our lives to God and pray for direction. My mother knelt on one side and Brother Woodie on the other.

That afternoon the speaker made a brief announcement about his college recruitment and urged anyone interested to please see him after the service. He also announced that he was going to Norfolk, Virginia, right after that; and if any persons needed a ride to places en route, he'd be glad to take them.

Wow! Dorcas and I lived "en route." And we both wanted to know more about Anderson College. So, we hung back and volunteered to be passengers.

When we approached the white '49 Ford to load up, we immediately noted that the back seat was crammed full of clothing, boxes, a pillow, and blanket. He opened the trunk to fit our suit cases in. It, too, was full. The man literally had all of his possessions in his car. We were both going to have to sit in the front seat!

Dorcas and I punched each other 'til she won, and I had to sit in the middle.

The preacher had an engaging personality; and since Dorcas and I both were chatter boxes, we were off and running. The banter was totally crazy. I lamented the difficulty of finding boyfriends who were entrenched "Church of Godders." Dorcas agreed.

Then the preacher said, "Well, why don't we start a Lonely Hearts Club for the

Berk's account of meeting Berny was a favorite sermon illustration. He told it like this:

My wife, Berny, comes from a part of the country not very well known. We met at a youth convention in Virginia. I was the speaker there. She came from one of the churches in the area. I met her, and we started talking:

I said, "Where do you live?"

She said, "I live in Roanoke."

I said, "Right in Roanoke?"

She said, "No, not right in Roanoke. A hundred and twenty-five miles from there."

And I said, "Well, what's the name of the town?"

"We live in Saltville."

"You live right in Saltville?"

"No," she said. "But that's where we get our mail. We live in Allison's Gap."

And I said, "Well, do you live right in the Gap?"

"No," she said. "Not right in the Gap. We live between Lick Skillet and Pump Log Hollow."

Which is true.

And the only thing it's close to is the ground!

Church of God. We could launch the group with just us three and even advertise in *The Gospel Trumpet*. We could make up our own motto. I could be the Field Representative. Berny could be the Secretary, and Dorcas could be Treasurer."

Our imaginations took turns in a hilarious ride that sped by in three hours. After stopping in Wytheville for dinner, I was soon delivered to the Woodies' doorstep. Dorcus had another hour to Lynchburg.

I thanked the preacher for the "lift" physically and spiritually. And went inside to regale the Woodies. What a weekend!

My work was before me. I had to tell my boss I'd be leaving in August for Indiana. I had the college application to fill out. I had to tell my boy friend about my recommitment, hoping he wouldn't be shattered. And I had to save money. How?

On Monday I witnessed to the whole office staff about my new vocation-to-be. I told H.L. that night. We both cried and vowed to stay friends. I scanned the ads for a second job and found one at the Patrick Henry Hotel Coffee Shop as a waitress from 5:30 to 9:00 five nights a week. I continued 9-to-5 at the office, leaving no time for play.

Intermittently, I was both overjoyed and scared. But I was determined.

Pursuit

On Wednesday morning, May 10, as I was leaving for the office, the door bell rang. It was the postman with a special delivery letter – for me. My very first. The postmark said Norfolk; no return address. I knew it was from that Anderson College recruiter. But why?

And what was that peculiar odor?

When I got to the office, I opened it, and . . . mercy! . . . whew! Took my breath away!

My fingers gingerly held a paper sack that had been used for stationery – reeking of onions and garlic! Crude printing chiseled a salutation: "Deer Lonely Hearts Club."

The malodorous missive was from him all right – that crazy recruiter. In the cleverly written note he introduced himself, extolling his attributes as a potential suitor. He signed it: "Your lonely little Petunia in an onion patch."

With the note was a brochure advertising an evangelistic meeting at the Colonial Place Church of God in Norfolk, Virginia. The flyer also included an address, a picture of the evangelist, and his name in bold type: Maurice Bergquist.

What a hoot!

Formulating an appropriate rebuttal took several days.

Invoking my best hillbilly idiom (I'd had more practice!), I extolled my virtues on a brown paper towel, smeared liberally with Limburger cheese, sealed in waxed paper, and sent pronto via special delivery to the address on the brochure.

So there! I'd never hear from him again.

On May 15, Monday morning, I was at my desk when the phone rang. I answered. "Department of Parks and Recreation."

Operator: "I have a long distance call for a Miss Bernice McIntyre."

I had never before received a long distance call. With my heart pounding, I said, "This is she."

If it was from Saltville, it could mean bad news.

"Miss McIntyre" – the voice was deep and stern – "this is the FBI. You have held up the mail in three states!"

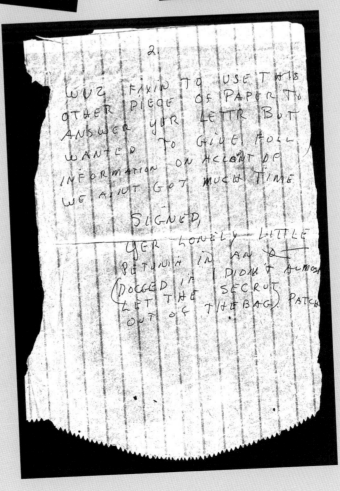

The Start of a Romance

Berk's First Letter to Berny *heavily perfumed with onion and garlic.*

mb and bm enterprises, BTO

MOTTO:

"By Bait Or Fate, We'll Get You A Mate"

THEME SONG:

"We'll Paper Your Walls With Your Love Letters"

Rev. Maurice Bergquist
FIELD REPRESENTATIVE

Miss Bernice McIntyre
EXECUTIVE SECRETARY

Miss Dorcas Preston
INSTIGATOR

Rev. Jack Woodie
Rev. W. C. Blair
CHARTER MEMBERS

Lonely Little Petunia
Onion Patch
Plumb Nearly, Virginia

Dear Mr. Petunia:

The MB&BM Enterprises, bto welcomes you into our "Lonely Hearts Club," You are our first male member and it gives us great pleasure to give you first and special consideration.

Since our club is still in the infant stages, we only have one female prospect. We could wait until we had more but since you are in such a hurry, I have submitted your letter and particulars to Lady Buttercup Astorbilt. She is a fine upright girl, is strong and healthy and is not afraid of work. Although she is not very pretty, she has a wonderful appetite and a special yearning for all vegetables in the onion and garlic category. She very much desires to become second mate in a Harvest Gang of your profession.

I am enclosing a letter and brochure for Lady Buttercup for your consideration. We wish you much success in your new endeavor and if this prospect does not please you, do not hesitate to call on us for further assistance.

Sincerely yours,

MB&BM ENTERPRISES, bto

Bernice McIntyre

Miss Bernice McIntyre
EXECUTIVE SECRETARY

Berny's Reply
"a la Limburger"

Stump #53
Grapevine 7
Hairpin Holler, Va.

Dear Petuner;

MAy I cAlL you by your FirSt Name? IT's secH a preTy naME FER a MaN That I cannot HEPT EsclaIMing o VeR it and PreNouncing It OveR and OveR in My MinD. When Sister McYNtire told ME that She had heerd from A Rael live man who wuz sorta intEREsted in My fuquliTieS, My Liver Turned OVer Twice and my Heart Went FLIppety LitTlE oLd FlOp. BUT the Real SEnSatIon come when I tored the Binder off and my SnOOt reTecTeD the StInK of ACROBATIC SPIRRITS OF NEW ERNIONS. TheN i noo i HAD fOuNd ThE MaN of mY dreamS. Did You no ThET there is Fifty-SEVen WaYs of Pre-Paring ERnionS? I Know 'em Ervery wun! SaY, HOw dId you ThinK yoU cud fOoL me abaouT the Kynd of a FaRRm you presessed? when the poisonality jest sticked Out moRe all OVeR Than It Did any PLACe else? I AIN't sew vurry bLUshy, but I CANSt ThunK ov Nuttin more ROMan-tick than SeTTing by the MoonLITE betwIXt rows and RowS of ErnIONs and Talking Over the Days Harvest.

ERefore I redulge In TelLing you al abaouT myself, You rest ESsured thet i woulk lake to Axcept yOuR teNder OrfeR and WoULD HaIR-LiP GEorGia before I Would FaIlure MyseLlUf. I Am 2o years goNe in A feW More Moons, red Hare, lite Bloo Eyeesplashers; 4 foot, 10 inchers heightY, and Way 147 BarelY. I hav all my teeth axcapt wun Gold One that Pap PAwneD to a FULlUR BResh Man in exchanGe fer a HAWg Bresh. Fir NiGh oN too aNNuals I hav been DePlOYeD As a TypEWriteR fer the Big City in A WRECkreation OrrfyCe, But I Can Tackle Country Work best. I got SenT to A cIty SchOol aNd CitiFieD Ways of Cooking VAttles, and soo-ing peice GooDs I LearnT/ ANd how To BuTchEr Frogs, put numbErs toGedder to make uddErs and learnt peculiar wayze to act sieh ez Eating Square MeAls At RouNd TablES.

Hyar LateLy I've fElT RighT Poorely Over my sHinister -HOOd but now ThanKs to Y-ou, I am MoRe PEART thAn ever. I ant never BeEn Uster much, so Jest Everything will be AllRight fer me.

I'lL be Oblidged to DeceAse thes, 'cause them Hawgs is a SquealLing down in the HoLLeR and hit Falls My LoT To go ketch the Graype vein and go sLOp 'em. I jest this Vurry Minit Herred my Mammy tell LUkey (my brudder) that one of my ANts from a RitZy HolleR is A CominG TomoRRow fer a XXX StaYing Spell uf A Weak er Too, I gess that MeaNs Pap'LL hav to PIPe Sum More DayLite in So!s

2

to MaKe an IMPreshion/ SeeM's lack WE 'JesT AllUs Have troubles and TribulatIONs here LateLy. AnY Day I axpect/ them revenOOeRs to come RidinG OBer the MOuntaiNS and Scatter Our CREmationS OverR the Land. Gues I had ortEr goe and ShIft inter Sum WorK. Hope I ant TalkeD as Much As A full GrowN WomAn.

WITH POPULATIONS OF THE HEART, I CLOTHES,

Jest LiL Ole,

Buttercup

PS I ThouGHt Yore Pitter was Real gEntEel like And yore HandpenciliNg most IntElligaBle.

Writ by maschine
Mae 11, 1950

Quickly, I rebounded: "That's funny, Rev. Bergquist. That letter never left the State of Virginia!"

"Hey, Kid, you win! I had to get out of the car by the side of the road to read it. I was afraid it wasn't Limburger."

"Don't mess with a pro," I said.

"Well, how about writing me a regular letter, and I'll do the same. Let's see how that goes."

"Okay."

He gave me his address in Anderson, Indiana – P.O. Box 67 – and we said goodbye.

Another special delivery came by the weekend. And Mrs. Woodie said, "Berny, you've got a feller."

"No, he's just interesting," I replied.

By month's end several more letters had arrived. Then a phone call brought the news that he was coming to Roanoke to see me for an evening over the Memorial Day weekend. Could I get a half-day off from work? He would be en route to Daytona Beach, Florida, to hold a meeting for White Chapel Church of God.

He came, ate with us, and I took him on a tour of the city. He left around midnight to drive straight through to Florida. Later I learned that he'd driven three hundred miles out of his way to see me.

During that first visit it became obvious that his was more than a platonic interest. Most definitely, a chemistry was there; and I found myself eager to continue the experiment.

He brought me a bracelet of scarabs (the sacred beetle of Egypt) linked with silver. I still have it, and will pass it on to my granddaughter.

Just before the Fourth of July, "Berk," as he was now known, called to say that he was coming to see me and was bringing another couple for me to meet. Fortunately, I was able to get a few days off from both jobs.

He arrived Saturday night prior to the Fourth with Polly (Mrs. Dale) Oldham – the ultimate preacher's wife – and her son, Doug, with his girl friend, Marilyn Marsh.

We all went to Virginia Beach for a couple of days, staying in the home of Rev. Weldon Lane. Berk and Doug were like brothers – the camaraderie between them was border-line insane. We had a ball!

We went to a huge amusement park, where I had an unforgettable moment. As I was ready to be strapped into a seat on the roller coaster with Berk, he handed me a ticket, and stepped back, shaking his head, "No." Who would have thought that this world traveler, who had flown across the ocean, was afraid of heights! I screamed alone.

July and August flew by, with letters and phone calls galore.

One day, sensing from all the attention I was getting that a romance was in the making, Mrs. Woodie said to me, "Honey, I hate to tell you this, but if you marry that man, your children are going to look like boogers!"

Moving to Anderson

September finally arrived. Over Labor Day I moved to Anderson, Indiana, and got situated at my new address: 212 West Eighth Street. This was the home of Mrs. Harriet W. Toner, owner of *The Anderson Herald*. Since I could afford only tuition, the College made arrangements for me to live there, to assist Mrs. Toner in exchange for room and board and a small salary.

Although Mrs. Toner was at that time in her eighties and needed live-in help, she was still quite active and drove her big Cadillac to the newspaper office every day. She was the town matriarch, a staunch Republican, and a force to be reckoned with. Although she was a Methodist, she knew and liked Church of God folks and wrote them up in the paper. She was good friends, for instance, with John Kane and John Morrison. In everything she did, Mrs. Toner had a commanding way about her. I loved – feared – and obeyed her.

Not until September did I see Berk. He blew through Anderson like a whirlwind to tell me that he was going to South America for a few weeks with Everett Minkler on a missions jaunt. After that, he said, he planned to enter Louisville Presbyterian Seminary to study for his Master of Divinity degree. After a few days with Dr. Dale and Polly Oldham (his "home" in Anderson), he was off to Lima, Peru. [Details of that journey appear in "Early Ministry."]

By the time he returned in October, I was a full-scale freshman, balancing college studies with duties for Mrs. Toner. Each morning I was up at 5:00 to get breakfast ready before walking uptown and across the bridge to the college. My classes began at 7:40 a.m. three days a week, with afternoon classes two days. I was home at noon to prepare lunch. Afternoons, when I didn't have a class, were given to study, library, and housework, before preparing dinner each evening.

Berk was in and out of town holding meetings and going to school in Louisville. Thus, I saw him only sporadically, although we supposedly were "going steady." In reality, my full schedule of work and studies left little time for social life or extra-curricular activities. But I was in the Drama Club, and through my English class I had joined *The Andersonian* staff as a columnist.

My column was a parody of an old radio program I'd heard as a kid about an Italian immigrant named Luigi, who wrote home to his mother, giving his version of life in America. In my adaptation, I was a hillbilly Southerner – something of a "Minnie Pearl" of the college set – giving my "Maw" back home in the mountains my interpretation of the citified ways of the Yankee kids. "Dere Maw" was pure "corn pone," but somehow my peers bought it and even thought some of it was true. Truth is, most of my material did come from real life!

One of my new friends was Jackie Monteith, who was engaged to Ernie Gross. I attended North Anderson Church of God with her, where her father-in-law-to-be was pastor. But on Sunday and Wednesday nights I attended Park Place services to hear Dr. Dale Oldham.

Over Thanksgiving Berk was doing a Youth Convention in Columbus, Ohio; and Jackie invited me to her home in Springfield for the holiday so we could go to the Convention from there. Jackie's mom and dad (Florence and Jess) became favorite surrogate parents, true saints and rescuers during my college days and thereafter.

The Convention was superb – well attended with many decisions made. But the North Wind blew in an incredible blizzard over the weekend. We were snowbound. Berk got only as far as Washington Court House, Ohio, before having to abandon his car and catch a train to Louisville.

Jackie and I were overjoyed to be stranded in the snow. We built real igloos, missed three days of classes, and finally caught a train from Xenia, Ohio, to Anderson.

Early in December Berk came by Mrs. Toner's to tell me that he was on his way to Topeka, Kansas. His stepmother had died, and he was going there for her funeral. It would be a particularly painful time, for she would be buried on December 16, the same day of his mother's death sixteen years before. He had not seen his brothers and sisters for several years and had mixed feelings about their reunion. This trip would also mean closure for the old house he grew up in. My heart wept for him as I watched him drive off in the cold.

Dr. Dale Oldham invited Berk to hold a meeting at Park Place Church in Anderson in the fall of 1949. Berk had no place to stay, so the Oldhams took him in. After that he "hung his hat" at their house when he was in town.

In 1981, during the first CBH Bible Conference at Montreat, NC, Berk led the large gathering in a song before Dr. Oldham began his conference. Dr. Oldham then opened with these remarks about Berk:

"I know him very, very well. He used to carry a key to our house. This was in his pre-marital days, and his idea of a good time was to go to Africa or England or around the world, and half the time I never knew where he was. I think he did – I'm not sure. But, anyhow, you'd get up in the morning and you'd see a coat hung over a chair, and Berk would be there. He had come in during the night and was sleeping. I think Polly and I really helped to raise him, but (chuckling) I don't want to take responsibility for him.

"Now, I didn't know he could lead singing, and he gets up here and leads a song. I never saw him do that before. It's amazing how a man can make progress down through the years. When I first knew him, he couldn't carry a tune in a basket, and now he is leading singing. Next, he'll be playing the piano. So the day of miracles is not past Berquist!"

Dere Santa Claus:

We have been asked especially to write you as the students and faculty of A. C. have moved here from so many different places that they are afraid you will forget where they live. Some of them are very bashful and unselfish and for this reason you may not know exactly what they want, so we have picked a few of these problem children and looked into their hearts to find out for you just what would make them happiest this Christmas.

Naturally, the first person we think of is Bumchen, as he is the first one we meet in the mornings and we think it is high time he received a dollar gift certificate from the Okay Barber Shop. "Honey-Voice" Buehler wants a portable mike so his voice will carry in sound-proof rooms. A nickel squeezer is urgently requested by the business office, so the Indian can ride the buffalo's back.

It has been revealed to us that it's Professor Nicholosky's burning desire to have a hand organ and a monkey to assist him in the choir; Mrs. Mayo doesn't want a thing but a new set of scales for "Snozz." Little Jimmie Macholtz says he can't go on unless he gets a Super Deluxe Bottle of HADACOL. And please don't forget a Toni kit for "Curly" Gressman.

Switzer has used her last pair of socks on her face so it might be a good idea to see that she gets a washcloth. And do you think you could grant permission for the girls in Morrison Hall to have hot plates? They're ruining their irons frying hot dogs on them. Would it be possible to have a new pack of dogs for the Snack Bar? The old ones that were keeping the place clean died last week. Oh, yes, we almost forgot to ask for dust rags for each mail box.

And maybe you could find a pair of stilts for Mrs. Ramsey so she can keep up with her husband. The art students exclaim in unison that "the keeper of the basket" is to have a pair of two-way stretch, hand-painted suspenders. Bob Deal makes bold to declare that he wants a real-life angel with blonde tresses in his stocking.

We can't get everybody in this letter, Dear Santa, but this present would benefit everyone. How about an electric Christmas for the college itself? The cafeteria, an electric stove; the maintenance department, an electric snowplow; an electric organ for the Rec. Hall, and an electric chair for the Judiciary Board.

For the girls on your list that just seem to have everything, why not present them with dust mops? Since some of them have learned that man comes from dust, they can't seem to keep their rooms clean at all. And for the boys, maybe a cake of Ivory soap and a tub of hot water would assure them of at least having a White Christmas.

That's all we have time for right now, Santa, so like Lady Godiva, we come to our close. Wishing you-all a Merry Christmas and a Happy New Year!

BERNY & JACKSON

P. S. (from Berny, herself)—

I have everything I need,
So it hain't fer myself
A gift I plead
But there's one thing
I'd ask fer Paw
Please Bring him a Son-in-law!

"Dere Maw" was pure "corn pone," but somehow my peers bought it and even thought some of it was true. Truth is, most of my material did come from real life!
— Berny Berquist

As the Holidays drew near, I knew I couldn't afford to go home for Christmas. But my sister Lois came to the rescue again, sending $40.00 bus fare to Norfolk, Nebraska.

Back from Topeka, Berk spent Christmas eve with the Oldhams. Then, early Christmas morning, he left them a note – "I've gone to Nebraska to be with Berny and her sister"– and set out cross-country once again to spend time with us on his way to California. He arrived the day after Christmas.

Berk was not a Christmas person. After his mother's death when he was twelve, Christmases were sparse and lonely times. His family did little to celebrate together. And after he left Topeka to go to college, he rarely went home for Christmas. He generally stayed in Anderson for the holidays, listed among other "displaced" students invited to homes of professors or parishioners for dinner. Many Christmases, he told me, he would just get on a bus or train and ride somewhere to avoid having to be part of a family during what was an unduly "awkward" time for him.

After the holidays I rode back to Anderson with a group of Nebraska kids – Laura Lee Makings, LeRoy Hoff, and Ken Cook. The trip was fun, but cold (broken car heater) and lo-o-ng. With the guys taking turns at the wheel, we drove straight through.

Upon return, I found Mrs. Toner hospitalized with pneumonia. Thus, for two weeks I stayed in the huge mansion on West Eighth alone. I was really scared there by myself. So, some nights I sneaked into Morrison Hall on campus to share quarters with Jackie and Colleen Morgan or Barb Bair and Alta Ruth Burt.

When Mrs. Toner returned home, the doctor recommended that she go to Florida for the winter, as she did not mend well. Consequently, I was suddenly homeless and jobless. Mrs. Toner helped me with some extra funds to get into the dorm. My dad came up with a boost on tuition.

And God opened a job for me with the Board of Missions. Some people in the office there had followed my "creative" jottings in the *Andersonian*, and two executives working on books needed ghost writers. So, I was hired, at seventy-five cents an hour, to compile their material and write chapters for them. The books were *Stewardship Enriches Life* by C.W. Hatch and *Evangelism* by Charles V. Weber.

In addition to writing, I handled mail room duties, along with some typing and collating and stuffing envelopes for mass mailings. E.E. Wolfram worked there, too, and was the top wit.

Dating "Mr. Church of God"

During the spring I saw Berk about once a month for two or three hours, when he would come barreling through on his way to or from a meeting. We did keep the mail man busy.

My roommate in Morrison Hall was Lawanda Koglin from Minnesota – a "no nonsense," conservative, brainy girl from a family of scholars. Her aunt, Anna Koglin, taught at the college. Violet Deubach, Dean of Women, thought a spirited, "liberal" girl like me needed a more sedate roommate to keep me in line. It counted for nothing with her that I was going steady with "Mr. Church of God" (a title given Berk by

(L to R) Berk and Berny with Betty Harp and Doug Oldham.

some of the ministerial students). Truthfully, I only stayed in my room to dress – and sometimes sleep. The rest of the time I visited other rooms of merriment. But "Kog" was a dear, and even laughed at our shenanigans sometimes.

In March, when Tom Smith, director of the national Youth Fellowship Office, married Clara Lorton, Berk was best man and Alta Ruth sang. We attended the round of showers and parties preceding the nuptials.

Then, in April, Berk escorted me to the Women's Banquet. Students were not allowed to date in two's or even ride to the banquet without a chaperone. I pled with Deubach for permission to go alone with Berk, but she refused. So, we double-dated with Doug Oldham and Betty Harp of Atlanta, Georgia. Afterwards we went to the Oldhams' for a while. Girls on campus had permission to stay out until eleven instead of ten-thirty, but Berk and I stayed out till midnight! I knew the night watchman, who also had deep respect for Berk, so he didn't turn us in. His name: Dale Whalen.

At the close of the school year, I returned to Mrs. Toner, who was home from Florida, fully recovered.

Berk and I saw each other for the entire week of Anderson Camp Meeting in June – for the first time, a whole week of every-night dates. I was caught up in a whirlwind of lunches, dinners, and after-church desserts, meeting his many friends. It was a glorious time, and too soon gone, as Berk, with the wind, was back on the road.

Mrs. Toner owned a vacation complex called "Shadow Trails Inn" on Walloon Lake, near Boyne City, Michigan. She asked if I would like to work there for the summer and take a friend. Would I! I had no job lined up. And the friend was Barbara Bair.

But first, I went to Springfield, Ohio, to be a bridesmaid in Jackie and Ernie's wedding. Berk was to have been a groomsman, but his summer was booked solid with youth camps, camp meetings, and revivals.

After the Gross-Monteith nuptials, Barb and I were chauffeured to Boyne City by Barb's boyfriend, Eldon Williams. Walloon Lake was a gorgeous setting – greenest of green trees, bluest of blue skies – the lake rimmed by stands of birch trees with glistening white bark. Ruthven H. Byrum, art teacher from Anderson College, came for two weeks and painted landscapes.

The inn, consisting of a lodge with dining room and separate log cabins, ran on the American Plan: families stayed one-to-two weeks for one fee, which covered lodging, beach, lake, activities, and three meals a day. Barb and I worked breakfast, lunch, and dinner. Between meals and after dinner we were free to enjoy the sun, water, and boating. Sometimes, to earn extra money, we baby-sat for folks wanting to go into Petoskey to the movies. We enjoyed a wonderful camaraderie with our co-workers. The managers, housekeepers, the bus boy, and other waitresses were like family. We ate together and shared great times of joy and fun.

At the end of August, Florence Orr, Barb's and my favorite teacher from Anderson College, came to fetch us. She was our English teacher and lived in chaperone's quarters right across the hall from us. Miss Orr was our "haven of everything." We fled to her quarters to eat . . . to cry . . . to share! Truly, she was "a perfect woman, nobly planned to warn, to comfort and command."

With our earnings at Walloon Lake, Barb and I saved enough to start the first semester in September. Barb got back in Morrison Hall. But I, because Morrison was full, moved into North Hall, a large old house on High Street converted into a dorm.

My new roommates were Janie Bradford and Beth Shutjer. What a trio we were! Janie was an artist and writer with an insane sense of humor. Since Janie was from Alabama and I was from Virginia, we flew the Confederate flag from our window. Someone suggested that she and I collaborate on a column for the *Andersonian*. ("Dere Maw" had long since died from "exhaustion"– exhausted material!) Our column, entitled "Jest - US," was a hit.

Again, I was fortunate to find employment to help with expenses. I worked with Lewellyn Studio in downtown Anderson every afternoon from 1:00 to 5:00 for $1.00 an hour. Tony Lewellyn was a master photographer. His wife, Sammie, was manager and bookkeeper; and I, the receptionist. They became another family for me.

Before long, however, the dorm clamor and my work schedule began telling on my grades. So my advisor recommended that I try living in a private home again – away from the temptation of merriment. One possible live-in arrangement opening soon was with Robert and Dorothy Nicholson. Wow! Nick, who was now Professor of Music at the college, had been Berk's roommate when they were students there. Laura Lee Makings, who had been living with the Nicholsons, was to marry Doug Oldham on

November 30. Berk was to be Doug's best man.

On December 1, I moved in with the Nicholsons and was adopted into yet another family. My room with breakfast was $4.50 a week, but some weeks I did so many household chores and baby sitting with two-year-old Paul that I didn't owe anything.

Living with the Nicholsons made courting Berk much simpler. The Oldhams lived only five or so doors away, so when Berk was in town he could walk over; and he and Nick had such great fun.

That Christmas I went home to Virginia. Berk had a meeting in South Carolina. The day after Christmas, he drove to Saltville to meet my family and spend a few days. I was mortified because we didn't have indoor plumbing.

Berk drove me back to college, and we plunged into our second semesters with a fury, balancing study and work. I continued working at Lewellyn Studio, in addition to my responsibilities with the Nicholsons. Berk continued seminary studies in Louisville during the week with meetings every weekend.

Rocky Road to Romance

Berk's rigorous schedule put our courtship on a rocking sea. He tended to overload himself. He took twenty hours of school work and booked his weekends heavily. He would leave Friday after class, drive to wherever, and then drive back to Louisville after church on Sunday night, sometimes barely getting to class Monday morning. Because of the strenuous schedule, he slept through some classes, he said, and was always behind on homework and papers.

Sometimes he would forget commitments or double book. Dr. Oldham would get calls from distressed ministers and then call me. Or I'd get a panicky call from some minister asking if I knew where Berk was.

I saw him about once a month. Intermittently I would get two to three letters a week and a phone call or two. Then two weeks would pass with no word at all. Reaching him was difficult, as his dorm had only a hall phone.

When he got "maxed out" with overdue school work, he would hole up and cram to catch up, totally withdrawn from everyone. After months of this off and on routine, I was totally frustrated.

> ### Looks Can Be Deceiving
>
> *When Berk was attending Louisville Presbyterian Seminary in Kentucky (1950-52), his only source of income was from week-end revivals. He would leave Friday afternoons and return Sunday night after the last service. His primary geographical focus was Ohio, Indiana, or Kentucky – churches within some sensible driving distance. Sometimes, he had to leave school early or even skip Friday's classes to get to his scheduled meeting.*
>
> *On one such occasion, he booked himself for a meeting in Michigan, a considerable distance from Louisville. Leaving Sunday night, it took him until 5:00 A.M. Monday morning to drive back. As he had a 7:00 A.M. class, he didn't dare go to bed. So, he stopped at a local all-night "greasy spoon diner" to have breakfast – especially coffee.*
>
> *Sitting on a counter stool – trying desperately to fight off sleep – he dozed off, and his nose hit his coffee, startling him awake. As he jumped awake, he glanced over at the only other customer at the counter and saw it was a drunk who had come in to sober up, whereupon the drunk said to Berk: "Buddy, we're gonna have to quit this kind of life. It'll kill us!"*

In March, a situation developed that put an additional strain on our relationship. I was Program Chair of the Women's Student Government Association banquet. Everett Minkler was coming from California to Emcee. I had asked Berk be my escort, but he was booked for that weekend. So I sought an alternative solution.

I was a P.E. major. One of my teachers, Athletic Director Ernie Rangazas, was single, but dating a young lady from North Carolina. Since we needed a certain number of chaperones for the banquet to satisfy campus rules, it seemed reasonable that, since I was going steady and Ernie was committed to someone else, he might do double duty as a chaperone and as my escort.

Ernie agreed. Berk approved. We were all set.

The Banquet was scheduled for Saturday night at the Edgewood Country Club. On Saturday morning I received a call from Berk. He was at the Oldham's. He had canceled his Saturday evening meeting, deciding to escort me to the banquet after all.

I was stunned. Berk meant well, of course. But his "surprise" placed me in an awkward dilemma. I saw no ethical way, at that late hour, to cancel the arrangement I had made with Ernie Rangazas. To make the predicament worse, one of the athletes called me at Nick's.

"The whole team is watching you," he said. "They don't want the coach made a fool of. So, are you going with him or "Mr. Church of God?""

After I spent a couple of frustrating hours with Berk, he said he understood. But we were estranged. Ultimately, I went on to the banquet with Ernie, not knowing whether my relationship with Berk would land or crash.

March and April were tumultuous. Separation with only letters and phone calls wreaked havoc on the relationship.

In May two independent film directors, friends of Everett Minkler, came to do a film about Anderson College. I was hired as a script girl for them, in addition to my college and studio duties. Lead director for the project was Al Baldecchi, who earlier had done a film for Everett and Berk, entitled "Mission Crossroads," about their travels in South America. [Details of that journey appear in "Early Ministry."]

After Camp Meeting in 1952, I traveled with Blanche DeYoung to Daytona Beach, Florida, to find work as waitresses. Leroy Fulton drove us down. His wife, Jeanne, was already in Daytona working on the beach for his folks at their concession stand of umbrellas and rafts. It was a fun-filled summer. Blanche and I stayed with Joe and Lou Espey, pastors at White Chapel Church of God. We worked the 4 p.m. to 12 a.m. shift at Howard Johnson's. During off hours we worked on our tans.

Berk was well into revivals and camp meetings again. He spent a week in Daytona in the middle of August, and then took Blanche and me to Miami for the International Youth Convention, where he was a speaker.

I had decided not to return to college. I simply did not have the finances. Everett Minkler had written to ask if I would stay with his wife, Ruth, in California while he traveled with Berk and C.E. Byers to mission stations around the world. Ruth had been ill and needed help. Thrilled at the prospect of spending time in California, I said yes!

In Miami, Berk and I said, "'Til we meet again." Then I went home to Virginia to prepare for California.

On October 6, 1952, after working a month in my father's store to earn train fare, I caught the Super Chief from Chicago to Pasadena. Immediately upon arrival, I fell in love with California. Ruth was a gracious hostess, and we became good friends. I attended Highland Park Church, where Denzel Lovely was pastor. And I found work as a long distance telephone operator in the Pasadena office. I loved that, too. Bill Allison, a friend from college was attending school there, as well as Ellen and Quentin Withrow, college friends of Berk. I met the entire Minkler clan and was duly adopted.

Shortly after I arrived, Berk, Everett, and Brother Byers set off on their expedition to visit mission stations around the world. Weekly, I heard from Berk; Ruth heard from Everett; and we compared notes on their thrill of serving together as they journeyed along. [Details of this journey appear in "Early Ministry."]

Meanwhile, I did some traveling of my own. Berk and Everett's film director friend, Al Baldecchi, showed me around California, including the many locations in and around Hollywood where he had filmed small independent movies. I also went on excursions with two friends from the telephone company who had started coming to church with me. We had the same two days off each week and spent the time seeing all the sights – mountains, seaside, Hollywood, Los Angeles, and surrounding towns.

With much assistance from Al Baldecchi, I directed the church youth that year in a Christmas pageant. It was a hugh success.

Everett returned just before Christmas. Berk would follow in January, arriving in Los Angeles to conduct a revival there at Highland Park. Everett had become like a father to me, so on his return I poured out to him my pent-up frustrations about this "on going" relationship with Berk that wasn't going anywhere.

"As I see it, the man simply wants to travel incessantly and do his own thing, then show up to see me when he has time, and he expects me to be there."

Tears stung my eyes as the words tumbled out.

"I'm not going back East to be a 'Camp Follower.' I love California. I have new friends, a new job, a new church. I'm happy here. I love Berk, Everett. But two and a half years is all the time I'm willing to give to a futile relationship."

Everett said, "Berny, just tell him how you feel when he returns, because he thinks you are going back to Anderson so you'll be close. I'll back you all the way."

When Berk arrived, he presented to me a lovely pendant watch from Switzerland and a cameo from Rome.

For once, Berk had not given his clothes away on the mission field, as he had to have preaching and school clothes. After the revival at Highland Park, he would be heading back to Louisville for second semester and a full slate of meetings. But his shoes were worn all the way through the soles. As Amos and Andy used to say, "You could read the newspaper through them." So I bought him a new pair of navy blue suede shoes. And he had the old ones resoled.

The revival started with great response on a Sunday morning.

Wednesday night of the meeting came, and he had not yet said a word about "us." After church that night we sat talking in Joe and Mary Minkler's driveway, where I was staying while he stayed at Ruth and Everett's.

I told him exactly what I had told Everett.

After a long silence, he said, "Berny, I'm as broke as the Ten Commandments. I don't have a car. I have to preach this meeting to get my fare back to Louisville. I don't have school money. But I have meetings waiting. I can't buy you a ring. But I do love you, and I do want to marry you. And I promise you that the marriage will be heaven compared to this rocky courtship."

Then it was my turn for silence. I sat there in absolute shock for several minutes before I said, "Yes."

Then we both cried buckets. I sat up the rest of the night. And I found out the next day that he did, too.

Thursday night Denzel Lovely announced our engagement from the pulpit. Berk and I both were beaming.

The meeting ended Friday night, and Berk flew out Saturday morning for Louisville. We would not see each other again until June, the month of our wedding. There was much to do – but with lighter hearts and so much joy! The next months flew by in a whirl of plans as we bombarded each other with letters and occasional phone calls.

Ruth's sister, Velma, was an incredibly gifted seamstress. In trade for my doing her house work, washing, and ironing on my days off from the phone company, she agreed to sew my wedding dress, with hoop and pantaloons, the headdress and veil, and my trousseau dresses. We shopped Fabric Row in Los Angeles for bargains, then worked zealously through February, March, and April. Velma was also a superb cook – married to an Italian – and taught me to make "real" spaghetti and meat balls.

Meanwhile, back East, Berk was running his marathon of school and meetings. He bought a new Plymouth Belvedere and was becoming solvent.

Planning a wedding by mail was rough, with so many people to contact for both of us. But, finally, the wedding party was chosen; songs were selected; and the myriad of other decisions made. Separated by three thousand miles, we both were in a frenzy. By late spring, I was strung tighter than a banjo. Even a mouse tippy-toeing across a shag carpet would shatter my nerves and trigger tears at any moment.

The telephone girls and the church ladies in Pasadena gave me showers.

In Anderson, where the wedding would take place, Ida Byrd Rowe and Polly Oldham were helping Berk with preparations. A somewhat flustered Berk attended Park Place Church's shower for "us" with me in absentia, since the schedule would not allow time to do it after I arrived in June. Berk opened all the gifts and sent me a detailed list of every one, with addresses for "thank-you's," along with a list of three hundred names for invitations! My friends at the telephone company helped address envelopes. Eloping was looking better all the time!

But we survived. June came and, amazingly, we were ready.

I caught a ride back to Indiana with Cecil and Lois Dixon, Everett's sister and brother-

Berny's Parents

Rev. Mary Mayo Moses
and J. M. ("Marty") McIntyre

Mary Mayo Moses was born in Loudon, Tennessee, near a town called Sweetwater, near Knoxville. She was the oldest of Martha and William Moses' fourteen children, but only eight survived infantile and childhood illnesses.

Her father was a tenant farmer. As far as my mother remembered, they never owned a home. Because of the family's bleak finances, she quit school at age fourteen to be "hired out" by families with newborns, to look after mother and baby for two to four weeks. Her pay, a whopping $6 a month, she turned over to her father.

When she was sixteen, she went to a tent revival somewhere in the Loudon area where evangelist A.G. Riddle of Atkins, Virginia, was spreaching. She – needy for spiritual food as well as physical and emotional attention – was captivated by the Church of God message, which she always described as "The Truth." A couple of nights into the meeting, she went forward and "was gloriously saved." And, as she often said of the experience, "I saw the church."

Impressed with the zeal of the young girl, the Riddles took her into their home as a hired girl, to cover room and board, while they tutored her in Bible study and doctrines of the Church of God. While basking in the services at the Riddle's church, she felt called to the ministry. Brother Riddle helped her gain admission to a school in Berea, Kentucky, to pursue her quest for religious education.

She stayed in Kentucky for about a year; then began traveling all over the Virginia area – Atkins, Marion, Christiansburg, Saltville – as a "girl into lady" evangelist. Advertising was by word of mouth, travel arranged by the parish that sent for her. She stayed in homes, mostly the pastor's, until summoned to another revival. On separate occasions, she took short-term pastorates in Elliston and in Chatham Hill until those congregations found pastors. Chatham Hill was just seven miles from Saltville and Allison's Gap. That's how she came to that area.

When my mother married my father in 1927, he already had two children. She intended to have these as her "own" and did not plan to have others. But God, nature, and life had other plans. In 1929 my brother Gerald was born. In 1930 I arrived. Just when I turned seven and Gerald was nine, and Mother had ventured back into nearby parishes to do a variety of services, she found herself to be in the "family way" again at age 40. My sister Noby was born September 8, 1938. And to compound Mother's "change-of-life surprises," my brother Johnny came calling on September 3, 1940. I had two live dolls to play with, and Mother's ministry was side-lined again. She always gave her family top priority.

Mayo Moses McIntyre

My mother was the most energetic, hardest working woman I have ever known. She literally worked until she dropped. My childhood was dotted with remembrances of people coming to our house for prayer and counseling.She taught a Sunday School Class in Allison's Gap for 50 years.

Mother was also called out into the night many times to pray for the sick. A knock would come at our door (there were no phones), and she would hurriedly dress and either walk or be transported to the house where the sick lay. Sometimes she would sit up all night. Sometimes I went with her, and it was through these experiences that I gained first-hand glimpses of ministry-in-action to the sick.

Many times persons were healed; but sometimes they died. Mother participated in hundreds of funerals – for the sermon, scripture, or prayer. My brother John, a gifted pianist at an early age, had been taught a selection of hymns by his piano teacher so he could accompany mother to the funerals. She preached funerals for saints and sinners alike. One of my fond remembrances of her ministry was a funeral she held for a bootlegger who was, you might say, "killed in action." The funeral was held in his home. Suspecting that this man was not transported straight to heaven, Mother simply "preached to the living." At the end of the service she issued a plea for family members who did not know where they would go if and when they went into eternity. Before she could offer the closing prayer, those family members came forward, knelt around the open casket and were saved before the casket was borne to the cemetery.

Mother lived to be 89. Though never bed-fast, she was slowed by congestive heart failure, arthritis, and diverticulitis. In reflection, she continues to teach us. And we remember every season of her long life.

Marty McIntyre

Certainly, it was a tragedy, but even more so, when it became evident that in this brief union, Sarah had conceived a child. She was already deeply troubled about how to support herself – much less this coming little stranger.

At that low point in her life, her best friend, a maiden lady named Alice Rumbley, came to live with her to be her companion and chief "load lifter." They lived in a small shack, which they finally lost. In desperation Alice and Sarah "hired in" at Saltville's only Hotel. Sarah was the cook; Allie, the maid.

It was into these cheery circumstances on April 30, 1898, that John Martin McIntyre was born. An aftermath of winter and a prelude to spring!

In the olden days, church was about the only "outlet a feller had." Marty, in fact, could hardly remember not being in church. Many of the old-time hell-preachin' evangelists would hold a meeting and not have another one booked. So they would have to stay put until some other church would be in need of a "stirrin' up." Sarah, Alice, and Marty would sit at the back of the church at meetings and wait to see if the preacher had a place to go – which was never. So they graciously gave him a place to stay until he was sent for again.

Marty married Fannie Mae Myers and fathered two children, Woodrow and Lois. When the children were ages three and five, Fannie Mae succumbed to tuberculosis.

Fannie Mae's best girl friend was a young lady evangelist, Mayo Moses, who held meetings in the area. She came to visit Fannie when she learned of her illness, sitting by

My father, Marty McIntyre, was indeed a self-made man. He had no choice, for he had no father. Sarah McIntyre was a bride of only six weeks when her husband, Martin McIntyre, dropped dead at the woodpile.

Berk's Tribute to Berny's Dad

(Excerpt from *When You Need a Friend*)

When he died in 1966, he left behind him an estate consisting of $10,000 on the books (grocery bills people owed him) and eight dollars in his checking account.

His gift to me was an example of how people ought to feel about money and what they ought to do with it.

To get the whole picture, you have to understand that in those days Saltville was a company town. The Company controlled almost everything in the town. People lived in Company houses and bought their clothes and their food at the Company Store.

For months on end the only personal cash Marty McIntyre would have would be the money he charged himself for his own at the store. This way he would have cash to put in the offering at church. Everything else was charged to the account at the store and then deducted from his pay, which was given in Company credit.

When Berny was ten, her father asked her one morning, "How would you like to go to the circus in Bristol?"

"I'd love it, but we don't have the money."

"Everyone ought to be able to go to the circus at least once in their life," Marty said. "This year it is your turn to go. Wait here a minute."

So saying, he went upstairs to his treasured coin collection.

In a few moments he returned, holding in his hands three shiny silver dollars.

"Here's enough to get in and to have some money for popcorn and cotton candy."

As Berny told me about this experience, I couldn't help shedding a few tears – tears of joy for being able to know such a man. Of course, spending three dollars for recreation when there are other needs seems like foolishness. He might have saved those three silver dollars. Today they are "collectors' items." Their value would have increased several times.

In fact, they might still be sitting in some bank vault, because no one would want to spend them since their value is bound to increase.

That could have happened, but it didn't, because Marty McIntyre realized there are some things worth more than money – things like the feelings in the heart of a little girl who learns that her daddy thinks more of her than of a few silver coins.

As I write these words I am sitting across from the old swivel chair in which Marty used to sit to figure his acher bedside and interceding for God's healing touch. The end came instead, with these two friends holding hands.

Mayo accepted the pastorate of the First Church of God in Allison's Gap. It was a tough task for a man, much less a lady. More people sat on the banks and bridge outside the church than in. Marty became an usher and chief order-keeper. During a particular revival, it became virtually impossible to have church because of the outside clamor of "sinners" and the inside "pew carvers." Mayo prevailed upon Marty for help.

The next night two empty pews were roped off. No one seemed to know why, and curiosity ran high. Suddenly, in the middle of a rousing "Jesus Saves" number, a white-robed band solemnly marched in and took the "reserved" seats. Not an eyebrow twitched nor a cud of tobacco moved. 'Twas the Klu Klux Klan in person! Marty was a member, but no one knew, not even Mayo. Suffice it to say, the service was a success, with many wayward and penitent souls finding the help they needed by being enabled to listen.

Marty leaned on the preacher lady, and the preacher lady leaned on Marty; more than anyone else dreamed. 'Twasn't deemed proper in those days for a lady minister to have any interest that was outside the Lord's work, but Mayo did. Marty had captured her heart. They carried on a secret courtship by mail; and on August 24, 1927, two years after Fannie Mae's death, they slipped away to Appomattox, Virginia, to be married.

From that point on Marty and Mayo shouldered together their most significant roles in ministry. Marty was employed in the grocery department of Mathieson Alkali stores for a total of twenty-one years – ten or twelve of those as manager of the Allison Gap branch. In later years, he became owner of his own grocery in partnership with John Henry Elmore. Many poor, needy, and unfortunate people were fed physically by Marty and spiritually by Mayo.

Marty and Mayo always tithed. They felt an inordinate loyalty to whatever man God had in the pastorate at the time and tried in every way to undergird him and his ministry. The McIntyres always had open house for preachers – for if you ran a grocery store, you could always eat.

They, also, kept the evangelists, to help out the pastor. Many an evangelist left Saltville with a full stomach, a sack of offering, and a set of underwear, socks, and shoes from the "company store," charged to JMM.

Marty was a trustee of the church board, mostly in the role of treasurer. Every time his term expired, he would be re-elected. He was a modest man, quiet in speech and manner. His role in church was always behind the scenes – he shunned publicity or special recognition. When called upon to pray in church, his voice hardly rose above a whisper. He was more a "do-er" than a "say-er." His children can never remember eating a meal without his thanking the Lord "for the blessings we are about to receive."

Eventually he semi-retired from grocering, but never from church. He passed away on September 12, 1966, from congestive heart failure. But for his family and all who knew him, he remains in their hearts as the true spirit of giving!

counts. He was a good business man, but he was also a generous one.

During the hard times Marty would often see a father standing in the store, knowing he hadn't enough money to buy the things he needed for his family. Marty would go to the meat counter, pick out a chicken or a roast and wrap it. Then he would hand it to the man saying, "Sam, this is Saturday night and I'm not sure our refrigeration will hold this meat until Monday. Why don't you just take it home with you and have it for Sunday dinner. That way I won't feel bad about it being wasted and you'll have a good dinner to boot."

When Sam had left the store, Marty would go to the record book, record the sale, and sign his initials, JMM, charging it to his account.

It is not easy to give a gift and give dignity at the same time, but Marty knew how to do it.

In those days there was not much organized charity or community planning for people who were in need. Marty's store became a focal point for personal charity. At Christmas time it was particularly important to see that everyone had at least something extra to eat to remind them of the holidays. He saw to it.

One year the local people decided that they ought to organize and try to see that everyone got some help during the holidays. Hi Henderson was chairman of the committee. Being the funeral director in town, he knew more people than almost anyone else.

He came to Marty's store.

"Marty, we need your help to provide some food and coal for needy families here in Saltville. Will you help us?"

"Let me see your list of families."

List in hand, Marty squinted at the names. Then he took his pencil from the pocket of his apron and began to mark the names.

"I've already taken care of this one, and this one, and this one, and this one. It's already done."

There is a verse in the Bible that talks about this kind of friend:

. . . If a man has enough to live on, and yet when he sees his brother in need shuts up his heart against him, how can it be said that the divine love dwells in him?

1 John 3:17 (NEB)

My father-in-law, Marty McIntyre, never spoke loudly. He didn't need to.

Maurice Berquist

Coordinator of California Ministries
1953 – 1955

5
California

Camp Meeting in Ottumwa, Iowa, was but the first stop in an evangelistic tour of the United States. For the rest of that summer, it was "home on the road." Home was our 1953 Plymouth Belvedere, with our clothes hanging in the back and in suit cases. My only house work was to dust the dashboard and, of course, do the laundry at our hosts' homes. After a city-wide tent meeting in Auburn, Indiana, we did the South – meetings in Alabama, Louisiana, and Mississippi. Then we traveled to Bristow, Oklahoma, to do the State Camp Meeting. Warren and Margie Anderson of Jamestown, NY, were the song directors.

Berk preached three services a day. We had a great response for about four days. Then a committee came to Berk and took him to task for wearing a wedding ring in the pulpit. It seems he was the first to wear a wedding ring there, and as a "man of the cloth" it wasn't proper. Besides that, his little bride was worldly. She wore a string of pearls (my wedding gift from Berk) and lipstick (Tangee Natural).

Berk rose to the task. He was wearing the ring, he said, as "a symbol of his belonging to someone," and he was not taking it off. They backed away and the meeting continued to bless.

Cruising Route 66

From Oklahoma we headed to Seattle, Washington, for a Youth Convention in early August. I remember long days traveling Route 66 and the welcome motels where we could take a bath or shower and bask in being alone. We were "company" all the time, staying in others' homes, sharing meals and bathrooms. Privacy was bliss!

But we really saw the country: Idaho, Utah, Montana, Wyoming, Colorado, New Mexico, Nevada – those wide open spaces and incredibly blue skies. We visited Portland and Seattle and fell in love with the lush greenery of the Northwest.

I remember hundred-mile stretches between gas stations. Our car had no air conditioning. And Burma Shave signs broke the monotony of long stretches of road. I kept a log of expenses. We had no bank account and, of course, no credit card. Everything was cash. And Berk always got his pay check cashed before he left for the next meeting.

After the Seattle meeting, we made the long trek in reverse, back to Indiana. We had to pick up belongings and wedding gifts stored at Mom Rowe's house and then head for Kentucky. Berk was enrolled in his last year at Louisville Presbyterian Seminary. We had yet to find an apartment, and I needed to look for a job.

On our stop-over in Anderson, we stayed with Nick and Dorothy and visited friends around town. We had barely lighted when Berk received a phone call from Herb Joiner in Whittier, California. A group of ministers there had met and decided to start a missionary/minister's training school. It was to be called "World Evangelism Institute." He wanted to know if Berk would fly out to confer with them and if he might be interested in coming there as a teacher if the school

became a reality. The proposal immediately captured Berk's imagination. Yes, he would meet with them and pray about a future there.

Our plans were again put on hold. Leaving me at Nick's, he was gone a week; and when he came back he was all agog! He had been offered the post of Area Administrator for Southern California, plus the thrill of being at the threshold of an exciting new challege: starting a school.

Of course, I was ready to go. I loved California! Leaders at Anderson College, however, were less than enthusiastic. Some took Berk to task, stating emphatically that any adjunct Church of God school or college should be initiated from Anderson. Dr. Dale Oldham, Berk's surrogate father and mentor, advised strongly against Berk's going. He felt it unwise for Berk to get mixed up with the new school. Besides that, he wanted Berk to complete his graduate program at Louisville Seminary.

But Berk was a man of his own mind. He followed one Voice, the inner voice of God, speaking to him alone.

We left Anderson a week later, pulling a U-Haul behind the trusty Plymouth, cruising back across dear old Route 66.

August, 1953

Chicago, Illinois
Sunday morning

Dearest Berny:

Sitting here in the terminal waiting for the 10:25 to L.A. I have a vaguely familiar feeling. Typewriter on my lap, kids on the seat next peering over on the paper, the general clutter ald flutter of a busy city. I write the words that I have written so many times, "Dearest Berny." How much different they seem now. Life with you is no longer a dream. Instead of a mountain of bright anticipations, we have more than three months of happiness, three months of being proud of you as my wife, three months of laughing and crying over the very same story or poem. A million sentimental things that would look rediculous if anyone else were to read them.

I wish you were here now to share in the first part of a bright dream that is bigger than our own lives together. I wish you were beside me now drinking coffee in the airport cafe, watching the rich and the poor of the earth, feeling the exhileration of a project that will bless millions. I cannot think of life apart from you. And I want you to know that on this Sunday morning I love you.

Plane arrives L.A. 3:45 today. Would you get Nick to take my dirty shirts to the Chinaman...that way they will be ready whatever happens. If you need any more money for anything, borrow it from Dorothy or someone and I'll get it to you. I left twenty for you on the dresser.

Gonna mail this before the plane leaves.

Yours,

M

Ministry in California

In California, we stayed with Ruth and Everett Minkler until we could move into our first apartment in October. Berk's state office was right downtown in Los Angeles, at Third and Spring Streets. As he did not have a secretary, I was it. Since the state ministry was low on funds, I was not paid. But I went to work every day.

After spending the summer in our car, living in an apartment was luxurious. We loved company and, as we had only one bedroom, we accommodated overnight visitors by our going over to Everett and Ruth's, letting guests have our bed.

On weekends we traveled to different churches in our district. During the week Berk met with Herb and other ministers to flesh out plans for the school. Berk edited and published a World Evangelism newsletter and realized his dream of a daily radio broadcast. He was "in his element"– preaching and writing and creatively putting together "a new thing."Like a high-flying eagle, he was soaring on wings of faith and enthusiasm!

The institute became a physical reality when the committee took possession of an abandoned army barracks in Anza, California, near Arlington and Riverside.

Fall came . . . Thanksgiving . . . and Christmas, our first together. It was exciting to be a part of a dream materializing – the beginning of a school. Berk went to Anza several times a week for meetings and to teach.

Students were arriving and looking for work. Among them was Doug King, a young Canadian who had been converted under Berk's preaching at a youth convention in Toronto, Canada, in 1950. Nineteen years old, Doug rode a bus from Indiana to California to study for the ministry at WEI. He had $10 when he arrived. We took him to our apartment, fed him, got his clothes cleaned, and deposited him at Anza. He was like our son. He married there, graduated as a minister, and traveled in evangelistic work with his wife, Reva. He and Reva would later spend two summers and two Christmases with us in Daytona when evangelistic pickings were lean. Later he did pastorates in California, but eventually stepped out of pastoral ministry when he became a sales representative for real estate and Church bonds. He remains a close friend to this day.

Another of Berk's recruits dear to our hearts was a boy named Gerald Marvel, who "rode his thumb" west from Indiana to sign on at the school. Like Doug, Gerald also met his future wife, Rena, at WEI. They made an exceptional team, developing over the years an exemplary pastoral ministry.

After Christmas, it became necessay to close our downtown office, combining it with the college facilities at Anza. Berk was running out of funds and sponsors for his broadcast, and we needed to cut costs. We made the move in March.

Then, I found myself unwell. For some crazy reason I was dizzy and nauseous. After I missed a few days' work, the mystery was solved: I was pregnant. What timing! In April we moved into the army barracks, trading our cute little apartment for one bedroom over the gym/study hall of the school. Our bath was shared with the students.

Berk said one time, "If I took Berny to Africa and put her in a mud hut, she'd wax the floor and put up curtains!"

That's exactly what I did. It was an ugly room. A long pole that stretched wall to wall held our clothes. A lady in the Riverside Church donated an iron bed and mattress. Another gave us a bedspread. I bought curtains at Woolworth's, waxed the rough boards, and put down a throw rug. A doily, a lamp, a few pictures – and it was home.

The students took turns preparing meals. One crew cooked; another cleaned up. I took my turn planning menus. Our speciality was "Kentucky Round Steaks" (hot dogs wrapped in bacon with potato chips and beans doctored up with ketchup). We sang, played games, ate, and laughed together. Appropriately enough, given that we were living in barracks, we were awakened every morning to the sound of a bugle – playing "Taps"! Nobody could play "Reville."

Berk did a lot of counseling and teaching. I became a surrogate mother/teacher to the girls. Four nurses, already RN's, came from Jamestown, New York, to study for the foreign field. We became really good friends.

June came. Our first anniversary. Berk was slated to preach at Anderson Camp Meeting. Of course, I couldn't go. Berk flew there and then drove back with Joe Bellamy, pastor of the Highland Park Church. I hated being apart on our special day, but knew we'd catch up.

Summer brought a whirl of activities. With Berk's state work and the California Camp Meeting, we were constantly on the go. Berk preached most Sundays, especially at the college church at Anza. He also had all the budding preachers practice there. And plans were escalating to open Arlington College in the fall. Yes, World Evangelism Institute had blossomed into a full-fledged school!

The college was running out of housing. So, when we learned that Warren and Rita Brock, from Baldwin Park, needed a house sitter for the summer, we

Vol.1 No. 1   *World Evangelist*   March 12, 1954

Christians Thrill to a New Venture of Faith

By Herbert Joiner

These articles [adapted from the first issue of the newsletter Berk edited in Southern California, *World Evangelist*] capture the enthusiasm and excitement generated by the project he was called to lead in California – a new approach to evangelism training. The school Berk helped get underway, World Evangelism Institute, became established within one year as Arlington College, which served the Church of God many years before merging with Azuza Pacific College (now University.) Today Azuza continues to serve the Church with distinction in the training of leaders for ministry.

Where in the whole world could the church find a more glorious opportunity for evangelism than in Southern California? Why should it be surprising that the Spirit of God has seized upon the Church of God for a vigorous and daring thrust into this the fastest growing population area in America?

The dreams and prayers of thousands of Christians have been and are being answered by the miraculous activity of the Holy Spirit.

A new thing has come.

Many long months of prayer, searching, and probing to determine the will of God have led to the launching of one of the most thrilling ventures of this generation. WORLD EVANGELISM is its name. Young as this program is, its accomplishments are already many.

It the Spring of 1953 . . . WORLD EVANGELISM launched a . . . leadership training school under the name Southern California School of the Bible. It offered 8 courses over a period of 12 weeks. That school issued 229 credits.

In the Fall of 1953 the same type of school was conducted under the name California Christian College. It enlarged the curriculum to 18 courses, 4 of which were on the college level.

In September of 1953 Christians of this area sponsored a huge evangelistic rally in Trinity Methodist Church (Dr. Bob Shuler's) in downtown Los Angeles. Nightly attendance was in excess of 1,000. Dr. Dale Oldham, Maurice Berquist, Jerry Carey, and Herbert Thompson were the evangelistic team.

An even larger evangelistic campaign opens on April 19. Major members of the team will be Dr. Dale Oldham, Warren Anderson, and Herschel Rice. This campaign will be folowed by a tremendous 3-weeks' push in Long Beach Municipal Auditorium this Fall.

Several months ago the various factors of this gigantic evangelistic movement were gathered up in one organization called WORLD EVANGELISM. Maurice Berquist is its Executive Director. Other officers are Herschel Rice, President; Everett Minkler, Vice-President; and David Martin, Secretary-Treasurer.

Also serving on the Board of Directors [for WORLD EVANGELISM] are John Neal, Lawrence Strobel, Mark Denton, and Charles Benson. As President of the Southern California Association of the Church of God, Herbert Joiner serves as an ex-officio member of this corporation.

The purpose of WORLD EVANGELISM is to offer to qualified ministers and laymen intensive training in 6-week units in the fields of practical evangelism. WORLD EVANGELISM will return many of these leaders to their home churches for more fruitful service. It will place others in strategic positions around the world to serve as lay missionaries while holding civil service or teaching positions as a means of financial support.

WORLD EVANGELISM INSTITUTE (WEI) is the training agency of WORLD EVANGELISM. This school is absolutely a move of faith. No charge is made to any worthy student. Lodging and meals are provided. Students do field work in he churches of this area. This school is entirely dependent upon contributions of individuals and churches for its support. The officers of WORLD EVANGELISM INSTITUTE are David Martin, President; Herbert Joiner, Dean; Gunnar Jorgensen, Registrar. Instructors are Maurice Berquist, Herschel Rice, J.G. Beecher, and Herbert Joiner.

This issue of the WORLD EVANGE-LIST . . . reports the activities of WORLD EVANGELISM INSTITUTE in detail. Wesley and Jean Lancaster have already gone to Alaska as full-time missionaries sponsored by WEI. Jim and Elizabeth Chapman have come from Virginia to prepare for active service in the evangelistic field. Blanche de Young, a recent graduate of Anderson College, is enrolled preparatory to full-time service. Don and Arlene Goens will be going to Japan in the next 4 months as full-time WEI missionaries. Don has an A.B. and M.A. from Nazarene College of Pasadena and has done work toward a doctorate at University of Southern Claifornia. Bill Williamson has come from Seattle to train for "Skid Row" service. Gerald Davis has come from Alaska. Such devotion [and] such enthusiam defy description. . . .

What will become the full scope of WORLD EVANGELISM? Nobody knows. Every step thus far taken has been a step of faith. Space will not permit a recounting of the many miraculous answers to prayer that have blessed this venture. Suffice it to say that all who have had vital contact with WORLD EVANGELISM from its inception know beyond any shadow of doubt that it enjoys the benediction of God. Through this daring venture God has captured the imagination of many thousands of Christians. Churches have been genuinely revived. Hope runs high. Young men and women are stepping out on faith to answer the call. Their daring matches that of early pioneers who "by faith . . . crossed the Red Sea as if on dry land . . . by faith conquered kingdoms, enforced justice, received promises, . . . won strength out of weakness."

Editorial

By Maurice Berquist

From the icy wastes of Alaska to the craggy mountains of Virginia has come an overwhelming response to World Evangelism. By long distance telephone, by letter, and by personal conversation has come an avalance of questions. What is World Evangelism?

The first answer to the question is, "World Evangelism is the only commission of the church." This is a trite answer. But something has happened. A stethoscope has been placed on the heart of the church and has discovered that the Christian people are desperately concerned to evangelize the world. Multitudes of young people wait eagerly for "marching orders" from God.

In answer to the cry for some way to attack the gigantic task of evangelizing the world a movement called WORLD EVANGELISM was born.

The term "movement" is not a mistake. In the past three months many things have

Statement of Policy

of the Association of the Church of God of Southern California

The following statement of policy submitted by the special study and planning committee was unanimously ratified by the Association of the Churches of God in Southern California on October 17, 1953, at Whittier and on December 2, 1953, at South Los Angeles at a record attendance of the Association. Members of the planning committee were D. Martin, J. Neal, D. Lovely, M. Denton, L. Strobel, C. Benson, E. Minkler, and H. Joiner, Ex-officio.

. . . "World Evangelism," is not to contradict but to supplement and implement existing programs, and to initiate further activities in fields which existing agencies are not set up to handle, such as

(1) Short-term training for personal witnessing of self-supporting lay missionaries.
(2) Correspondence courses.
(3) Refresher courses for ministers and gospel workers.
(4) Leadership training classes.
(5) Evangelistic rallies.
(6) Sunday School promotion and improvement.
(7) New churches.
(8) Means for areawide interchange of information, activities, news.
(9) Centralized headquarters for all So. California Church of God activities.

Directors of World Evangelism

(Top, L to R) Herschel Rice, Pomona pastor, is the newly elected President of World Evangelism. David Martin is President of World Evangelism Institute and Secretary-Treasurer of World Evangelism. Everett Minkler, President of California Marble Company is Vice-President of World Evangelism. Mark Denton, Glendale pastor, is a member of the Board of Directors.

(Bottom, L to R) Other members of the Board of Directors are Charles Benson, pastor at Pacific Beach; John Neal, South Los Angeles pastor; Lawrence Strobel, President of Western Arts Publishers. C. Herbert Joiner, Whittier pastor and President of the Southern California Association of the Church of God is an ex-officio member of the Board of Directors.

---

been moving. Scores of people have been moved to pray with a fervency never known before. In answer to their prayers automobile wheels began to turn. All across the country young people quit their jobs and moved out by faith to prepare for their real life's work, "Evangelism." Revival has come to many churches who had thought it impossible.

The international office of World Evangelism is in Los Angeles, California. But the program which has risen miraculously during the past three months did not come from an office. It was born out of the fervent dreams and prayers of ministers, students, businessmen, and housewives. And out of the concern of God Himself for a world desperately in need.

It beame readily apparent that the initials of World Evangelism were W.E. As the army of the concerned prayed, men began to wonder, "What shall 'WE' do?"

In those letters are the answers to many quesions. They are not limited to what "I" can do. Nor are they waiting on "You."

What can "we" do together? World Evangelism is eager to augment and supplement any program that spreads the gospel around the world. National and local church leaders have rejoiced to see a spirit of daring and adventure in the work of evangelism.

We are convinced that every Christian must be an evangelist.

World Evangelism does not plan to call or send missionaries. This is the work of the Spirit of God. But we are praying that God will raise an army of engineers, school teachers, typists, clerks, businessmen, and full-time gospel workers who will volunteer to be trained as "World Evangelists." Unless thousands of 24-hour-a-day Christians are sent in the next few years, the greatest opportunity of the century will have been squandered. World Evangelism does plan to provide, free of cost to worthy students, a six weeks' intensive course in "Evangelism" as a "basic training" for full-time service on the front lines of World Evangelism.

I Trust
By Doug King

Jesus tells us in His word that if we have the faith of a mustard seed, we can move mountains. Somehow God has planted this faith in my heart, and that is why I am attending WEI.

A few months ago the Berquists left Anderson, Indiana for California with a vision of a thrilling evangelistic movement. They told me briefly about it before they left . . . I wrote and received a couple of letters from them and somehow I felt like I wanted to go out, but I couldn't make up my mind.

I really prayed about it and in February, I received another letter; then decided to go. Many people thought I was taking the wrong step; but I knew it was God's will and that everything would work out.

I left Anderson on faith and the Lord has really supplied my needs out here. I haven't regretted a minute of it. The school is a thrilling experience. We have just begun and there are great things ahead of us.

World Evangelist   Vol. 1, No. 3, 1954

Year of the Pioneer
by Maurice Berquist

My grandfather Swanson owned some land in Kansas. Yet he never paid a penny for it. It was his more truly than the people who bought it from him when he moved into the little city of Chanute because the farm was too much work for an old man. So the old homestead moved away from the land.

The strange part of all this is that he was a son of the Sunflower state in a way I will never be. He was born in Skoning, Sweden. I was born in Topeka, Kansas. It belonged to him rather than to me, because he developed it. With his young bride he came to the windswept plains of Kansas. A house was made of sod. Then the fields were plowed and planted. Barns and fences came. Cattle grazed on the pasture land. The Government gave him the land, because he conquered it.

Those were bitter days; I have heard my mother tell of it many times. "He would go for weeks," she said, "without enough money to buy a postage stamp." Sickness and drought took their toll again and again. But Grandfather Swanson stayed on. The land belonged to him. And it still does.

There's a different name on the deed now. A modern highway cuts across the section and busy people in shiny cars whirl by. But the land belongs to the pioneers . . . those who subdued it and developed it.

This is the year of the Pioneers in the Church. Especially it is the year of the pioneers regarding Arlington College. September 30, 1954, will see young people from all over the United States registering for classes in a new school. On Monday following, they will begin their classes. For the most part they will look like the students of all the other classes that will follow them.

There will be some who are young – some who are older. Some will have previous college experience and others will have come directly from high school. They will be just a typical group of Christians attending a Bible school.

One thing, however, they will have that they can never share with another class, the "Pride of the Pioneer." The college will be in a large measure what Emerson said any situation is – "their lengthened shadow." They will blaze a trail in which thousands of other feet will walk. They will lay foundations on which countless others will build their lives. They will be, in time, that grand army of adventurers of whom millions will say wistfully, "I wish I had been one of them."

But the pride of pioneering is not all. There is a price. This is no task for the half-hearted drifter who waits for a gentle breeze of fortune to waft him into the harbor of success. Pioneering is for the courageous.

Arlington College does not offer an easy, breezy vacation in ivy covered halls. For the pioneer of this glorious first year there will be the inconvenience of a bustling building program, the frustrations of a thousand new adjustments, and the dogged discipline of the army of "pace setters." But these people will love it all. For they are pioneers.

To these whose names and faces I do not yet know, I dedicate a story.

A small boy with his sister were trying valiantly to climb to the top of a mountain near their home. The little girl complained that the way was too difficult – she could never make it to the top.

"I know a short cut," suggested her brother. He led her through brambles and over some rocks.

"You said you knew of a path to the top," she cried while trying to get her breath. "There is no path here, just the rough places."

Reaching his hand to his sister, the hardy lad said, "I know, but the rough places are what you climb on."

A salute to the climbers – a salute to the Pioneers. The future belongs to them. And Arlington College is a part of the future.

Berk, the Pioneer

Those who called him to Southern California knew Maurice Berquist to be a catalyst and a motivator.

Once he was sold on a idea, Berk's enthusiasm was infectious. He was fearless in charting new territory, undaunted by impossible odds, for he believed unwaveringly that if the cause was right, God would even the odds, making even the "impossible" do-able.

During his lifetime he would be involved at some level in the founding or preserving of at least three other Church of God schools. To these enterprises he invested himself fully in fervent prayer, hard work, and personal finances.

Arlington College (1954 - 1968)

The school Berk helped launch in 1953 in Southern California, World Evangelism Institute (WEI), became established within one year as Arlington College, a four-year liberal arts school, specialing in "practical training for service in the church at home and abroad."

With C. Herbert Joiner as President, Arlington College opened on September 30, 1954, offering Bachelor of Arts degrees in Bible, Religion, Christian Education, Music, and Social Studies. Also available were diploma programs: Ministerial (3 years) and Christian Education (2 years).

Azusa Pacific University

In 1968 Arlington College merged with Azusa Pacific College (now Azusa Pacific University), a fully accredited interdenominational Christian school with a strong Wesleyan tradition since its founding in 1899. At the time of merger, Arlington President Dewayne B. Bell served as Assistant to the President and Director of College Relations. Fred Shackleton, Dean of Arlington, became Coordinator of Graduate Studies. Azusa's affiliation with the Church of God continues to this day.

volunteered. A real house – with a yard and a kitchen. Doug King moved in with us. Then, in August, Everett and Ruth Minkler asked us to house-sit for them while they made a tour of mission stations around the world to scout out missions projects that might involve students and graduates of the school.

With the move to the Minkler home, we came up in the world fast. I was now waxing marble floors. And company came pouring in.

Joe and Lou Espey came from Florida with Bill Ellis in tow and stayed a week. Doug King stayed there most of the time. Richard Lee Meischke (known in his radio ministry as Dick Lee) moved in for a month or two. Dick was a great help to Berk with the radio program. A man named Phil Kerr was doing a weekly Christian musical at the Pasadena auditorium, and Dick was able to round up some of the featured singers to be on Berk's broadcast. Doris and Fred Shackleton and their two kids (one is "the" Martin Shackleton at Mid-America Bible College) moved in for three weeks while they taught at the college. Doris was expecting in November – I, in December.

These were all wonderful guests, sharing both chores and expenses. And with Fred's musical touch, the Minklers' piano and organ came alive and the house rang with music and singing. Sometimes we'd be up 'til midnight. I always made dessert and coffee. Berk and I loved the fellowship of these friends.

The week of November 7 Berk started a revival with Herschell Rice in Pomona. We drove the sixty miles back and forth each night. That was a regular routine for Berk: office or school by day; preaching within driving distance at night.

Marty

On Thursday (November 11, 1954) I awoke around 4:00 a.m. with an ache in my side. I sat up a while; but when the pain grew worse, I woke Berk. False labor pains, obvously. Berk called the doctor, who suggested we come in, and he would give me a shot to stop the labor because, in his words, "the baby wasn't ready yet."

It was pouring rain in Pasadena. We had a thirty-minute ride to Burbank, arriving at St. Joseph's Hospital at 6:30 a.m. They whisked me upstairs and sent Berk off to drink coffee, saying they'd be back with me later.

I remember an injection and the examination, and I went to sleep. That's all I remember until 1:30 that afternoon.

Berk later filled me in on the rest of the story.

He was sitting in the lounge drinking coffee and dozed off. At 8:45 a nurse shook him awake.

"Are you Mr. Berquist?" she inquired.

"Yes."

"Will you please come with me. Dr. Walker would like to talk with you. Your wife has delivered."

"Delivered what?"

"Her baby. I'm taking you up to see her."

"What did we have?" Berk asked, in a daze.

"I'm not allowed to say," she replied. "We've made mistakes."

"Is my wife okay?"

"Yes."

They had arrived at the OB suite, where Dr. Walker was waiting.

"Mr. Berquist, you have a son. He is little – 5 lbs. 2 oz.– and has to be incubated. He has a slight breathing problem, which bears watching. Your wife shouldn't have delivered yet, but she was ready when she got here. We had to work fast. We gave her a spinal and sodium pentethol, so she'll be out until noon. I suggest you come back at the 2:00 p.m. visiting hours. Would you like to see your son?"

"Yes."

Berk said a nurse came out with this tiny bundle. She uncovered every inch to show Berk the baby was okay. His legs were the size of Berk's thumb.

Later that day, I was awakened by a nurse, wiping my face. I had a splitting headache, and she was rousing me.

"Mrs. Berquist, I want you to wake up. It's almost 2:00 p.m., and your husband is standing outside with a big bunch of roses.

"Why?" I asked.

"Well, you delivered."

In shock I patted an empty stomach. "What did I have?"

"A tiny boy. We'll be in to show him to you."

At that moment Berk came striding in with a smile to match the stride, and, in his hand, a dozen red roses.

"Wow," he said, presenting the flowers, "you don't fool around, do you? Where's all the travailing in birth?"

We were both overjoyed. Maurice Martin Berquist was here!

I was in the hospital six days; Marty had to stay an extra week. When we went to pick him up, he weighed 4 lbs. 14 oz. We were parents and we weren't ready.

Berk and Berny in their trailer with Baby Marty (seven months old).

The doctor quarantined Marty and me for one month because he was six weeks premature. I couldn't take him out, nor could he have visitors because of the risk of infection. As Berk often told in sermons, Marty was awake about every two hours for nearly two years. It truly was a vigil.

In early December, when the Minklers returned to Pasadena, we went to Riverside to stay with a family there. Then, after Christmas, the Vernon Thomas family in Madera loaned us a 27-foot house trailer that was "home" for the rest of the winter.

On the Road Again

By spring Berk was ready to get on the road again. I wanted to stay put. But at that time I didn't know about all the personal monetary sacrifices he had made to keep the radio broadcast going and all the revivals he had booked for the future to catch us up financially. He was winding up his administrative assignment; the radio broadcast had been sidelined for lack of funds; Arlington College was off and running, and Berk was eager to get back to "just preaching."

We drove to Nebraska and Oklahoma for meetings, then back to California. Marty was a fussy baby. He took about all the time we both could give. I was quite thin . . . and tired. In fact, I was tired all the time. In March I was so run down I finally went for a checkup. The doctor said I was badly in need of vitamins. Turned out that I needed more than vitamins – I needed two cribs! The stork was going to come calling again, and we hadn't invited him.

On May 1, 1955, we pulled out into Los Angeles traffic, towing our silver bullet. Berk had never pulled a trailer before, and here we were heading out toward Route 66 again – this time with one and one-half babies! Destination: Houston and Gulf Coast Bible College, where Berk would conduct a seminar for ministry students.

Our trip across the desert was unforgettable!

One morning as we were streaking down Route 66 – headed for Houston – Marty developed "the runs"! It was hot and humid. The car had no air-conditioning. I was nauseated with morning sickness and Berk had the windows down. The diaper pail was filling up – no disposables in those days. Service stations were a hundred miles apart, so there was no place to wash out the diapers. In the stifling heat, the smell in the car was becoming unbearable.

On a long, barren stretch of road, Berk suddenly slowed down, stopped, and said, "I'm gonna bury those diapers!"

He got out of the car, grabbed the diaper pail, dug a hole, and gave those "bird's-eyes" a decent burial.

"Let's hope we have a prosperous meeting," he muttered as he got back in the car. "I'll buy another dozen before I'll endure that!"

I "urped" up my breakfast and we journeyed on!

In Houston at last, we parked on the College grounds near the church. Max Gaulke, the college president, greeted us warmly. It was already 90 degrees in Texas! He asked Berk if he could please have his seminar notes, so he could have a course syllabus typed up for the students.

"I don't have any," Berk replied. "You'll just have to get them as I speak."

"You mean you're going to lecture the way you preach — without notes?"

"That's the only way I operate," Berk said.

I thought Max would faint. Berk was talking to one of the most organized of church administrators.

Max solved his dilemma by taping each lecture and having a secretary take notes — like a court stenographer — then type it up and hand it out the next day. He got his syllabus!

Berk also preached every night at the church.

Morning sickness hit me full force. I was so sick every morning, Berk hired a college student to take care of Marty while he lectured. Then he took the afternoon shift. I was able to revive myself enough during the day to take over during the evening service. Dr. Loren Rohr checked me over and had a long talk with Berk about getting Marty and me "off the road" as soon as possible.

We managed a couple of revivals en route to Anderson Camp Meeting: one with Tom and Mary Lee in Tulsa, Oklahoma; the other with Woodrow Starkey in Vincennes, Indiana, where we were guests in the home of Lowell and Dorothy Wilson. By the time we got to Vincennes, Marty was sick with fever and had tiny blisters on his face and body. In spite of all our precautions, he had picked up chicken pox from the Lee's children in Tulsa! Only 6-1/2 months old, he gave new meaning to the word *fretful*! We were so thankful to the Wilsons for two more pairs of adult arms to help.

Lori

After Anderson Camp Meeting we left the trailer in Anderson and headed for Saltville. Acting on Dr. Rohr's advice, Berk was taking me home to Mother! My family hadn't seen Marty yet, and I was going to "stay put" all summer. Little Marty was welcomed warmly. I rested and helped Mother with her chores. Berk was in and out all summer, but Marty and I stayed in Saltville.

We left early in October, headed for Indiana — Huntington and Fort Wayne — to hold meetings. Then we moved on to Anderson to look for a place to live. Mary and Joseph had to find a stable and a doctor. We had left Marty with Mother.

We rented an apartment from Tom and Clara Smith, who were on a teaching assignment in Portland, Oregon. I went to Dorothy Nicholson's Dr. Donaldson for a checkup. He said I would deliver within ten days. That was October 15. Dorothy was expecting at the same time.

Meanwhile, Berk was finishing a revival in Huntington. He closed the meeting on Sunday night, October 22. We had a few days to catch our breath.

Dorothy and Nick celebrated Gary's arrival on October 24.

Lori Ellen made her debut at 3:30 a.m. on October 26, 1955. She weighed a "monstrous" 5 lbs. 12 oz. and was a little doll.

When the nurse handed Berk his new daughter for the first time, he looked into her tiny face and said, "Now, here's another woman for me to try to understand."

Some time later, Berk captured memorable moments from their first years together in this poem he penned for Berny.

* * *

Diapers in the desert,
Cornbread on the lake,
Stories from the mountains,
Rosie's birthday cake;
A hundred thousand reasons
To make each moment shine;
So here on Feb. the 14th
Be my valentine.

Birch bark thank you letters,
Bills upon the first,
Liking Filet Mignon,
Hating Liverwurst;
A hundred thousand reasons
To make each moment shine;
So here on Feb. the 14th
Be my valentine.

Tears at Grampa's funeral,
Laughs at Everett's jokes,
Taken from a note book:
"Honey, buy some Cokes";
A hundred thousand reasons
To make each moment shine;
So here on Feb. the 14th
Be my valentine.

Admitting to Miss Clairol
A few new strands of grey,
Asking God for courage
To face another day;
A hundred thousand reasons
To make each moment shine;
So here on Feb. the 14th
Be my valentine.

Struggling over textbooks,
Baking "homemade" bread,
Hoarding up three dollar bills
When someone was wed;
A hundred thousand reasons
To make each moment shine;
So here on Feb. the 14th
Be my valentine.

Saving for a cookstove
Smaller than a stamp,
Thinking of the Waldorf
As a "place to camp";
A hundred thousand reasons
To make each moment shine;
So here on Feb. the 14th
Be my valentine.

Berk.

Having no help at home, I stayed in the hospital six days. Berk left the day after I was settled to get Mother and Marty in Virginia. When they returned, Marty didn't know me and wouldn't come to me. He clung to "Maw Maw" for dear life.

Berk left for the West Coast when Lori was two weeks old. Mother stayed a week and went back on the train. I was devastated at times. My wealth was in the loving neighbors on Seventh Street. The Oldhams lived two doors up; the Nicholsons two doors down; and the Reardons next to them. Across from Reardons lived the T. Franklin Millers. They all visited.

Dr. Dale tried to get Berk to cancel the West Coast meetings and stay home with his family. Marvin Hartman was leaving Park Place to take a pastorate in Michigan. Dr. Dale offered the associate position to Berk, but he was deeply committed to go evangelize.

I had no car and couldn't drive anyway. Earl Gadberry delivered my groceries; a college girl helped me on Saturdays; and a dear saint named Titia DeYoung came every evening and spent the night. Someone came every day. Jo Jo Baxter came after work almost every day to bathe and hold Lori. And a new "old" friend named Pearl Reardon, Dr. Bob's mother, came by daily. A young semi-

Baby Lori joins brother Marty on the road with Mom and Dad.

nary couple, George and Ruth Reed, lived in the downstairs apartment. They also checked on me every day, and Marty spent hours with them.

Berk wrote every day, but he did not get back home until December 10. The first Sunday he was back we took both of our children to Park Place Church to have Dr. Oldham dedicate them. Then we packed our belongings, hitched up the trailer, and headed to Virginia for Christmas. As Willie Nelson would say, we were "on the road again."

Home on Wheels

After the Holidays we struck out for Louisiana, then on to Oklahoma City and Tulsa. The rest is vague, but we were busy. Sometimes Berk drove all night to get to the next meeting in time. Marty rode in back in a Porta-Crib; Lori rode in my arms.

The trailer was a blessing for its privacy and a place for storage, but it was a pain to park and hard on gas. We blew two trailer tires that winter and they were costly. I looked for laundromats along the road, as we had no facilities in the trailer. It was also hard to heat. Having taken our bed out to accommodate two cribs, we slept on a fold-out couch. Sometimes we **wanted** to stay with the pastor.

We were holding a meeting for Sister Logsdon, a lady pastor in Tulsa Oklahoma. During the night there was a snow fall, and we awakened to a cold trailer. Underneath, Berk found the fuel line frozen.

So we moved in with the Logsdons. Theirs was a beautiful home with the first radiant heated floors I'd ever seen. It was heaven – walking on warm floors.

One night after church I was caring for Lori, and Berk was trying to get Marty to bed. But Marty was fussy, crying and croupy. Berk was walking the floor with him, patting and bouncing.

Sister Logsdon said, "Brother Berquist, would you like to rock him?"

"Yes," he replied, "but I couldn't find any rocks!"

We all collapsed in laughter.

Poor Berk was exasperated. Marty was such a "daddy's boy." He would hardly let anyone touch him but Berk, and I had my hands full with Lori. It was such moments as this when mirth was our only salvation.

We took turns having colds. The stress of travel and freezing weather took their toll. Many times, as we were zipping through little towns and residential districts, I'd pick out a house with a lamp in the window and pretend that it was ours and that we could pull in the driveway. Of course, in that dream house would always be a washer and dryer!

Spring found us in New Albany, Indiana, holding a revival for Thurman and Teenie Hall. Thurman and Berk had been roommates, along with Robert Nicholson and Art Eikamp. Thurman was really sharp and a "preaching machine." He and Berk delighted in each other's company. Teenie was a great help with the kids, even getting a baby sitter so we could get away for a shopping spree in nearby Louisville, Kentucky.

While we were in New Albany, Joe and Lou Espey stopped by. They were on their way to Anderson, Indiana, to candidate for the Northside Church of God. Joe asked Berk if he would be interested in White Chapel in Daytona, Florida.

Berk said, "Yes, I would. I have to get my family off the road. And after this winter, I'm looking for a warm place. Have the pulpit committee contact me."

"Well," Joe laughed, "I have to see if I make this vote at Northside. The church in Daytona doesn't yet know that I may be leaving."

Answering Another Call

We had a couple more meetings in North and South Carolina. While on the road, we did receive a call from Daytona to come and "try out" for the pastorate. We went in May and stayed with the Espeys.

I remember Berk's sermon.

"I'm not preaching to 'try out,'" he said. "You people know me. I have preached here many times. My focus is not to impress you, but to preach the Word."

He then preached a message entitled, "Are All the Children In?" and quoted a poem by that title. The emphasis was on how God wants all of his children in the Kingdom of God and, shepherd-like, seeks for them until they are all accounted for.

Response was wonderful, with many coming forward for prayer. That night the church voted, giving us a 98 percent vote. We had a church – and a home.

On June 13, 1956, our third anniversary, we were headed for Daytona Beach. We pulled into the yard on Bellwood Avenue on June 14. The people had restored the little white parsonage beautifully. Every room had been painted. The kitchen had new cabinets and flooring. The pine floors in all rooms had been sanded and refinished. It was sparkling clean. We had bought a few pieces of furniture, and a group gathered to help us unload.

I had the most wonderful feeling of security. The little house was right behind the church. I could hardly wait to get settled and make it our very own. The kids could have their own room – and Berk could stay home!

"Honey," Mrs. Woodie had said when Berk first came calling, "I hate to tell you this, but if you marry that man, your children are going to look like boogers!"
A dear soul she was, but no prophet.

Pastor "Berk"
White Chapel Church of God
Daytona Beach, Florida
1956 - 1977

6
Daytona

On June 14, 1956, we moved from our "home on wheels" into White Chapel's parsonage on Bellwood Avenue. The small white clapboard house with its tin roof sat on cinder block underpinnings. With three small bedrooms, two closets, one bathroom, a living room, kitchen, and two screened-in porches, it seemed like a palace compared to life on the road. A small gas space heater in the living room provided warmth. No air conditioning – just fans. On the back porch stood a Bendix washer – the ultimate joy for someone who had stopped at laundromats cross-country for three years!

After living in our car, in a one-room apartment, in army barracks, in other people's homes, and in a trailer we towed from one end of the United States to the other, it was wonderful to live in a real house with curtains and lamps and beds that belonged to us.

We had scarcely been in Daytona two days when company started coming.

Wilson and Lettie Cooper and son Tommy from Drexel, North Carolina, were first to knock at our door. Next came my brother John, who stayed the summer to help with the move and to play the organ for the church. At the end of five weeks we had entertained twenty-seven overnight guests!

Those first weeks were exciting and fun. Everyone who came bought groceries and helped with chores – including baby sitting. Our children, both still in diapers, were carried around like dolls. Marty was twenty months old; Lori, eight months.

Of course, everyone went to the beach – and took us. It was "Picnic and Sunburn City." Marc and Esther Fulton's umbrella stand was the gathering place.

Believe it or not, a few times Berk and I actually spent the night with Buddy and Vera Simmons on Big Tree Road because our house was overrun with guests. Then we'd come home early enough to fix breakfast for everyone. I learned to cook huge portions and made gallons of tea. Rice and beans were standard fare. They do swell, you know! And it was a good thing!

On one of those rare mornings when we had the house to ourselves and could linger in our pajamas over coffee, Berk commented: "We've had to jump into our clothes before breakfast so often with guests in the house, it feels practically indecent to be sitting here in our pajamas!"

Finally, in spite of the continual influx of guests, we managed to settle in.

At long last, life for us began to seem "normal." Berk was busy trying out all his ideas and sermons on the congregation; I was basking in homemaking; and the children were thriving on being in one place. Like most preachers' wives, I dutifully took part in the "Missionary Society" (as it was called back then) and joined a ladies' prayer group that met weekly. During preaching services Marty, Lori, and I stayed in the nursery most of the time, so Dad could keep his job.

First parsonage – next door to the church.

The parsonage sat right next to the church. In fact, the back door of our house was just steps away from the back door of the church. Being that close to the church was a plus in that I couldn't drive, and Berk could come home for lunch and assist me with our young children. On Sundays I could put a roast in the oven and check it between Sunday School and church.

On the other hand, its proximity to the church made our home "everybody's home." It wasn't uncommon to find a stray teenager or two in the kitchen groping in the refrigerator for a Coke or a left-over chicken leg. And whenever members – or even hitchhikers – came to the church looking for the pastor, if he wasn't in, they came to the house. Privacy was nil. Early in the morning I dressed for the day and straightened the house fast, lest we be caught "untidy." Increasingly, church and parsonage became one and the same. Our living room, for example, was soon home to a Sunday School class, all church rooms being full.

We also continued to have more out of town guests than we ever imagined. It seemed that most of the people to whom we said, "Come see us," did. And as company by the carload continued to pour in from all over the U.S.A., the need for an extra bathroom was paramount. Many mornings Berk headed for the church with towel and shaving items to clean up there, because our bath room had a line waiting.

After a year or so of the wearing, hectic schedule, I developed a peptic ulcer from the stress. We talked about finding a larger house nearby (but not "too" near), so we could relax a bit and have another bathroom. But we really had no funds. Berk's salary was $85 a week; we had no savings account; and the church couldn't afford another parsonage.

We dreamed of buying a small starter home on our own, to build some equity for retirement some day. We knew of many pastors who had lived in parsonages all their lives and thus owned no home of their own to live in when retirement came.

Two years passed and the pace only intensified.

One night the phone rang, and I heard Berk talking – animatedly – to our friend Lowell Wilson from Vincennes, Indiana. At first the conversation was cheerful (Lowell was always full of jokes). Then the talk grew serious and mostly one-sided – from the Indiana side.

I heard Berk say, "Well, that sounds wonderful. I'll pray about it and call you in a day or two after I talk with Berny."

When Berk hung up, I was naturally curious.

"What was that all about?" I asked.

"Well," Berk replied, "Lowell is chairman of the pulpit committee, and he offered me the position of senior pastor there in Vincennes. It's a flattering offer and almost indecent. The board is offering a salary of $125 per week, plus health benefits. And they have just purchased ground to build a new parsonage. Lowell said, 'Berny can have her choice of house plans, and select the carpets and appliances.' And Lowell will give me a new car to drive every year."

Lowell owned a Cadillac-Pontiac dealership. Berk drove cars so worn out the dogs wouldn't even bark at them.

"Whoopee!" I cried. "Let's go! While you pray, I'll pack."

My materialistic nature emerged full force. It was a dream come true. For the next few days I was elated – mentally decorating as I sailed through the daily chores.

Then one night Berk said, "Honey, I want to talk to you. I know how much your heart is set on moving. And I want to have something better, too. But that call from Indiana is like bribery, and I can't be bought. I'd love to go to Vincennes, and I'd love

94

being close to Lowell. I'd love to see you have a nicer house. But God isn't through with me here. When we came, He gave me a vision for this place; and we haven't scratched the surface here yet. I have a dream of building a larger sanctuary; we're overflowing now. And I have a dream of building a Christian school. I'm going to earnestly pray for us to find a larger house here, and I'll do all in my power to make your dreams come true, if you'll be content and trust my vision."

Tears gushed down my face. The weight of disappointment felt so crushing. But I loved Berk, and I trusted his vision of God's call on his life. I knew when I married him that, above all, he had to be true to whatever ministry he felt God directing him to do. And I had made my vow "to follow a man who followed a Man." Though Berk's decision was painful to accept, I had to admire his resolve. And deep down, I knew he was right.

So, I laid flowers on the grave of our move.

One year later, in 1959, we found an old two-story house – a real fixer-upper – across town on Lexington Drive for the astronomical price of $5,700. We saw lots of potential in that old Spanish adobe hacienda with its red tile roof. The church people pitched in to help us paint and redecorate. In no time the "ugly duckling" old house emerged as a "swan," sporting even a new "Florida room" added onto the back. With the additional space and an extra bath, it was a dream come true.

The new location was ideal for Marty and Lori. They spent hours fishing in the backyard canal. And North Ridgewood Elementary School, where both were enrolled, was just a few blocks away.

We stayed eight years there. Then, in 1967, our dream of equity was further realized when we bought a 4,000-square-foot home on Ridgewood. By the time we left Daytona in 1977, it was paid for; our "nest egg" was secured. Berk's promise to me had been fulfilled.

During our years in Daytona God blessed Berk's ministry. The church grew. The larger sanctuary was built. Warner Christian Academy became a reality.

And other personal benefits came to our family. Our children went from grade school to college without ever having to change churches or friends. I went back to college to earn a degree in nursing. We even got better cars and enjoyed warm winters in the bargain.

All of these blessings happened by our "staying put," because Berk listened to God instead of "other voices" promising material wealth.

Third parsonage, on South Ridgewood (1967).

95

Celebrating White Chapel's Twenty-Fifth Anniversary

In his first year as pastor, White Chapel celebrated twenty-five years of life as a congregation. Berk used the occasion as an opportunity to honor the legacy of those who had gone before, while introducing the church a-fresh to the surrounding community. A commemorative booklet he prepared for the celebration tells both stories.

The Story of White Chapel

How does a church come to be? How did this particular congregation come to be? May I invite you to a journey across twenty-five years:

Twenty-five years ago, South Daytona was a sparsely settled community within the city limits of Daytona Beach. At the time, Grace (Mrs. James) Beville and Miss Hattie Beville became burdened to improve the religious training of the children of the community. So they announced the beginning of a Sunday School.

The only place available was an abondoned tenant house on Beville Road. There was more to do than simply move in. The house had to be rid of fleas, plunder, and dirt which had accumulated through the years. But with the labors of Mrs. Ada Graham, Mrs. A.J. Pinkerton and her family, plus the work of two teachers, the house was cleaned. Both teachers and students could sit on the floor for Sunday School. Soon James Beville and A.J. Pinkerton secured lumber and built benches.

Attendance grew until every family within reasonable distance was represented. An adult Bible class was started. Then a young people's class. Two teachers were added to the staff, Mrs. Ada Graham and Mrs. Olive Mobley. Visiting ministers held services occasionally and at one time the Reverend Clyde Stepleton drove from New Smyrna Beach at regular intervals to pastor the work.

In 1937 the school was moved to an abandoned American Legion hall in South Daytona that later became city hall. W.O. Moon came and held a revival meeting at which time conviction settled upon a number who later were saved.

Early in 1940 L.S. Mowrey came to pastor the little flock. The state Missionary Board paid half his salary. In April a tent meeting was begun and several were saved. When the tent became too warm, the Beville brothers volunteered a double garage which was remodeled to become a little chapel. Here the Sunday School met until the new church was built. Six times the little congregation moved; and when the new church was built, it felt very happy to be settled.

In the years that followed Brother Mowrey's departure in 1943, the congregation has been led by a number of ministers: N.J. Jones, Ralph Poole, Florence Moon, H.H. Vines, and Joseph Espey. Under the leadership of Pastor Espey the present building was begun and completed.

The growth of the church has not been a steady, continuous climb in numbers and spirituality. But times of discouragement have served to strengthen and challenge the church.

Today we meet to pay tribute to those whose lives are invested in this most important work. Let us remember that none who has worked in this church is unknown to God.

*When the Bevilles moved to Daytona in 1912, they were the only Church of God family there. In 1931, James Beville married Grace Graham, a former Gospel Trumpet worker, who soon started a Sunday School, from which the church grew. **BELOW:** In 1976, during the 44th Anniversary Celebration of the church's founding, members who attended the original "White Chapel" Church gather on the steps of the old building (at that time painted red and known as "the Little Red Schoolhouse" because of its use for pre-school classes). With the group (front row, center) is founder Grace Beville, holding a portrait of her husband, James.*

The Coming Thing

This is "the coming thing." I use the phrase from a friend of mine who commented on the rapid growth of our congregation and this movement in the stream of Christianity. "What you are doing," he said, "seems to be the coming thing."

What did he mean? What does it mean that there is a church in South Daytona? Have you ever asked yourself, "What is the difference between this church and all the other churches? Why do they call it the CHURCH OF GOD? How many members are in it? How long has it been here? What are the beliefs?

If you have asked any of these questions you can be proud of yorself. They are intelligent questions. I can't answer all of them. One in particular is hard to answer: how many members are there in this church?

We do not have any membership roll. You can't join anythng if you really wanted to. Not that we think you are not good enough to be a part of the church. Rather it is because there is no one good enough to take you in. Christ must do that.

The reason we go by the name Church of God is that we want it to be just that – God's church. The Bible says, "The Lord added to the church daily such as should be saved." (Acts 2:47) He is truly the only one who knows who should be in the church. If you are a Christian, you are already in. There is nothing more to do.

Is this something new? In a way, yes. But it is new merely because it has been forgotten. It was the way they did it in New Testament times. We believe that this pattern will return and become normal in all true churches. In that sense it is as modern as tomorrow.

Do we have a creed? Yes. It is the Bible. It contains the will of God and the plan of salvation. Read it yourself and pray for the Minister as he preaches about it, and you will learn to undestand it.

I think you will understand why most folks feel right at home the very first time they come to White Chapel. We welcome you to the services of the church and to the SERVICE of the church. The Minister is here to serve – that is, to minister. He is happy to help you.

Twenty-five years have gone since the first little Sunday School was held in South Daytona in 1932. Now we have a beautiful church building. But it is almost inadequate for our growing needs. The future is glorious. Do not spend your time lamenting WHAT THE WORLD IS COMING TO, but rejoice at WHAT IS COMING TO THE WORLD.

LEFT: The original church building, built in 1941 by Rev. L.S. Mowery. Originally called "First Church of God," the church was renamed "White Chapel" in 1946 by Rev. Ralph Poole. Berk led a revival in that building in 1950.

In 1940 Rev. Mowery had built the parsonage, the same one the Berquists moved into 16 years later. Berny and friend Blanche De Young stayed with Joe and Lou Espey in the parsonage when they worked in Daytona during the summer of 1952.

RIGHT: White Chapel Church of God as it was when Berk became pastor there. This, the second sanctuary, was built while Rev. Joe Espey was pastor. The dedication for this new facility was held May 6, 1956, just before Berk took over leadership of the congregation in June.

Royal Positions

During our first few years in Daytona, while Berk was caught up in pastoral duties and his dreams for expanding the church, my primary focus was to settle down (after three years on the road) and be wife and mother.

Whenever anyone asked me if I liked being a preacher's wife, I'd say, "No, but I like being Berk's wife, and if I please him, I please the Lord."

Almost everywhere we had traveled, people would ask, "Do you play or sing?" and I'd reply, "Neither, but I can roll my eyes."

Sometimes they laughed, and sometimes they'd cluck their tongues and lament the fact that such a fine upstanding preacher would pick such an untalented wife.

Because our children were so young when we first arrived, I had to put them in the nursery. And because there was no appointed nursery attendant, I was "it." I stayed with them so they wouldn't be afraid – and before long I had lots of company. Most of the babies and toddlers left there were children of choir members or instrumentalists. I served, so they could serve. I felt good about that.

Soon I had a teenage helper or two. I bought diapers, lotion, milk, Kool-aid, and cookies. Our little members grew in number as the church in general grew.

When our big church building emerged, the nursery was placed in a larger room way in the back of the sanctuary, with built-in cribs, toys galore, small sinks and toilets. We had lots of volunteer helpers, but sometimes they didn't show. I would be sitting in Church wearing my Sunday-go-to-meeting dress (instead of my usual smock), and there'd be a tap on my shoulder from an usher with this message: "Miss Berny, the attendant didn't show up today. They need you in the nursery." Sometimes I felt honored, but other times I felt martyred. I wanted to dress up and "play lady," too.

Many times visitors would say to Berk, "Which lady here is your wife? Is it the pianist or organist, the soloist, or the choir director?"

He'd say, "None of the above. She's in the nursery, caring for the children."

In this position I became better acquainted with most of the families than Berk did. I often accompanied expectant parents to the hospital and paced the floor with the fathers – sipping black coffee and awaiting the bundle of joy. I'd have in my possession a pink or blue Testament to present to the proud parents.

I stayed in the nursery for eleven years. Then the board hired a Seventh Day Adventist lady to take on this noble task.

One Sunday morning – before I was demoted from my job – I was all alone in the nursery with five or six toddlers and a couple of infants. No teenager or assistant

"Miss Berny" No Run-of-the-Mill Pastor's Wife

More than a little unorthodox and zany, with a heart of pure gold! – Pastor Berquist's "better half" brought a whole new definition to the role of "First Lady of the Parsonage." Whatever other minsters' wives might bring to the gift mix for ministry with their husbands, Berny's was a ministry of compassion and laughter. Whatever else she might bring to congregational life in Daytona, foremost were her caring heart and her indomitable sense of humor and fun!

Clockwise from Top Right:
1. *Berk and Berny at the Junior-Senior Banquet (1969).* ***2.*** *Nancy Hughes can't take much more of Berk and Berny's "Gong Show" performance on harmonica and comb with waxed paper for the WCG All-Church Banquet (1976).* ***3.*** *Berny shows off her change in swim attire for the move from Florida to Indiana (1977).* ***4.*** *"The Require Sisters" (L to R: Berny, Louise Hardy, Helen Stephens) lip-sync their rendition of "Sugar Time" for the Junior-Senior Banquet (1976).*

Berk and Berny made a perfect team. Both were "people persons" who enjoyed spending time with their parishioners, having friends over for dinner or for dessert after church, making themselves available to become involved in the lives of their flock. Both were great storytellers, and could always sense a good story in the making. For both knew that the best stories came from real life. Berny had a "sixth sense" about people and situations, and some of Berk's best sermon illustrations came from her – certainly some of his funniest!

They were evenly matched with humor and sharp wit. Berny's ability to see "the funny," even in the direst of circumstances, is a gift from God and a blessing to others. The Bible says, "A merry heart doeth good like a medicine." Berny was good medicine – for Berk and for White Chapel.

came to my rescue. I had my martyr hat on – big time. But I decided I could cope.

About then came a knock at the door, and there stood a couple I'd never seen before, with two little girls in tow. I introduced myself as the minister's wife. They seemed surprised to meet me there. I asked the ages of the little ones.

"Five and six," they answered.

Our cut-off was age four. But because they were new and the little girls had never been in church before, I decided to keep them, as they could help with other children, coloring and passing out Kool-aid. And such good little helpers they were!

Then came the hitch. When church was over, everyone picked up their children – except the new family.

We tidied up the play room. And waited. It became 12:15. Then 12:25. I grew more and more exasperated, and my martyr hat almost grew horns.

Finally they came. It was apparent that they had been crying.

When I got to the sanctuary, very few people were left; and Berk was looking for me. When he asked why I was so late, I related rather heatedly the scenario of the new people and their "too old" children, and the late pickup.

He reached out and drew me close and said, "Honey, you're an angel. That new couple just got saved – on their very first Sunday. And if you had not taken the little girls, they might have misbehaved; and the parents would never have heard the sermon."

I took off my martyr hat permanently that day and never again lamented my lack of musical talent. Esther 4:14 took on a new meaning for me: "And who knows but that you have come to a royal position for such a time as this?"

That couple, Joe and Neva Bailey, became pillars of the church. Neva taught Sunday School. Joe, an astute businessman and owner of a pre-cast concrete company, helped Berk launch Warner Christian Academy by chairing the board, providing invaluable business acumen and financial assistance, as well as the concrete materials for the buildings. He also influenced the church to provide health insurance and a pension plan for us.

And the little girls, Aven and Rondi, attended Warner Academy, then went to Warner Southern College, married, and now have beautiful families of their own.

Every once in a while, even now, I run into one of my "nursery babies." Many of them I am always pleased to discover, have entered the ministry or are actively involved laypersons in the churches they attend. Of course, Berk's influence on their lives had a lot to do with that. But I like to think that something I may have said or done for them back there in the nursery also had a lasting effect.

Cross Bearing: Your Turn or Mine

God doesn't take away our cross, but he sends other Christians to help carry it. Sometimes we carry, and sometimes we are carried.

When we were living in California in 1954 and expecting our first child, I had gotten established with an OB-Gyn Clinic in Burbank. Because California was so nomadic, the clinic's rules were that all pre-natal fees had to be paid by the third visit. We had no medical insurance, so we paid up front from our savings.

California living was much higher than anticipated, but we had managed to keep ahead in our bank account, even though I did not receive a salary.

Berk had a daily radio broadcast, "World Evangelist," that he dearly loved. The program was paid for by the listeners, with some State and individual church funding. But eventually, because there were so many projects and so many hands reaching, including the college, funding for the radio program fell short. Berk was left to keep the broadcast afloat solely through listener donations. Unfortunately, that was not enough; and it soon became apparent that he would have to go off the air entirely.

I didn't know it at the time, but he took our personal savings to bail out the broadcast, thinking that he would catch up when "promised donations" came in. It didn't happen. Berk didn't tell anyone about his sacrifice. He just prayed about it.

Our baby was due around Christmas, but Marty made an early debut on November 11, six weeks early.

I stayed in the hospital six days. It depleted our bank account. Marty had to stay an extra week in the incubator because of a respiratory problem.

Berk was able to pay my hospital bill, but didn't know how he was going to pay for Marty's. St. Joseph's in Burbank demanded cash upon dismissal. And the costs were mounting.

One day as Berk was praying in his office, he received a phone call.

"Brother Berquist, this is Delbert Miles. I'm from Mark Denton's church in Glendale."

"Yes," replied Berk. "I remember you. You are a contractor."

"Yes," Delbert continued. "Brother Berquist, I have just had my devotions, and while praying, God laid on my heart that you need help. I know your wife just had a baby, and I feel I'd like to help you with your hospital bill."

Tears flooded the phone as Berk responded.

"It has to be from God, because I was just praying also. My wife is home, but there are complications with the baby, and I am in a financial bind."

"Well, I am going to come over to the office and give you a check. The Lord has blessed my business."

He did come and gave Berk a check to cover my hospital bill and Marty's. We didn't see Delbert much after that, but we never forgot this act of obedience and love prompted by God.

Nearly two years had passed. We were living in the parsonage in South Daytona. Around 2:00 one morning our phone rang. Berk groped for it in the dark. I got up, knowing that at this hour there was never good news. I feared the call was concerning my family in Virginia.

"Yes," I heard Berk say. "Of course, I remember you."

He listened a minute or two, then said, "I certainly will. My wife is up and we'll pray right now. Please write me your address and telephone number so we can keep in touch."

With that he hung up and turned to me.

"That was Delbert Miles from California. He's the one who "paid us out" of the hospital. His wife has cancer, and he is calling for prayer."

We knelt and Berk prayed fervently for Wilma's healing. A few months later we received word that she was totally healed. We weren't a bit surprised.

Back at Golgotha so many years ago, a man named Simon carried the cross for Jesus. And Jesus has been in charge of cross-bearing ever since, delegating the turn of responsibility to each of us as He sees the need.

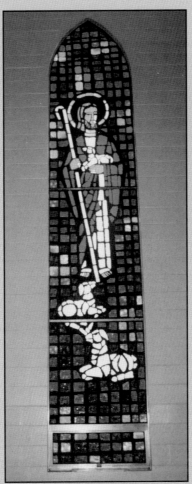

The Man with Blue Hair (Berk speaking)

We had an artist in our church in Daytona: Saul Chaftez, a Jewish man who got saved there. He was very talented, and he taught me a lot about art. To start with, I knew nothing about art. I'm still no expert in it, but thanks to Saul, I know more than I did.

One day in his studio I watched as Saul painted a man's portrait. He was painting in the hair. Looking at the man sitting for the portrait, I would say he had brown hair. But to my utter amazement, Saul was using red . . . orange . . . blue . . . all kinds of colors as he painted the hair!

Finally I said, "Saul, that guy doesn't have blue hair . . . or red hair . . . or orange hair. He has brown hair."

"Okay," he said, "I'll paint it brown."

Then he filled his brush with brown paint and painted over the hair.

"Wait a minute," I said. "It doesn't look like that!"

"No," he replied,"of course it doesn't. Now, go look at the man's hair."

I went over to the man and looked closely at his hair. Was I in for a surprise!

Honestly, if you look at human hair – untouched by Miss Clairol – you, too, will see that in anyone's head of hair there are many, many colors. And when all of these colors are used in painting the hair, it looks natural. Paint it solid brown, and it looks like a piece of carpet. Real hair is not that way at all. Check it out sometime. It is totally fascinating to see all the colors that are there that make for reality.

Likewise, we can look at other things with the eye of an aritst – and we preachers, as sermon illustrators are supposed to be artists. We can learn to see, not merely

generalities, but the subtle details – the colorings and shadings – that make people unique.

AT LEFT:
Portrait of Berk
by Saul Chaftez

Berk, the Preacher

Berk was already a masterful preacher before we went to Daytona, but while we were there, he honed his preaching gifts to a fine art. One thing he worked hard to overcome was his natural tendency to use big words. As a school boy, thanks to Chester Edwards, his mentor while growing up in Topeka, he had developed a life-long fascination with words and languages. His studies in Latin equipped him with a huge vocabulary, which he drew upon with ease.

Early in his preaching career, however, Berk discovered that many of those impressive words just sailed right over the heads of his audience. Since his driving passion was communicating the gospel, being understood was more important to him than impressing anyone with his genius-level vocabulary. Thus, Berk took it as a personal challenge to simplify his words, his manner, his style of presentation. As he was fond of saying, "If you can't understand me, you shouldn't be loose on the streets!" A favorite story he told on himself was this:

I grew up as, you might say, an intellectual type. I mean, I used to read the dictionary and I used a lot of big words. And it was impressive. Several years ago when my son and daughter were in junior high school, they were going through my study one day. In some old files they found a recording of a speech I had made in college for one of my classes. That was before tape recorders, so it was on a 78 RPM disk. The kids had put it on the record player and were listening to it when I walked into the room.

Teasing them, I said, "Who is that? Guess who it is."

They couldn't guess.

"Well, guess," I persisted. "Listen. Guess."

Still they couldn't guess.

Finally, I said, "Well, that is your father."

And my daughter, Lori, the younger of the two, spoke up and said, "Wow, Dad! Back then you were smart!"

Well, I listened to that speech; and I knew what she meant. I was using a lot of ten-dollar words and long sentences with involved construction. Fortunately, I'm smarter now than I was then. That speech was so complicated, I could hardly understand it myself!

Preaching like Jesus

As anyone who ever heard Berk preach well knows, the mainstay of Berk's riveting preaching style, other than his preaching without notes, was his stories. Painting verbal pictures that were unforgettable, he skillfully wove together the Biblical text with real-life stories – stories always with an emotional impact that plunged his audience into gales of laughter or left them brushing away tears. It was masterful. No one did it better.

But not everyone appreciated his light touch with Biblical truths. His affinity for humor made him appear frivolous to some. He was a gifted speaker, they said, but could not be taken seriously as a theologian. Those who followed Berk's preaching, however, held quite a different view. Many recognized that his greatest gift as a preacher was his ability to put deep theological truths into language common people, even children, could understand. Truly, he was a disciplined scholar of the Word. Nevertheless, Berk had his critics. And he always gave them a hearing, whether or not he took their advice. One day he came home from church more than a little shaken by a lady in our church who had taken him to task about his preaching. Later, he told in sermons and conferences that her criticism did him a great favor:

> *In the past when I was characterized as a "storytelling preacher," I took it as a great affront.*
>
> *"I really preach the gospel," I protested. "I don't just tell stories."*
>
> *I remember one time a woman in my congregation took me aside and said, "Pastor, you know I love you . . ."*
>
> *After you have pastored for a while, you know that those words more often than not are preface to a lot of trouble. So I braced myself.*
>
> *"I love you," she said, "and you are a good man and all that. But I have trouble with your preaching."*
>
> *"Well, I have trouble with my preaching, too; but I'm trying to remedy it."*
>
> *"You preach the gospel all right," she said, "but you tell too many stories."*
>
> *Then came the boom: "Why don't you just preach the Bible like Jesus did?"*
>
> *Well, I took the woman's suggestion to heart and started a personal study of how Jesus preached. Try it yourself. Read the Gospels. Guess what you'll find.*
>
> *He told stories! Only he called them parables.*
>
> *In fact, the Bible says that "without a parable he didn't speak to them" (Matthew 13:34, NKJV). If he couldn't paint a picture, he didn't tell it.*
>
> *Ever since then, I stopped telling stories. I tell parables!*
>
> *And I've been indebted to my critic for her sage advice.*

"Why so angry, Berk?"

Another characteristic of Berk's preaching in his early years of ministry was a hard-edged, sometimes cynical tone, accompanied by sudden bursts of loud, angry shouting at key points in the sermon. The effect was jolting; sometimes, distracting.

Berk, no doubt, acquired the style in part from patterning himself after preachers he heard speak when he was a lad in Topeka. Animated elocution, with leaping and shouting to emphasize key points was not uncommon back then. But most of it came from Berk's passion about the gospel and his compulsion to impress upon people the truth of their lost or complacent spiritual condition and the urgency of their doing something about it NOW. He wanted to "wake people up" – literally and figuratively.

Whatever the reason for taking that approach, Berk apparently was not aware of its negative effect. Then a friend dared to confront, and it made a real difference. Berk later wrote about the experience in his book *When You Need a Friend*:

> *While David Grubbs was pastoring in Kingsport, Tennessee, he invited me to come to his church for a series of special services. I arrived on Saturday night, had time for some leisurely conversation, prayer and study, and a good night's sleep.*
>
> *Sunday morning the church was filled. The spirit of the people was warm and accepting. I enjoyed preaching and felt certain that his revival would be productive and inspiring. The people listened and were responsive.*
>
> *After the service Dave and I walked to the parsonage. I waited for some comment form him about the service. I wasn't consciously angling for any praise, but I was probably expecting it. It didn't come.*
>
> *"Berk," Dave began, "who were you mad at this morning? Did you have an argument with your Board of Directors just before coming? What's the matter?"*
>
> *"I'm not mad at anybody. I have no problems at home; everything is going well."*
>
> *"That's good. But you sounded as if you were down on the whole world this morning. And you sounded as if you thought the whole church was down on you. We're not. We love you. We want to hear you preach. We even paid your air fare to come preach to us. So don't be mad at us."*
>
> *I was speechless.*

That afternoon, I spent some time all alone looking at myself, listening in my memory to my peaching. Dave was right.

Without consciously wanting to, I had pcked up all the bad habits of preachers I had heard. I was an amateur Captain Blackcloud, a prophet of doom. I must have thought that this was the right way to preach. But the more I thought about it, the more I recognized things in my preaching that were totally negative, totally paranoid, totally unlike the kind of preaching I really wanted to do.

I changed. That night I changed. Granted, I had a hard time moving to the sunny side of the street in the preaching business; but whenever I find myself because of weariness or frustration slipping into the old patterns, I hear Dave say, "Berk, who are you mad at?"

In that moment, I thank God for friends who care enough to confront.

Poverty Games

Berk found "parables" everywhere. Many came from his days of growing up "poor" in Topeka, because most adults in the 1950's and '60's had had similar experiences and related to those days back in the '20's and '30's. He had a plethora of "poor" stories that surfaced not only in sermons, but also when entertaining guests in our home. We would all compare "poor stories" about growing up in hard times. Little did we realize the impact those stories were having on our children.

While the chldren were small, they both played a game called "I Am Poor." Berk added their stories to his "repertoire" of sermon illustrations and wrote about their poverty games in *When Financial Pressure Becomes Unbearable*.

When Lori was six or seven, she and her closest friend, Karen Van Hoose, came walking through our living room with an air of dejection that would be more appropriate for a man on the way to the gallows. Their shoulders drooped, their feet dragged, and their faces were masks of despair.

"What in the world are you girls doing?"

"We are playing poor."

That was a new kind of game for me, so I asked, "How do you play poor?"

Lori spoke: "We were at Karen's house drinking Cokes and watching color television. We decided to play poor, so we are looking sad and have come to our house to drink a glass of plain water and watch black and white TV!

Marty's dramatization was more upsetting. I noticed him going from door to door in our neighborhood. Since he was only four I thought I had better follow him to see whether he was a precocious brush salesman or was looking for a new home. I listened to his request.

"I am Marty Berquist. Could I have a piece of bread?"

It was pitiful.

As soon as I heard, I stepped out from behind the bush and said, "Marty, let's go home. If you need a piece of bread, I'm sure we can find one . . . and we will find it at home."

Berk, the Songwriter

In 1966 we had in our employ a minister of music, a young man of musical genius named Ray Cantwell. In addition to directing the choir and leading worship, Ray could sing, play piano and organ, and was a gifted composer. He and Saul Chaftez became soul mates, for Ray, too, could paint and sculpt. He, in fact, worked with Saul on the windows, which for both became an obsession.

Ray brought out a new talent in Berk. Inspired by Ray's ability to compose music, Berk turned his talent for writing poetry into song writing. Lyrics just poured out of his head and onto Ray's fingers, as Ray set them to music. Together Berk and Ray wrote a Christmas Cantata called *God Lit a Star* (1966) and an Easter Cantata in 1968 called *Rex Mundi* (King of the World). They wrote more than thirty-three songs. The sheet music was printed by our own White Chapel Press. We even bought a typewriter that typed out the notes! Of all their songs, Berk's personal favorite was "On Bended Knee."

Sacred Songs
by
Maurice Berquist
Ray Cantwell

Unworthy Am I
Beyond Forever
Sharing His Load
Great Big Heaven
Why Was I Born?
On Bended Knee
When I Think That
the Lord Loves Me
He'll Never Let Me Fall
Lead Me All the Way
Lord, Is It I?
Be Thou My Song
Behold Your King
The Carpenter's Son
Lord, Send Me
Roll, Chariot
and 18 more

Christmas Cantata, God Lit a Star.
Cover design by Saul Chaftez.

White Chapel and Gulf Coast Bible College

Another of Berk's great passions was challenging young people to respond to God's call on their lives. A firm believer in the value of Christian schooling, he encouraged the youth at White Chapel to look beyond high school to a Christian college. The closest Church of God college in the South at that time was Gulf Coast Bible College in Houston, Texas.

In the fall of 1966, David Brown, Fred Gilmour, Jr., Martha Rosenbaum, Jennifer Burdine, and Jim Harvey – all from White Chapel – enrolled in Gulf Coast Bible College. Nathan and Lois Brown, with their son Mark, joined son David in Houston in 1967. Mark finished his senior year of high school there, and in 1968-69 all three Browns – Nathan, David, and Mark – were studying for the ministry. By 1971 those representing White Chapel at Gulf Coast, besides the seven previously mentioned, were Margaret Watkins, Ron Kern, Lou Isenberg, Carol Stephens, Larry Van Ness, Dottie Cavender, and Nancy Morgan.

While our "kids" were in Texas, White Chapel found ways to give extra support for GBC. The WCG had monthly pie socials, and a monthly Sunday night offering was designated for the college.

In 1971 six of our students graduated. Berk and I drove out to Texas to celebrate not only their achievement, but his. He was invited to be the Commencement speaker, plus GBC bestowed on him an Honorary Doctorate degree.

Nathan and Lois followed us "home," and Nathan became Berk's associate pastor and right-hand man. While in this position Nathan wore every hat imaginable – preacher, teacher, carpenter, singer. Whatever dream or project Berk envisioned, Nathan picked it up and helped achieve it.

One of Berk's greatest delights were these, and other young people after them, who grew up in the church under his ministry and became men and women of God through his challenge to "Go ye into all the world and preach or teach the Gospel." He considered these, more than buildings, to be the true fruits of his labor.

111

White Chapel parishioners at Gulf Coast Bible College in 1968. (L to R) FRONT: Dave and Jennifer Brown, Dottie Cavender, Martha Rosenbaum Black, Nancy Morgan Boozer, Jim Harvey. BACK: Ronnie Kern, Fred Gilmour, Larry Van Ness, Nathan Brown, Mark Brown.

Berk, the Dreamer . . . Warner Christian Academy

Because of his strong commitment to Christian education, starting Warner Christian Academy was for Berk one of the most significant achievements of his ministry at White Chapel. Mary Lou Sempsrott, our good friend and first-grade teacher at WCA for twenty-six years, captured the spirit of the adventure in a brief history of the school she wrote for the dedication of the new high school building in 1986.

As she noted, Berk had for years toyed with the idea of of starting a Christian school. When he finally put the idea before the congregation, Bess Cook and Mildred Ellis did some preliminary research on how it might be done; but, in Mary Lou's words, "time passed and the idea was tabled . . . but not forgotten. God was working in minds and hearts to begin the ground work for His school."

Then, one evening in prayer meeting, dear Elizabeth Marwick, a frequent visitor to the congregation, stood to share that God had "laid it upon her heart to donate $2,000 toward the funding for a school."

Sometime later, Berk shared another dream: "That 1,000 workers would be sent from White Chapel into Christian service." Among those who stepped forward to accept that challenge was Martha Rosenbaum. "She was anointed by the church and placed her life in God's hands for missionary service." She chose to attend Gulf Coast Bible College, where she met and married David Black. As a part of his college work, David did a study on how to operate a day care facility and start a church school. And during that time David and Berk talked about the possibility of starting a day care and school at White Chapel.

After graduation, Martha and David returned to South Daytona to lead the opening of Warner Christian Academy in the fall of 1971. David directed day care for 20 - 30 pre-schoolers in "the Little Red Schoolhouse" behind the church, while in the church nursery, Martha taught a class of 9 eager first-graders: Todd Atalek, Rhondi Bailey, Gretchen Cook,

The old White Chapel, with its gleaming doorhandle of solid brass, gains a new life as "the Little Red Schoolhouse," birthplace of Warner Christian Acaademy.

112

Warner Christian Academy

Berk's dream of a Christian school serving the community of Daytona Beach came true in 1971. Here, in Berk's own words, is the way it began:

Who can say where a miracle starts? Does it start with a flash of fire from the sky, or does it start with a quiet dream in the mind of a child? A dream flashing across the idle mind of a child leaves so little in its wake that the child scarcely knows he has dreamed. But the footprints are planted on the mind that will make a path for future deeds. A miracle is born, first of desire, then dreams, then deeds. Who dreamed the first dreams of Warner Christian Academy?

As I sit here writing, a score of faces flash across my mind. Each of these persons was involved in some way with the miracle of Warner. Each dreamed, dared and worked. But God gave the miracle. To Him be the glory. Of course, God didn't do it all by Himself. He used people. All kinds of people. Even people who didn't particularly want to be used.

Marty for example. On a bright Saturday morning I asked Marty to go with me to the old church.

"I need help," I pleaded.

"For what?"

"I'll tell you when we get there."

When we got to the church I walked to the front of the battered white building that stood forlornly on the back of the lot. In its early days it had housed the congregation of White Chapel Church of God. In fact, its austere and puritan whiteness had inspired the name, White Chapel. The name was still used, although the congregation had grown until it was housed in a spacious sanctuary that seated more than a thousand worshippers. The now shabby building reminded me of John Greenleaf Whittier's schoolhouse: "Still sits the school house by the road, Like a ragged beggar sunning." No one cared for the little chapel any more. It had served as sanctuary, youth chapel, store-house, nursery, and printing room. On this Saturday morning no one used it. The only attention it got was the complaints of the beauty-minded saints.

Marty and I stood in front of the old building for a moment; and then I went to my car, got some old rags, polish and steel wool. I began to polish the brass handle on the front of the door. Marty watched. Then he helped.

Then he asked, "Why are you doing this? No one uses this building any more."

"You'll see. Just keep polishing."

Soon the gleam of the brilliant brass began to show through the tarnish and dirt.

"This is solid brass," Marty said. "You don't see many like this any more."

"No you don't."

We worked for an hour or more. Soon the massive old door handle glistened. It looked strangely out of place on the door with peeling paint. Our work was done and we stood to admire it.

"Now what do you think of the door handle, Marty?"

"It looks great, but why did we do it. It's a waste of time. It's out of place."

I felt inspired to preach a little sermon. Sermons, I have learned, are not extremely popular with one's children.

"Marty, have you ever heard the operetta *H.M.S. Pinafore*?"

"No, what is it?"

"Well, I am not going to sing it for you, but the story line tells of a young man who enlisted in the King's Navy. His first job was to polish up the handle on the big front door. He attacked this job with such enthusiasm that he was promoted and eventually became Captain of the King's Navy."

"That was the refrain: ' I polished up the handle on the big front door.'"

"So what has that got to do with this? We just wasted a Saturday morning polishing this piece of brass."

"Ah, here's the important thing. No matter how bad something is, if you begin to improve it, you start a whole new chain of events. In this case, someone will notice that there is something different. And they will ask why. Then someone else will begin to think that maybe the rest of the building needs help as well. Something great will come from this."

And something did.

Soon the little building was ready for children to come and put their little hands on the shining brass door handle . . . a door handle that would open a whole new world to them.

What wonderful things God has done through this school. What great days are ahead for it.

As I write these words, I am three thousand miles from the sandy beaches of Daytona, but I have left there a great many years of my life, a great many hours of labor, and a great many hours of prayer.

I regret none of it. To have invested a part of one's life in the dreams of God is to have a strange kind of treasure in this movable feast we call "life." I encourage thousands of others to invest in these dreams.

Tammy Gibson, Harry Lesh, Wayne Parrish, Troy Sharpton, Cathy Summers, and John Yonkosky. Two of them, Gretchen Cook and Troy Sharpton, would complete all twelve years of their education at WCA.

Heading the cafeteria was Lois Brown, Nathan's wife, as chief cook, with Betty Simmons, Lois Hardy, and Babe Sharpton soon coming on board to help her. Eventually, Babe became director of food services for the entire school.

So many people caught the vision and contributed to the school's success. Reid Hughes, astute business man and politician, chaired the founding school board. Serving with him were Nathan Brown, Fred Gilmour, Sr., Fred Kern, and a young first-timer, Norman Riley.

Another influential person in the life of the church and school was Berrien Becks, an attorney whom Berk met in the 1960's. Berk's secretary at the time, Lou Isenberg, worked half-days for both men. She suggested that Berk consult Berrien on several legal matters, a contact resulting in instant mutual admiration. Berrien became a close friend and an invaluable asset in all legal matters, donating his time and his services. Though he was a member of another church, Berrien attended all of our dedications and special events. Even after we left White Chapel, we kept in touch. When Berk started his missions to India, Berrien was on hand as a sponsor, even for the last journey. He is still there now – for me, and I thank God for him.

WCA's office command post was staffed at different times by Judy Sipes, the first school secretary, Charlotte Hogan, and Linda Kress. Dottie Cavender Arington also worked in the office. Nancy Pike, who became the school's accountant, "could collect money from a rock." At stressful moments, Linda Kress' undaunted sense of humor kept everyone sane. On a day when Murphy's Law was in full force, she just might answer the phone by blurting out: "Warner Christian Calamity. May I help you?" Her

MIRACLE CHILD
By Berny Berquist

Commencement Address Commemorating
the 25th Anniversary Year of Warner Christian Academy.

I am here tonight not to honor the Senior Class of 1996 or to challenge them on to new heights. That has already been done. I am here to honor the birthday and anniversary of a miracle child named Warner Christian, whom I have watched grow up from a dream in a man's heart to a healthy youth of twenty-five.

I did not really want this child. When Berk came home twenty-five years ago and announced the impending birth of this miracle child, I was less than enthusiastic. I was forty years old and had just started back to school, to Daytona Beach Community College to earn a nursing degree. Our two children were finishing high school. The church was growing, was fairly solvent; and I didn't want to begin another project with its inherent financial involvement and congregational upheaval. I hated to see Berk taking on another hat.

But take it on, he did. I thought he would be shot down, but instead he was lifted up! As in the movie "Field of Dreams" – but long before it came out – he had caught a vision and knew in his heart, "If you build it, they will come."

Berk was always a visionary, a dreamer. He thought thoughts that were beyond our imaginations and brought ideas into simple words and challenges that caused others to dream their own dreams; and through God's Spirit, he lit fires in their hearts. He saw things that we did not see and lived in a realm we did not understand. But, he was a shepherd and we followed.

In Berk's own words, "A miracle is born, first of desire, then dreams, then deeds." From the day that Marty, our son, and his dad polished the door handle on the old White Chapel Church, it was blessed. It sparked dreams in all who scraped, painted, sawed and nailed to make "the Little Red Schoolhouse" ready for those nine eager kindergartners whose little hands would open the brass door handle and become history in the making.

This miracle child could have been aborted, but its star shone so brightly it was full term before anyone could blink. When God takes over in the fatherhood department, it is out of human hands. Jesus was a Miracle Child. Just think how much poorer the human race would have been had he not been born.

sense of fun, her creativity and love of students, and her ability to cope with adversity endeared her to everyone.

Originally, the plan was to add a grade or two each year as needed. But growth came instantaneously when another Christian school in the area closed, and WCA was asked by the community to pick up many of those students. Thus, WCA, in its second year of operation, opened the school year with grades K-9 and over 200 students!

By the third year, enrollment had climbed to 440. That year, athletics were added to the extra-curricular program, with Bill Yates as athletic director and coach for the boys' teams; Martha Black coached the girls. Another of our Gulf Coast graduates, Freddie Gilmour, Jr., returned to teach physical education, science, and social studies. In time, we also had an excellent full-time music department under the direction of Kent and Kathy Shoop, who also served as ministers of music for the church. And we were blessed with "special angel" remedial teachers for students with learning problems.

Because of rapid growth, a full time supervisor for the elementary department became essential. That position was filled by a gem of a lady named Esther Fedor, and the department flourished under her leadership. Cancer came calling and whisked her away – much too soon – but her imprints remain on the school and on the lives and hearts of everyone she touched.

White Chapel's church facilities, with "the Little Red Schoolhouse" out back, provided the first home for Warner Christian Academy.

Warner Christian would not have grown, had not so many of you caught the vision also. You were the board who voted to go ahead, the businessmen and women who gave unselfishly, the teachers who sacrificed by teaching for so little. You were the ones who worked the rummage sales, the suppers, and auctions; and were volunteers of every kind. There were no little jobs.

The second year, with the closing of another Christian School in the area, we had the opportunity to encompass some of their enrollment and thus started the 1972 year with grades K through 9 and 228 students. We were up and growing. The third year our enrollment was 440 with twelve grades. Houses came down and buildings went up. Grass became barren and so did carpets. It was hustle, bustle, and tussle. We became athletic and scientific. We became Eagles long before we could fly.

Berk wore three hats: pastor, principal, and professor. By the time we left for Anderson, Indiana, in 1977, "Little Warner" was six. We had an enrollment of 649 and our third graduating class.

Berk was excited about his new opportunity with Mass Communications; but, oh, how he hated to leave his child, "Little Warner." He was so anxious that it would continue to flourish. And it did, thanks to all of you who stayed and prayed. I salute these pastors – Dale Whalen, Marvin Cain, and Roger Stamper – who kept alive the flame Berk lighted – who nourished the child. The flame flickered a few times; the child floundered. But now in the apt hands of Pastor Robinson and Headmaster Dr. Richards, the flame glows even brighter.

Since Warner Christian was our third child and our Miracle Child, I feel that Berk would like to leave more than labor, dreams, and prayers. He would like to have left some monetary investments, as well. So, I have come here to make provision in my will to have "Little Warner" made a recipient as our third child, an equal share upon my death.

I salute all of you who have kept our Miracle Child, Warner Christian, alive.

Jeremiah 29:11 states, "For I know the plans I have for you, says the Lord, plans for good and not for evil, to give you a future and a hope."

Graduates, never quit dreaming! Have miracle children of your own.

Thank you very much. God bless you all!

The same could be said for Janie Stark, who took the reins as Pre-School Director in 1973, guiding that department for 23 years. Janie exemplifies the loving, caring, gifted, and dedicated Christian teachers who believed in the school with all their hearts and made it work.

A spirit of excitement permeated the school, though teaching conditions at the outset were far from ideal. Starting a school is not for the faint-hearted. As with any creative project, the chaos endured by both the school and the church in those early years would try the heartiest and most enthusiastic of spirits. Space was a major problem. Classes met everywhere, including the balcony, the sanctuary, the narthex – even Berk's office. Jokingly, he told of being afraid to leave his office to go to the bathroom, lest a class take over his space while he was gone.

But the school's wonderful teachers were, for the most part, undaunted by what they lacked. Howard Bird, for example, whose classroom was a postage stamp surrounded by temporary walls at one end of the noisy cafeteria, said, "Just give me a piece of chalk and a blackboard and I can teach anywhere."

Mary Lou, in her historical piece, noted that the old choir rooms adjacent to the small chapel (the older sanctuary) were used for P.E. dressing rooms for girls and boys. "We had no lockers!" she says. "Many a Sunday morning worshipper was greeted by the smell of old gym clothes and tennis shoes left by some absent-minded student. Many a time, a stale lunch was found on Sunday morning, left in a hymnal rack behind a pew. But through it all, God was blessing; and we all made do with the little inconveniences of a busy church and school."

Though the church was solidly behind the school, over-crowding did put a strain on tolerance and understanding. Berk had to continually run interference with the church folks, reminding them what was at stake: saving and shaping of the souls and lives of children. In light of the eternal significance, he would point out, surely we could overlook a peanut butter and jelly sandwich left on a pew.

Guiding Principles

From the outset, the school made neither apology nor concession for it's Christ-centered approach to life and every academic discipline. At its twenty-fifth year, the school had served 12,622 students from all over the South Daytona area with roots in over fifty churches. The faculty and staff have daily devotions during which time they pray for students and their families. Students attend a required weekly chapel program and study the Bible daily.

From the beginning, Warner Christian Academy was designed to be a school "where Jesus is Lord and students are led to develop spiritually, academically, socially, physically, and in service to others." A later pastor, Kerry Robinson, said it well: "We want . . . to meet individual needs of students and families (in a place) where we can teach young people to make a difference in the world for Jesus Christ."

Berk, the Principal

Berk loved the school, because he loved learning. When David Black left after two and a half years, Berk assumed the role of president and principal for an interim. As principal, his most difficult responsibility was discipline. He hated being "the judge." So many of the little "perpetrators" were from one-parent or dysfunctional homes, and most of their infractions seemed to be bids for attention. Berk, the psychologist, realized that. So when a discipline case was sent to him, he merely sat, talked, and prayed with the child. There were no spankings.

Berk enjoyed eating in the cafeteria, so he could watch the different classes come and go. But so many little ones came by to touch him or sit on his lap, he couldn't eat. Untimately, he would have to retreat to the kitchen, where he ate his lunch sitting on the freezer while Betty Simmons and Babe Sharpton served him.

Berk inherited another role when the Spanish teacher left suddenly. He had never taken Spanish; but because he had such an intuitive, linguistic ear in other languages, he took on the challenge and taught by staying one lesson ahead of the class.

What I Learned in the Principal's Office

At the heart of Berk's great success both as a preacher and a teacher, was his innate love and respect for people of all ages. He found people fascinating and always looked to learn something from everyone he met, even a child. He was then eager to share his discoveries with others in sermons and seminars, for his philosophy was that we are all on this human journey together, so how can we help one another. From a discipline problem at school, he made a profound discovery about the Power of Listening, which afterwards became a frequent theme in sermons and seminars.

One day while I was acting principal of our school, a young man walked into my office with a note from his teacher. He was in junior high at the time.

"Here's a note from my teacher," he said.

The note was brief: "Dr. Berquist, here is Jeff. Either he goes or I go. Signed (the teacher)."

I seated the young man beside my desk, and I asked, "What seems to be the problem?"

"I can't get along with this teacher. And she obviously can't get along with me."

And I said, "Tell me about it."

Now, I have never done this before or since, but, as it happened, I had just bought a new tape recorder, which was lying on my desk. The salesman had told me it would pick up conversaton in ordinary tones, so I just pushed the button to record as I listened.

About thirty minutes later Jeff finished his conversaton with me, and I wrote a note to his teacher – "I think Jeff will be better. Keep trying"– signed my name, and sent Jeff with it back to his room.

After he had gone, I wanted to check my recorder; so I rewound the tape and played it back.

To my amazement, on that tape all I had said for thirty minutes was "Uh huh . . . uh huh . . . uh huh, uh huh . . . Hm-m-m." The rest was Jeff talking, while I listened. I remembered scratching my head a time or two, but that didn't show on the recorder.

That night Jeff's mother called me late and said, "You talked to my son today."

"Yes, I did."

"What did you say to him?"

I said, "What do you mean?"

She said, "Well, he came home from school today and said, 'Dr. Berquist has got to be the smartest man in the world.'"

Well, that was a new accusation and, granted, a minority report; but she went on:

"What in the world did you say to him? He is just . . . changed."

Then I said to her: "Frankly, I have to make a confession. He came into my office today greatly perturbed – as was his teacher. I had just bought a new tape recorder, and when he came in I pushed the record button, and when he left I played the tape back. All I said for thirty minutes was "Uh huh" while he talked."

"You mean you listened to him for thirty minutes?"

"Yes, I did."

"We never listen to him." she said. "He's always talking."

In my role as principal, I felt much more at liberty than I did in my role as pastor. As principal, you can tell the truth; as pastor, your approach is to sugar coat it a little and wait for it to go down. So I put on my "principal's voice" and said, "Has it occurred to you that the reason he's always talking is that nobody listens?"

That idea had not occurred to her.

So I said, "Try listening. It might do you both good."

Well, I tell you with a fair amount of pride in the system that it turned his career around. He graduated from our school; went to college, where he became an outstanding student; is now pastoring a church and doing well.

I became consciously aware that day that the simple act of listening can make a difference in people's lives. It costs nothing, but can yield big dividends for the Kingdom.

The students never knew, and they had such fun! Berk's enthusiasm for language study was infectious, and his creative mind kept lessons lively and interesting.

But the discipline problems just about "did him in." He felt that the children being sent to his office were misbehaving for a reason, and one day it occurred to him that the problem might somehow be tied to their ability to read. So he had the teachers test all the students in reading achievement and discovered that, on the average, children in the school were reading two years below grade level! Since most students came to WCA from public schools, it was obviously a problem the school had inherited, but could do something about.

Berk immediately initiated an innovative remedial reading program. He hired a young, vivacious "reading expert," whom he coached in setting up a program to convince the children that reading was easy and fun. The program was a phenomenal success, boosting grades and cutting down on discipline problems as children were better able to understand and keep up with their classwork. Students were doing better, teachers and parents were pleased, and Berk was happy to be "holding court" less often.

As the school settled into a well-organized routine, Berk's duties lessened. In the fall of 1974, Jim Rudolph came on board as principal and administrator.

An Emerging Campus

In response to swelling enrollments, the board approved a building program for the school. In addition to classroom buildings, the school eventually boasted a first-class gymnasium, home of "the Eagles," built under the supervision of Nathan Brown.

When Barry Sempsrott painted the school mascot, the Eagle, on the wall of the gymnasium, he dedicated it "to the memory of Barney Riley, friend of the Eagles." Barney never missed an athletic event at the school, whether or not his grandchildren were playing!

Before long, we were into all the big school stuff: basketball tournaments, Homecoming Kings and Queens, Christmas pageants, science fairs, and Junior-Senior banquets (in lieu of a prom).

Taking Jericho

Knowing that the school would ultimately need more space, Berk challenged the church to pray for a cause that had "IMPOSSIBLE" written all over it! For years they prayed and, then, God moved. Berk would share the testimony of this experience many times afterwards at preaching engagements around the country:

The night was hot and I felt uncomfortable sitting there in my car.

Of course, I might have been more uncomfortable if one of my friends had asked me what I was doing there, at that time of night. As it turned out, there was nothing to fear. Only God knew that I was there. And, of course, He knew why I was there.

Across the street from where I was sitting, the neon lights blazed, outlining the figure of a scantily clad young lady. The "night club" was crowded. Inside the garishly painted buildings were scores of people who were trying to add a little inspiration to their lives by drinking and inflaming their unholy desires by watching the "exotic dancers."

Early that evening I had met with the city council of South Daytona, trying to urge them to at least curb the hours of operation of this infamous place, located a few hundred feet from my congregation. In spite of my urgent pleadings, things seemed destined to continue as before.

By all standards, my attack was not terribly threating to the business people who were intent on making as many dollars as possible from the evil that lurks in men's hearts. Had someone pointed me out to them, I am sure that they would simply have smiled sympathetically. "Right forever on the scaffold; wrong forever on the throne."

A few years have passed. I am writing from memory. Some memories stretch back over a few years; some go back only a few days.

Let us start with the recent memories. A few days ago a friend handed me a copy of the Daytona Beach News-Journal. *Headlines declared that the Drive-In Theatre (the property on which the night club had been located) was sold to White Chapel Church of God. The eight acres would be used as an extension for the Christian School, Warner Academy, now in its eighth year, with more than 800 students.*

I was invited to come speak at a dedication of this land for Christian purposes. "We want to walk over and claim the entire operation for God," my host said.

More memories. I remembered the times I drove by this spot asking God to release our community from its degrading influence. I remembered walking over the grounds quoting God's promises to those who move forward by faith.

Now, like the people of God who marched around the walls of Jericho to watch them fall, I had seen God's plan and power revealed. In a little while, these grounds will be hallowed by the happy chants of children and the concerned instruction of their elders. The time will come when the old days will not be remembered by anyone. Except me.

I do not think I will forget. I don't want to. There are too many other places around which God's army needs to march.

118

The Dream Goes On

It is a great tribute to the caring people of White Chapel that even after Berk took another ministry assignment, their dedication and commitment to Warner Christian Academy continued. In 1980 the "Little Red Schoolhouse" was replaced by the Ken Kress Memorial Child Care Center, a project led by Dale Whalen, who followed us as pastor. Freddie Gilmour, Jr., and his father, Fred, Sr., were contractors for the project. Reid Hughes made the lot available by trading one of his own for it. The Gilmours poured the footers, and Joe Bailey's precast company put up the walls. Bill Appenzeller donated and installed the windows. Frank Garmon and Ron Welborn put in the plumbing. Charles Farmer did the electric work; Jerry Koontz, the heating and air conditioning. Berk was invited to speak at the dedication of the facility.

Ken Kress, the late husband of WCA secretary Linda Kress, was a special friend who died much too young. He was a prince of a fellow, who devoted himself to a bus ministry for children. When Ken died in 1980, Berk wrote a poem celebrating Ken's contribution to the church and to the children. Shared at Ken's memorial service, the poem said in part:

Kenny agreed to work in the bus ministry,
Spending his Saturdays
Piloting a bus as large as a dinosaur
Up and down the streets of Holly Hill
Inviting kids to come to Sunday School.
It wasn't that he liked wrestling that monster
Through the narrow streets.
It wasn't that he enjoyed knocking on doors
And talking to strangers.
It was just that he felt it ought to be done
And he was someone who could do it.
. . . . .

If faithfulness is the only coin
That will buy heaven's real estate,
Then it is my guess
That Kenny has just moved into
Heaven's largest mansion.

Dale Whalen also led the congregation to begin construction of the new high school building in 1981. At that time enrollment had reached nearly 1,000 and the school was operating on double shifts to accommodate all the students. The Junior High/Senior High complex was completed in 1986 under the leadership of Pastor Marvin Cain. On the building committee were Fred Gilmour, Jr., Ron Welborn, Art Morris, Richard Poore, Norman Riley, Stan Hoell, Ren Bruning, Roger Stamper, Nita Garmon (Berk's long-time secretary), and Walt Sempsrott. Berk followed all of this progress from Anderson, Indiana, with tears of joy. These who had been a part of our congregation during our pastorate were continuing to bless! Berk was invited back for the dedication.

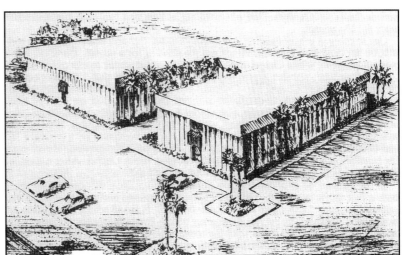

RIGHT: Warner Christian Academy's Junior High/Senior High Complex, dedicated, March 9, 1986. Today WCA boasts three educational buildings, two libraries, two gymnasiums, and separate outside playgrounds on a 15-acre campus. In addition to basic academics, the program includes science and computer labs, foreign languages, music, and an extensive athletic program. The school, fully accredited, has held to a high standard of academic excellence for students, with 90 to 100 percent of its graduates each year pursuing higher education. Berk would be proud of that achievement.

Warner Southern

While Berk was busy preaching and teaching, another dream emerged. Warner Southern College was established in 1968, and Berk served on the Executive Committee of the founding Board of Trustees. To Berk's delight, Leroy Fulton was named President. Leroy was one of Berk's converts and was called to the ministry under Berk's influence.

Nina Ratzlaff, in her book about Warner Southern entitled *Through Faith and Faithfulness*, states that during this period many sacrificed time away from their homes and jobs, to plan, meet with committees, and visit churches to tell the story of the college and arouse interest in supporting the school with prayer and finances.

As they traveled together throughout the Southeast, these college promoters had a great time with one another. Nina records that "on one all-night trip Maurice Berquist played his harmonica and Dick Smith sang. They tested each other on who could remember the words to the most Church of God songs and also on which songs came first in the hymnal. James Chapman was known as the driver with the 'heavy' foot, for he received the most traffic tickets from the thousands of miles he traveled in his enthusiasm for the college."

Berk with Leroy Fulton, President of Warner Southern College.

After Warner Southern was in operation, White Chapel kids no longer had to go as far as Texas or Indiana to attend a Church of God college. First to enroll from our church was Bob Sharpless, who worked as a maintenance man at the college during his years as a student there. Others attending through the years were Peggy, Tommy, and Becky Brown; Brian, Jeff and Tanya Hogan; Gary and Tracy Garmon; Sandy Farmer; Barry Sempsrott; and the Bailey girls, Rhondi and Aven.

Letters in Flight

Our church and school kept growing. But no matter how fulfilling or challenging the "home-front" pastorate and school were, Berk never lost his evangelistic zeal and booked himself to preach and teach for as many seminars, revivals, and conventions as the board would permit. When Berk accepted the call to White Chapel, it was agreed that he could be away for a specified number of Sundays each year for speaking engagements. So when he got calls to go somewhere to preach, he went. But, inevitably, when he announced that he would be gone on a particular Sunday, some people would corner him and make him feel as if he were deserting the ship. He found the criticism totally frustrating. He was merely taking days already allotted to him. The home ministry team was more than capable of handling every kind of situation in his absence. What could he do to appease these people? In his words:

> *I could have become defensive and said, "Look, you told me when I came here that I could have six Sundays to preach away from home, and I'm just taking them. I'm here the rest of the time working my heart out for you people."*
>
> *But I didn't say that. I listened. And what I heard beneath their words was a feeling – the motive behind their criticism – that said, "We feel deprived, cheated, when you are away."*
>
> *Then, out of that bad experience, came a wonderful idea.*

When I went away, I developed a habit of writing letters back to my people. I'd take along a mailing list, and on the plane out of town, I would start writing. In a week's time, I'd write anywhere from fifty to a hundred and fifty letters to my people back home. Not long letters, mind you – a page maybe. I don't write well at best. You might describe my handwriting as a hieroglyphic scrawl. And when I'm in a hurry, I don't write even that well! But you know what? The folks in my church came to look forward to those letters. Years later, some were still saving them . . . still trying to read some of them! Seriously, in time, it got to where they actually liked for me to go. They enjoyed getting the mail.

For the rest of his life, Berk wrote thousands of letters on napkins, restaurant placemats, airline "barf bags," church bulletins, whatever was at hand to scribble on when he thought of someone. Some of them, done in "Berquist scrawl," were barely legible. But most were keepsakes for delighted recipients, who knew from the treasured missive that they held a special place in Berk's heart.

Putting Mom Through School

In 1967 I went to a vocational school to earn a surgical technician degree. I also learned to drive!

After a year's training, I graduated and started working as a surgical technician (scrub nurse) at Ormond Beach Memorial Hospital. Although it was fulfilling, I wanted something beyond the operating room. All I saw there were people sleeping; I wanted to be a part of their recovery. So, in 1970 I enrolled in Daytona Beach Community College as a full-time RN student.

In the interim we moved again to the twelve-room, two-story house on Ridgewood. In addition to keeping house and attending classes, I worked half days for my nursing instructors, typing syllabuses. Berk was my greatest encourager and mentor! He got Marty and Lori, now high schoolers, off to school each day; helped me with the household chores; and studied with me. He was such a scholar that I teased him about taking my state boards and passing.

> *"My wife's a nurse, so I can be sick for nothing. And I'm a minister, so she can be good for nothing!"*
> *– Berk*

Marty graduated from high school in 1972 and entered Anderson College that fall. Lori and I were "seniors" together – high school and college respectively – and we both graduated in May of 1973. I was exhausted and exalted, for I was chosen to represent my nursing class in *Who's Who in American Junior Colleges.*

Berny Berquist, RN

Berk started guiding some Holy Land Tours in the 1970's. I went on the first. He took Marty as a graduation present in 1971, and likewise for Lori in 1972. I had to stay behind that year to study for my Nursing Board exams. But in May of 1973, Berk took both Marty and me to Israel and Egypt – this time, *my* graduation present!

By September of 1973, I was working in the intensive care unit at Halifax Medical Center. And though both of our children were now away at college, we didn't have time to suffer from "empty nest syndrome."

While I was engrossed in my new ministry, Berk continued building, preaching, teaching at Warner Academy and a Sunday School class, plus doing a weekly radio broadcast. We were each other's best audiences. I was always eager to hear his latest stories. And he enjoyed my experiences as a nurse. One of his new lines became: "My wife's a nurse, so I can be sick for nothing; and I'm a minister, so she can be good for nothing!"

Berk's years of preaching at White Chapel bore the fruit of many changed lives, heartwarming stories of people who found help and a true friend in Jesus Christ, and endeared themselves to our family. There would not be room in ten books to include them all, but these two are representative of the many.

Welcome to Heaven: Smoking or Non-Smoking

The Pappy family started attending White Chapel in the 1970's. Hubert and Merle were realtors and Rosalie, their daughter, was a tax accountant. Shortly after they came, Merle was stricken by a heart attack. At first, she was in intensive care in critical condition; then she graduated to stable status, and finally was sent home to heal further.

Rosalie was physically handicapped with cerebral palsy and had need of her mother's assistance for her nightly shower. This posed a problem while Merle was hospitalized, but was solved by several of our church ladies, including me, who took turns nightly with this task. We also provided food and shared in Merle's care until she was able to solo again.

One Sunday evening Berk preached a sermon entitled: "The Altar Sanctifies the Gift." The gist of the message was based on Matthew 23:19:

"For which is greater? The gift on the altar, or the altar itself that sanctifies the gift?"

Berk's message was that whatever gift or problem you have, bring it to the altar, lay it before the Lord, and leave it there. He will answer . . . deliver . . . take away . . . forgive . . . or bless. Whatever! Just leave it there and let God take over.

After the sermon Berk opened the altar to those who wished help. Merle Pappy went forward, and I slipped out of my pew to pray with her until Berk was free. Usually I returned to my pew after Berk appeared, so the seeker could have privacy. But Merle asked me to stay. She looked up at Berk and said, "Brother Berquist, do you really believe what you preached tonight?"

"Why, yes. If I didn't I would not have said it," he replied.

"Well," continued Merle, "I have a problem. You two know full well what I've just come through. But what you don't know is that I have smoked most of my adult life. I gave it up all the time I was hospitalized and thought I was totally free of the addiction. Then I came home, found my cigarettes in the drawer, and I'm on them again. Hubert and Rosalie are aghast. I know what it's done and will do to my health, so I want you to anoint and pray for me to be totally delivered."

With that statement, she reached in her purse and laid a pack of Luckies on the altar. And she said, "Here, Brother Berk, take these home with you; and I'll never buy another pack."

Berk prayed. Then handed back the cigarettes.

"Merle," he said gently. "I have a better idea. You take these home; and every time you start to smoke or light up, look up and ask God if it's okay. He'll never give you permission."

Then, with a twinkle in her eye, Merle said, "Brother Berk, do you think there'll be smoking in heaven?"

"I don't think so," he grinned back. "It bothers me where you'd have to go to get a light."

Merle was delivered. That was more than twenty years ago. And for the past ten years she has been inhaling the purest of air – celestial!

Birthday of Joy

"Practice random acts of kindness and senseless deeds of joy."

People all over read these words on cards and bumper stickers and are spurred to do favors for others with no premeditation – just a nudge from God.

One of the favorite stories going around is about the lady in San Francisco who headed across the Golden Gate Bridge in a bright red convertible. Just as she was one car from the toll both, she noticed the bumper sticker ahead of her and read the above words. It sparked her heart; so she reached in her purse, handed the attendant a $20 bill, and said, "I'd like to pay the fare for the next six cars behind me. Just tell each person that the lady ahead of them paid their way."

Imagine the smiles of the travelers as they each received that message and journeyed on!

We had a moment like that in Daytona, one of my favorite memories of an impulsive "act of kindness."

The year was 1970. On December 23, I became 40 and I was not elated.

I was a Surgical Technician at Ormond Beach Memorial Hospital. Christmas was upon us, with church activities paramount; and Marty and Lori were in high school. We lived in a twelve-room house, and I was weary from a 7 a.m. to 3 p.m. shift, plus holiday baking, cleaning, and shopping preparatory to Christmas. I felt like a pie cut into six pieces to be served to twelve people.

Being born so close to Christmas is not a plus. But after we were married Berk always made it special. This particular birthday we, as a family, decided to go to our favorite Chinese restaurant, "The Lotus," on Sea Breeze Boulevard. We ordered the family dinner for four and were merrily chomping away.

Suddenly we were interrupted by a cheery, "Hi there, Berquists, what are you doing eating out so close to Christmas?"

We looked up to see Joe and Phyllis Bryant – one of our delightful church couples.

Berk quipped back, "Well, this is a very sad occasion. It's Berny's fortieth birthday, and we're out commiserating."

"Oh, I'm so sorry," Joe exclaimed. "I'm headed down that road myself and you have my deepest sympathy."

After chatting a bit, they went on their way.

We waited for the check. When it did not appear, we arose and approached the cashier, a small Chinese man. When Berk inquired about our check, the man bowed deeply with his hands clasped and said:

"Oh, so solly, sir, for your great sollow. The man and lady who just went out said you had grief in your family – so they pay your bill."

We left the restaurant wreathed in smiles.

This gift – the Bryants' random act of kindness – has been packed carefully in my memory box and has warmed me every year as I have unwrapped it for each birthday since.

A Cherished Christmas

In December of 1976 I was working at Halifax Medical Center in the Intensive Care Unit. Our work schedule had been posted for the month, including New Year's. Below this schedule was the edict that there would be NO extra days off, other than our allotted ones. And no excuses for absences. Sickness had to have a doctor's excuse, and we'd be better off if we just called in dead.

On the 13th I arrived at 10:40 p.m., walked into the nurses' lounge to retrieve my cap and stethoscope. Our charge nurse was there and greeted me with these words: "Berny, you won't believe what we have here tonight. A 15-year-old girl shot herelf and is brain dead. She's on a respirator; has a heart beat, but that's all. The family won't give permission to turn off the machine, so she has to die "on her own."

As the shift gathered for assignments, the charge nurse read the list of patients, assigning to each nurse her charges and listing the diagnosis and care measures needed. Coming to "Debbie," she said, "I know none of you want this case, because it's a heartbreaker."

Then she looked directly at me and said, "Berny, I'm giving her to you. She will be your only patient. She probably won't make it through the night, and I need your strength and skills as a nurse, a minister's wife, and a mother of teenagers."

The assignment was heavy. My charge was a beautiful girl with long, golden brown hair hanging to her waist. My nursing duties were to turn her every two hours, plus vital signs and respirator care. My heart was broken as I carried out my tasks.

Every now and then the family came in for fifteen minutes to bend over the bed to hug, pat, and talk endearments to her. There was no reponse to touch or voice.

Jim Smith, the hospital chaplain, was there, as well as the family minister. From them I gleaned the details of how this tragedy happened.

"Debbie" was a student at Sea Breeze High School. She was a well-rounded and popular honor student who somehow had got in with the wrong crowd and was caught smoking marijuana in the girls' locker room. She was suspended and sent home. That evening her parents had a family conference to decide her punishment. There was , it seems, an up-coming Rock Musical in Jacksonville that she had tickets to and was eagerly awaiting the event. Her parents decided to take away this privilege to discipline her. She ran from the meeting into her father's study, opened a desk drawer, grabbed a loaded revolver, and shot herself in the right temple – in minutes.

I watched the family as they agonized over this pain. I listened as they begged her to come back. I heard her father say, "Daddy is so sorry. It's going to be all right." And as I watched I, too, cried and thought about my Lori and some turbulent years we had passed through with her. Lori had a few escapades that her father and I had to deal with, and she went through some angry and rebellious times. But we all survived – through fervent prayers and the Lord's mercy.

Debbie lasted through the night, and I went home. Before going to bed, I shared the tragedy with Berk, who also wept, shaking his head in disbelief, when I related the night's scenario. We talked about what the Bible says about "reproving a child," and how the parents surely felt justified in meting out that particular punishment. But now . . . this terrible guilt they'd have to live with.

When I awakened around 4:00 p.m., I called the Intensive Care unit to check on Debbie and learned that she had died at 9:30 a.m. I felt relieved that it was over.

On December 16, when I again reported for night duty, a pall of sadness still hung over the Intensive Care unit. The charge nurse came in and said, "I don't know what is going on here, but this case is worse than the one before. We have another suicide attempt. This time a 15-year-old boy, another discipline problem. He tried to hang himself in the family garage."

This is his story. "Billy" was from a family of six children. After school they all had chores to do before dinner and homework. Billy shirked his chore, it seems, and when his father found it undone, he spanked him and sent him to the garage to sweep it out. Supper time came and no Billy. Thinking he was just pouting, the father went out to fetch him. He found Billy hanging by his neck from a harness hooked to the rafters. He was not dead, but unconscious. At the hospital he had been placed on a respirator. Though he responded some, he was found to be badly brain damaged.

As we listened to the report, I looked pleadingly at my charge nurse.

"No, Berny," she said, "I'm not going to do this to you again."

Several nights passed. We did turns taking care of Billy before he was moved to a regular unit and then on to a long-term facility. He would be a "vegetable" the rest of his life.

On December 20 I was having breakfast with Berk at a little local cafe we frequented after I got home and before he went to the church. Our children were both in Anderson College in Indiana. Berk told me that Lori had called the night before to say that she would be catching a ride home for the holidays, but Marty couldn't come because he had only two days off and not enough time to make the trip.

I was crushed. All I could think about were the two teenagers I had just cared for, and how fortunate we were to have gotten our own safely this far. And I started crying.

"Berk," I sobbed, "there isn't anything I want for Christmas, no gift that would mean as much to me as to be together this Christmas. I want both my children home. I want to sit at the Christmas table and hold hands as a family and thank God for sparing us, for honoring our faith, and bringing us thus far. I want to gather my chicks under my wing. I know we don't have flying money for Marty. But I want him home, even if it is only for two days. I'll give my whole pay check."

It took some doing, but Berk flew Marty home for those two days. I had to work on Christmas Eve, but we had our festive, traditional Christmas all together – safe and thankful. Though we did not know it at the time, it would be our last Christmas in Daytona. (We moved to Anderson, Indiana, in the summer.) But, for me, this was the "warmest" and most blessed Christmas we had ever had.

God's Call to Another Challenge

In 1976, for the first time, Berk began having serious thoughts of leaving White Chapel and Warner Academy. At long last, he felt that his ministry in Daytona was fulfilled and that God was leading him in another direction.

Warner Press had called him as a candidate for the editor's post. The position of Executive Secretary of Mass Communications was also open. Berk had served on the Mass Communications Board for several years; thus, when the Board approached him, he agreed to pray about that position, as well. Either of these assignments afforded the opportunity to work in areas of ministry Berk was passionate about: communicating the Gospel through writing and through radio.

In March of 1977, Berk flew to Anderson to be interviewed by the Mass Communications Board. At first he had refused their offer; but after praying about it, he finally told the board: "If I get a vote of 100 percent, I'll know it's God's will."

Because we had stayed in Daytona so long, and so many of our friends had short pastorates, Berk liked to tease them with this old story:

Back in the days before modern transportation, a certain minister was known to change pastorates rather frequently. In those days when one moved, they loaded up a wagon with horses pulling it. Piled on the wagon were all the household goods, sometimes even live stock. Well, this preacher, it seems, had a flock of chickens. And, whenever he got ready to move, he would tie the chickens' legs together to keep them from escaping. This fellow moved so often, it was said, that every time he went out in the yard to feed the chickens, they automatically rolled over on their backs and stuck up their legs to be tied. They thought it was moving time again!

As Berk left for Anderson, he said to me, "You stay by the phone, and I'll call you as soon as the verdict is in."

With my heart pounding on the day of his meeting, I sat awaiting the call. The phone rang. It was Berk. The first words I heard when I answered were: "Berny, this is your 100 percent husband. Tie the chicken legs!"

Saying Goodbye to White Chapel

Berk's being tapped for the Mass Communications ministry was exciting for us. His work in Anderson, however, would not begin until July 1. Nevertheless, he had to resign as soon as he got home, because Mass Communications was announcing his appointment publicly the next day. It was hard for us and for the church to have such a long waiting period. Yet, it was a good time to affirm the deep love we shared with the people there and the many friendships that continue even today.

We had much to do. Our house had to be sold. I had to resign from my nursing position. Many ministry details had to be wrapped up for whoever would follow us. So many "goodbye's" to be said.

It was an exciting and bittersweet time.

We had to return to Anderson in June for Berk's ratification by the General Assembly at the International Convention. I flew up a week ahead to house-hunt and to help Lori, who was graduating from Anderson College. Berk drove up in time for the graduation exercises.

After Berk's ratification, Camp Meeting week became a blur of meetings, receptions, and dinners. CBH hosted two receptions – one honoring Dr. Eugene Sterner, who was retiring from the CBH microphone as Speaker and another welcoming Berk to the CBH family. In off-hours we rode with real estate agents to look for a house. We finally settled on an old home in Edgewood (1301 Winding Way) – a Williamsburg style two story that would be home to us and all our antiques.

Then we went back to Daytona for our final two weeks.

As the finality of our leaving settled upon us, we asked ourselves, "How do you pack up and finalize twenty-one years of a life poured out. How do you say 'goodbye' to all the wonderful people who let you fulfill your dreams and who have been so faithful?"

These were the people of our first and only pastorate, who truthfully had let us grow up in their midst, forgiving our many mistakes and celebrating our victories. This church had suffered with us through all the birth pangs of growth and regrowth. Together we had shared times of grief and joy in a plethora of deaths, births and weddings, and a thousand other unforgettable moments.

Again we asked, "How do you just walk away?"

You don't. For to be a part of such a church is to have your heart walking outside your body for the rest of your lives. This was home!

White Chapel bade us farewell with a love offering and a gala banquet. To keep it light, the board appointed our favorite comedian, Charlie VanHoose, to chair the farewell. And he made it a "roast." So we were warmed by the laughter and spoofs of all our years there, making a difficult time easier.

Marty and Lori were both there to pay tribute to the church people who had "raised" them from babies to college students. They were thrilled that the move to Anderson would once more place the four of us all in the same town. But "home" for them would never again be the sandy shores of Daytona Beach. They had to move on with their lives, also; but carried with them the best memories ever.

When we pulled out for Anderson that July, we cried all the way to Georgia. Guess north Florida needed the water! The chicken legs were tied; the ark was loaded. But we marked signs all the way, so we could find our way back.

The Berquist family – Berny and Berk, Marty and Lori – leaving Daytona for new challenges in Anderson, Indiana.

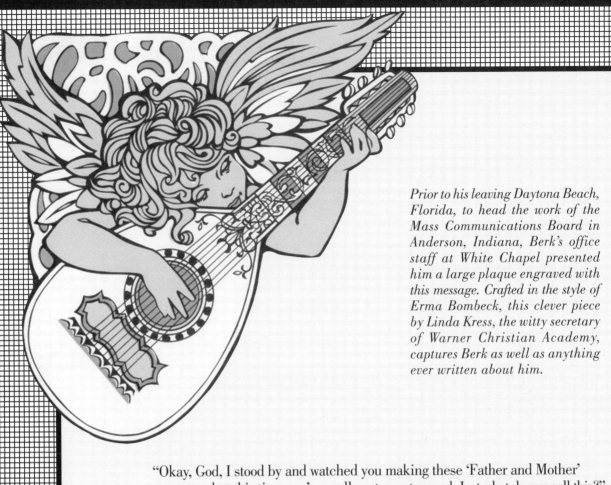

Prior to his leaving Daytona Beach, Florida, to head the work of the Mass Communications Board in Anderson, Indiana, Berk's office staff at White Chapel presented him a large plaque engraved with this message. Crafted in the style of Erma Bombeck, this clever piece by Linda Kress, the witty secretary of Warner Christian Academy, captures Berk as well as anything ever written about him.

"Okay, God, I stood by and watched you making these 'Father and Mother' creatures, but this time you've really got me stumped. Just what do you call this?"

"This, Angel, is about to be my finest creation – my 'top of the line' model of mankind, so to speak. I'm using all the best ingredients – the pure Swedish extract, for example."

"A nice touch," said the Angel.

"I thought so," said God. "I have great plans for him; but, first, I thought a humble beginning would be good. It would not only build his character, but also give him an endless range of 'poor stories' to share with his listeners."

"He sure is a big one, God – he'll never fit in a Volkswagen, that's certain. And just look at the size of those hands! I think he'd make a good carpenter."

"No, Angel, I've got other plans for those hands – instead of pounding nails, they'll pound the podium when he gets fired up; but they'll have other uses, too – he'll lay them on the sick, fold them in prayer, touch the cheek of a little four-year-old, or caress his favorite rosebush. He'll write sermons, songs, and poetry; and the fingernails will get more than their share of printer's ink."

"But, God, don't you think the shoulders should be streamlined? They're much too broad."

"They'll have to be, Angel. He'll have to carry the burdens of many people – the sick, the tired, the discouraged, and the lonely; and the frame must be big enough to house his enormous heart."

"Sounds like he's got a tough job ahead of him – are you sure he can handle it?"

"Oh, yes," God smiled. "I plan on sharing the load with him."

"But the face is all wrong – it's both rugged and gentle."

"That's the way I wanted it," God said, "a reflection of the inward spirit of the man, a gentle strength."

"Well, you have to admit, you went overboard on the nose!"

"Well, maybe just a little," God conceded.

"I've got to admit though, I kind of like him," said the Angel.

"You haven't seen anything yet!" smiled God. "He'll be blessed with a variety of talents. He'll be able to fill a church with his eloquent preaching or empty it with the simple toot of a harmonica. He'll be able to recognize the smell of Boston cream pie from 50 feet away, fall asleep virtually anywhere, and be able to change the key of any song in the Church of God hymnbook. A red-haired beauty from the foothills of Virginia will make the perfect helpmate, and it might be a good idea to give her a sense of humor.

"I plan to give him an outstanding intellect; he will be able to produce some of the great thoughts of his time. We will walk together, and I will share my innermost feelings and thoughts with him so that he can communicate them to people."

"But, God, in view of all this, how will you keep him humble?"

"Why, Angel, I thought you would have guessed – I'll give him a church to pastor! And if that doesn't get the job done, I'll even throw in an office staff!"

And the Lord saw that it was good – and He named his creation *"BERQUIST."*

Linda Kress
June 1977

Berk as Tour Leader
1971 - 1992

07
World Travels

While pursuing his vision for White Chapel in Daytona Beach, Berk's zeal for evangelism never abated; neither did his concern for missions. He led our church people, for example, to build two churches for Japan right in the midst of our own building campaign to enlarge White Chapel's facilities.

In 1959 he encouraged me to accept an invitation to attend the World Conference of the Church of God in Essen, Germany. He was eager for me to experience the kind of excitement he had felt in his travels to learn about the worldwide ministry of the church. My traveling companion was Margie Van Ness; our tour host, T. Franklin Miller. We visited eight countries in eight weeks. The trip, however, was no vacation. Mrs. Toner, owner of the *Anderson Herald*, asked me to chronicle the journey. She ran the articles in their entirety – some on the front page of the *Herald*, along with my picture. Friends I met and traveled with and the experiences we shared still warm my heart.

Then, in the Seventies, Berk found another way to spark the involvement of our Daytona flock in missions. From personal experience, he knew that the best way to stir excitement about missions is to see first-hand the work being done and the needs of missionaries and ministers on the field. And what better way to give people deeper insight into Scriptures than to visit the lands of the Bible. Combining travel, Bible study, and missions awareness – leading tour groups was Berk's "cup of tea."

1975 – Around the World

In the fall of 1975 we shepherded a group of twenty-one (counting Berk and me) on a month's journey around the world. With us from White Chapel were Patty Blair and her mother, Ruth Drake; Marion Cherney, Etna Caldwell, Nancy and Buddy Hughes, Nell Crowe, Maxine Burdine, Harry and Ann Gregory, along with the Lowell Wilsons from Vincennes, Indiana, and seven hearty souls from other places.

We left on September 8, from Daytona Beach via New York to Rome, then to Athens, and on to Cairo. In each country we did the usual highlights, enjoying the reactions of our flock at each new wonder . . . the Coliseum . . . the Parthenon . . . the Pyramids.

Then, on Friday, September 12, we left Cairo at 7:30 a.m. bound for Jordan and arrived at 9:30 a.m. We were herded into the passport and luggage-search arena and kept there two hours. With growing concern I watched Berk talking intently with the officials. Finally, to our shock, we learned that Berk and six others of our group were being denied entry into Jordan because their passports had Israeli stamps on them from a previous journey. Jordan was angry at Israel that day and would not admit anyone into Jordan who had previously been in Israel. The officials refused to let Berk or the tour guide call the Embassy.

I was aghast. But what happened next plunged my heart to the soles of my feet. Berk handed me the airline tickets for the remaining fifteen, putting me in charge. And I had never been in Jordan before.

"Be brave and don't worry," he said. "You'll do great. I'll see you in Jerusalem."

I reached out to clasp his hand. The airport security man slapped it away. And with that, the police hustled my husband and six others to a plane going back to Egypt.

I didn't dare act as scared as I was. I gathered the remaining sheep together and told them that we were in a hostile land, and that I needed their full cooperation and their prayers. I asked them all to be sweet-spirited and polite, lest we raise any more ire.

Our Jordanian tour guide got us out of the airport and to the chartered bus waiting. At the hotel, I gave out room keys and got everyone settled in their rooms. After lunch and naps, we were treated to an expedition through the bazaar; but my concern for Berk and the rest of our group took the edge off shopping that afternoon.

Next morning we traveled to Petra, that ancient city carved out in a canyon of rose-colored stone. I led the pack on horse back, as Arabs saddled us up and led us single file down the treacherous path – two miles down to the city and two miles back. All the travelers were valiant. And cheerful. The city was awesome; but again, the absence of Berk and the others dampened the joy of being there.

The next day was Sunday – reunion day! We arose early, breakfasted, and were bused to the Allenby Bridge, from whence we would be taken to Jerusalem. At the bridge our luggage was scrupulously searched, and I filled out papers. The air was thick with tension. We held our breath.

Finally, our bus was allowed to pass to the middle of the bridge, where we were stopped again. More officials got on, moved solemnly up and down the aisle looking us over, had me sign more papers, then let us continue. On the other side of the bridge, we changed to another bus waiting with our tour escort. When we were safely ensconced on that bus and finally on our way to Jerusalem, we all applauded. As tension fell away, the gang gave me hugs, and we sang heartily, "We're Marching to Zion."

From its perch high on a hill overlooking Jerusalem, the Intercontinental Hotel looked like the gates of Heaven as we approached. We pulled up to the entrance, and there stood a haggard Berk. We all cheered and he was soundly hugged, while I basked in all the compliments the fearless fifteen were giving me! In their view, I had earned my wings as a tour leader! But my heart ached for Berk and the others and what they had gone through.

Berk had barely slept since we had been separated. The police took all the money from his wallet – about $200. Luckily, I had the travelers' checks, tickets, and other passports with me. He had to charge $2,100 on American Express for airfares for the seven. They had flown back to Cairo, where they sat up all night there in the airport before returning to Athens and flying from there to Tel Aviv.

We spent three days in and around Jerusalem, touring the usual Holy Sites – thankful to be safe and together again.

New Delhi, Agra, Calcutta, Bangkok, Hong Kong, Tokyo, and Hawaii awaited – with no more major mishaps to spoil the joy of the journey.

1976 – World Tour of Mission Stations

Undaunted by our trouble in Jordan, we sallied forth on another month-long trek around the globe on November 1, 1976. This time, because of wars and rumors of wars overseas, we had only thirteen "pilgrims." Among them were Emmy and Gerhard Schmidt, Marion Cherney, Etna Caldwell, and Gerry and Charlie Allen. A major focus of this journey was visiting mission stations in Nairobi, Bombay, Bangkok, Hong Kong, Manila, and Australia.

After a two-day lay-over for sightseeing in London – I remember waking up to the news that Carter had become President-Elect on November 3 – we flew to Nairobi. I was excited to be going there. Berk had always glowed about Africa. Nairobi was a cross-cultural sea of people in every mode of dress imaginable. Equally colorful were the

What Seeing Missions First-Hand Has Meant to Me

[Excerpts from an article written by Berk for *Project Partner News*, April, 1976.]

You are stooping to enter a mud hut in Egypt. Or you are swaying on a subway strap in Tokyo. Suddenly you look up to see the face of your companion, Phyllis Kinley or Ernie LaFont, and you realize that missionaries are real people who live in a real world. . . .

A typical answer to the question "What impressed you most in your visit to Israel?" is this: "I guess it was the feeling I got when our plane landed in Tel Aviv and I walked down the stairs and started walking to the terminal."

"And what was so special about that?"

"Really, I couldn't tell you. It was just that all the things I had read about and heard about were not merely pictures on the calendar or in the Bible. It was the sudden realization that these lands and people are real."

And that is the main value of actually "seeing" and being involved in missionary work. It is gaining a deep sense of the "reality" of the struggle to plant the seed of the gospel. Some of the most dedicated workers for the cause of world missions have scarcely ventured beyond their home country. I am thrilled that they have a vision that reaches around the world. But there is another dimension that will make them even more aggressive for missions. It is the experi-

ence of actually seeing and touching some of the places where their prayers have gone.

On a recent trip around the world, I had the pleasure of traveling with some outstanding workers for the cause of missions: Janet Miller of Oregon, Pearl Winterfield of Montana, Daisy Shriner and Ann Denlinger of Michigan. These ladies had invested their lives in teaching and working for the cause of missions. . . .Naturally, in their minds they had made the journey to the mission fields a thousand times. But they found a particular delight in seeing what their prayers and work had accomplished. . . .

One of the most faithful workers in my own congregation, Joe Bailey, is in the construction business. He makes precast concrete panels for many public buldings. So he knows how to read blueprints and sketches. But when he came home from his first trip to Greece and Israel, he said,

"If I had enough money, I would have a large ship come right down the Intercoastal Waterway (which is about two blocks from our church) and load the entire congregation on it. Then I would take them where I have been and let them see what I saw. The church would never the same."

And I think he is right.

flowers. Hibiscus, jacaranda, and bougainvillea were in full glory, as it was summer there. My Virginia accent stood out in sharp contrast to the English spoken there with a clipped British cadence.

After a night in Nairobi and an over-night adventure watching wild animals at the Tree Tops animal preserve two hours out of the city, we re-boarded our vans for a 250-mile journey to Kisumu - Kima and M'Whila hospital. We traveled through incredible country. Cows, goats, and sheep grazed on verdant plains. We passed through villages of thatched huts and palm trees. Lunch by the roadside consisted of boxes of sandwiches, fruit, cheese and crackers, petit fours, and Cokes.

We were really "chowing down," at our make-shift picnic spot, when out of the bushes appeared a little native about 5 or 6 years old with ragged clothes and runny nose. We kept on eating, and children kept appearing until they numbered 10. That's 20 pairs of hungry eyes watching us eat! Suddenly not hungry any more, we gathered up remnants and whole portions and gave it to them. They were not the least bit shy. We followed them into the bush and saw their cow-dung and thatched hut with accompanying outhouse, cooking pot, and cow. And their mother smiling, toothless. It was a priceless moment, giving insight into real life in that part of the world – an experience not included on the basic tour itinerary.

At M'Whila Hospital, Darlene Detweiler, a college friend who was the RN there, gave us a tour of the primitive facility with its iron beds and rough plank floors. In the maternity wing mothers in bed, with their newborns swaddled in muslin, held out their babies for us to hold. Mothers bring their youngest child with them when the time comes to deliver. Thus, the room was also full of toddlers being cared for by a young girl. If a mother brings a sick child to the hospital, she stays there with the child until it gets well.

Back on the vans, we headed for our mission post at Kima, to visit with the George Bucks and Edna Thimes. We didn't see all of the mission, however, because dusk was upon us and it started raining. Our bedroom at the Kisumu Hotel, with the mosquito net canopy over the bed, looked like something out of *The Arabian Nights*.

Next morning we headed for the Nairobi airport to catch our flight to Bombay.

Scenery was much the same until we approached a town named Nakuru. Suddenly in our view was a bountiful mass of incredible flowers. Gerry Allen, one of our most avid photographers, was riding the jump seat by the driver and snapped away at this Garden of Eden. In the background was a huge house, obviously a wealthy estate with gates and guards.

We stopped at a roadside place, had a cold drink, and resumed speed. But ahead was a road block. A policeman flagged us down. We weren't really speeding. Our dark-skinned drivers got out of the vans to speak with the police, and almost turned white. The problem?

"Lady in van take picture of summer home of the President just as he was coming out. No photos allowed."

With that, the police took Gerry's camera and insisted that we turn around and return to Nakuru to the police station.

Berk tried to explain that she was only aware of the beauty and had no knowledge of the house's ownership. We had to go back any way. Berk asked us to remain in the vans and pray. He and Gerry went in and asked them to take the film and forget it. The officials stalled. Berk feared we would miss our plane, but finally they relented and let us go.

Berk told us later that while he and Gerry were in the station, the police brought in two little boys about ten years old. The officers took two cane poles off the wall, had the boys drop their pants, and gave them a sound beating. This punishment was for pick-pocketing. Gerry and Berk thought they would be next.

We were supposed to be in Nairobi at 1:00 p.m. We arrived at 2:30 p.m., elbowed and pushed through customs, and barely made our 3:00 p.m. flight.

Had we known what lay ahead, we might have opted for jail in Nakuru. We arrived in Bombay at midnight. By this time the dampness of London had caught up with us, and several of our group were sick with sore throats and colds, including me. Berk was first in line with passport and health certificate. He failed yellow fever. We had been told in the U.S. that yellow fever vaccinations were no longer required. The folks at customs in India thought differently, particularly since we had been to Africa. India denied us passage. All arguments were in vain.

It was Sunday morning. We couldn't get out of the airport to get a room. Our travel agent couldn't help. Finally, Air India gave us free Cokes. Our people were tired, scared, and sickly. At 3:00 a.m., after trying several airlines, Berk negotiated with British Airways to fly us directly to Bangkok at 6:15 a.m.

Putting the unpleasantness of Bombay and the disappointment of missing the Taj Mahal behind us, everyone loved Bangkok. The gold-gilded palaces were awesome, and the sampling of Thai culture at the Rose Garden – everything from traditional folk dances and a Thai wedding to an elephant ride – was spectacular. Our group was ecstatic. Also in Bangkok, we visited missionaries Mac and Jean Johnson at our Mission complex there. We toured the church and school and ate a real "American" meal, with the first iced tea we had seen since leaving America.

On October 12, we arrived in Hong Kong. What a city! Noisy. Busy. Crowded. A mad house of wall-to-wall signs, shops, cars, and people – 4.4 million people! We enjoyed its panorama of mountains, sea, fishing boats, and, of course, shopping!

Our group fell in love with our missionaries there, Dr. and Mrs. Peter Jenkins. Dr. Jenkins looked like a British explorer with his white hair and beard, white shirt, shorts, and knee sox – and delightful British accent. He headed the Haven of Hope Sanatorium, a hospital built mainly for tuberculosis patients. At one time TB was the Number One killer in Hong Kong. Little wonder. Cigarette smoking is rampant.

The hospital also manages a home for retarded and handicapped children that started when impaired or disfigured children were left on the door step of the hospital, abandoned by their parents. Ten little ones were there at the time of our visit. Another wing of the hospital housed healthy children from three months to four years, highly unusual. They were there because their mothers were in the TB wing for treatment. The hospital cared for the children until their mothers were well.

Manila was our next stop. We toured the city and visited the American cemetery where 17,500 of our boys were buried during World War II. Our missionary there, Dr. Rolando Bacani, took us to their church Wednesday night and Berk preached.

Then it was on to Sidney, Australia, where we spent some time with missionaries Austin and Nancy Sowers. A wonderful tour of the city included the famous opera house and spectacular views of Sydney's beautiful harbor. On a ride into the country, we saw vast grazing lands and herds of sheep. Another delight was visiting the Koala Park to see koala bears and kangaroos.

We concluded our trip with the unique sights and sounds of New Zealand, visiting Auckland and Rotorua, where we saw the Argodome, hot mud pools and geysers at a thermal reserve, and enjoyed exhibits and entertainments featuring the village life, culture, and crafts of the native Maori people. Thanksgiving dinner at our hotel featured steak instead of turkey.

On November 30 we were home again in Daytona Beach, our minds and bodies reeling from all that we had seen and experienced, but enriched by the journey.

Oh, Jerusalem!

Six times I was privileged to travel with Berk to the Holy Land. And each trip was "made" by the people we traveled with. Incredibly special moments – memories and forever friends – are the rewards of these pilgrimages.

We toured the Coliseum and the Vatican in Rome, and the Catacombs. In Athens we saw the Parthenon on the Acropolis and heard Berk preach on Mars Hill. In Cairo we viewed museums, the pyramids, and learned to ride a camel. But everyone's favorite place on any of our journeys was always Jerusalem and all the Holy Sites in the surrounding areas.

To see the walls of Jerusalem for the first time – at night with torches burning in the niches – always brought tears to every eye. To walk the streets of Jerusalem, down the Via Dolorosa, retracing the steps of Jesus is awesome.

Ride a camel? Nothing to it.
Berk takes the lead with style!

There is just something about Jerusalem.

Israel is now a super modern country, built on the stones of Biblical times. It is a state bordered by four Arab nations, each taking turns at being hostile. Israel presents a contrast of cultures – old and new; rich and poor.

Relive with me a typical Holy Land journey:

Our Mercedes-Benz bus zooms us past old Arab villages, refugee camps, and defiant new Jewish settlements. We move from terraced rows of olive trees to the lush vegetation of leafy, fruited date palms. Fields of rocks. Cotton fields. Orchards of oranges and grapefruit. Factories, apartments, and recreation parks – all rising proudly from what was once a malarial waste land.

A sleek Cadillac speeds by a lone Bedouin and his camel. A huge truck marked "Coca-Cola" lumbers past a donkey laden with cement sacks.

We pause in our journey beside the quiet waters of the Jordan River, marveling that it is neither as deep nor as wide as we had imagined it would be. As we gaze upon the peaceful scene, one of our pilgrims asks to be baptized; then another and another. Berk is only too glad to wade into the chilly waters and re-enact the holy ordinance. We who watch imagine how it must have been the day Jesus waded into the gently flowing stream to be baptized by His cousin John.

Berk wades into the Jordan River
for a baptismal service.

After a lunch of Saint Peter's fish beside sparkling blue waters, we board a boat to skim over the Sea of Galilee to Capernaum. This same sea Jesus walked on now has boats passing us with water skiers in tow.

We swing toward the barren Golan Heights and stay at a thriving Kibbutz, to feast on fresh veggies, fruits, and turkey. We view their pet ducklings, rabbits, lambs, and deer – drinking in the peace and tranquility, yet, knowing that only a few steps away is a bomb shelter.

On another day, we drive into the desert on a winding road through the hills of Judea, down to the salt-rich sulphurous Dead Sea. The water is blue, but a finger dipped into it comes out with an oily feel. Some bathers sit upright in the water without sinking, a miraculous defiance of nature because of the incredible buoyancy of the dense salt water. As we wade and fill our souvenir bottles, we stand side by side with Yemenite women in full-length dresses and scantily clad young girls bathing and floating.

A cable car – not for the faint-hearted! – bears us aloft to the remains of Herod's palace fortress, Masada, where in AD 73 some 900 Jews chose suicide over surrender.

Berk at the Mount of Blessing
by the Sea of Galilee.

Back in Jerusalem at the Dome of the Rock, we watch barefoot Moslems kneel in the mosque; we stand by the wailing wall to see yarmulked Jews reciting their prayers; at the Church of the Holy Sepulchre we see Christians lighting candles.

We experience a heart-wrenching visit to the Yad Vashemn, the memorial museum chronicling the history of the Holocaust.

My personal favorite spot in Jerusalem? The narrow streets of the Old City, where one can buy anything from an Aladdin's lamp to a T-shirt, inscribed with "Coca-Cola" in Hebrew. Or, to capture the true irony of this city whose name means "peace," one can buy a shirt with "Shalom"(peace) written on it, in view of boy-like soldiers who patrol with guns. Souvenirs for Jerusalem pilgrims range from Mother-of-Pearl jewelry to embroidered Bedouin caftans, sheepskin coats, olive wood nativity sets, and even Welcome Signs that say: "Shalom, ya' all." All these items are offered for sale by Arab vendors who swear they wouldn't give a lower price to their mother!

Our guide tells us that Jerusalem's trash cans have all been removed to prevent the deposit therein of terrorist bombs. Yet, we feel a greater sense of safety when we walk its streets than we feel in our own home towns.

Jerusalem – indeed, all of the Holy Land – evokes deep-seated emotions from everyone who goes there, even as it did for Christ who wept as He looked upon the city from the Mount of Olives and said: *"O Jerusalem, Jerusalem, thou that killest the prophets, and stonest them which are sent unto thee, how often would I have gathered thy children together, even as a hen gathereth her chickens under her wings, and ye would not!" Mattew 23:37. (KJV)*

Another place evoking deep feelings is the Church of the Nativity in Bethlehem. One November as our group stood around the manger, holding hands, and singing "Oh, Little Town of Bethlehem," the birth of Christ, our precious Lord, seemed oh, so close . . . so real. Having experienced prior to visiting Bethlehem the full scope of His life and sacrifice for us magnified the moment, for in Jerusalem, we had worshiped in the Upper Room, prayed on the Mount of Olives, visited the courtyard and the dungeon of Caiaphas, the high priest; we had stood on the very pavement where Pilate had Jesus flogged and where He shouldered the cross; and we had traced His steps along the Via Dolorosa; we stared in horror at the skull-like visage of Golgotha; then we had seen with our own eyes the empty tomb!

Berk loved to travel in the Holy Land. He loved to study there. And he loved to share the experience with others. For no one can visit Jerusalem, and the land from Dan to Beersheba, and ever be the same again.

Lessons from "the Pit"

Pilgrims with Berk in the Holy Land always carried home unforgettable moments of insight and inspiration to be replayed each time a particular Bible story or passage of Scripture comes to mind. For one group such a moment occured at a site just outside the walls of Jerusalem, the house of Caiaphas the high priest. Everyone knows well the scene with Peter in the courtyard, where he denied the Lord three times, as Jesus foretold. But less known to most people is a place inside the house – the dungeon where prisoners were chained to the wall or were flogged with their arms stretched out and chained between two pillars or where they were cast down into a dark pit, to await their fate – alone in total darkness. In that place, after appearing before the chief priests and the Sanhedrin, Jesus was spat upon, beaten, and left for the night.

Today a rough-hewn stairway allows pilgrims to actually descend into the pit, and there Berk read Psalm 88 and spoke of the night when Jesus was imprisoned in this place and may well have uttered the words of this ancient Psalm as a prayer in His hour of extreme despair and darkness. The mood of the place made the words sink deep as Berk spoke of times in life when we find ourselves in the pit of despair . . . when we we are in the dark and feel totally alone . . . when times are bad and it seems that every friend we have has deserted us. As Berk spoke, himself overcome by emotion, tears flowed freely as every person standing in that place personally entered into the alone-ness of Jesus on that night of his arrest, when he was abused by his enemies and abandoned by all whom he had called "friend."

"Jesus knows," Berk said, "what it is like to be 'in the pit,' abandoned . . . alone. He was there. And because he walked that journey, none of us ever have to face 'the pit' in our life's journey alone. Jesus will be there. He will never forsake us. For after his resurrection He said, not only to his disciples, but also to us . . . *be sure of this – that I am with you always, even to the end of the world."* Matthew 28:20 LB

Frank Elgar's beautiful and moving prayer sealed the moment in our hearts, to be remembered and treasured to this day.

Lessons from Calvary

Berk's knowledge of the Bible and his fertile imagination gave all who traveled with him eyes to see beyond the obvious things the average tourist might see – to touch the past in a way that made it come alive again, even amidst the ruins and the clamor of present-day life.

Berk is speaking:

Have you known what it is to have a broken heart? Have you known what it is to see all the dreams of your life shattered by a sudden tragedy? Have you heard the voice of Jesus saying to you as He said to Mary, "Why weepest thou?"

God is near to us in our sorrow. Perhaps more than at any other time.

Christianity was not born in an ivy covered seminary. It was born in a world filled with the clanging armor of occupying armies, squeezed to despair by oppressive taxes, and frightened by rulers who were madmen. The cross on which Jesus died was not a polished oak cross located between the piano and the organ in a sunlit cathedral. Jesus was crucified between two thieves just outside the garbage dump.

This fantastic truth leaped into my mind one night in Jerusalem. After a day of touring with members of my congregation, we returned to our hotel for the evening meal. Most of the people were so weary that they went to bed, but I decided to take a little walk down the street toward the Damascus gate. As I was leaving the hotel several persons asked if they could go with me. The group grew to include a dozen or more.

A Holy Land Sampler

Clockwise from Top Right:

(1) NC tour group hosted by the McCalls with Berk as resource leader; January 1986.
(2) In the garden near the empty tomb, Berk leads Communion for the 1979 group.
(3) Berk and Berny at the Great Pyramid in Egypt; January 1981.
(4) Daytona Tour Group; October 1972.
(5) Berk baptizes daughter Lori in the Jordan River; October 1972.
(6) Berk and Berny at the Dome of the Rock in Jerusalem; December 1979.

As we walked down the street we came to the bus station which is on the back side of Gordon's Calvary, the spot believed by most evangelical Christians to be the place where Christ was crucified. We had visited the Garden Tomb and the skull shaped hill called Calvary earlier in the day. Now we found ourselves standing in the parking lot of the Israeli bus company. The air was heavy with deisel fumes. Blaring horns echoed against the sandstone cliff. Roaring motors and screeching brakes added to the din. I gathered my little group close to me and spoke to them of the things that were passing through my mind:

"This is a view of Calvary that most people never see. There are no reverent pilgrims taking pictures. There is no air of holiness or sanctity. No hymns are being sung. But this is probably what it was like when Jesus was crucified. Donkeys stumbled by, loaded with merchandise. Merchants shouted and slaves swore. In those days people thought no more of seeing a body on a cross than a fisherman thinks of seeing a worm squirming on a hook. Even thieves were put to death for their crime, small as it was. It was at a place like this that Jesus died."

I started singing: "On a hill far away / Stood an old rugged cross, / The emblem of suffering and shame; / And I love that old cross / Where the dearest and best / For a world of lost sinners was slain. / So I'll cherish the old rugged cross . . ."

Our voices rose in the night air, drowning out the clamor of the bus station. That was a moment I shall never forget. I do not want to forget it because it reminds me that God is present when He seems most out of place. True, He may be found in the muted music of the cathedral and found in the quietly flowing stream, but in such a place even a pagan feels a sense of calmness. It is in the storm of life that I need to hear His voice. And it is there that I do.

Lessons from the Empty Tomb

A highlight of all our trips to the Holy Land was visiting a hillside believed by many to be the skull-shaped hill where Jesus was crucified and, adjacent to it, a garden containing an empty tomb that many believe is the actual tomb that for three days held the body of Christ.

In this special place, whenever possible, Berk liked to hold Communion for our tour groups. He sometimes shared about previous visits to this place. In 1952, he wrote about two of them in a letter to Kenneth Hall for publication in *Youth* magazine:

Located outside the wall of [Jerusalem] is a simple little garden. . . . Inside the garden . . . is a cave – in its day it was a tomb. Scholars know this was the tomb belonging to a noble family. Many scholars believe it was the tomb of Joseph of Arimathea – the tomb from which Christ was resurrected. There is a great deal to support that belief. A door opens into a little ante-room. In front of the door is a large groove in the rock in which the door-stone was rolled. Inside, along the side of the tomb, there is a shelf where the body was laid. Whether or not we could confirm our views . . . all of us felt that this is . . . the kind of place where Christ was buried. We prayed together within that empty tomb. And somehow, it seems to add something to prayer to be praying in Christ's empty tomb.

Paul told us that if Christ is not risen, then our faith is vain and our preaching is vain. And we are still in our sins. But if the tomb is empty, then our faith is real and our hope is genuine. It is the sort of thing you think about when you stand praying in Christ's empty tomb. . . .

The first time I visited this place several years ago I, like all tourists, wanted to take a picture of the empty tomb. . . . I wanted a picture just to remind me of what I had seen. So I snapped the shutter of my camera.

When I returned to the States, I was showing my pictures of the Holy Land to some friends . . . the Mount of Olives, the hills of Judea, and other things tourists usually take pictures of. Then came the picture of the empty tomb. It was almost too dark to make any showing at all. The brown walls of

138

the tomb were almost lost in the shadows. The only thing that was distinct was a bright patch of sunlight on the floor. The sun was streaming through the open door. As photographs go, it wasn't much.

"What is this?" my friends asked.

"This is the tomb of Christ."

"I can't see anything but the bright spot," someone said.

Just as I started to explain where the walls of the grave were and how sunlight had streamed through the open door to ruin the picture, I thought better of it.

"As a matter of fact, that is all I can see, too – nothing but the bright spot."

As I meditate on it now, that conversation may have been a similar to the one Peter and John had on Easter Sunday morning so many years ago. Their hearts were heavy with sorrow as they approached the tomb of Christ. Their dreams were buried in the tomb with their Savior. This was the darkest day of history for them.

Peter, being the bolder of the two, ventured in. He saw the empty tomb, the grave clothes lying on the shelf where Christ's body had lain. Then, perhaps, he saw the same patch of light on the floor that I witnessed. When he came out, to John he said, "All I can see is the bright spot."

Indeed, it was the brightest spot of all history. This, the light of an empty tomb.

The Traditional Site of Warner's Baptism

Daniel Sidney Warner

In 1979 we saw a site no other group has ever seen, before or since!

There's nothing like travel on a bus to bring a group of folks together. And after a week or two of close fellowship and shared experiences, bus trips over the hills and valleys of Israel were delightful times filled with singing, light banter, and laughter. Sometimes, to my chagrin, Berk played his harmonica. There were also times of quiet, when folks were immersed in their own thoughts or lightly dozing, as the case may be.

On this particular trip we had a guide who referred to himself as "Tony Baloney." He was full of stories, some of them "tall tales." But on the first day of our tour he went to great lengths to explain that on a few occasions he would be able to point to a place and say with certainty, "This is the spot where this or that event took place." However, more often than not, we would hear phrases like "Tradition says this is the place," when no proven evidence exists to verify a location beyond all doubt. And Tony was true to his word as we visited Biblical sites all over Israel.

Late one afternoon, after a full day of touring, the bus was approaching the Sea of Galilee. We would have one more stop before arriving at our hotel in Tiberias for the night. As the bus lumbered along, a hush had fallen over the group. Some were quietly talking, some dozing, some just watching the beautiful green hills of Galilee roll by. Suddenly, as the bus rolled to a stop, Tony stood up and said, "We are here at a place few travelers get to see – the traditional baptismal site of Daniel Sidney Warner!"

The group sat in stunned silence at the unexpected announcement. Daniel Sidney Warner, "founder" of the Church of God movement, baptized **here**. WOW! You could have heard a pin drop. Then, after several moments, Berk exploded with laughter, and the rest soon followed suit, realizing that Tony Baloney had "pulled one over on us!"

Truth is, Daniel Sidney Warner was never in the Holy Land. Though he had always wanted to go, he never made the trip. But therein lay the greater mystery: How did Tony

Berk and Berny on bus with 1979 tour group.

139

Baloney know about Daniel Sidney Warner in the first place? Clearly this was an "inside job." Someone in the group obviously "clued Tony in." But who? We spent the next three days trying to guess which one among us was the perpetrator. Turned out to be the one we least suspected: Don McCall.

And being the gentleman that he is, he never once said, "Gotcha!"

Berk – the Haggler

I loved shopping in the Old City of Jerusalem. But I always took Berk along. I simply did not have the expertise, or the gall to bargain. And that's the only way shopping can be done in the Middle East. No one – but no one – is expected to pay the asking price for an item. You are supposed to haggle, or "Christian them down," as the case may be.

My Berk was a haggling pro.

"You're kidding," he'd say. "That price is for five, right? Not one."

Then he would counter with an offer so small that I would shudder with shock and shame and slink back to the hotel. I knew full well that Berk would have a ball, gesturing, practicing his "Arabic indignation," and that he would eventually agree on a price and return triumphantly to our room, armed with his treasures.

On one of our journeys leading a tour group, Berk was doing a seminar for Egyptian ministers at the mission headquarters in Cairo, leaving me to herd our people through the bazaar. I spied a beautiful alabaster vase and a bust of Nefertiti. I asked the price.

"For the vase, $20, and $20 for the Queen," the shopkeeper replied.

With Jordan and Jerusalem still ahead, I didn't want to drop $40 in Cairo, so I simply started to walk away.

Then the Arab called out, "$35."

I hesitated.

Marian Cherney and Betty Simmons called to me that the bus was loading to take us back to the hotel. So I hurried on.

"$30.00," calls Abdul.

I'm sorry. I must go," I replied. "My bus is leaving and I can't tarry."

He followed me, clutching the objects d'art.

"No place in Cairo can you buy such quality, lady."

"Sorry," I countered. "I only have $20" (to put into the Egyptian treasury, that is).

Preaching in Cairo

Berk often took groups to visit the Shoubra church in Cairo or invited missionaries Jim and Betty Albrecht or Russell and Sharon Scaggs to come speak to the groups.

BELOW: Berk preaches at the Shoubra church (1986), with Pastor Mounir Riskalla translating.

ABOVE: In 1979 Berk led a conference for Egyptian pastors. At Berk's right is Jim Albrecht, then missionary to Egypt. At Berk's left is Mounir Riskalla, pastor of the Shoubra congregation in Cairo. Far left, front row: Pastor Daoud Yousef, who translated for Berk. Sixth from left, front row: another translator, Pastor Morgan Ibrahim and his wife Enaam (Grace) of Alexandria. Not pictured: Collie Shirrell and Don and Maxine McCall, tour members who accompanied Berk to the meeting.

How Berk Learned to Haggle

Berk could haggle with the best in the shops and bazaars and in the streets of foreign cities. But he learned the hard way. On his first trip to Europe, though forewarned, he was not prepared for his encounter with those smooth-talking, Academy Award-winning street hawkers who besiege tourists. His initiation took place in Italy in 1947. He often shared the story:

The Piazza surrounding the Cathedral [in Milan] is patrolled by venders who flock down upon each unsuspecting tourist like chickens descending from the roost at feeding time. While I am conscientiously opposed to squandering money on useless souvenirs, I decided to blow in the price of a little blue picture book. Primarily I wanted to see if I could wheedle the book for less than the price at which it was ordinarily offered. So . . . I now give you Lesson One in the gentle art of wheedling:

A vender has just sidled up to you and offered you a little cheaply bound blue book.

"It is only three hundred lira."
Shrug shoulders. Keep walking.
"For you, I make it, say, two hundred and fifty."
Arch the eyebrows in a superior way.
"I give it to you for what it cost me, two hundred lira."
At this point you stop and show the faintest sign of interest. Then you say gravely, "One hundred lira."

"Oh, senor, you joke, of course. I give it to you for what it cost, two hundred lira."

At this point you walk away and forget the whole deal. But not for long. In an instant your vendor friend has caught up with you. His face is sad as though he had contracted laryngitis on the day he was to sing the part of "Figaro."

"Senor, I lose money, but I give it to you for one hundred and fifty."

You feel as if you are pouring salt into his lacerated heart, but you reach into your front trouser pocket and come out with the fabulous amount. You are a little remorseful that you have been so mercenary. Almost apologetically you take the little blue book. Before giving it to you, however, the vender has fondled it lovingly as though it were the last photograph of his deceased mother. But he takes the money and surrenders the book. Sad eyed he departs.

When he is about five paces away, your conscience jabs you a little and you decide to run and give him an extra fifty lira. But as you turn, you see him rub his hands together gleefully just before pouncing on another tourist.

You have gone not more than ten paces when another fawning peddler comes up to you offering the same little blue book for **one hundred lira**. *At this point you mutter something or other into your stubble about the deceitfulness of human nature and stride on.*

He startled me by saying, "I'll take it, but you starve my children."

I rushed back and signed a travelers check, while he hurriedly wrapped my bargains in newspapers. Then I ran for the bus. A feeling of elation heightened my color. I had learned to haggle. By myself. And I was righteous in my joy!

A week later we were back in New York City for a few days of R & R. Our group had dispersed, headed out to their homes in various parts of the country. Berk and I decided to take a few days in New York City, do some "touristy" things and perhaps catch the post-Christmas performance at Radio City Music Hall.

At the airport we went through a cafeteria line to get breakfast. When we got to the cashier, she looked at my food, tallied it up and said, "That will be $5.28, please."

Slyly, I looked up at Berk and said, "Do you reckon she'd take $4?"

* * *

Berk and I have treasured warm memories of all these trips and the wonderful friends from all over the country who shared them with us.

Our last tour was in the spring of 1992, with pilgrims from Wichita, KS; Lake Charles, LA; and Vero Beach, FL. That trip was all the more special because, on June 13, Berk and I celebrated our Thirty-Ninth Wedding Anniversary (our last together) cruising the Nile.

Berk and Berny cruising on the Nile River in Egypt and celebrating 39 years of marriage.

Executive Secretary-Treasurer
Mass Communications Board
1977 - 1984

8
CBH

Taking only our summer clothing, we moved to Anderson in July of 1977. Our other possessions remained temporarily in Daytona, because our house in Anderson would not be vacant until October. At first we "set up camp" at a small motel down town. Later we accepted Greg Hammel's offer to move in with him until our house was ready for occupancy. Greg, being single, had rooms to spare in the house he bought while attending seminary in Anderson.

These were exciting days for us. *Christian Brotherhood Hour*, the international radio ministry of the Church of God, was entering a new phase of activity and growth. The work begun in 1947 as the brain child of Dale Oldham and Richard Lee Meischke had flourished in the thirty years of its existence, twenty-two of those years as a ministry of the Radio and Television Commission (established under the Executive Council in 1955). In 1976 the General Assembly had awarded agency status to the commission and ratified James Earl Massey as the new radio voice of CBH, upon the retirement of Dr. R. Eugene Sterner from that post.

Dr. Dale Oldham

As the first Executive-Secretary of the newly formed Mass Communications Board, Berk did a good bit of traveling at the outset to orient himself more fully to the work and to get some projects moving. I traveled with him on weekends, glad for a respite from nursing.

Since 1965 CBH-Spanish, with Fidel Zamorano as speaker, had been reaching out to Hispanics in the United States and in Central and South America. One of Berk's early assignments involved traveling to Mexico City to confer with pastors translating CBH into Spanish. At the school in Saltillo, he was invited to do his Blessing lectures from Psalm 103 for Bible students and ministers. Thrilled with the opportunity to practice his Spanish, he did a bang-up job, sometimes "overtaking" the interpreter and spieling right along with his extraordinary linguistic ability. His stint as the self-taught Spanish teacher for Warner Christian Academy paid off!

Dr. R. Eugene Sterner

In Anderson we chose to worship at Park Place Church, the fellowship Berk had known during his college years and afterward when he became an "adopted son" of Dale and Polly Oldham, who pastored the church in those days. Many of our friends from former years were still a part of this congregation, as well as many of Berk's peers in the Executive Offices. For me, it was a welcome change to be just a preacher's wife – not the pastor's wife. The big reward was getting to sit with Berk in church again, just as in our courting days.

Dr. James Earl Massey

Keith Huttenlocker, our pastor, was a gifted pulpiteer, and sweet-spirited. We were so blessed by his sermons. Associate pastor Ron Duncan, his wife, Martha, and their children, Becky and Andrew, were like our own kids. Another joy was being a part of the Pathways Sunday School Class, taught by Dr. Gene Newberry. Pathways was a big family of the most gifted people imaginable. Each class session was a rich time of warm fellowship and rewarding Bible study. Truly, a little congregation within itself, the members saw to one another's special needs, whatever they might be. Though we were often on the road, Berk and I were fully adopted into the circle, as if we were always there.

On October 1, we moved to our home on Winding Way. Marty had enrolled for his senior year at Anderson College and was living with us. Lori lived in nearby Alexandria, working as a receptionist for the Gaithers. While I was immersed in unpacking and setting the house in order, Berk was totally absorbed in his new venture into the world of broadcasting. Having worked with radio programs of his own in California and in Daytona and having served on the Radio and Television Commission since 1971, Berk knew a good bit about radio ministry going in. He enjoyed thoroughly learning the day-to-day operations of CBH and meeting the creative challenge of exploring ways to expand Church of God ministries in mass communications at home and abroad.

By Thanksgiving we had our first snow. What a change from the sands of Florida! We frantically sought long undies to underlay the polyesters.

In February 1978, we attended the National Religious Broadcasters Convention

The Lost Wedding Album
By Berny Berquist

Berk and I had a favorite quotation: *"A coincidence is a small miracle in which God chooses to remain anonymous."* Time and again, circumstances in our lives proved that quote true. This story is my favorite.

While we were in Daytona, as we were moving from one house to another, our wedding album was lost. All of our wedding pictures were wrapped up in that little blue album of 5 x 7 black and white photos.

Lewellyn Studio in Anderson had done the album.

While I was enrolled at Anderson College in 1951-52, I had worked as receptionist in the studio each afternoon after classes. When I came back to Anderson to be married in June of 1953, Lewellyn Studio did the photos for us. They also gave us a sizeable discount on the album as a wedding gift.

Because of our tight budget for the wedding, Berk and I were not able to give pictures to the wedding party or family members. Consequently, we were the sole possessors of any of the photographs. We carried the album everywhere – in the car and later in the trailer – as we traveled around the country. We also had them with us in Daytona.

But in November of 1967, when we moved from the house on Lexington Drive to the larger house on Ridgewood Avenue, in the transfer of books and personal belongings, somehow our treasured album was lost in the packing boxes.

We didn't actually discover the loss until the spring of 1968, amidst preparations to celebrate our fifteenth wedding anniversary. We were going through boxes looking for pictures, but the wedding album was not to be found.

"Where did we put that wedding album?" I asked Berk.

We scoured the house searching for the little 5 x 7 blue leather album, but it had vanished.

The next day, realizing that further searching was futile, I called Tony Leweyllen, who was still in business, and shared my predicament.

"Sweetheart," he said, "I wish I could help you; but we never keep negatives after ten years. You've been married fifteen.

Those negatives were destroyed five years ago."

I was sick. But that was that.

When Berk came home that day, he pulled from his billfold a wallet-sized picture of me in my wedding dress. Sensing my pain he said, "Here, honey, you can have this enlarged to an 8 x 10, so we will at least have that."

We mourned the loss. But, we knew that others had lost photos in fires or other tragic circumstances. So we took it in stride.

Later I found another wallet-sized photo, this one of Berk and me together; and that helped ease the pain somewhat.

When we moved to Anderson in the summer of 1977, I naturally looked up our old friends, Tony and Sammy Lewellyn. Though now in their 80's, they were still in business part-time. Because of poor cirulcation in his legs, Tony could work only a few days a week.

Soon it became apparent that Tony would have to have surgery on one of his legs, for he had no feeling from the knee down. Sammy

Berk's wallet photo (actual size).

called me to come talk with them about the surgery since I knew a surgeon who attended Park Place Church. She wanted my opinion of the surgeon and the surgery.

in Washington, DC, with CBH board members, their spouses, and CBH speaker, James Earl Massey, and his wife, Gwen. How thrilling it was to be part of that assembly of broadcasters, senators, entertainers, and Christian leaders. Days and nights were jam-packed with spiritual inspiration, practical seminars, and things to see and do in Washington.

Then a major snow crippled the Midwest, closing airports in many states, including Indianapolis. None of us could get home. As convention rates did not accommodate past our allotted time, we were all scrambling to make other arrangements. Berk and I took the train from Washington to Philadelphia, where we enjoyed a visit with my brother John until we could get into Indianapolis.

Headlines in the Anderson *Herald* read: "Anderson is closed."

By the time we got home we were utterly astounded at the banks of snow. The sands of Daytona had shifted, indeed. By May we had had twenty-two snows!

But spring did come, and we loved the seasonal changes. In March I took a nursing position, caring for a paraplegic man near our house on the night shift four days a week, remaining free to travel with Berk on weekend assignments. Berk was elated to have popular newscaster Mort Crim join the production team as announcer for CBH-English and to have Paul Yerden, long-associated with CBH in various roles, come on board to handle details of program production.

I told her that the surgeon, Dr. Ken Schemmer, was well-qualfied; and if he said surgery was needed, they should follow his advice.

Then I called Dr. Ken personally to ask about the procedure and make an unusual request.

"I wonder," I asked him, "that since I am a surgical technician and also an RN, would it be possible for me to scrub in with you for Tony's surgery. I'd like very much to be with him for the procedure."

"I'd be more than happy to have you come in," he replied," and will make arrangements for you to do that."

So I was there when the amputation took place, holding Tony's hand. And I accompanied him to the recovery room, so that he would see a famliar face when he awakened. He was scheduled for intensive care, but there were no beds. The staff nurse asked Sammy if there was a possibility of having a private duty nurse to sit with Tony.

"Oh, yes," I said, before Sammy could speak. "I'm it."

So I changed from green scrubs to basic white and sat the night vigil with him.

Tony did not mend well from the surgery. A few days later, on a Sunday morning, he sucummed to a pulmonary embolism.

As I was getting ready for church, Dr. Ken called to advise me of Tony's death. He asked if I would meet Sammy's minister at her house to relay the sad news.

Immediately, I changed my plans. After joining the minister at Sammy's home, I then took her to the hospital. After that I helped her make the necessary calls to relatives and the funeral home. She was distraught – in no state emotionally to make those calls for herself.

Going home just long enough to confer with Berk and pick up some clothes, I stayed with Sammy a couple of nights until her stepson, Stephen – like his dad, a photographer – and his wife, Lois, could come down from Chicago. I did the usual things friends do in times of need – answering the phone, preparing meals, running errands.

Naturally I went to the funeral.

As the days passed, I took Sammy out to dinner. And I stayed with her on some of her lonely nights until she worked through the worst part of her grief.

Then I moved on to other private duty assignments.

A couple of weeks after Tony's death, Sammy called to ask me to go with her to the studio, to sort through some of the files and records to decide what needed to be saved or discarded. She didn't want to go alone.

Hundreds of envelopes of negatives were filed in rows on metal shelves, like books in a bookcase. While going through the files, checking dates to see who should be called and which files should be discarded, I noticed that one envelope had fallen down on the floor behind the case.

Reaching down to retrieve it, I was absolutely shocked to read these words at the top of the envelope: Berquist / McIntyre wedding, June 13, 1953.

Chills ran over me.

"Sammy," I yelled, "you're not going to believe this! Our wedding negatives . . . they're here!"

"Oh, my goodness," she exclaimed, as she ran into the room. "It's a miracle! Tony never kept anything over ten years! Now you will have your wedding album again. I will send these negatives to Stephen to have them reprinted. Yes, you will have your album. That will be my way of paying you back for all you have done for me since Tony's death."

Steve not only duplicated the album, but embellished the gift by selecting for me a top-of-the line white one embossed in gold, with 8 x10 photos – and not just a select few, but all of them. That was his way of saying "thank you" for the care I had shown his father and mother.

Miracle or coincidence?

The parable of the lost coin (Luke 15:8-9) recounts the story of the woman who lost a coin and swept her entire house until it was found, then called all her friends in to share her joy.

"Rejoice with me," she said, "for I have found that which was lost."

In that spirit of joy, we celebrated the return of our long-lost wedding album – all the more precious to me now.

We both looked forward to the International Convention, our first "Camp Meeting" since moving back to Anderson. So many friends came from all over! We had a house full of guests and loved it. I cooked for days in advance. We even bought an extra fridge for the basement to store all the goodies. It was the first of many annual reunions with treasured friends from all across the United States. Two special visitors every year were Joe and Mary Minkler from California. We also regularly entertained an entourage of Daytonians.

At right: Berk and Berny celebrate their Twenty-fifth Wedding Anniversary with Dale and Polly Oldham (1978).

Traveling Can Be Hazardous to Your Wealth

CBH had come a long way since Richard Lee Meischke and Dr. Dale Oldham launched the radio ministry in 1947. When Berk took the helm, *Christian Brotherhood Hour* was heard in two languages (English and Spanish.) Much of Berk's attention would be given to expanding the radio ministry in other countries. In February of 1980, Berk and I traveled to Germany and Italy in response to two such broadcasting opportunities.

Richard Lee Meischke (known in business as J. Richard Lee) was co-founder with Dr. Dale Oldham of the CBH radio broadcast.

We would stop first in Ostia, Italy, to deliver a check to Pastor Franco Santonocito, to help him purchase a radio station. In January of 1980, Franco had notified his friend Tony Romano in Decatur, Illinois, that he could buy a radio station in Ostia for a down payment of $3,000. Tony called Berk and the two of them were able to raise that amount with several phone calls to interested angels. With this station, Franco would set up 24-hour Christian programming and broadcast the CBH message weekly in both Italian and English. What a ministry opportunity!

Walentin Schule CBH-Russian Speaker

Our second stop would be Pforsheim, Germany, to deliver equipment that would enable Pastor Walentin Schule to beam the first CBH message in Russian behind the Iron Curtain into the Soviet Union. In 1975 in Germany, a chance meeting with Peter Tjart, professor of German and Russian at Anderson University, was the first indication to anyone in America that more than 60 secret Church of God congregations, with over 3000 believers, existed behind the Iron Curtain! These churches were begun after World War I by five converts of missionary William Ebel. Walentin and some of his relatives were allowed to cross the Russian border into Germany in 1974. At Pforsheim, they and several other Russian immigrant families established a Church of God. Walentin, with his father and his brother, started sending tracts and pages from the Bible to friends and relatives behind the Iron Curtain, in churches that had no access to religious literature. Then he sent tapes of sermons, messages of hope. Response was so tremendous that he thought of having a regular radio broadcast. He obtained access to broadcast over the powerful Transworld radio station in Monte Carlo that covers eleven time zones of the Soviet Union; but he had no money to buy the equipment needed to record and transmit programs. Enter CBH. Berk made several phone calls to individuals and churches to secure funding for the necessary equipment, which Mass Communications then purchased.

Thus, with great excitement and anticipation, we began our journey.

After flying to Frankfort, Germany, we boarded a train for the trip across Switzerland into Italy and to Rome. We had a compartment to ourselves. In the dining car, we feasted on a delicious dinner. And, since we had flown all night the night before, we converted our seats into beds and turned in by 8:00 p.m. Around midnight we were awakened by the conductor, to see our Eur-rail tickets and passports. Berk handed him the tickets; I reached under the seat, retrieved my purse, and handed him the passports. The train stopped at the border of Italy to change crews.

We resumed our sleep. My eyes were so heavy. Around 4:00 a.m. I awakened with a dry throat and a bitter taste. Thinking I'd go to the bathroom to get water and re-brush my teeth, I reached under the seat to get my purse (wherein lay my toiletries and cosmetics) – it was gone!

I stood up, shook the blanket and my coat, then dropped to my knees, doing a thorough under-the-seat check, to no avail. The purse had vanished! I woke Berk to tell him. He helped look. Nothing.

Then we realized the horrible truth: we had been robbed in our sleep! I had been carrying only $50.00 in ones, but our passports and the "rest of my life" were in that purse: credit cards, nursing license, social security card, and all the other essentials that only women carry.

Immediately, Berk went to inform the conductor. They stopped the train. That woke the other passengers. And when 'roused, all who had been sleeping found that they, too, had been robbed. I then didn't feel quite so stupid. Cameras, purses, and small travel bags were reported missing. The theft occurred after we had changed crews and entered Italy. We surmised that it had to be an inside job. Only the conductor had seen where I kept my purse. Furthermore, everyone who was robbed had eaten in the dining car. Later we learned that quite possibly a sedative of some kind had been slipped into our beverage or food to promote drowziness. That kind of thing, we were told, does happen in Italy. Why else would that many people sleep through the robbery? Luckily Berk had our tickets, traveler's checks, and Franco's check in his inside coat pocket.

Needless to say, when we pulled into Rome, we were sad sacks. Franco met us, and we joined the line at the police station to file a report. Then we trudged over to the embassy to have pictures made and get new passports. Franco canceled my credit cards, and we shopped for toilet articles. I nearly fainted when I saw my passport picture. My hair looked like it had been done by Stevie Wonder!

We stayed with the Santonocitos for a couple of days before traveling on to Pforsheim. Such considerate hosts they were, so sympathetic to our misfortune. Berk bounced back fast, but I mourned my loss the entire Roman stay.

By the time we got to Germany, I had recovered enough to enjoy once again our reasons for the journey. We enjoyed the gracious hospitality of the Schule family. It was an incredible thrill to deliver the transmitter and be a part of an outreach that would penetrate the Iron Curtain.

When we arrived back home in Indiana, we discovered that whoever stole my purse had started to work immediately. "He" or "they" had charged $7,000 on the two credit cards. Since we had canceled them in Rome, I only had to pay a $50 deductible to Visa; nothing to American Express. It took until May, however, to finish with all the paper work relating to the robbery.

In June reports came from both the Schules and the Santonocitos that the broadcasts were flourishing. Our arduous journey was well worth the end result. Untold listeners were now being told. And we'd like to think that, in some small way, those broadcasts helped bring down the Iron Curtain not too many years later.

New Challenges and Innovations

Berk's responsibilities for Mass Communications – launching new stations, travel, fund raising, public relations, planning innovations, and office work– proved more demanding than he could manage alone. Thus, the Board brought on an administrative assistant to free Berk for more field work. Working first as Director of Operations and Long-range Planning, later as Associate Executive Secretary, Gary Moore was for Berk a true godsend, an invaluable partner and friend.

Gary came on board in the summer of 1980. His administrative and creative gifts were put to immediate use, helping Berk with new ministries such as publication of *People to People* (the CBH newsletter); weekend workshops on communication; distribution of the *CBH Study Bible*, with study notes edited by James Earl Massey; the Bible Study Conference at Montreat; fundraising, production, promotion, and follow-up for a television special, *The Doctor Is In*; and production of an audio cassette study series featuring James Earl Massey on the topics of prayer and Bible study and Berk doing *The Secret of Communicating* and *The Power and Magic of Blessing*.

Gary Moore

Credit is also due the excellent office staff, who kept day-to-day CBH operations running smoothly while tackling an array of new projects. When Berk arrived in 1977, Gail Smith was the administrative assistant and Margo Royer was in charge of station relations. Neal Moore was producing *Directions*, a fifteen-minute youth broadcast. Later, Margo Royer served as office manager (1978-80), followed by DonDeena Johnson (1980-82) and Dana Yerden Stuart (1983) in that role. Jerry Kolb (1979) and Ken Neiman (1980) were part-time accountants. Other staff during Berk's tenure were secretaries Chris Smith (1980), Donna Alfieri (1981), Diane Koeth (1981-82), and Christy Overby (1983). Secretaries for CBH Spanish were Doris Doty(1980-81) and Debbie Yerden (1981-83). Shirley Wright did mailings (and has continued to do so: 1976-99, 23 years).

Also significant was the eleven-member Mass Communications Board, who served with Berk and Gary during this time of change and innovation. On the Board when Berk took office in 1977 were Gordon Powell, Jim Edwards, Bill Ellis, Ken Schemmer, Leonard Freeman, Mary Bowman, Robert Culp, Gary Ausbun, and Edna Edwards. Others who came on the Board as original members rotated off were Paul Kendall, Courtney Duff, Bernard G. Mendenhall, Jim Sanders, Laura Withrow, Paul Yerden, Tom Malbone, Dean Schield, Betty Thompson, and Les Decker.

Don and Maxine McCall at Montreat in 1981; they proposed the idea of a CBH conference.
Below: *Berk, on harmonica, leads the troops in a rousing Friday night "Jamboree."*

Above: *Evening session of worship and Bible study in Anderson Auditorium.*

Below: *Former CBH speaker, R. Eugene Sterner and his wife, Millie, in Anderson Auditorium.*

Dr. Sterner helped refine the concept of putting CBH in touch with the grassroots through a retreat based on a long-standing CBH slogan: "The Word of God Unites."

148

CBH at Montreat – Making the Grassroots Connection

One of Berk's concerns at CBH was developing a close partnership with people at the grassroots level who were both audience and supporters for radio and other minstries. In 1979 he asked two of our most creative friends, Don and Maxine McCall, to be field representatives for CBH. In that role the McCalls took the CBH story into churches and gathered ideas for other mass communications ministries needed in the field.

Bainstorming sessions with the McCalls always energized Berk. For example, Maxine was the first to prod Berk to start writing books to reach more people with his empowering ideas on "The Power of Blessing" from Psalm 103 (later published as *The Miracle and Power of Blessing*), "How to Understand the Whole Bible" (published as *When the Bible Seems Confusing*), and a study on dreams he called "Nite Life" (the nucleus of Berk's last book, *The Secret of Immunity*).

From the McCalls came an idea that has blossomed into an enduring partnership between CBH and people in the field. Picking up on the CBH slogan, "The Word of God Unites," the McCalls suggested a four-day ecumenical retreat offering in-depth Bible classes taught by outstanding communicators of the Word. In return, CBH would have opportunity to share "up close and personal" the story of CBH and other ministries of the Mass Communications Board.

*Above: The Christian Brothers and Carolyn. Together and separately they came to lead worship and conferences at Montreat. (**L to R**) Doug Oldham, Dean Schield, Carolyn Patty, Ron Patty, Ernie Gross. Conferees never let Ernie get away without singing "This Old House."*

CBH BIBLE STUDY CONFERENCE
Montreat, North Carolina
September 16-19, 1981– Present

Above: Assembly Inn and Lake Susan at Montreat.

Below: CBH Conference Pioneers celebrate 10 years of perfect attendance in 1990.

(From left) Dr. Dale Oldham, Dr. R. Eugene Sterner, and Dr. James Earl Massey

Speakers for CBH English

CBH Ministry Team

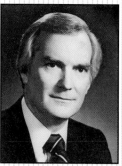
David Grubbs followed Dr. Massey as Speaker.

Mort Crim, noted reporter and news commentator, joined the team in 1978 as announcer for CBH.

Fidel Zamorano Speaker, CBH Spanish

Vocalist Doug Oldham, with the program from its beginning in 1947.

Bill Gaither Trio: (L to R) Bill and Gloria Gaither with Gary McSpadden)

Inspiration for the idea came from two sources: the Praise Gathering (hosted by Bill and Gloria Gaither, Bob Benson, Ron Huff, and others) and Dr. R. Eugene Sterner. While Gene and Millie Sterner were interim pastors at the McCall's home church in Drexel, North Carolina, Dr. Sterner shared with them one evening his regret of not having the opportunity during his tenure as radio speaker for CBH to minister to people in his radio congregation in a retreat setting.

"You can touch hearts in a retreat setting in a way not possible from the pulpit on Sunday morning," he said. "The real key is in-depth study of the Scriptures."

With Berk's approval, the McCalls garnered support for the conference from North Carolina and neighboring states, presenting a proposal that ultimately was approved by the Mass Communications Board. Thus, in 1981, quality Bible teaching in a retreat setting became the grassroots connection to bring CBH and people together in partnership for ministry – a partnership that today draws participation from coast to coast and Canada and undergirds approximately one-fourth of the CBH budget.

A unique national television special

THE DOCTOR IS IN

FEATURING
CHARLES SCHULZ
and the "Peanuts" Characters

THE BILL GAITHER TRIO
DOUG OLDHAM
SANDI PATTI
DR. JAMES MASSEY
DR. DAVID GRUBBS

Based on a new book by
DR. MAURICE BERQUIST

Television – *The Doctor Is In*

Exploring possibilities in television for CBH was a major goal of the Mass Communications Board during Berk's tenure. Two television spots were filmed and made available for churches to place on local television stations with "trailers" tailored to feature the local congregation.

But the major thrust into television the Board aspired to was the production of a one-hour

The Doctor is In
by Maurice Berquist

WITH ILLUSTRATIONS FROM THE "PEANUTS" COMIC STRIP BY CHARLES M. SCHULZ

prime-time TV special. It was uncharted territory for the Church of God, just the kind of project that sparked Berk's creativity. In 1979, after much thought and prayer, he seized upon a concept for both a television special and a book.

Inspired by the comic strip *PEANUTS*, by Charles Schulz, Berk envisioned communicating a message of hope and healing to a world of broken and hurting people. Taking his cue from Lucy's counseling booth, Berk's idea was to project the reality that God Himself – the Great Physician, the Eternal Healer of all physical and psychological ills – is the Doctor who is always "In." He saw the popular *PEANUTS* characters – Charlie Brown, Snoopy, Lucy, Linus, and others – forever struggling with everyday problems, but often finding solutions with spiritual undertones. Undeniably the most widely read item in newspapers all across America, reaching literally millions of readers – the strip frequently carried a spiritual object lesson or innuendo. Knowing of Schulz's Church of God background, Berk thought, "Who better to partner with on a communications project than Schulz?"

According to Gary Moore, the Board shook their heads in disbelief; but Berk sold the idea. He also gained an audience, and a lasting friendship, with "Sparky" Schulz, who did agree to participate not only in the book, but also in the accompanying television special, *The Doctor Is In.*

Of his relationship with Schulz, Berk said in a newpaper interview: "We had a great meeting of minds, and I really like the guy. I know now why I like Charlie Brown so much. I spent a lot of time getting to know him before we ever began discussing the book. I didn't want just to use his art, but wanted his character and personality to be a part of the book also. Schulz is a delightfully literate man. He reads in every field and has a wide range of both interests and knowledge."

For the prime-time special, Berk recruited some of the finest talent the Church of God had to offer: the Gaither Trio, Doug Oldham, Sandi Patty, and others. James Earl Massey and David Grubbs filled cameo speaking segments, as did Charles Schulz and Berk himself. At Anderson "Camp Meeting" in June of 1981, Berk, Gary Moore, the CBH Quartet, and David Grubbs launched both the book and the filming project. People attending the convention were invited

Charles Schulz, who collaborated with Berk on the television special and the book The Doctor Is In.

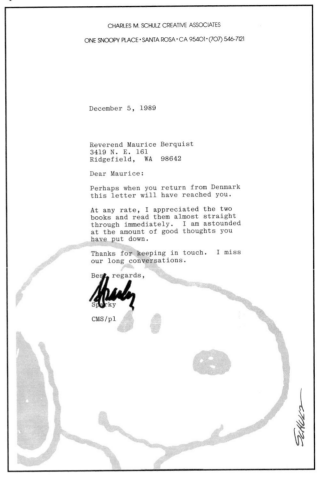

CHARLES M. SCHULZ CREATIVE ASSOCIATES

ONE SNOOPY PLACE · SANTA ROSA · CA 95401 · (707) 546-7121

December 5, 1989

Reverend Maurice Berquist
3419 N. E. 161
Ridgefield, WA 98642

Dear Maurice:

Perhaps when you return from Denmark this letter will have reached you.

At any rate, I appreciated the two books and read them almost straight through immediately. I am astounded at the amount of good thoughts you have put down.

Thanks for keeping in touch. I miss our long conversations.

Best regards,

Sparky

CMS/pl

ABOVE: Berk and Schulz kept in touch after their work on The Doctor Is In.

Dr. Murphy interviews Berk on Channel 40 - Indianapolis about the book and TV special. The program had been named a finalist for the 1981 Religion in Media "Angel Award." Within three months of the program's debut, 64,000 paperback "gift" copies of The Doctor Is In *had been sent to responders, and it was being carried as a "book club selection" or catalog item for at least ten national Christian book stores.*

to participate in the live filming of various segments of the production at several locations.

By October the production was "in the can." The CBH team then embarked on a marathon of fall "preview parties" around the country to advertise the TV special to local congregations and solicit support for airing the program over television stations around the country for several weeks, starting January 2, 1982. They also discussed how CBH could assist local congegations with follow-up on responses from viewers after the program aired in their areas.

Gary recalls the tour's hectic pace: "We were in a different town every night for at least three weeks."

In mid-November, Berk became ill with a respiratory infection in Sikeston, MO; and was ordered to bed by a doctor there. But the next weekend he was back on the road

Right: Berk enjoys a jam session with Gerald Marvel on guitar (left) and Ron Fair on harmonica (center) at Anderson Camp Meeting in June of 1983.

The Libary for Living series also carried the theme of the TV special: The Doctor Is In . . .
- *When You Feel Rejected by Family*
- *When You Feel Like a Misfit . . .*
- *When Nothing Seems to Go Right*
- *When Divorce Strikes*
- *When Someone Hurts You*
- *When You Pray and Nothing Happens*
- *When You Need a Friend*
- *When Financial Pressure Becomes Unbearable*
- *When You Lose a Loved One*
- *When You Need Direction*
- *When You Seek Healing*
- *When The Bible Seems Confusing.*

with Gary in the mid-West for a CBH rally, a communication seminar, two other services, and a Premiere Party in Chicago. Then he was one day home and back out again. To the McCalls he wrote, "Would you listen to a few words from the center of the whirlwind – I'm not sure whether I'm coming, going, spiraling, or circling."

The grueling schedule continued into the spring and summer of 1982.

Even into 1983, the pace never abated. By then Berk had completed a second book, *The Miracle and Power of Blessing*, and was writing a series of twelve small books, the *Library for Living*, that CBH would use to raise funds for more airings of the television special. Given the challenge of producing a book a month for the "Library" series, he asked Gary to teach him how to use a computer for writing manuscripts. Breaking Berk in on the K-pro proved to be the biggest challenge Gary faced in all his years at CBH! Meanwhile, the two of them were also conducting "People to People" communication workshops on weekends around the country – all part of an intense promotional campaign for the television special and an expansion of Mass Communication ministries.

And while Berk loved doing it all, it was almost his undoing.

Derailment!

Berk returned home from a meeting on August 8, 1983 (his 61st birthday), more exhausted than usual. On August 9 his tiredness kept him sleepless all night. The pain in his left shoulder persisted. When I arrived home the next morning from work, I found him flushed and instantly sensed something out of the ordinary. Over Berk's protests, I immediately called our physician, Dr. William Anderson. I told him that I feared Berk was experiencing an impending heart attack and that I needed to get him to the office pronto. Protesting all the way, my "Stubborn Swede" drove us there. Since I had been up all night working, he feared I'd run off the road.

The doctor was waiting. He hustled Berk right to the ER, where fast test results showed that I was right! Berk had an evolving infarction. By that time, he was having chest pain so severe the doctor had to use IV morphine to stop it. Further testing showed coronary artery blockage requiring surgery. Our world was topsy-turvy again.

On October 10 Berk had a quadruple bypass at St. Vincent's in Indianapolis. He was subsequently out of the office (doctor's orders) until January 1, 1984.

Gary literally took over. Already an office whiz, he now proved his speaking prowess by traveling to fill Berk's engagements. Meanwhile, I had a restless, sometimes angry, and extremely impatient patient to contend with at home.

Three weeks after surgery Berk had lost thirty pounds and looked great. His strength gradually returning, he walked a little each day until he could do a mile.

By the last Sunday of October we were ready for our first visit to Church. For an imprisoned Berk, it was "freedom day"! We walked into the Pathways Class just as they were beginning. All of our friends – who had visited, sent flowers and cards, and prayed – stood and applauded.

It was a moment frozen in time.

I Never Thought about Jonah Before

Berk wrote this article for People to People *a few weeks after his near-death experience from a heart attack*

It's strange that Jonah is called a "minor prophet" because he is much better known than any of the major prophets.

Everyone knows about Jonah and the whale, or as the Bible more accurately describes it, "a great fish." I suspect that millions of people who know the story of Jonah would be surprised to discover that it is in the Bible.

Of coure, I have known about Jonah since my earliest childhood when I was shown a picture (not a photgraph) of a bearded man standing on the shore of the sea. As I recall the Sunday School picture now, his robes didn't seem to be wet, although he had just been cast out on the land after a three-day ride in the fish's belly. I marvel at that, since Jonah lived long before drip-dry clothes were invented.

Now that I think of it, this picture and Jonah himself might have made a greater impression on me if I had seen a little more evidence of his harrowing expeience. I guess I was too young to know that artists sometimes improve the appearance of their models, making them look like the "person they have become" rather than the "person in the process of becoming."

Let me talk about that.

About four weeks ago, I came home from a three-week preaching assignment. As I started to resume my office acivities, I became ill. I am almost never sick. I couldn't believe that I was. But when the chest pains persisted, my wife hurried me to the doctor, who promptly rushed me into the hospital, where I was treated for a heart attack.

The latest diagnosis is that I have not had any serious damage, but I have to wait for futher testing to be sure.

In spite of my plans and pleadings, my whole preaching schedule was cancelled for two months. At the moment I am home, as I will be for at least three more weeks.

I understand better how Jonah felt as he was suddenly detoured from his own direction and put out of circulation for a while.

The Bible simply says:

"From inside the fish Jonah prayed unto the Lord." (Jonah 2:1)

I can imagine it now. The ribs of the fish were like the arches of a chapel, and the seaweed all around was like floral decorations on the altar. Of course, the thing that really made the place holy was that Jonah found a new level of prayer in his despair.

That's a lot easier for me to undertand now that I am "waiting" on the Lord.

Waiting comes hard for people who are accustomed to working and working.

Of this experience, more lessons have been learned during my days in the "Submarine Cathedral" than I can tell about here. My priorities have changed. My compassion has changed. My praying has changed. And, hopefully, my future is changed.

Like Jonah in the fish's belly, I am looking forward to the time when I can be out on the dry land again, even if I have seaweed hanging from my ears.

I'll be ready to preach again. And preach better.

"Jonah's Submarine Cathedral"
as interpreted for Berk by Barry Sempsrott.

Since Berk could not yet take on active assignments, he spent days reading and writing. While recuperating from surgery, he finished the *Library for Living* series. This treasure trove of instruction and inspiration drawn from his life and years of experience as a pastor and evangelist was good therapy during this trying time. He also wrote many letters, limericks, and other poems in response to flowers and cards he had received. But he was champing at the bit to get back to work.

In November of 1983 we set out on a two-week's Amtrak trip to Los Angeles, Portland, and Seattle. We took a sleeper on the northern route out, via Chicago to Seattle. After a visit with the Tallmans there, we traveled to Vancouver, Washington, and Portland, Oregon, to visit the Marvels and the Warmans. Our last stop was Los Angeles to visit the Minklers before returning, via the Southern route, to Indy. It was a wonderfully relaxing, fun trip that "took the bite" out of Berk's boredom.

That December Indiana pranced out its coldest winter – snows, ice, freezing temperatures to 22 below zero. Although Berk was medically and physically sounder, his big enemy was shortness of breath. Earlier bouts of pneumonia had wreaked havoc on his lungs, and the cold weather worsened his condition.

CBH – Mission Accomplished

In February of 1984 we flew to Seattle to install Jim Lyon in his first pastorate: Woodland Park Church of God. The Western Washington Association had been courting Berk's favor to come out there in the near future to be their State Coordinator, so he had an interview while there. We talked about it on the way home.

Berk was feeling the pressure of ever-increasing responsibilities and expectations in the Mass Communications endeavor. In addition to writing and producing the television special, he had been instrumental in launching new international broadcasts, had written fourteen books, and produced two advertising spots for television. He had expanded radio programming, developed audio-cassette study programs, and conducted communication seminars around the country. He had helped establish the CBH Bible Study Conference at Montreat as a grass-roots connection for on-going support of CBH ministries. In short, he felt that in seven years, rather than the ten he had expected to stay, he had completed all he could do. And midwest winters were proving to be unbearable to his health.

He also had a yen to stretch his evangelistic legs in a different venture. Hence, the Western Washington administrative job challenged him. We both had loved the beauty of the Northwest; so, nomadic souls that we were, we decided to go for it.

Berk resigned, effective July 1, 1984. Dave Grubbs was still the speaker for CBH-English, but Gary Moore had already returned to Portland, Oregon, to work with Warner Pacific College as Vice-President of Business and Management.

Our seven years in Anderson had been fruitful and fulfilling. Saying goodbye to old and new friends, the wonderful church and college community, and our beloved house on Winding Way was sad and difficult.

Berk delighted in the camaraderie of all the agency executives with whom he had been privileged to serve. Among them were Robert Reardon, Bob Nicholson, Paul Tanner, Ed Foggs, Dave Lawson, Don Johnson, Harold Conrad, Marvin Hartman, Arlo Newell, Don Noffsinger, and others from Warner Press who had assisted in the publication of his books. He had enjoyed especially the brainstorming at Friday luncheons.

On June 19, 1984, CBH honored Berk with a banquet, attended by former and current members of the Mass Communications Board, executives from other church agencies, members of the CBH production family, and former CBH speakers – R. Eugene Sterner, James Earl Massey, and Dave Grubbs. Spouses were also included, of course. Many gracious remarks were made about Berk, his years of service to the church, and his labors and accomplishments for CBH and the Mass Communications ministry of the church. Particularly touching was a tribute by Doug and Laura Lee Oldham, declaring Berk to be "an international art treasure in the Kingdom of God."

Lori's Wedding

On May 1, 1986, Lori called from West Virginia.

"Mom, put Dad on the other line. I want to talk to you both – together."

"Okay. We're ready– shoot."

"Jack and I are going to get married in one month. Can you handle it?"

Momentarily speechless, I gulped twice and finally respnded, "Yes." But my mind was whirling back to 1981, when we traveled the wedding path with Lori and Jack once before.

The date had been set: October 30, 1981. I had gone down from Anderson and worked a week on all the preparations. The dress was chosen; bridesmaids' dresses in the making. The

At the wedding of Lori Berquist and Jack Evans on June 1, 1986:
(L to R) Berk, Berny, Lori and Jack Evans, and Marty Berquist.

program had been selected and the reception paid for. Invitations were addressed and stamped, but, fortunately not mailed, for on October 1 they called it off. Their reason was commendable: they felt they were not ready. Now, five years later, they had both matured and were at last ready for the commitment of marriage.

Needless to say, we were in high gear. I flew back east in mid-May to help with organizational details for this "Day of Days." Berk then joined us for the big event.

On June 1, 1986, our beautiful little girl married her "Prince Charming" in the church there in Scott Depot, West Virginia. A proud dad gave her away and shared in the ceremony with Pastor Oliver Hogue. Grandmother McIntyre, Uncle John, cousins Gina and Zola, aunts Noby and Lois, and a host of friends – including some from Daytona – were there to share the joy of the newlyweds and to wish them well.

"Camp" Adventures

For three summers I was privleged to work with Iris Swisshelm as camp nurse for up to sixty handicapped campers (ages eighteen to sixty) at Camp Long, a large city park with camping facilities. We stayed in cabins with sleeping bags and carried out a full program of activities and planned outings, as well as dispensing medications and treatments as needed. Wonderful times! . . . filled with heartwarming moments and stories of these my special people – God's little ones – to hold in my heart forever.

Berk was also involved in "camping." One of his greatest achievements of our Western Washington years was planning for and purchasing a permanent camp ground in Easton, Washington. Formerly a boys' camp called the Double K Ranch, the facility featured wonderful buildings, trails, and outdoor wonderment in some of the most beautiful scenery, mountains, streams, and woods imaginable. His original idea was to sell off one-acre plots to interested investors on which to build their own log cabins, with all plans and construction according to strict zoning regulations. It didn't work out that way; but Western Washington does own this incredible property, now called Camp Kachess; and it is used year-round – not just for camp meeting, but also for youth camps, conventions for adults and teens, and, of course, ski outings.

Moving to Vancouver

In 1987 we ended our three-year contract with Western Washington. On August 8, Berk turned sixty-five. Believe it or not, he was eager to arrive at that age! As he had it figured, with Medicare and Social Security, he would have a little leeway financially, and more than anything he wanted to "free lance" as an evangelist again. But where to settle as a home base?

Seattle was financially implausible. But we loved the Northwest, and all our "stuff" was out there. Finally, we decided on Vancouver, where Gerald and Rena Marvel pastored. The Marvels were treasured friends from Arlington College days and long-time supporters of Berk's ministry. Theirs was a wonderful church.

Great friends. Wonderful pastor. Spectacular area. Why not?

And we got to build our first new house. We moved to Vancouver in August and almost immediately our house was started. We met a great new friend, Doris

Berk and Berny "at home" in Ridgefield, a suburb of Vancouver, Washington.

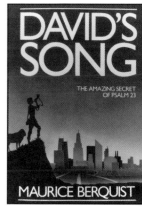

Olson, who was heading to Hungary for the summer. For three months we rented her house while ours was under construction. By Thanksgiving of that year, our home was a dream come true. We had chosen a charming Victorian farm house, implementing as many of our ideas as possible and accommodating the best of our furnishings. I used touches here and there of a pastoral decorating motif of sheep and green pastures to commemorate Berk's most recent book, *David's Song: The Amazing Secret of Psalm 23*, scheduled for publication in 1988. The effect – sometimes whimsical, sometimes peaceful, sometimes spiritual – gave the house an aura of tranquility, making it the restful haven I wanted it to be for both of us.

Lori and her husband, Jack, flew out for Christmas. Not only did we have a new house, but when we unwrapped our package from them, we discovered that we would be unwrapping a grandchild in August of 1988. What a Christmas!

Lake Charles Interlude

On New Year's Day, 1988. Berk received a call from Lake Charles, Louisiana, asking him to be interim pastor there. He accepted their plea for help, and flew there January 15 to stay a month or so. I was to follow. My real self wanted to stay and decorate and put away. But God had other plans, for 1988 turned out to be our most "trying and flying" year.

Instead of joining Berk in Lake Charles, I boarded a plane to Philadelphia to help care for a friend of my brother John. His business partner, Steve Freedman, had lung cancer with a "few months" prognosis. I was to stay two weeks to nurse him through some chemo and radiation. But while I was there, Lori almost lost their baby, so I flew down to West Virginia to minister to her. Then it was back to Philly for another week.

In March I returned to a Vancouver socked in by drizzly, chilly, gray weather – too wet to put in the landscaping – while Berk was basking in the bayous of Lousiana, loving being a pastor again and eating Cajun food. Finally, I did get to spend Easter with him and his new flock, which included old friends from our Daytona days – Bob and Vida Pompelly. Once there, I could easily see why Berk was so content. He was living in their completely refurbished parsonage, with a car thrown in.

Inspired by the Southern flavor of Lake Charles, Berk seized upon the idea of becoming "Mr. Hospitality." He decided to host dinners at the parsonage, playing the double role of both host and chef. He started out practice-cooking, with some prepared food, some help from those carrying in, and some "grudgingly stolen," recipes from me. During his months as interim pastor there, he entertained about 200 people, bringing together every age group and peer group imaginable. His project was a heart-warming success. No wonder they wanted to keep him.

While helping the Lake Charles pulpit search committee and preaching, Berk also had to fulfill other previously made commitments around the country. So our lovely little house in Vancouver just sat and pouted. I did get a yard seeded in April.

Then, in May, Mother became ill. I flew to Virginia for a two-weeks' stay that mushroomed into five, as she was hospitalized.

June marked the end of Berk's "Magnolia Mission," when the church in Lake Charles called Cliff Sanders as pastor. Near the middle of June, Berk was preparing to go to Anderson, as he was on the camp meeting program committee, and I was hunting a part-time job in Vancouver, when a phone call came from John in Philly. Steve's death was imminent; would I come? On June 13 Berk and I flew out on different planes to our God-appointed destinations. It was our Thirty-fifth Wedding Anniversary.

The rest of the summer was a whirr and blur. After Steve's death I was back in Vancouver, but barely unpacked, when Lori decided to unwrap the package two weeks early. On July 31, 1988, Mary Lauren Elizabeth became an awesome reality. Berk was holding camp meeting in Alabama, but came to West Virginia as soon as his responsibilities were over. A visit I had planned for two-weeks stretched into a month when Lori developed toxemia and needed help longer.

Wearily I flew back to Vancouver at the end of August. Berk was home, too, and we were saying to one another: "What a year! Now, we can stay home and get more of our things unpacked . . . ."

But the respite was short lived. September found Berk back in Anderson for a program committee meeting. I had Iris down from Seattle and was thinking of taking on some private duty work, when a call in the night on September 3 brought the sad news that my mother had passed away. Life plans detoured again, as I stayed two weeks in Virginia, saying goodbye to our faithful matriarch and helping the family.

I had flown 55,000 miles that year to help family and friends.

In October I applied for and got work as a charge nurse, part time, at a nursing home called Fort Vancouver Convalescent Home. And, with just a few interruptions, I worked there until the fall of 1989.

Preaching Conferences and Interim Work

Meanwhile, Berk was doing what he loved best next to preaching – teaching others how to preach better. He and his preaching buddy Gerald Marvel did several preaching seminars, including a week-long summer course at Mid-America Bible College. Here were two of the most skilled preachers in the Church at large sharing from their life-time of study and experience ideas covering every aspect of preaching from being confident in the call to preach to preaching without notes. The series was a great success and was later converted from conference tapes and Berk's notes into book form by Maxine McCall, using the title Berk had chosen: *A Handful of Stars*.

Berk did a short term interim at Elkhart, Indiana, and another at Johnson City, Tennessee. He also continued preaching for camp meetings in various states and serving as a leader for the CBH Bible Conference in North Carolina. For a couple of summers he did month-long stints in Wichita, Kansas, as Pastor-in-Residence while Pastor Ray Cotton, on sabbatical, studied at Fuller Seminary.

In 1989 he made two trips to Denmark – in July and again in November. He wanted so much to help re-energize the churches there, to help them set some goals and move forward. He preached revivals, led Bible studies, and conducted conferences for pastors and lay leaders. Especially gratifying was learning that they

Gerald Marvel (L) with Berk in Vancouver.

were translating his book *The Miracle and Power of Blessing* into Danish, with the project more than half complete.

During the July journey, he took time out to visit Sweden, his mother's homeland. Though unable to locate her homeplace or any relatives, he did see the hills where she grew up – scenes he heard her describe many times when he was a boy.

He returned home from Denmark on December 11, with barely time enough to unload and repack his bags for his second expedition with Howard Baker to India.

Even in retirement, my errant Swede was hardly ever home; but when he was, he enjoyed to the hilt being in Gerald Marvel's congregation. We both attended Rena's Sunday School Class and considered her one of the finest teachers we'd ever known. Berk went to both the 8:30 and the 11:00 a.m. worship services. He took great delight in Gerald as a preaching colleague. He, like the rest of the congregation, was moved to laughter, tears, and awe as Gerald depicted the Gospel in his simple, direct, totally captivating style.

He and Gerald were kindred souls in their passion for preaching. Berk lived and breathed sermons. He saw "parables" in every-day living; and, much to the chagrin of our children, just about everything that happened in our family found its way into a sermon. He genuinely loved people, and he believed that God could help them if they could hear and understand the simple Bible message. All his life Berk continually honed his natural gift of story telling to make the gospel relevant and clear to everyone. As he often said, "If you can't understand me, you ought not to be loose on the streets." Gerald shared Berk's philosophy, and whenever they were together they talked incessantly about preaching and how to do it better. Sometimes they met together between services to talk about the message. Berk was inspired by Gerald, and Gerald always said that Berk was his greatest supporter and encourager. Theirs was a great friendship.

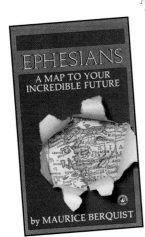

Another couple in the congregation very special to us were Dale and Marilyn Warman. They supported Berk on all his trips to India and joined Berk and Howard Baker in India on one trip to dedicate two churches the Warmons had funded: one in honor of Dale's parents, the Warmans, and one in honor of Marilyn's parents, the Trudgeons. Both couples were pioneer Church of God pastors. We also admired the Warmans for their leadership in initiating and guiding L.I.V.E (Laypersons in Vital Exchange) Ministries, a weekend witnessing program that is now revitalizing congregations all over the country.

Not only do Dale and Marilyn support missions and lay ministries, but they also have made possible some special times of respite for their ministers. Berk and I spent several weekends at their beautiful home in Cannon Beach on the Oregon Coast. Berk loved to go there to write. One manuscript he worked on there was *Ephesians: A Map to Your Incredible Future*, published as a teaching tool in 1989. Berk presented it at Anderson Camp Meeting in 1990 as a three-day Bible study series. We were also privileged to spend three weeks in in their condo in Kona, Hawaii, where Berk wrote the bulk of his last book, *The Promise of Immunity*, based on Psalm 91.

Berk's life was full during our years in Washington, but little of our time there was spent together. We discussed his frequent absences and lamented the fact that all his opportunities were back East. In all of our married life, Berk was away from home more now than ever.

Once in a while
A door opens.
For a moment we look on a new world,
A wider world,
A world of wonder.

It happens in childhood sometimes.
Looking into a mirror
The little girl in pigtails
Sees a dream.
She sees a beautiful princess
Descending a circular stair.

A lad with freckles
Peers over the steering wheel
  of the family car
Parked in the driveway.
He feels like a champion driver,
Screeching his way around the track.

Fantasy opens doors for the rest of us
Sometimes.
Not often.
It happened to me.
Let me tell you how it happened.

In our home in Indiana
Near the light switch in the
  breakfast room
Was a small picture.
Beautiful, but small.

A rock jutted out of the water,
Like a thumb poking out of a glove.
Blue and white the waves crashed
Against the protruding rock.

"Do you know what that is?
  a guest asked.
"A picture of a rock in the ocean,"I said.
"Well, yes, but a very famous rock.
It is called Haystack Rock,
Off the coast of Oregon."

"Sometime I would like to see
The real thing," I said.
"It is hard to squeeze the ocean
Into a post-card sized picture."

Then it happened.
Friends made it happen.
I found myself looking out their window
At Haystack Rock.

Gibralter-like it stood.
Waves crashed around it
And the sky stood blue above it.
Birds flew around it,
Possessively,
Claiming it as their
Castle in the sea.

"This," I thought, "is reality.
So much grander,
So much larger
Than I had dreamed."

But I mused on
As I rested in this castle by the sea.
I thought about heaven
And eternity.

I look at the pictures
Painted with words
In the writings of John
Or the great Apostle.

The frame is too small.
They can't get it all in.
Nor could we understand it
If they could.

Just as I waited,
We must wait.
And just as I found myself
On the beach,
Looking at Haystack Rock,
We will one day see
Reality.

For we shall stand on the shore of eternity
And glimpse heaven.
Our tiny pictures
Will be left behind,
For we shall see Jesus
As He is.

This, too, is a gift.
A gift of a friend.

Maurice Berquist
for Dale and Marilyn Warman
April 23, 1985

LEFT: Dale and Marilyn Warman below their vacation home at Cannon Beach, overlooking Haystack Rock.

Haystack Rock

Alone it stands amid the waves;
*   It scorns their snarling cries.*
Winds whistle 'round its rugged face,
*   Above are leaden skies.*

Yet still it stands, a mighty rock
*   Thrust upward from the sea,*
Unchanged, unmoved throughout the storm.
*   As Jesus is to me.*

The years pass on relentlessly,
*   The seasons come and go.*
The Rock of Ages stands unmoved.
*   That's all we need to know.*

Maurice Berquist
October 27, 1986

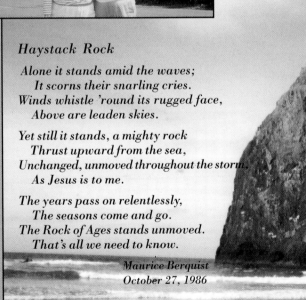

*Berk with
daughter Lori
1991*

"Papa" Berquist
Pastor / Evangelist at Large / Grandfather
1991 - 1993

10
Wichita

We spent Christmas of 1990 in West Virginia with Lori, Jack, Lauren, and a new baby-to-be. Berk was totally charmed by Lauren, who had "Papa" wrapped around her little finger.

Come February, Berk asked me what I would think about moving to the Midwest, so we could be nearer the family. Ray Cotton had approached him about moving to Wichita and serving on staff there as Minister-at-Large or Minister-in-Residence.

Kansas!

Never in my wildest dreams had I ever imagined moving there. Anderson, maybe, which was so central, or Florida, which was so warm. But Kansas? Mercy!

When Berk started out as a young evangelist, he had held many meetings in Wichita, especially for E.E. Kardatzke, who had signed him up for Anderson College. Through the years he had often returned to hold youth camps, conventions, revivals, and seminars. He loved the church there and had watched with fascination as Ray took the burgeoning congregation to new heights and built a huge facility seating 3,000. In 1991 Central Community Church had eleven pastors and was viewed as a model church in its outreach and amenities.

Berk saw the move as a golden opportunity to work with a truly innovative staff. So convincing was his spiel to me that I mentally packed while he pursued further conversations with Ray and his administrative associate, Mark Deffenbacher, about possibly accepting the offer.

I couldn't believe that I would be tearing up another playhouse! But neither of us wanted to stay so far away from our family any longer. As he did with every decision, Berk submitted the matter to prayer. We would put the house up for sale as a fleece. If it sold quickly, that meant we were to go.

Meanwhile, back in West Virginia, Matthew John Christian Evans made an early debut on February 10. I flew out quickly. As usual, Berk was gone – but this time to Tennessee, putting him close enough to drive over to see his namesake. We were all delighted with our new baby. I spent two weeks with the Evans four, then hurried back to Vancouver.

On March 1, our house sold, and at the asking price. The fleece had taken. We had to move quickly, for the new owners wanted possession by April 1. Our next step was to fly to Wichita to meet the congregation and look for a place to live – again!

A fascinated Lauren absorbs a lesson from "Papa" on the joys of playing the harmonica.

Berk and I met there in mid-March. (I don't remember where he flew from). We were introduced to the staff and the congregation, and Berk preached. After a few days of making the circuit with real estate agents, we found a condo just to our taste (with much re-doing, of course) on a golf course very near the church. I might add that I was completely taken away by the church facilities, services and programs, and the wonderful staff. I felt immediately at peace.

"On the Road Again" Reprise

Our last Sunday in Vancouver was the Easter early service. Our furniture was on its way to Kansas, and we spent Saturday night with the Marvels. After the first service, we said our "good-byes" and pulled out in our trusty blue Ford, across the Cascades to the plains of Kansas. Were we crazy?

As we drove along, heading for yet another chapter to unfold, it all felt strangely familiar – like that first summer in 1953, when we started out across the USA in our '53 Belvedere: New horizons awaiting . . . new opportunities . . . starting over . . . yet without one doubt and with the same excitement I felt as that naive twenty-two-year-old when I said, "I do," to a man who boldly said, "Come away with me, Little Girl of the Hills, and I'll show you the world, its wealth, and its thrills." How much more could these brown eyes see?

The great states of the Northwest to the Southwest seemed to zoom by. Spring was just emerging in Idaho, Montana, Wyoming, and Colorado as we trekked on. We listened to tapes, talked, had quiet times, and I read to Berk. Once he reached down and took my hand and said, "You're something else. No other woman in the world would pull up stakes so cheerfully and tear down the erected 'manses' like you, and never look back!"

I choked up a little, for I had felt some pain in saying "goodbye" to lots of cute little rooms. But I managed to smile and respond, "Well, I'm still just following a man who's following a Man."

Wichita – Settling In

We arrived in Wichita on April 3, 1991, and stayed with Ray and Janet Cotton a few days until the moving van came. April 8 was "unpacking day," as we moved into the condo at 100 South Maize Road.

My challenge of transforming another "ugly duckling" into a "swan" required that we endure a brief period of chaos to re-carpet and change avocado appliances and fixtures to almond. A minor inconvenience, for we loved the location – right on a golf course, with church, bank, and grocery store all within a mile. I was as excited as if it were our first home.

Berk was eager to get started in his new role as Evangelist Teacher-In-Residence. Being no stranger to Central Community Church and Wichita, he blended in beautifully. He held Central Community to be one of the most innovative and effective ministries in the Church of God and the United States. He considered it an excellent place to invest his time and energy, in addition to all the ways he felt he could learn from such a gifted staff. One of his goals was to develop and present specific Christian Education seminars. He would substitute for other teachers and fill the pulpit whenever Pastor Ray had to be away. He was also to write and promote the church, especially

for the "Successful Church Ministries and Leadership Renewal Conference" held annually in October.

Berk settled in easily with the staff, holding his own, while trying not to be overwhelmed by such a gifted peer group. He was eager to learn as well as teach. And the staff broadened their circle to include us in every way. We had, indeed, found a superb new family.

Hearts and Hands and TLC

We had only been in Wichita two weeks when Mother Nature issued a wake-up call. We were in tornado country! From hurricanes in Florida to earthquakes in California – now twisters!

I knew the sky was unusually dark and the wind more fierce than usual, but what was that siren? Berk came running to me upstairs and said, "Get into the basement quick – that's a tornado warning!"

We cowered down in his study for an hour, listening to the wind, rain, rattling windows – and the radio. Finally came an "all clear" signal, and we emerged to skies less grey, but still somber. We heard that the worst damage was east of us and were thankful that Providence spared the church. And us.

That week we learned something else about our wonderful church. They were outgoing and profusely generous in giving for community endeavors. A "Hearts and Hands" ministry was in full bloom. Eleven of our church families were hit hard by the tornado. Thankfully their lives were spared, but they lost all their possessions. Donations poured in. The church gym was full of used appliances and furniture, food, and clothing. So abundant was Central Community's response that the church called the Salvation Army and Goodwill to come and replenish their coffers from the bountiful supply.

And we were yet to discover another ministry far-reaching in its impact. Called T.L.C. (Together Loving Christ) groups, Central Community's small group ministry was formed to bring people closer together, to pray, share, and see to one another's welfare on a one-to-one basis, lest anyone be lost in the vastness of such a large church. Like Berk, I was fascinated by these small groups and their outreach, which truly were the catalyst for the church's phenomenal growth.

Melodee Schaeffer asked me to co-teach one of these groups – a women's group that met in a home each Thursday morning. What a fabulous opportunity to get acquainted! I was scared, but jumped in anyway. And I found new sisters and daughters immediately. We bonded like magic. Melodee suggested study books for the group's approval. Each week we had homework, then came together for a time of sharing and prayer, making requests and celebrating answers. And, for those who could stay afterwards, lunch provided a wonderful time of fellowship. Later, I came to realize that I was not brought into this group by chance. God was at work. These ladies were to be my salvation – and I thought I was theirs.

Another group that became very precious to me were the young ministers at Central Community and their wives. The wives invited me to join them for monthly luncheons or breakfasts at different houses, making me feel very much a part of the staff. Ray and Janet Cotton, Mark and Judi Deffenbacher, George and Pat Skramstad, David and Michelle Boots included Berk and me, and sometimes Gramps (E.E.) and Grammy (Vera) Kardatzke, in their frequent get-togethers. We were delighted to be with E.E. and Vera Kardatzke in their retirement years. When we lived in Daytona, E.E. and Vera often visited for a couple of weeks in the winter, parking their Airstream nearby. Through the years, they had been great friends and mentors. It was good to enjoy close fellowship with them once again.

Another exciting discovery for both of us was a phenomenal Sunday School class taught by Dr. Jon Kardatzke, his wife Lorna, and Bruce Pearson. Every week they made incredibly interesting and challenging presentations, with headliner guests like Florence Littauer, James Dobson, and Gary Smalley. In addition to the class itself, they hosted an annual Marriage Enrichment Seminar, open to the entire city. Attendance at that time would swell to 1,000, and they would have to use the sanctuary for the overflow. The regular Sunday School class ran around 300. Jon is an unexcelled teacher, and Lorna, who is an improvement even on the virtuous woman of Proverbs 31, has managed to keep Jon humble in spite of all his attributes.

Derailment and Recovery

In June of 1991, Pastor Ray was awarded an honorary Doctor of Divinity at Anderson University. As many other staff members were also attending Camp Meeting, Berk opted to stay in Wichita to preach in Ray's absence and help keep the ship steady. On the last weekend in June, Anderson University President Jim Edwards came to Wichita to preach and to re-enact for the church the presentation of Ray's degree. That same weekend – on Saturday, June 29 – Berk flew in from Daytona, where he'd been conducting a seminar. He complained of an "unrelenting headache" and slept most of Saturday afternoon, attributing it to extreme fatigue. He had literally "preached his head off" in Daytona, he said. He always took on an arduous schedule whenever he went back to Daytona Beach – so many hands reaching after twenty-one years of knowing him as pastor.

I was busy that Saturday afternoon. Lorna Kardatzke and I had volunteered to prepare and serve a dinner for twelve at the Cottons' home that evening to honor Jim and Deanna Edwards. Berk managed to get to dinner, but his pain persisted. Dr. Jon Kardatzke's presence at the dinner was a boon. He gave Berk some pain medications, and the pastors – Ray, Mark, and George – prayed for him.

Berk slept all night, but was still in pain upon awakening Sunday morning. I called Dr. Jon, who suggested that Berk stay home and in bed. By noon Berk was worsening. He was flushed, incoherent, and unsteady on his feet. His eyes were extremely sensitive to light, and the left eye had a puffiness and droop.

Growing increasingly alarmed, I called Jon and Lorna to please come over and help. One look was all Jon needed. He immediately put us in the car, with Lorna driving, and ran to the phone to alert the Emergency Staff at St. Francis. I feared an impending stroke. Somehow we got there, and the emergency team rushed into action. X-rays showed clearly that Berk had a sub-dural hematoma (blood clot) on the left side of the brain and was bleeding internally. He was losing consciousness and was unable to respond properly to questions asked. Emergency surgery!

Jon called his TLC group and placed messages on the pastors' phones. (They were away at an entertainment park for the annual All-Church Picnic). My life was on hold. But for such a trauma to hit, God had us in the right place.

I called my children and sisters for prayer. Before the forty-five-minute surgery was over, the waiting room was filled with our staff family. First came Dale and Judy Lewis; next the Skramstads; then the Deffenbachers. I have never felt such a warmth of support.

Around 9:00 p.m. the doctor came out to tell us that he had been able to remove the clot, stop the bleeding, and thwart any paralysis. We whooped – though not too loudly. What a relief! God is so good!

At 10:00 p.m. they rolled Berk out – bright as a star – his head swathed like a Swami. He didn't remember any of Saturday or Sunday; didn't remember coming to the hospital. He did remember the headache and was shocked at actually having had brain surgery.

Jon told me later that when he first saw Berk that day, he feared a brain tumor. He also said that I had saved Berk's life by being persistent in getting him to the hospital. The pastors left and I sat the night vigil by his bedside until George and Ray came to get me the next morning.

Hospitalized for a week, Berk was borne aloft by all the attention: flowers, cards, and daily visits from the staff. Another faithful visitor was Teri Kardatzke Mesner, a tremendous cheerleader, for she, too, had recovered from brain surgery.

He had a good recovery, but was basically quarantined for a month. That meant canceling a couple of meetings, which, of course, drew Berk's ire. His Swedish temperament disliked being "managed" by anyone in any way – no matter the circumstances. This situation was almost a repeat of the "imprisonment" heart surgery had inflicted upon him, and he was not pleased.

He was unable to fill the pulpit when Ray took his sabbatical, a void covered by other staff members and added concerts. Mid-August was freedom time. Berk held the Colorado State Camp Meeting, and I went along to see that he rested between speaking times. "We" did fine. By September he was unharnessed and fulfilling his duties, including the CBH Bible Conference at Montreat, North Carolina.

Marty's Wedding

On September 28, 1991, Marty, our first-born, was married to Sharon Reid in a lovely ceremony in Bloomington, Indiana. The wedding was a small, family affair. Once again Berk squeezed into a tuxedo to serve as best man and to share in the ceremony. Lori brought the grandchildren – little Lauren was flower girl – so it was a joyous family celebration for us all.

We also gained two additional children to love, as Sharon brought to their union two sons from an earlier marriage: Ryan (thirteen) and Shane (eleven). We had wondered if Marty at age thirty-six was ever going to "tie the knot"; but on this day, he made up for lost time by presenting to us not only a beautiful daughter-in-law, but a ready-made family to boot. Our circle was growing.

ABOVE: Marty and his bride, Sharon Reid.
RIGHT: Berny, Marty, and Berk.

Back in Wichita, things were bustling in preparation for the "Successful Church Ministries Conference" in October. It was our first experience with this event which drew hundreds of participants from all across the United States. It was a great time seeing friends from all over. Berk conducted a Communications Seminar, and we enjoyed so much keeping guest speaker Robin Wood in our home.

Thanksgiving was spent with the Deffenbachers, the Skramstads, and the Cottons. At Christmas we headed for West Virginia to spend the holidays with the children and grandees.

Answering Calls from Florida

Berk was quite concerned about Daytona Beach. White Chapel was without a pastor, and he was worried about the church and school being "shepherdless." We also wanted to spend some time with Berk's former secretary, Nita Garmon, who was gravely ill with cancer. Thus, we headed for Daytona after Christmas and spent New Year's Eve with our beloved former-and-forever parishioners. We stayed a month in Daytona in an apartment. Berk spent his days seeing to the affairs of church and school, and I visited as many of the flock as possible. It was a precious and productive time. We all rejoiced when Kerry Robinson accepted the call to pastor "our flock." He arrived to take the helm on February 1.

With light hearts we drove back to Wichita via West Virginia to see Matthew, our grandson, celebrate his first birthday. He took his first wobbly steps into Papa Berk's arms.

Back in Wichita, I still had much work to do on our condo before it could be dubbed a "full-fledged swan." This time I had chosen an angel motif, with muted shades of ivory and soft blue, inspired by a line from Psalm 91, the scripture basis for Berk's latest manuscript, *The Promise of Immunity*:

Berk and Berny with grandchildren, Matthew and Lauren Evans.

For He shall give His angels charge over you, to keep you in all your ways. They shall bear you up in their hands, lest you dash your foot against a stone. (Psalm 91:11-12)

But the first order of business was fresh laundry for Berk. Within a week of our return, my knight-errant was off to Florida again, this time to Vero Beach. Leaders from that congregation had sought his help in finding a pastor, and he felt drawn to that call. Thus, he took up temporary quarters in Vero Beach to serve them as interim pastor, and in doing so became a part of another fabulous congregation. The rapport between Berk and the people, the board of elders, the pastoral and office staffs, and the programs of this church, was immediate and long-lasting.

At the time, I was totally baffled at this man's wanting to be the "answer" to so many churches. Why, I wondered could he not be content with just one? I was at war with myself. Still heavily involved with and committed to my TLC group, part of me wanted to stay in Wichita with my new friends, while part of me wanted to be with Berk on the sands of Florida.

Ray Cotton seemed content to loan Berk out to Vero while they did their pastoral search. The problem was, it seemed to me, that the Vero folks were so comfortable and happy with Berk, they weren't looking too hard and, for various reasons, kept turning down those who candidated. Berk would think they were all set with the right one, and something would go wrong. He would just get back to Wichita, and a call from Vero would say, "Come on back, Berk. This one didn't work out."

When he returned to Vero in the spring, I decided to go along. I spent Easter with him there. I heard music minister Mark Hanson's rendition of "Watch the Lamb" and met the congregation. Then, I understood. No wonder Berk was captivated, I thought. These people are treasures!

I met the "snow birds" who migrate from the North to escape "old man winter." They call this club of senior citizens "the Elderberries." I met priceless people like the Pressleys, Blakes, Griffiths, and Browns. The Baileys and Henleys were already long-time friends (from Drexel days). The pastoral staff was exceptional: Jay Colkitt in administration; Grant Powell (whom we had known as a lad) in Christian education; and Mark Hanson, music and worship. These talented ministers were backed up by an excellent office staff and an exceptional Board of

Elders, headed by Harvey Dodson and consisting of Tom Burdsall, Dave Murphy, Art DeGrazia, John Rodgers, Doug Milton, Leroy Pressley, and Art Cardiero. They were the wind beneath Berk's wings, and they made him fly a lot!

In May of 1992 we co-hosted a trip to the Holy Land and Egypt with Floyd Diehm and Mark Deffenbacher, pastors from Wichita. Our group was a marvelous meld of Wichita and Vero Beach people. The trip included a very special romantic moment for Berk and me: on June 13, in Egypt, while cruising on the Nile, we were treated to a lavish buffet luncheon and one dozen roses from our tour group. It was our 39th Anniversary . . . and our last.

The Promise of . . . What?

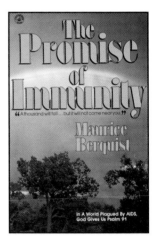

Berk's newest book, *The Promise of Immunity*, was to be unveiled at Anderson Camp Meeting, with Berk there for a special autographing session to mark the occasion. We flew in from Cairo on Monday, unpacked, re-packed, and flew out to Indiana on Wednesday. We were weary travelers – talk about jet lag! We had it coming and going! Berk started coughing and got a slight temperature on the plane. By the time we got to Indianapolis, he was dragging.

Eldon and Barb Williams met us at the airport. Berk slept all the way to Anderson. As soon as we got into the Williams' house, I called the doctor's office for an appointment; but they were closed until Thursday morning. Berk sat up all night with fever and congestion. Tylenol PM had no effect.

Next morning, we called and went straight to Dr. Anderson's office. I told him I feared pneumonia. Dr. Anderson listened to his lungs, did a chest X-ray, and shook his head.

"Berk," he said, "that's the most pneumonia I've ever seen. Both lungs. I have to put you in the hospital for aggressive IV antibiotics."

So Berk never got to the campgrounds. He was in the hospital a week; had lots of visitors from all over. The main teasing he had to endure was missing his book-signing, and the book's title didn't help – *The Promise of Immunity*.

After Anderson Camp Meeting, Berk was in Vero more than Wichita.

I lucked out on a nursing job that proved to be my most magnificent assignment. On July 6, 1992, I became the private duty nurse for one of Wichita's most notable ladies: Mrs. Olive Anne Beech, of Beechcraft airplane fame. Mine was the 11 p.m. to 7 a.m. shift four to five nights a week. For me, it was a perfect job with a perfect lady. It filled the lonely nights when Berk wasn't home, gave me some legal tender, and provided another satisfying and purposeful outlet for ministry.

Celebrating "Three Score and Ten"

Celebrating Berk's 70th Birthday with a surprise party at State Camp Meeting in Lake Wales, Florida.

Berk celebrated his 70th birthday on August 8, 1992, in Lake Wales, Florida, doing the Florida Camp Meeting. I had alerted the staff there so he would be well feted for the big day. Then, when he returned home, we would celebrate more grandly with our staff in Wichita. Upon his arrival a few days later, he was showered with 250 cards. I had a special dinner ready – a home-cooked Swedish dinner just like his mother used to make, with all his favorite dishes – including Boston Cream Pie! Little did we know this birthday was to be his last.

September was Montreat time, with a gala bash there to commemorate his birthday as well. Berk was dearly loved by the CBH Bible Study conferees, some having attended every year since its beginning. Everyone (except Berk) received a note in the registration packet that a surprise party for Berk would take place Friday evening, during the Southern Hospitality Jamboree, which Berk himself usually hosted. Amazingly, not one of the several hundred people there breathed a word to Berk. So the party took him totally by surprise.

AT RIGHT:
Berk, in his "Friday night Jamboree garb" at the CBH Bible Conference at Montreat, NC, is surprised by a "Three Score and Ten" Birthday Celebration in his honor. (September, 1992)

He was toasted and roasted and loved and hugged. As a fund-raising gesture for CBH, the group auctioned off several sheets of totally indecipherable scribbles and doodles Berk had made that week during his conference, "How to Understand the Whole Bible." Artist Dick Maloney, who had illustrated *The Miracle and Power of Blessing,* submitted a delightful cartoon sketch of Berk for the auction.

Berk with Maxine McCall at the "Successful Church Ministries Conference" in October of 1992.

Berk took possession of a T-Shirt that proclaimed, "It took me 70 years to look this good!" And many there had penned notes of love and warm wishes that were collected and presented, giving him an abundance of wonderful sentiments to read on the flight home.

October rolled around and it was "Successful Church Ministries" time again. We had a wonderful enrollment. Berk had written promo letters and recruited widely. Many came who had never attended before – Canadian delegates, for example, and a slew of North Carolinians who'd never seen so much sky. Our Florida visitors were not amused at Kansas' gift of a light snow as a greeting the first night. Maxine McCall, leader of the North Carolina delegation, and her mother, Minnie Belle Cooper, were our gracious house guests. Ray Cotton and the Central Community team were in top form for their presentations, and Berk did a superb job with his conference series – closing his last session to a thundering standing ovation.

Then, for Berk, it was back to Vero – another pastoral candidate didn't get the vote! Berk had been approached by the Board of Elders to think about serving on staff there as "Pastor to the Elderberries" six months of the year, November through April. He thought about the offer so seriously that we bought a condo in Vero Beach that November, with the idea of living in Vero during those months and renting the condo out the rest of the time. The other half of the year we would live in Wichita to fulfill his quest there.

Berk came home over Thanksgiving holidays and announced the really good possibility that Ken Long from Bellingham, Washington, would be assuming the Vero Beach pastorate. Berk was elated, as Ken was one of his "golden-haired boys" from our Western Washington days. The church had big plans for a school much like Warner Academy, and they definitely wanted Berk on board for advice.

Back home for Christmas, Berk brought good news: Ken would definitely be taking the helm in Vero. Because of my work, Berk's short time off, and snow piling up in West Virginia, we did not visit the children for the holidays. We had just seen the family a few weeks before, when my brother Gerald had died on November 7. And Berk was preparing for his third mission to India with Howard Baker, to be gone three weeks from January 21 through February 17.

Although Berk's ministry opportunities frequently pulled him away from our home in Wichita, I was content there. I liked my job, I enjoyed tremendously my TLC group, the staff was like family, and the church was booming. It was a good place. And God surely knew when He sent us there that one day I would desperately need the strength of this wonderful congregation.

To Berquist from Berquist
12/14/91

I defy the doubtful watches.
I defy the prince of night.
I defy the threat of aging,
I step boldly in the light.

It is not the years that weary,
Nor the quiet pace of time,
Nor the work that looms before us
That ends our upward climb.

But I know of a river
That springs from deep within;
It defies the outward desert
And makes us new again.

Each day is filled with promise
And like children hard at play,
We run to meet the challenge
Of the mystery of today!

Wearing the ceremonial "garland of welcome," Berk takes a break with a glass of tea at one of three churches where he spoke on February 7, 1993.

Berk in India
1986, 1990, 1993

11
India

Berk was always excited about going to India. There was a lure, a "calling," that was hard for me to understand. I do know that he felt a great sense of accomplishment in going there – the needs were so vast and such gratitude was expressed for even the smallest effort. He basked in being able to minister to the people and their pastors.

We were living in Seattle when Berk started traveling with Howard Baker on regular trips to India. Their journey generally lasted three weeks. They traveled to Cochin for the annual Church of God Convention at the end of January. This large gathering, spanning three days, was open to all – including ministers, laymen, and women. Attendance usually ran between 800 and 1000.

After the convention Berk and Howard and whoever else might be traveling with them would visit various villages, holding two or three nights of evangelistic meetings at each one. Most places had no church buildings, so brush arbors designated the place of worship. Once they met in a rice field, with a brush arbor for the pulpit backdrop. Each night the audience in that place numbered from 5,000 - 10,000 people. A powerful amplifying system carried Berk's voice for miles, so that all who came could hear.

On one expedition, Berk became burdened to raise money to give bicycles to ministers who had no other mode of transportation. Buses did not run in many areas, and he noticed that many seemed to be arriving at the convention on foot.

When he asked P.V. Jacob, native leader in South India, how the ministers were getting to the convention site, P.V. confirmed Berk's suspicions.

"They walk," P.V. said, "some coming from as far as twenty miles away."

Back in the States, Berk raised enough money for 100 bicycles at $200 each to be purchased in India. On their next trip, in 1990, he was looking forward to seeing the ministers riding to the convention rather than walking, many of them barefoot.

A Ministry of Soles
"How beautiful are the feet of those who preach the Gospel." (Romans 10:15)

As Mahatma Ghandi stepped aboard a train one day in India, one of his shoes slipped off and landed on the track. He was unable to retrieve it as the train was moving. To the amazement of his companions, Ghandi took off his other shoe and threw it back along the track to land close to its mate. Asked by a fellow passenger why he did so, Ghandi smiled and replied: "The poor man who finds them lying on the track will now have a pair he can use."

In 1986 we were heavy into preparations for Berk's first journey with Howard.

175

While Berk was getting his tickets, visas, and passport in order, I was busy putting his clothes together. As wardrobe mistress for this global evangelist, it was my task to assemble light, washable, drip-dry, wrinkle-free, and serviceable clothing for his "flying ministry," with everything fitting into a 24" suitcase. I settled on gray and navy coordinates with touches of maroon, so that everything was interchangeable. When all the garments were assembled, I focused on shoes. He needed a pair of "preaching shoes" and a pair of walking shoes, as they would be walking quite a bit down dusty, unpaved roads and jungle paths.

He had bought new Nikes, but he needed dress shoes, preferably Hush Puppies in grey (so the dust wouldn't show). I searched the shelves at Nordstrom's, the Bon Marche and Penneys; but, alas, no size l2B was available. One day I decided to hit the outlet stores out at Southgate Mall. And there on a rack in Nordstrom's I found them – size l2B grey suede. Perfect!

Arriving home with this treasure, I proudly announced my find. Berk grinned an "I knew it" response, for he had often preached with pride about my "black belt" in shopping. As we were together sorting and folding the clothes to pack, I said to him most earnestly:

"Now, Berk, don't you give these shoes away. They are perfect for other trips on dusty camp grounds all over the country. These were hard to find; and, besides, what 'slight' Indian man could possibly fit into these gun boats?"

Berk had a history, long "before me," of giving his clothes to needy people before flying back to the USA from a missionary journey.

176

The Lure of India . . .

"Now, Berk, don't you give away these gray suede shoes," Berny had told him – hard advice to follow when leading a conference for ministers who walked many miles barefoot to attend.
Clockwise from far left: (1) Berk ready to travel; **(2)** Berk with Bible students at the convention in South India; **(3)** a roof-top service in Cochin; **(4)** Berk preaching with P.V. Jacob interpreting; seated: Dale and Marilyn Warman, travelers with Berk and Howard in 1990 to dedicate two churches they funded in honor of their parents; **(5)** ministers' conference; **(6)** young school girls with a meal of rice; **(7)** Berk speaks to Dale Warman as P.V. Jacob supervises preparations for laying the cornerstone for a new church.

His only response to my "wifely lecture" was a shrug.

Then, off he went, armed with the Gospel in his head and his coordinated wardrobe. I received glowing reports from him as he traveled those three weeks. Though the schedule was full and arduous, it was fulfilling.

I decided to surprise him when he returned to Seattle by meeting him at the airport. I rode the airport shuttle out and was standing at the gate smiling my brightest when he appeared. He was no walking advertisement for Brooks Brothers! Wrinkled clothes, hair standing straight up, and under each arm he was carrying a snack table top tied with ropes.

"Berk!" I called out.

Down went both tables and we hugged each other tightly.

As we hurried toward baggage claim, I noticed his shoes. His Nikes!

"Oh, no!" I exclaimed. "You gave away your Hush Puppies."

"Yes, I did," he replied gruffly; "and I don't want to talk about it!"

So I shutteth up.

Later that evening, after he had had a bath, a good nap, and we were eating our dinner, I said, "Okay, dear heart, tell me about the shoes."

"Well, we were in the Convention Assembly. Howard, P.V. Jacob, and I were on the platform waiting for the service to begin. The ministers were assembling slowly because of their modes of transportation. Some rode buses; some, old cars. Most came on bicycles, and some walked. There's no such thing as starting a service with all the delegates present.

"Deciding that we had better begin, P.V. rose to greet the audience.

"At that moment he noticed a certain minister who had been doing an especially significant outreach in his church. Thinking to have this brother pray the opening prayer, P.V. sent a runner down to bring him to the platform. After a whispered conversation between the runner and the preacher, the runner came back alone with this message:

"'Brother Jacob, the minister says he cannot come into the pulpit as he has no shoes. This platform is Holy Ground, and he does not feel he can pray here without shoes, especially in front of these American ministers.'

"At that Brother Jacob bent down, slipped his own shoes off, handed them to the man, and said, 'Take these to him.'

"Then the minister came striding forward in Brother Jacob's shoes and prayed the morning prayer."

Berk said he could hardly preach after that. And after the service, he gave his shoes to that minister.

"But, Berk," I finally stammered, "how do they make shoes like yours fit on such small feet?"

"Shoe shops there have toe and heel appliances that adapt," he answered.

In my mind's eye then there appeared a small Indian man – 5'7" or so – striding into his pulpit with size 12B Hush Puppies marching before him!

"The steps of a good man are ordered by the Lord: and he delighteth in his way."
(Psalm 37:23)

178

Whether speaking to a packed congregation, enthralling young and old . . . handing out Sunday school awards . . . trudging down dusty paths to preach in remote churches . . . dedicating a new parsonage funded by the Missionary Board for $1000 . . . or tooting his harmonica for the children – Berk loved it all!

Letter from India

Always on his journeys, to India as elsewhere, Berk wrote scores of letters to friends and sponsors back home. This letter written on January 20, 1986, captures some of his excitement about being in India and being a part of what God is doing there

India is a fascinating place, and this particular place (Cochin) is more than fascinating. As I sit here in the mission house in Cochin, the odors of night soil mingle with the fragrance of a thousand blossoms. The singing of the girls in the orphanage mingles with the honking of horns on the Delhi highway. Tiny ants swarm on the walls, and I try to forget the big roach I saw in the bathroom as I hung up my drip-dry shirt.

But you would love it. . . . We had a convention over the weekend, and I met about 80 of the 118 pastors in South India. . . .

Here in Cochin there are (1) a church, (2) a Bible training school, (3) an orphanage for boys and also for girls, (4) a home for destitutes – people rescued from the streets because of family rejection, (5) seven day schools with 165 teachers and 3000 students, (6) 118 pastors and congregations, (7) a printing instruction program and job printing, (9) a carpentry shop, (10) typing classes to help low caste and outcast girls learn a skill to get a job, (11) self-help farms, a rubber plantation, and other agriculture related training. . . .

I am up and ready for breakfast – tea and cornflakes with hot milk. Of course, all the milk we drink and the water we drink must be boiled; and I intend to watch that. So far, none of Pharaoh's revenge, or the curse of Krishna, or whatever it is called over here. . . .

Just wanted you to know that your prayers for me during these weeks are working.

Gotta go!

Love,

Berk

Of Bicycles and Rice

In 1993 Berk spent the early part of January working on correspondence and phone calls to his many sponsors about his return to India later that month. He was excited about seeing again the bicycles he had solicited funds for in 1990.

For this journey he felt led to provide rice for struggling seminary students, to help feed their families. Rice is their staple. Many WCG groups gave, as well as many individuals. Berk learned that in India rice could be bought in commercial 75-kilo bags (about 160 pounds) for $21.00. One bag would feed a family for about a year. Thus Berk wrote numerous letters to potential sponsors for the venture, soliciting funds for kilos of rice.

"It makes a 'swell' contribution!" Berk would say, chuckling at his own wit.

The minister in charge of the convention this year would be Dr. George Tharakan, who had assumed P.V. Jacob's position after P.V.'s untimely death in a car accident. Howard and Berk would miss P.V. He had been a great leader of the work in India, and a good friend. But they knew Brother Tharakan to be a capable leader who could lead the work forward.

I was able to take a few nights off to go with Berk to Kansas City for a weekend respite. Time was fast approaching for the India departure. We worked on wardrobe possibilities – the usual light weight garments and coordinates.

Berk got "all clear" readings on medical and dental check-ups. Dr. Jon gave him a cache of prescription medicines and wished him "Godspeed." At prayer meeting on Wednesday night before the trip, Mark had the ministers and lay people come to the altar and pray for Berk's journey and mission. Several gave rice money.

ABOVE: Top left: Berk displays one of 21 bags of rice sponsors bought for seminary students in 1993.
Top right and bottom left: In 1993 pastors in South India are making good use of the bikes Berk raised funds for after his 1990 trip.
Bottom right: Measure of a hand – Berk's and that of a child of India.

180

More than a preaching mission . . .
Meeting needs takes more than sermons and prayers. In India Berk demonstrated love in action through sermons, yes, and healing hands; but also through practical things like gifts of bicycles and rice.

ABOVE: Top left: Berk addressing the South India Assembly.
***Top Right:** Berk with national leader, Dr. George Tharakan.*
***Bottom left:** This elephant munching lunch outside the Mission House where Berk and Howard were staying not only found its way into Berk's letters home, but also sparked a sermon illustration.*
***Bottom Right:** Hiking back from one of the outlying churches where Berk preached one of his last sermons: on February 7, 1993.*

We spent Thursday morning packing and left home around noon to get him to the airport for a 2:00 p.m. flight. He wouldn't let me wait for the plane's departure, as I had been up all night and would be working again that night.

My friends Connie and Iris met him in Seattle, where he spent the night. The next day Connie put him on the plane. He called me before he took off – excited, rested. Singapore loomed ahead. Later, Howard would tell us that only Berk could get away with playing a harmonica on a 747 jet to combat the boredom of a seventeen-hour flight.

I was totally at peace with his going. I filled my nights with working, my days with sleeping, and my time off with TLC buddies. I received a letter Berk wrote en route to Seattle and two prose poems on a Delta napkin. The creative juices were flowing.

Several "rice donors" called to say that they, too, had received letters. Berk was feeling good and having a great time preaching, meeting the people, napping in the afternoons, and writing letters to thank friends back home for their support.

"Howard watches over me like a mother hen," he said in one letter.

Ten days into the journey, I baked cookies and bought Rock Cornish hens for the homecoming on February 17. It would be a late Valentine dinner. I had ordered a tie with books depicted on it for his Valentine gift.

During the week-end of February 6 - 7, I went on a cleaning spree, tidying up even the forbidden desk and office downstairs – where angels fear to tread.

On Sunday night, February 7, I had fallen into bed and was sleeping soundly by 11:00 p.m. The phone rang and rang. I groped for the light and saw that it was 1:00 a.m.

"It can't be a happy call," I thought, as my hand lifted the receiver.

My world of hopes and dreams was about to come to a sudden halt.

Monumental Joy

*The bronze plaque
says –
"Preach the Word."
Instead of a
monument to grief,
it is a monument
to joy!*

*Sunflowers on the
Kansas grave,
and the bronze plaque
will not show the world
that his work is
triumphant.*

*His ministry in
words and deeds
marches on –
For he will live
forever
in the lives of
those he touched.*

- Berny Berquist

12
Requiem

When I lifted the receiver, Pastor Ray Cotton was on the line. He said simply, "Berny, I have just received a call from Bettie Baker in Walla Walla, Washington. Howard has called her from India. Berk has had a stroke and it is rather bad. Howard wanted me to tell you and to come to your house, as he will be calling you in a half hour or so, and he wanted me to be with you."

With a pounding heart I dressed quickly and made the bed. It seemed only minutes until Ray was at the door. We prayed. I cried. And we waited. When the phone rang again, Howard was on the line.

"Berny, Berk has suffered a stroke, a cerebral hemorrhage. He had been doing great. Preaching the best! Resting well, exercising some, and taking his medicines. Yesterday was a wonderful day. He spoke three times and was in his element.

"After church last night we had a four-hour journey home by car. Berk was so happy! We sang all the way as we jostled along on the bumpy roads. I think he sang every Church of God hymn in the book, and for most of them he remembered all the stanzas.

"At one point I said, "Berk, I believe you're making up some of those songs."

"And he said, "I may be, but I'm having a good time."

"He slept well all night. At 6:00 a.m. a house boy brought our morning tea; and after drinking his, Berk went to shower.

"A bit later, I heard him stumble as he came back into the room; and I turned to see him slump over on the bed to one side with a dazed look on his face. I ran to him, realizing that something serious had happened. He could tell me his name, but his speech was slurred, and I could elicit little other verbal response. So I called the hotel desk for help. We transported him to the best hospital available. In half an hour he was unconscious. The hospital tests proved that he had indeed suffered a massive cerebral hemorrhage with total paralysis on the left side.

"He is on a respirator, and we have the best medical help possible. But he is losing ground. It does not look good. The doctors say he is 'brain dead.'"

I don't know what I said back. I numbly handed the phone to Ray, and the connection went bad. Ray prayed again. And then, as it was nearing dawn, he asked which of my lady friends would I like for him to send to stay with me.

"No one right now," I replied. "I need to call my children and brother and sister; then the Marvels and McCalls for prayer. But you can call Grace and some of my TLC girls, if you wish. I'll be all right."

I waited until he got out of the driveway before I screamed. I remember picking up the Bible and reading the 91st Psalm and crying aloud as I read Verse 10 – *There shall*

183

no evil befall thee, neither shall any plague come near thy dwelling" – and Verse 11 –
"For He shall give his angels charge over thee, to keep thee in all thy ways."

"Really, Lord?" I wept. "This is Berk's Psalm. This is your promise of immunity to him. What happened?"

"I am still here," He seemed to answer back.

I made my calls. The children were hurt and shocked. Gerald and Maxine both prayed over the phone for Berk and for me. And dawn had broken. Soon the house was bustling with my TLC girls – Melodee, Grace, Mary Jane, Joanie, Diane.

Hugs. Tears. Prayers. Coffee. And waiting.

George Skramstad came and took letters to be mailed. The phone had rung non-stop since 7:00 a.m. Pastors Ray and Mark arrived; and when I saw Mark's tears, I knew it was over. More tears and more prayer. The whole day was a daze – phone calls and visitors.

Journey Home

Ray had heard from Howard that it would be at least ten days before the body could be shipped home. So we didn't know how to plan a service or what to tell relatives or out-of-town travelers.

Pastor David Boots put a message on my answering machine stating that Pastor Berquist had passed away in India, memorial services were pending, and further information would be forthcoming. Central Community Church put one secretary on a special line to answer inquiries from out-of-town pastors and friends.

In this world of places where we have lived, I could not have chosen a place more special and precious than Wichita to have seen me through this valley. The pastors, the parishioners, the caring, the organizational qualities were unexcelled.

I was in a state of numbness, not knowing what I was doing or where I was going with my plans. But God provided guidance for me through the caring staff at Central Community, as He promised in Psalm 32:8: "I will instruct you and teach you in the way you should go; I will guide you with My eye." In particular, God used Mark Deffenbacher, our Minister of Administration, to steer me through innumerable decisions that had to be made.

By the time my children arrived, Mark had already called the funeral home to advise them of a pastor's death and the circumstances thereof. He also assured them that whatever my financial circumstances, the Church Foundation would back the costs until I was solvent.

Mark took Lori, Marty, and me to Rest Haven Memorial Chapel to select the casket and make other necessary arrangements to receive my beloved. We chose a sturdy oak casket and the proper vault.

Mark asked the funeral director, Mary Donovan, if it would be permissible to use their services for the funeral and a different place for the burial. Then he went on to explain, sharing something the children and I had not heard.

"We have grave spaces donated to Dr. Berquist through our Church Foundation," he said, "by Chuck and Donna Thomas at White Chapel Memorial Gardens."

Before Mary could answer, Marty, Lori, and I simultaneously burst into tears. It was a sign from Heaven! White Chapel was the church Berk had pastored for twenty-one years in Daytona Beach, Florida.

"Oh, yes," we said. And Mary Donovan agreed.

On Wednesday Mark called. "Berny," he said, "Howard has just called from India to tell you not to buy a casket, because the Indian brethren are making Berk one. He is too tall to fit in the Indian ones, so they have gone from parish to parish to collect money for wood and they are fashioning him a "custom made one."

"Oh, mercy! What will I tell Mary?"

"I'll call her and explain it all," he volunteered. "She'll understand."

"Well, tell her I do want the vault."

Marty and I went to Berk's closet and picked out a favorite outfit for burial. I chose to include his mother's Swedish Bible that she had brought with her via Ellis Island when she emigrated from Sweden. Inside it I placed a picture of all of us, including the grand-children. And in a pocket, I would tuck Berk's harmonica. He never traveled without it.

All we had to do now was wait.

By Friday Ray and the staff suggested that we move ahead to set the date for a memorial service, as so many from Indiana and other states had called. To further complicate the situation, there was an Air India strike, with no guarantee as to when the body would be transported. We set the date for Tuesday, February 16.

On February 13, I walked to the mail box and found there a letter from Berk.

He wrote, "I won't be home for Valentine's Day, so draw some money from the Berquist Books account and take someone you love out for lunch. Tell them it's from me and that I love them."

On the 14th, my children, their spouses, and my brother John went to Sunday morning services, then out to lunch. I watched everyone fumble for the check to see who should treat Mom. Then I grabbed it and said, "This is from Berk – and he loves you!"

With family and friends I shared letters and poems I had received from Berk earlier in his journey – each, like the Valentine note, written with the full expectancy of being home as scheduled on the 17th. With letters like these in my hands, how could I believe that he was gone?

On Monday, February 15, word came that the body had left Bombay and would arrive in Dallas on Wednesday night, the 17th. We scheduled a private interment for Thursday, February 18, at 1:00 p.m.

Howard Baker arrived with Berk's personal effects. What a treasure he was throughout this traumatic ordeal. What pain he suffered. A friend closer than a brother.

Wings

Wing it lady
Fly so high
Stars will marvel
As you pass by.

Let your dreams
Like rockets rise
Past the clouds
Of leaden skies

Leave behind
The plodding ways
Of those who never
Lift their gaze.

Break the chains
That bind your soul,
Let your spirit
Seek its goal.

As your happy Spirit sings,
I'll be the wind
Beneath your wings!

Berk

Written on a Delta Airlines napkin en route
to Seattle and on to Singapore
January 22, 1993

Celebrating His Life

Pastors George, Ray, Mark, and David planned a colossal home-going celebration for February 16 at 3:00 p.m.

Representatives from the Church of God Executive Offices in Anderson, former colleagues at CBH, state delegates, college presidents, friends from White Chapel, Vero Beach, and other places where Berk had preached or ministered braved the elements to be there to honor Berk and to support us, his family. Many others who tried to come were prevented by harsh winter storms that closed airports around the Mid-Western and Plains states. "Old Man Winter" had dumped six inches of snow over the weekend, and temperatures hovered around 15 degrees.

Berk's son-in-the-Lord, Gerald Marvel, delivered the eulogy, with other tributes spoken by Mark Deffenbacher, Ed Foggs, and Pastor Ray, who also shared a prose poem Marty had written. The service featured songs Berk loved best, including ones he had often heard his mother and father sing in Swedish during his childhood, old beloved hymns they had sung in Sweden. A moving two-minute video clip showed highlights of Berk's activities on his last mission to India.

After the service, out-of-town guests and relatives assembled in the church hall for a dinner prepared by the Women's Ministries.

Excerpts from Tributes Given at Berk's Memorial Service

Mark Deffenbacher: Welcome, in behalf of the family, to a celebration of the life of Maurice Berquist – author, pastor, evangelist, father, grandfather, husband, and affirmer for us all. Berk has touched the lives of people throughout the world, and I would like to share . . . just a few thoughts about him that have come to the family from people around the world:

From James Earl Massey, Dean of Anderson University School of Theology and Berk's colleague when they worked together for CBH: *"I admired his mind, his spirit, and I shall miss the intellectual camaraderie that we shared. We lived together, prayed together, planned together, and, perhaps soon, we will be together again. I look forward to that. Meanwhile, I mourn for you."*

From Mrs. P.V. Jacob of Cochin, India: *"We had a wonderful time with Rev. Dr. Berquist in our home during these last few days. I considered it a great opportunity to hear from him the last words of his inspiring message at the General Convention held in Ecclesia."*

And from Rev. George Tharakan, leader of the Church of God in South India: *"We express our deep sorrow in the sudden demise of our beloved friend, Rev. Dr. Berquist. He is a great man of God who loved the people of India more than his own life. He conquered our hearts with his simple behavior and lovely nature."*

Now, these words from Maurice Berquist himself as found in his book entitled *David's Song: The Amazing Secret of Psalm 23*: *"After a lifetime of following our Shepherd, the good news is that when death comes, we do not change shepherds; we merely change sheepfolds."* Let us now celebrate the life of our good friend Maurice Berquist, who has gone to another sheepfold.

Ray Cotton: Scripture tells us that "precious in the sight of the Lord is the death of His saints" (Psalm 116.15). And . . . this is a precious day as we come together to celebrate Berk's home going.

Some of us were concerned about Berk's going to India this last time; and yet . . . I don't think he would have had it any other way. . . . As Howard Baker, who was there with him, said, "I know that he was having the time of his life and was doing what he wanted to do, but, more importantly, what God called him to do."

Berk . . . was a great leader, because he could see things in a way so many people couldn't. Berk was not bound by traditions, by small thinking, by experiences, or by the past. He was always looking to the future.

Hillary Rice wrote in a letter to Berny: "I've known Maurice Berquist for over half a century. He was a maverick, and I love mavericks. He was a spiritual giant. I love spiritual giants. Maurice Berquist was an outstanding person . . . [he] had a heart for people everywhere."

Kerry Robinson . . . said in a note to the family: "We talk today about having 'a world view.' Maurice Berquist had a global view that began in the 1940's. . . ."

As Executive Director of the Mass Communications Board of the Church of God, [Berk's] most notable accomplishment was . . . the book and international television special *The Doctor Is In*, which he co-produced with Charles Schulz of *Peanuts* fame.

Also . . . an unforgettable preacher, his wit and humor charmed and enthralled, entertained, convicted, challenged, amused, and disturbed people all over the world. Of Berk's preaching, **Howard Baker** wrote: "Maurice Berquist had the unique ability to take the deepest theological concepts and translate them into every-day terms, even in countries like India or Africa, and still retain

The Service of Celebration
from death into life
for
MAURICE "BERK" BERQUIST
August 8, 1922 — February 8, 1993

Tuesday, February 16, 1993   Three-Thirty in the Afternoon
Central Community Church — Wichita, Kansas

A MEDITATION
Jesus said: "I am the resurrection and the life. He who believes in Me will live, even though he dies; and whoever lives and believes in Me will never die. Do you believe this?" John 11:25, 26
"For to me, to live is Christ and to die is gain." Philippians 1:21

THE PRELUDE .... Mary Eaton and Pastor George Skramstad, organists

THE WELCOME .... Pastor Mark Deffenbacher

A HYMN OF GOD'S PROVISION .... Hymn No. 461
"He Leadeth Me" - Bradbury

PERSONAL WORDS AND EXPRESSIONS .... Pastor Ray Cotton

A VOCAL SOLO .... Kim Noller
"Will There Be Any Stars In My Crown?" - Hewitt/Sweney

A UNISON READING .... led by Pastor Mark Deffenbacher
Psalm 91 - Responsive Reading #707

PERSONAL WORDS AND EXPRESSIONS .... Dr. Edward L. Foggs,
General Secretary of the Leadership Council of the
General Assembly of the Church of God - Anderson, Indiana

AN ANTHEM .... The Sons of Joy
"Grace Medley" - arr. Clydesdale
Michael Beaver; Larry Furnish; Ken Lygrisse; Dr. Ed Weippert

A VOCAL SOLO .... Pastor David Boots
"Wind Beneath My Wings"

their meaning." As **Berny** phrased it, "Berk didn't die with the music in him." He wrote nearly two dozen books and was working on several others, one of them being a book on Church Growth and Ministry, based on his experiences here at Central Community.

Berk was a great friend and encourager. . . . He loved people and he loved being around them. . . . He particularly loved pastors. Berk felt a keen sense of kinship with young pastors; . . . I would see him taking them under his wing, without their even knowing it – encouraging them, nurturing them, mentoring them – just as he did for me so many times. Berk was a mentor to so many of us. He was so perceptive. He could sense the situation, sense your need and your potential, and he would always have something good to give to you. It was those informal moments with Berk that I loved the best. It was fun to sermonize with him, to sit down and take an idea and develop it together.

He was so creative in how he communicated the Gospel of Jesus Christ. And somehow you could not be with Berk without feeling better about life and about yourself. Something about him forced you to stop being so preoccupied with your own little world and to remember to take time out to . . . smell the roses.

Berk wrote a lot of poems. In one of them he said:
So I will sing and I will play.
I'll try to live just for today.
I'll smile, whatever falls my lot,
Because today is all I've got.

THE MESSAGE .... The Reverend Gerald J. Marvel,
First Church of God, Pastor
Vancouver, Washington

A VOCAL DUET .... Marilyn Main and Kim Noller
"Precious Lord, Take My Hand" - Dorsey

A HYMN OF HOPE .... Hymn No. 493
"It Is Well With My Soul" - Spafford/Bliss
(sing stanzas 1, 3, and 4)

*THE PASTORAL PRAYER .... Pastor Ray Cotton

*AN ANTHEM .... The Voices of Central Community
"Hallelujah Chorus" (from The Messiah) - G.F. Handel

THE POSTLUDE .... Mary Eaton, organ

Pallbearers: David Boots, Marty Johnson, Blake LaMunyon, Kelly Landenberger,
Dale Lewis, Doug Peake, Kit Tabor, Dennis Turner

Honorary Pallbearers: Howard Baker, Ernie Gross, Dan Harmon, E.E. Kardatzke,
Arlo Newell, Forrest Robinson, Ken Tabor

Piano: Laura Bergquist

Attention: Family and friends from out of town are invited to a special dinner in
the Activity Center following the Memorial Service.

Pastor Maurice Berquist will be laid to rest at 1:00 P.M. at White Chapel
Cemetery on Thursday, February 18, 1993.

And I think he really lived that. Berk brought out the best in people; and I think that's why so many pastors and others looked to him not only as a mentor, but as a friend. . . .

When Berk traveled, which he did often, he always wrote notes to people in his church. Howard Baker observed that even with the heavy preaching schedule Berk had over in India, he wrote 52 letters that Howard counted. Today my secretary handed me a letter that came to me from Berk, one he wrote while he was in India. He said: "We feel that the timing here is excellent and we are able to be a blessing, so we are glad."

Finally, Berk was a great husband and father.

His son **Marty** wrote a little poem this past weekend, just recalling his dad. I want to share it with you. It's an imaginary phone call he is making to his dad up in Heaven:

Hello?
Hello . . . Dad?
Hi, Dad! Mom wanted me to call . . .
You know how she worries.

You sound great!
You got in when? Monday . . . about 10?
Is that Indian or Central Standard Time?
Time doesn't exist there . . .
I forgot.

Dad . . . Dad, can you turn down that music?

It's live?
Really . . . Sounds wonderful.

You got a what?
A new body?
You sound as excited as a little kid.
Same nose though . . . huh?
That's too bad.
It's great to hear you laugh again.

All those voices in the background . . .
They all know you?
That many friends . . . fantastic!
Better than you ever thought?
Now, that is saying something.

We have been what? Crying?
We've cried a lot, Pop.
We're thrilled for you, really . . .
But . . . it's all so sudden . . .

You have always been there to lean on . . .
You were the strength in our lives that never wavered . . .
That's all gone now . . .

We feel so alone . . .
And this hollow ache . . .
Who kisses that and makes it go away?

Your best friend promised to take care of us?
Completely?
Even our extended family?
Who is this guy? Give me a hint.

A Jewish carpenter's son . . . Of course.
It's just that He has been with us so long . . .
I guess I had started taking him for granted.
I'm sorry, Dad.
I think we know He loves us.

We really miss you, though . . .
You promise we'll get together some day?
I know, I know, it's not up to you.
We will do our best, Dad . . . we really will.
It might be a while, Pop, so don't wait up.
But stubborn Swede that you are, I'm sure you will.

What's that?
You've got to be going?
What? . . . Of course, I'll look after Mom.
She knows, Dad; she loves you, too.

I can hardly hear you, Dad . . .
We love you, Dad . . .
And we couldn't be prouder.

I can't hear you, Dad . . . Are you still there?
Of course . . . You'll always be.

Goodnight, Pop.
Goodnight.

- Marty Berquist
February 12, 1993

Edward L. Foggs: I am so grateful to be here this afternoon to share some thoughts about one whom we all esteemed so highly. . . . I first met Maurice Berquist when I was a student at Anderson College. I heard him speak in Chapel, and I never shall forget what he preached about: "Do Chistians Have Bad Dreams?" He was addressing the work of the Holy Spirit in the

[continued next page]

life of the believer. And it made an impact that has lived with me across these years.

I had the privilege of working with him closely as a leader in national church life. One thing was clear about Maurice Berquist: he was a man with a mission and with a ministry, and he did not see his assignment as chiefly pushing a pencil and shuffling papers. He was always about that which was creative in the life of the church. An imaginative and creative thinker, he had a way of taking simple things and giving them such meaning.

Every Monday all the agency staffs [in our building] come together for worship. One day Berk took a penny and several sheets of paper he had taped together, and he strung them out across the room and talked to us about investing that penny. If that penny had been invested at the time of Jesus, what it would be worth in the late 20th Century came out to be multiple trillions of dollars. Then, he went on, of course, to talk about investing our lives in the work of the Kingdom of God.

Maurice Berquist had a deep love and appreciation for the Word of God. I know of nothing he loved to do more than preach. . . . As Jeremiah said, "there was fire in his bones"; he loved to stand and proclaim the Word.

He had a keen sense of humor. Not all of us are gifted in communicating that which is serious in a way that we can both laugh about it and yet get from the "punch line" the meaning that was really intended. . . .

He had a Global Vision. He saw not just some small part of the Kingdom; but he loved the Church all around the world. . . .

He was a generous person. . . . On occasion he would walk up to me with a book he had been reading and comment about it and then say, "Here. Take it. It's yours."

And so today I am delighted to be a part of this celebration of the life of one who lived so well and who gave so much. In one way, his voice is silenced in death. But in another way, because he lived so well, "he being dead yet speaketh."

For myself and all of my colleagues and his colleagues in ministry, we join to say, "Well done." And may God bless our hearts with the memory of his life.

Gerald Marvel: God gave us Maurice Berquist and Berk gave God his life, and because of that we all walk closer with our Lord and Savior Jesus Christ. . . .

To talk about Berk's life is like going to the ocean with a little sand pail and trying to dip it empty . . . [his life] was so vast and so powerful and so penetrating. . . . His was a multifaceted life and was well done in all those facets. True of his life is the Scripture, "Well done thou good and faithful servant," for he was faithful to his vision; he was faithful to his call; and, most of all, he was faithful to Jesus Christ, his Savior.

Berk, always and forever, was the preacher. He started preaching in college as an evangelist; he preached in camp meetings and conventions; in seminars, city-wide crusades, and revivals in churches all across this land and, indeed, around the world. . . . Berk loved and was committed to the Chuch of God. . . .

Berk was a kind and tender husband and father. Berny, today I want to commend you in your marriage . . . for you had a unique compatibility that allowed him to be God's man . . . to all of us. It takes a special wife to be married to a man like that. And Marty and Lori . . . [he was proud of you] and loved you dearly. . . . You as a family are to be commended that you were willing to share him with a larger family, the Church.

Berk was also a student . . . truly, a genius. He had an extremely keen mind and . . . an insatiable quest for knowledge. . . . He read all the time . . . in every field. . . . And in everything he read he found concepts that could be used in ministry . . . particularly in preaching. He related everything in some way to preaching.

Also a student of the arts, he loved literature, especially poetry. He memorized hundreds of poems, and he loved to write poetry.

Berk was always a pastor. He loved people, he believed in people, he drew the best out of people, and he cared for people **everywhere** as a true pastor. Berk carried in his heart the needs of people . . . prayers for people . . . the sorrows and joys and thrills of people's lives . . . . Everything that people experienced, Berk experienced with them as a pastor. . . .

People treasure letters they received from Berk. My wife has every letter Berk ever wrote to her. He always started them the same: "My beautiful Rena." And Rena said to me, "You could take a note from that, Gerald, on how to address a letter to a woman."

Berk always remembered things about people individually. He never grouped people . . . or bundled them and labeled them. He took every person on his or her own worth.

Berk was a friend – best friend I ever had. . . . I first came in touch with Maurice Berquist when I was a sophomore in high school. He had just returned from a trip around the world and was preaching at the Oklahoma Youth Convention; and I went to hear this young man, who preached on faith. I remember going home from that convention thinking, "I'll never be a preacher, though I would love to be. But if I ever could be a preacher, I would want to be one like that man. . . ."

I have idolized Berk from day one to this very moment, and will as long as I live. . . . There has seldom been a month in my ministry that I haven't called Maurice Berquist just to talk. I remember as a young pastor in my first pastorate . . . being so frustrated. I said to him, "And another thing, Berk, about three of my church stalwarts sleep every time I preach." He said, "Don't worry about that, Fats (he always called me "Fats"); they trust you." So the next Sunday when I rose to preach and they checked out, I thought, "Check!" I've never forgotten that.

Berk gave good advice. When he was in our church, he often came to our first service at 8:30. . . . Then he would come hear me preach again, the same sermon, at 11:00. . . . Another preacher once said to me, "Aren't you intimidated with him in the congregation when you get up to preach?" I said, "Honestly, I'm not, for there is no man on earth pulling for me more than Maurice Berquist. . . ."

Berk was unconventional . . . unpredictable . . . and unpretentious . . . the only man I ever knew who could pull out a harmonica on a 747 flight and play "Stepping in the Light" and get by with it! And when he finished, he said, "Now get this, Fats"; and he played "What a Mighty God We Serve." I looked around – they would have had me arrested had I done something like that. But people were smiling knowingly, enjoying the thing. Totally unself-conscious, Berk was who he was, wherever he was, all the time.

His favorite poem was one by John Burroughs . . . that, for him, signified God's being in control of a person's life. He quoted it at your wedding, Lori. It also seems fitting for this day.

Serene, I fold my arms and wait, nor care for wind or tide or sea;
I rave no more 'gainst time or fate, for, lo! my own shall come to me.
I stay my haste; I make delays, for what avails this eager pace?
I stand amid the eternal ways, and what is mine shall know my face.
. . . .
The stars come nightly to the sky; the tidal wave unto the sea;
Nor time nor space, nor deep nor high can keep my own away from me.

And today he is with "his own."

So much of reality had not sunk in for me. I didn't see him sick or die. And, as yet, there was no body. I was in full denial. There I stood in my basic black dress with pearls, acting like the Jackie Kennedy of the Church of God, serenely poised in the receiving line and flitting from table to table at the dinner, hugging and greeting guests, while tears were raining on the inside.

Words of Kahlil Gibran echoed in my mind: "Your joy is your sorrow unmasked and the selfsame well from which your laughter rises is oftentimes filled with your tears."

The cellular phone rang in Mark Deffenbacher's pocket. He answered, then walked toward me as I sat with my family.

"Berny, that was Delta Airlines. We have a problem."

"They lost the body," I quipped. "Like Enoch, Berk has just walked away and was taken."

"No," he replied. "Delta can get it as far as Dallas tomorrow night, but no carriers that large come into Wichita. For you see, the coffin . . . it weighs 750 pounds!"

"How?" I exclaimed, my humor surfacing for a second. "He lost weighs before he left."

"I don't know," Mark continued; "but we have to send an ambulance down to Dallas to pick it up and bring it here."

A call to Rest Haven. Mary would send drivers down pronto and have him back in time for the burial. And it would only cost $500!

Well, I had saved on the casket.

On February 18 at 9:00 a.m., the phone rang. It was Mark.

"Berny, we have a slight problem."

"Oh, no," I answered, "he didn't get there."

"Yes, he is here. But I just got a call from White Chapel Memorial Gardens, and they wanted to know if you understood that a vault was included with the burial plot."

"Oh, my. What am I going to tell Mary? I've already bought and canceled a casket. Now I have to do the same with the vault."

"I'll take care of it," he responded.

My children and I continued our preparations to be ready at 12:00 to meet the church staff and my TLC ladies to go to the cemetery.

At 10:00 the phone rang. Mark again.

"Berny, we're at the funeral home – Ray, Howard Baker, Dennis Turner, and I. Berk is safely home . . . but we have a problem."

This time I had no quip. I just listened.

The Indian brethren did as good a job as they could, but the casket is too large for the vault, so the body has to be placed in another casket after all."

My tears flowed!

Mary Donovan had told us at the outset that, because of the long journey home and the less modern embalming and cosmetizing techniques of a foreign country, she would advise our not viewing the body. The children and I agreed.

Mark went on to say, "Berny, he looks really good. The casket is sealed, but there is a glass bubble top showing his face . . . and he fared well."

I listened as tears flowed to my collar.

"Well, tell Mary we need to buy the casket back. And Mark, how is he dressed? Marty and I picked out some clothes; but since I knew the casket would remain closed, we didn't send them."

"I wouldn't touch him," he replied. "The Indian ministers have dressed him in all white – a shirt and pants like they themselves wear. And they have draped a prayer shawl around his shoulders to symbolize a holy man."

"Well, he fell in battle for them. Don't touch him," I replied.

Lori had stood mutely by as I talked with Mark. After I recounted these latest developments to her, she said, "I hope Dad is enjoying all of this. Only he could orchestrate such a journey."

And we both smiled through our tears.

Later, as the family and I were riding to the cemetery with Mark, I asked him, "Why did that casket weigh so much? Was it made of stone?"

"No," he answered. "You're not going to believe it. We were all there when the

189

drivers took the 'box' out of the ambulance. The outer container was constructed of galvanized tin and fastened with large spike-type brads. The workers used a crowbar to pry it open and slide the coffin out. Inside the container, the coffin was emulsified with pounds of sawdust to protect it. When the job was done, the workers were covered literally from head to toe with sawdust! They had to use shop vacs to remove it."

That moment my mind traveled back again as I remembered Berk telling me how he, as a seventeen-year-old lad, had preached his first youth camp service on a sawdust floor at Goddard, Kansas. So . . . he started out on sawdust and ended up in sawdust. What a finale!

Directly behind the statue of Christ (above) stands a circle of cedars, fronted by a another statue of Jesus as the Good Shepherd (opposite page). Behind and to the right of that statue, marked by a vase of flowers seen through the trees, is Berk's resting place.

In the Garden of the Good Shepherd

The wind was up, as it can blow only in Kansas. The temperature was 18 above zero. Snow was over our shoe tops as we made our way from the cars to the gravesite. I held on to Ray and Mark as we stepped gingerly through the snow. Ray whispered, "Can we make this brief?"

"Please," I answered back, "even if you just say 'Jesus Wept.' We'll come back in the summer and have a good party for his birthday."

The committal was short. Then, we said final farewells to our sturdy oak.

I was alone in my thoughts.

I had stood by him, but never in his way. Words of Kahlil Gibran again came to mind:

> *And stand together yet not too near together:*
> *For the pillars of the temple stand apart,*
> *And the oak tree and the cypress grow*
> *not in each other's shadow.*

And now, the cypress must grow on.

My thoughts whirled as I retraced my footsteps to the car. And a favorite quote of Berk's came to mind – this from Thomas Wolfe's tombstone: *"The last voyage, the longest, the best. Death bent to touch his chosen son with mercy, love and pity, and put the seal of honor on him when he died."*

Berk's mission was accomplished. Mine had just begun.

Epilogue

Remembering that "a coincidence is a small miracle in which God chooses to remain anonymous," I marveled at these "coincidences" of Berk's home-going:

He was born on August 8 and died on February 8.

He was born in Topeka, Kansas; buried in Wichita, Kansas.

His first passport was dated 1947 – embarkation: India; his last passport, 1992 – embarkation: India.

His only pastorate was White Chapel in Daytona Beach; his final resting place: White Chapel Memorial Gardens.

One of his books, *David's Song*, tells of the Good Shepherd's everlasting love. The gravesite God chose for Berk through the generous love of some friends lies directly behind a beautiful, serene statue of Christ in an area of the cemetery called "The Good Shepherd Garden." A circle of trees – cedars of Lebanon, mute reminders of his many pilgrimages to the Holy Land – surround the gravesite, creating a private sanctuary. A simple bronze marker captures Berk's life-long passion and mission:

Preach the Word.

Encore

Not even the presence
of the coffin
under the canopy
spoke finality
to me.
My mind beneath
its false acceptance
could not bid
farewell.

Presently
his quiet limbs
will stir,
I thought,
in my pain of denial.

He had simply walked
across the stage,
played well his part,
and bowed to his
last curtain call
with great
aplomb!

And I, in the audience,
front row, as usual,
was the first to rise
for the standing ovation,
as I yielded him to
Heaven.

Berny Berquist
July 1994

The Main Event
This Is It!

Berk was a traveling man, so our correspondence was vast. And interesting.

Some of my main sources for stationery headings were from the comics and cartoons from magazines. One time I clipped a cartoon for him from an issue of *Good Housekeeping*. It depicted a bride on her wedding day walking down the aisle on her father's arm, heading for the altar under a wedding canopy. She was in full bridal regalia – the satin dress, train, and veil attached to a tiara. But the tiara was perched on top of hair curlers about the size of soup cans. The father's look registered protest.

The caption underneath said, "But, Daddy, I want to look nice for the reception."

I sent it to Berk, because he hated hair curlers. Early in our marriage he wrote "Beauty Shop" in our budget. And it seemed to him that our daughter Lori spent half her life putting up and taking down her hair.

As soon as the missive arrived, he called me.

"Honey," he said, "I just got your letter, and I have the greatest sermon illustration. It's a classic!"

"Oh? I just thought it was funny because of Lori's curlers," I answered.

"No, that's not it," he said.

"You see, this is the most important, the happiest day of a girl's life, when she is her most beautiful. There she is at the ultimate moment, and **she doesn't know it**. She's waiting for the next event, not realizing that **this is it! This** is the time to take her hair down.

"That's a whole sermon.

"People spend their entire lives waiting for the right time – saving up for that trip . . . that car . . . that house . . . for retirement – and they don't know how to seize the moment. When it comes, it's too late. The time is now!

"A surfer waits for the perfect wave and misses some good ones while waiting for the great one to come along. Do it now – while you can. That's the message.

"The reception is now."

I was pleased to have given him such a good illustration. And he did preach on it many times, encouraging people not to plan so far ahead that life passes them by while they are waiting for a bigger event.

It's strange how a mind works. So many times a wild thought will surface at an inane moment. It often happened with Berk and me. We were both blessed with merry hearts, and our sense of humor often brought us through the worst to the best of times. We were each other's best audience, and sometimes we didn't dare look at each other, lest mirth should erupt inappropriately.

That cold day in February, 1993, I walked an aisle of snowy footsteps, holding on to two pastors' arms, as I approached the canopy where the casket awaited. Pastor Mark looked down at the snow covering my patent leather pumps, and said, "Berny, your feet must be freezing. Don't you have any boots?"

"Yes," I replied.

Then suddenly, out of nowhere, I heard myself saying, as I looked up into the blue sky and smiled, "But I wanted to look nice for the reception – Berk's reception."

This is it!

From Tears to Triumph
Berk's Legacy

Three weeks after Berk's death my door bell rang; and when I answered it, the mail man stood there.

"Mrs. Berquist," he said, "Have you had a sorrow? Did that nice man die? I have never delivered so much mail to one house, even at Christmas."

In a month's time, I had received over 500 letters and cards.

"Yes," I replied, "he passed away on the 8th while on a mission to India."

"He was a prince. He came out of the house on Christmas Eve as I was delivering mail and asked me to wait a moment. He then dashed into the garage and brought me a book he had written about blessing people and also handed me a $20 bill and said, 'Bless you, my friend, and Merry Christmas.' That was the last time I saw him."

In the weeks and months after Berk's death, the children and I found solace and strength in the countless kindnesses shown to us by the Central Community Church family and through the mountain of cards, letters, and the many phone calls of love and encouragement that poured in from around the world.

Mid-America Bible College expressed an interest in becoming the repository for Berk's extensive library. Over the years he had collected thousands of books. He had given away hundreds of them, but the rest moved with us from Daytona to Anderson to Seattle, to Portland, to Wichita. I asked Maxine McCall to come help me sort through Berk's papers and to box up hundreds of books to ship to Mid-America. In addition to housing the Berquist Book Collection, Mid-America established a scholarship in Berk's honor. The college also furnished Maxine tapes of the preaching seminar Berk and Gerald Marvel did for the college in 1988, as she undertook to complete for Berk the manuscript he had begun on preaching: *A Handful of Stars*.

In Berk's files we found chapters he had written for at least a half-dozen other books: *Paul's People Principles*; *Principles of Prosperity from Proverbs*; a sequel to the *Miracle and Power of Blessing*; *The Sensuous Bible* (using the senses to more fully understand the Scriptures); *Keep It Simple, Williams* (angel letters to a new convert); an untitled piece about *"power principles"* affecting work in the church; another on *"church growth"* (based on experiences and observations in Wichita).

Berk's mind never stopped working. Even on those rare occasions when we went on vacation, he was forever scribbling ideas on yellow pads or pounding the keys of a cheap little typewriter he'd pick up at a sidewalk sale or flea market. There was comfort in knowing that his fertile mind had planted all around the world seed thoughts of these and countless other God-given concepts – life-changing ideas that had taken root in younger minds, inspiring them to be more effective workers in God's Kingdom and to grow "thought gardens" of their own.

Tributes that poured in after his death, as well as some we had kept from earlier times, gave testimony to the powerful and lasting effect Berk had on people's lives. Here is but a sampling of those tributes and fond memories:

There was a commotion in Heaven as a legion of angels departed, ordered by God to India, to the bedside of a great saint, Maurice Berquist. In the hospital room angels watched in love as the doctors worked feverishly. Suddenly the archangel at the bedside nodded. The angels hurried back to Heaven. And after a final look, the archangel moved with the speed of a thought to the throne of God. Bowing low, he smiled.

The Father of all creation turned to His right. Immediately Jesus arose. In an instant He entered the hospital room of His friend Maurice with whom He had spent many happy hours. Jesus moved to the foot of the small bed and, ignoring the doctors and nurses, reached out His hand, which Maurice grasped eagerly.

As they started to leave, Maurice looked back for an instant. The emergency crew was still working, but it was over. Together

Christ and Maurice moved to the Gate of Death, where Satan stood cursing in rage and anger. As Jesus and Maurice started through the gate, Maurice, being the humorist he always was, shouted in Satan's face, "Old devil, long since I told you so. Where now is the sting of death . . . where the victory of the grave?"

Then, still grasping the hand of Jesus, his longtime friend, Maurice stepped through the gates of pearl onto the street of transparent gold to be carried away to the door of his mansion at the corner of Eternal Joy and Rejoicing streets.

Jesus spoke as they stood by the door: "Maurice, it's true. You ran a good race; you finished your course; you have won it all. Enter into the palace prepared just for you since the beginning."

With a smile and a wave of his hand, Maurice stepped inside. AMEN.
    - Ken Tabor

Songs of Love and Grief

One way Berny worked through the grieving process was by writing poetry. Over the years she and Berk had exchanged poems – not only on special occasions, but as little surprise tokens of affection that she might tuck into his suitcase or he might attach to her pillow, to be found when she returned home after a night shift of nursing.

Pulling together his poems to her and writing new ones of her own brought both comfort and healing for a loss too deep to express any other way. I asked her permission to share some of these, for the insight they give into the great love they shared, and also for the universal feelings they contain of love and loss. MM

Good Morning, Magnolia
The sun has come out,
The choice is before me
To smile or to pout.
I could try to match
Tom Selleck for looks,
Don Trump for money,
James Michener for books.
But instead, I'll just boast
About my cute wife,
To whom I am married
Most of my life.
Wallpaper or collards,
Or designer clothes –
What she is up to,
Nobody knows.
Love,
Berk

(Berk often called Berny "Magnolia" – both delicate and strong.)

How do I know who I am
Without you?

A hand is made for touching
And until it clasps a hand
How does it know what it is?

An eye is made for seeing
But until it looks steadily
Into another's eyes
How does it know what it is?

A heart is made for loving
And until it finds
Its love returned,
Can it know it is a heart?

You are the mirror
In which
I have found myself.

Berk

Did Martha wear a bow-tie
And an apron edged with frills?
Or did she wear a housecoat
And dust the window sills?

Did Mary cultivate her mind
And don a "holy look,"
So busy with her high I.Q.
She never learned to cook?

How blest I am, mortal man,
How blest I am to find,
A wife with Martha's cooking skills,
And Mary's brilliant mind.

MB

Dusting Prayer

Often when I dusted I would change
The placing of a picture or a chair
And wait his cheery admiration, hoping
He would say: "Oh, that's pretty there."

He said I had a way of bringing beauty
To the barest place; and however much
Of loveliness a room might claim, it gained
In warmth and decor from my touch.

But now . . . I hardly change a thing –
Each chair and picture stays in place,
For I have only the echo of his words
And a million memories of his face.

Perhaps I've erred, but who is there to say?
For time and time again, I breathe a prayer
That soon I'll see him smile and hear him say
That Heaven is lovelier, because I'm there.

BB

It was a sad and lonely day,
When the loved one flew away.
As a world pushed us apart,
I felt the anguish in my heart.
Half of all my life is gone,
A crippled man must carry on!
Half of what I thought was me,
Has for the moment ceased to be.

Maurice Berquist

This poem – one of two written for Berny on a Delta Airline napkin enroute to Seattle and from there to Singapore and India, January 22, 1993 – took on a prophetic meaning after his death.

Is this, then, "good-bye"? – this empty aching,
This feeling of despondency and loss,
As if we two were walking side by side,
And suddenly the earth has opened wide,
And swallowed you – as if from deep sleep,
I stretch my hand to you and, in despair,
Find only emptiness and silence there?

So, this is "good-bye" for now,
And as my heart is breaking,
I clasp your invisible hand,
And smile into remembered grey-blue eyes,
Then, turn and go my way,
As you went yours,
Saving my tears to shed behind closed doors,
Uncertain as to the road I'll be taking,
But knowing as I look back,
I shall see your silent presence
Still keeping step with me.

Berny Berquist
February 1993

For Berk

I would not have you back on earth,
Your body racked with pain –
I know that longing for your mirth,
Your companionship, is vain.
And yet, when I sit wondering
As night is merged with day,
It seems your spirit comes to bring
The words you cannot say.

Berny

I learned just tonight of Berk's passing. I am a bit stunned. You see, "I take Berk with me" many times as I minister to people. Sometimes it's his humor. (Just last Sunday night I referred to his quip about Paul's thorn in the flesh: "**Grace** is good enough for you!") More often it's some insight he shared with me at one time or another. I have learned more really profound, practical things from Berk than from anyone I've ever known . . . since childhood.

It was Berk who taught me to be myself in the ministry. It was Berk who taught me how to minister to, and with, what he called "power people" in the church. It was Berk who gave me the courage to break the bonds of tradition which had limited my effectiveness early in my ministry. I owe him a lot. . . .

I will also smile as I recall good times and funny expressions – like his reference to the "single sock eater," that menace in the washing machine and in the church.　　**- Will Hughes**

A devoted disciple of Jesus, an ardent gospel worker, an eloquent speaker, a prolific writer, Rev. Dr. Morris Berquist, the apple of our eyes is now no more. The sudden and unexpected departure of the divine from this world of mortality to that of unalloyed celestial happiness and glory has thrown us into a world of loss, of grief, and of vacuum. While he was with us during the general convention, he enriched our knowledge of biblical truths with his rare skill in unravelling their mystery. . . .

A man of strong physique and dynamic personality, of prophetic vision, of unequalled intellectual powers, Rev. Berquist evinced uncommon biblical fervour in his speeches at convention meetings and unparalleled skill in expressing his ideas. He rendered meritorious service to the Church of God in South India, sacrificing his precious time, health, wealth, and even his life, and this deserves to be written in "letters of gold' on the pages of the history of the global Church of God.　　**- Rev. D. S. Dass**
In a letter to Howard Baker
from Kerala, South India

I t was with deep regret that we received the news of Berk's death. . . . It seems like only yesterday that you arrived in Tulsa in that '55 Chevy pulling the travel trailer, and I backed it into our backyard and hooked you up to our sewer and water. Marty almost cut a tooth gnawing on my thumb.

Our Gary woke you up rather early one morning as he went around the yard calling for his little turtle. "Turtle! Turtle! Berk never forgot that. He said he could just see that turtle, with squinched up face, calling back, "Boy! Boy!" . . . .

In Goshen, IN, one evening we answered a knock at the door, and there was Berk, looking for a place to spend the night. The next morning after he left, we found a pair of socks he had left.

I also remember chauffeuring you and Marty to Kansas to pick up Berk from a meeting. We were eating lunch when Marty knocked over a glass of water across the table toward me. I was out of the booth in a flash – didn't get a drop on me. And Berk said, "You can sure tell Tom is a father with reflexes like that!" . . . .
　　- Tom and Mary Lee

M ontreat will never be the same without "Berk" We looked forward each year to being in his conferences. He always saw the funny side of things. But in addition to making you laugh, he could also be serious and bring tears to your eyes.

Berk, we will miss you; we have lost a "Dear Friend."
　　- Virginia Blevens

O ver a lifetime Dr. Maurice Berquist has been an incomparable friend to thousands around the world. For years to come he will be thought of with deep admiration and appreciation.

His career as a preacher, evangelist, and leader has been a phenomenal journey of faith, hope and love, giving help and encouragement to so many.

Dr. Berquist was a VOICE; most of us are echoes.

He was an ORIGINAL; most of us are copies.

We shall long be indebted for his Christian world view. He articulated the Christian world view as the interest in persons and the positive affirmation to human life and culture which derives from the Christian faith. Always, he believed, it shares with others the motive of discovering and supporting whatever enhances human existence, but is distinctive in finding the source and goal of human powers in God, the Creator, Redeemer, and Spirit.

Dr. Berquist held a deep conviction that while secular forms of humanism focus on "merely" human interests, deliberately excluding transcendent factors from consideration, the Christian world view seeks an understanding of the whole range of human experience in the light of God's revelation to humanity in the person and work of Jesus Christ, whom he served so faithfully.

We shall always be encouraged by his benediction:
"The Lord watch between you and me,
while we are absent one from the other."

– E. Joe Gilliam

I trusted Berk in major decisions. I have continued to look to him, to this very day. The church has lost a pillar. I have lost my mentor. The Lord willing, I will be able to pass on to others what was passed on to me by a faithful, reliable man of God.

"And the things you have heard me say in the presence of many witnesses entrust to reliable men who will be qualified to teach others." 2 Timothy 2:2.　　**– Ken Long**

T he fact that people called him "Berk" says so much. He made you feel comfortable enough to call him "Berk" – not "Dr. Berquist"! Many learned Bible scholars and teachers who have a "Dr." by their name want you to use it, and you would not dare call them by their first name, let alone a nickname.

Berk's Bible teaching was simple, but profound. He taught deep Biblical truths, but never got you lost in theology. You could relate to his message, and you would remember the lesson because it was so easy to understand – like The Doctor Is In, with the simple Charlie Brown characters used to illustrate the book.

I remember the many "drawings" Berk used with his lessons. He would always laugh about his "art," but he was a wise man – he knew that people remember what they "see" more than what they hear . . . it sinks in.

In preaching, he would often read a passage of Scripture to put the message in context. But then he would pick out a single verse or phrase – something you could remember – and focus his sermon on that one thing. I remember him preaching one night in Drexel [NC] on Ephesians 3:20: "Now unto him that is able to do **exceeding abundantly above all that we ask or think**, according to the power that worketh in us . . . ." What a sermon!

– Helen Clarke

Dr. Berquist was an extraordinary personality . . . . His ability to put deep theological concepts into everyday terms helped him simplify and relate answers to the complexities of life, to help people live a meaningful life in harmony with others, whether they live in India or Africa or in the United States. All of us can also testify that Dr. Berquist never spoke a negative word about others.

Like ABRAHAM, he went where he was called, and was faithful in all things.

Like MOSES, he led the people of God from doubts and fears to confidence for success in the face of any difficulty.

Like JONATHAN, he met many a discouraged brother, and cheered him by giving him strength from God.

Like DAVID, he sang the church to victory, and shouted in the battle of blessed triumph.

Like ISAIAH, he constantly pointed the church to brighter days and better things in the future.

Like DANIEL, he was true throughout life to the teachings of his boyhood days.

Like MALACHI, he believed in bringing all the tithes into the storehouse.

Like JOHN THE BAPTIST, he delighted to cry out to the multitudes around the world, "Behold the Lamb of God."

Like JOHN, he believed with all his soul that Jesus Christ was the Son of God, as was evidenced in his last message, taken from the Book of Isaiah, Chapter 53, and Luke 3:4-6.

Like PETER, he honored the Holy Spirit by teaching the doctrine of the operation of the Divine Holy Spirit upon the souls of men.

Like PAUL, he rejoiced that Jesus Christ died for all men; and he was willing to go into all the world to tell them.

Like JESUS, his Divine Master, whom he followed daily, "he went about doing good."

Like ENOCH, "he walked with God, and he was not, for God took him."

– Howard Baker

Maurice Berquist was a visionary. The openness of his theology was unique. He had a broad view of the Christian concept – his concept was of a loving God who embraced all people.

His concept of education was to provide quality education in a very moral climate, but not strictly to evangelize through education as many Christian schools attempt to do.

In the early days of Warner Christian Academy, he sometimes dozed off during conversations because he had foregone sleep to visit the sick or counsel the distraught – whether they were church members or not.

– Reid Hughes

I enjoyed listening to Dr. Berquist while in Kerala. God's message through Dr. Berquist was so deep in thought and expression, and I could feel it came out of his great sense of humility and rich experience in his ministry for the Lord. Truly he worked for God till the last of his breath. I am sure he must have loved India so much that he chose to come for his last trip to this land of ours.

Even though I met Dr. Berquist only that time in Kerala, yet I could see he was a very sincere worker and a humble man of God, and I was very much impressed and inspired. He shall remain as a symbol of inspiration to us here in India, and our hearts shall be the living tombstone inscribed with the name of Dr. Berquist. The Crown of Glory is waiting for Dr. Berquist in Heaven.

- Rev. S. Dexter Kharmawphiang
In a letter to Howard Baker from Meghalaya, India

Years ago at the Oregon camp meeting was my first introduction to Maurice Berquist and his unique preaching style. . . . I can still remember clearly several of the messages he preached that week, like the one about the danger of "doing your own thing" and another in which he illustrated salvation and the advocacy of Christ with a folding chair.

During the morning sessions Berk shared about blessing. I sat with my mouth open hearing him recount with obvious delight the story of the poinsettia which responded to a positive attitude (and an occasional glass of iced tea). That material became the book I still enjoy reading.

When we later pastored in Lake Wales, I was on the mailing list for your church newsletter from South Daytona. Many weeks Berk's column was my life line to God. I was young and inexperienced. His freedom to be himself in spite of how others may have perceived him was always helpful. His ability to find spiritual truths in the most unlikely and commonplace events was a gift.

– David Shultz

When I was a teen in Sikeston, Missouri, and at East Prairie Camp Meeting, Berk greatly influenced my life with sayings like, "If you don't make a plan for your life, then you will become the victim of the first person who has a plan." His messages helped guide and shape my life and gave me a vision for the future.

Now in full-time Christian service, having the privilege to work alongside him at Vero Beach has meant so much to me personally. Maurice Berquist's ministry and life have been deeply implanted in many of us . . . and his heart will continue to live in us for many years to come. **– Mark Shaner**

Brother Berquist has always been a part of my life. He was my pastor in Daytona Beach from the time I began going to church as a baby until I was 17 years old. . . and he is greatly responsible for the person I am today. . . .

At Warner Christian Academy we had the privilege of learning from Berk seven days a week. . . . More than my pastor, more than my principal – he was my friend. Through the pivotal years of high school, his influence kept me striving to be what God would have me be.

It was Berk's referral that helped me come to Sneads Ferry, NC, my first pastorate. . . . I will always treasure the camp meeting he held for us in May, 1992. I had Berk in Sneads Ferry for a week and only had to share him with a typewriter he was using to write his latest book. He took the opportunity to give me a three-hour crash course in homiletics. The wisdom he shared greatly changed the way I approach the ministry and preaching. I am certain that I learned more in those three hours than I did in my last year of college.

I will treasure my last memories of Berk. I saw him while attending the "Church Growth Seminar" in Wichita in October, 1992. As I visited with Berk and Berny in their home, along with Maxine McCall and Brian Hogan, I couldn't help feeling the unity we all shared. It was more than friendship; it was the unity of serving and giving our lives to the work of God.

I will greatly miss Berk, but I know that his ministry lives on through his books and, more importantly, through the lives of the people he touched. I thank God for Brother Berquist. May we all learn from the way he lived. **– Gary Garmon**

My favorite adult when I was a child was my Uncle Berk. As a missionary evangelist before he married my Aunt Berny, he traveled to exotic places around the world preaching the gospel of Jesus Christ. Once he brought my two sisters and me bracelets from Siam and my brother a leopard skin wallet from Africa.

Although most people considered him homely with his big ears, long nose, disproportionate face, and tall lanky frame, I thought he was beautiful. His example taught me that inner beauty was much better than outer handsomeness. I loved his kind quiet manner, his soft gentle blue eyes with their affirming look, his engaging smile, and his blond hair that disclosed his Swedish ancestry.

After he married my Aunt Berny and they had two children, . . . he took a pastorate . . . in Daytona Beach, Florida. There also my family moved in 1960, when I was an impressionable thirteen. Every Sunday for the next two years, I sat spellbound by his unique sermons in the congregation at White Chapel Church of God. He was a great storyteller who could find a sermon illustration in anything from telephone lines to a pebble on the beach. He showed me that serving the Lord was not just an exciting way to live, but the only way to have a fulfilling life; and I dreamed of marrying a man just like him when I grew up.

As a minister/missionary/writer, he was a quiet, contemplative person, very hardworking and preoccupied with his thoughts, spending many hours studying in addition to counseling others. The hand of God had to be protecting him to do the work he was doing. For example, once when my sister and I walked to his house after school, he took us home. He had been working very hard for long hours and was exhausted when he drove us about five miles across the city on a typically hot Spring day in Florida. As he drove, he began to nod. My sister and I watched his eyes close and his head drop several times, but he drove steadily on, never missing a traffic light, never weaving to right or left, never missing a turn. Sometimes his eyes seemed to be closed for blocks at a time. My sister and I nudged him a few times, and he would open his eyes and smile and mumble something about being sleepy. We were too reticent to make a commotion to get him awake. I was terribly relieved to see our house finally come into view. When we ran inside we told our parents that God must have driven us home, because Uncle Berk slept most of the way. That was only one of many times God protected him until his work on earth was finished.

– Zola Noble
Written for an assignment in a writing class
a couple of years before Berk's death.

No role was too small for Dr. Maurice Berquist, founder of Warner Christian Academy and pastor of White Chapel Church of God in South Daytona for 21 years. . . .

Transients would stop daily at White Chapel for food, gas, bus money, etc. Rev. Berquist had told his staff always to show such people to his office, and they never left empty-handed. Often he took funds from his own pocket, seldom using the expense account.

As a counselor, he seemed always to have someone waiting to see him. People who were hurting took priority. He was a patient listener. His genuine compassion caused him to empathize. He ended each session with a prayer that touched hearts and heaven.

It was my privilege and honor to work by his side each day as the administrator of his church and of Warner Christian Academy. We who have known and loved "Berk" have been enriched by our relationship, by his messages, his writings, and his life. His ministries salvaged thousands of lives and homes.

– Jim Rudolph

In Japan people are the most valuable of all national art treasures. We in the Church of God have in Maurice Berquist a true international art treasure.

He was a pioneer. He was a jet-setter before the term was coined – as usual, ahead of his time. For years he carried a key to our home, coming and going in the middle of the night – many times going to preaching missions and missionary journeys that carried him around the world.

Those missionary journeys brought him into an experience with the gift of languages before **that** term ever became controversial. His superior intellect, his spiritual compassion, and his intuitive understanding of the people, coupled with the spirit of the Lord, gave him a comprehension of most languages in the countries where he traveled. It was this comprehension which enabled him to minister more effectively than perhaps any other man in our communion, in like circumstance.

These same qualifications led many of us to believe he was "spaced out" even before that term was originated. He saw things we did not see – he frequently lived on a plane we could not understand.

He thought thoughts that were beyond our imaginations, and then he brought all of these things into simple words that caused us to dream our own dreams and, through God's Spirit, helped light fires in our own hearts.

So, Berk, on this warm afternoon of June 19, 1984 – we hereby salute you and declare you to be an art treasure in the Kingdom of God.

– Doug and Laura Lee Oldham
Presented in 1984 at a banquet honoring Berk
for his service to CBH ministries

Berk. That's all you have to say to thousands of people all around the world to conjure up an image of a friend.

Berk . . . head cocked to one side, a wry smile and sparkling eyes, as he took his time waiting for the exact words to open a conversation or humorously put you in your place.

Berk . . . preacher, counselor, author, poet, world-traveller, dreamer, philosopher, husband, father, friend.

Berk . . . compassionate, generous, persevering, intelligent, well-read, witty, loving, and the list goes on.

Anyone closely connected to CBH has experienced Berk, and that is one of life's treasures. He was one of the instigators and great supporters of our Bible Conference at Montreat, and all alumni of Montreat know that it will never again be quite the same. Just last September we had the delight of honoring Berk and celebrating his 70th birthday during that conference. I'm so glad we did.

He worked diligently to initiate our Russian broadcast. It had been almost twenty years since our first foreign broadcast, CBH-Spanish, was begun. His dream and efforts to produce a broadcast that would reach into then-Communist U.S.S.R. were brought to fruition in 1984, and that accomplishment led to a new excitement and new frontiers in the CBH ministry. In rapid succession since then we have added Arabic, Portuguese, Indian, Chinese, and Swahili broadcasts. And the dream goes on. . . .

Maurice Berquist has ministered in so many ways, to so many of us. Our loss is great.

Goodbye, friend. Our consolation is that we'll see you later.

– Dwight Dye
Berk's successor as agency executive
for Mass Communication ministries
of the Church of God (Anderson, IN)

I have many memories from my time of working with Berk at CBH. Berk was the smartest person I ever had the privilege of working with and also the humblest. He has probably influenced my life more than any other person. I will forever be guided by the simple faith that he had in the Lord. He simply took God at His word – believed it, preached it, and practiced it.

More than once people told us we would never pull off the television special, but we always stuck together and believed God would see us through. And He did. In airing the special, we almost went broke with success. To gauge the number of viewers, extend help to viewers, and provide local congregations a list of names and addresses for follow-up – we offered a complimentary copy of the book, The Doctor Is In. Each responder to the 800 number cost us $1.00. The "experts" told us to expect between 15,000-20,000 responses. We had more than 70,000 calls! Thus, we actually had to cancel some air time buys to pay for the responses.

While producing and promoting the television special, we were on a grinding schedule. And Berk was working long hours writing books for the Library for Living series, to raise additional funds to buy television time. Consequently, he fell asleep easily – even in Board meetings. One time we were meeting with a salesman in Berk's office; and while the salesman was making his presentation to us, Berk fell asleep.

Berk had a reputation for being "absent minded." And, from time to time, he would do something to earn his reputation. One day we received a package at the office. When we opened it, we found one of Berk's shoes. He had left it at one of his speaking engagements.

Berk hated to say "no" to anyone, particularly if it was an invitation to speak or teach. Because of that, and his lack of attention to details, he was constantly double-booking himself. I ended up with many speaking assignments because of this.

One of the hardest things I ever did was to teach Berk how to use a computer. He was determined to learn how to use one, but he was so "right brained" that it was absolutely comical sometimes – other times, it was just pure frustration.

Berk used to joke about singing the same way he preached – "without notes." We had a tape in the office of one of his speaking engagements where the sound man did not shut off Berk's microphone during the altar call hymn. We used to play it in the office when we needed a good laugh.

Helping to edit most of the manuscripts Berk wrote during the four years we worked together was a great privilege and learning experience. He would get more ideas and sermon illustrations from a walk around the block than most of us will get in a lifetime. We would both look at the same things, but he would get so much more out of them. He truly looked at things through the eyes of Christ.

– Gary Moore
Reflections from his years as Berk's associate
in the Mass Communication office, 1980 - 84

B rother Berquist had many gifts – his great intelligence, his ability to present the profound in a way that even the most unlearned could understand and remember; the ability not only to preach and teach, but to write. And how thankful we are for his gift of praying for the sick. He once said that the people he liked to pray for best were children and those in a coma. That really said something to me about how we, as adults, limit God.

But the quality that endeared him to so many was his genuineness. He was "real," and he had the ability (often with humor) to help us as Christians see our areas of – to coin a word – "fake-ness."

– Bertha Sue Deal

O ne of his many contributions, and one that might be easily overlooked by the larger church body, was Maurice Berquist's ability to be a mentor to others. . . .

As a young pastor, in 1986, I was glad for an opportunity to be in the company of Maurice Berquist. He and I were traveling, by car, from the Billings, Montana, airport to Sheridan, Wyoming, where I was pastor of a newly planted church. We had barely started down the highway when Berk said, "Bob, did you ever stop to think that the only thing you can learn is what you already know?"

As you can imagine, that was the basis of some pretty interesting discussion on the way back to Sheridan. And that incident was typical Maurice Berquist. He stretched his mind in many directions, and he wanted to be sure those around him were stretching their minds, too.

The days Brother Berquist spent leading a retreat for Wyoming pastors were enriching for all of us. After the pastors' conference he stayed with us in Sheridan to speak to our young congregation. His encouragement and guidance were invaluable helps to the church and to me as a church planter.

"Remember to spend as much time as you can in reading and study when the church is small," he said. "The by-product of church growth will mean less and less time for you to invest in study and preparation." Such insights have been valuable guiding principles in pastoral ministry.

"Berk, I've tried preaching without notes – but I'm always afraid of forgetting a major point," I lamented. Berk smiled and said, "I've forgotten things lots of times. I'd start out saying, 'Now, Paul had three things to say about this.' So I'd talk about the first thing a little while; then I'd expound on the second principle a while. But about then I'd realize that I'd forgotten entirely what the third thing was. So I'd say, 'Come back tonight and I'll tell you about the third thing Paul says about this." His good-natured encouragement was the catalyst I needed to develop the discipline of preaching without notes.

Maurice Berquist shared his perspectives with humor, insight, and conviction. Time spent with him was like an internship in finding sermon illustrations in every situation.

– Robert L. Moss

D r. Berquist, a successful pastor, prolific writer, evangelist, and conference leader, has traveled around the world sharing the Good News with the most unshakable faith and positive attitude. He left a legacy that will be hard to follow, and his absence will leave a void in the church. His honesty, humor, and humble approach always were refreshing. He was a friend, a mentor, and an inspiration with his unwavering commitment to Christ, and his willingness to give his last breath for the Master. He died in the field, doing what he always wanted, serving Christ.

– Bill Konstantopoulos

H e could reach out to people in a way no one else could. When you put the brand "brilliant" on someone, it tends to spill over and blot out any loving human touch. But he never tried to impress anyone with his intellect. I'm not even sure he knew how brilliant he was.

You could share anything with him and you would know with certainty that it would never go further. He was caring and deeply spiritual. If you were around him any length of time, you'd say, "God sent someone special my way."

– Charlie Van Hoose

In Memoriam

In the months that followed Berk's death, friends continued to undergird our family with phone calls and letters that meant so much.

My brother John offered an apartment in his townhouse in Philadelphia that gave me the security of family and a location closer to the children and grandchildren. I moved there in August of 1993.

During the year several churches, including Vero Beach, and the CBH Bible Conference at Montreat held memorial services for Berk. We could not attend them all; but Lori and I, with the grandchildren, were guests for a special service at White Chapel in Daytona Beach in April of 1993, marking the 61st Anniversary of the church we had pastored for twenty-one years. At that time, the congregation conferred upon Berk posthumously the title "Pastor Emeritus," reconsecrated in Berk's memory the beautiful stained glass windows he had dreamed into existence, and unveiled two portraits of him – one that would hang in the foyer of Warner Christian Academy and another, by Saul Chaftez, that would hang in the church narthex.

The Mass Communication Board established a Russian Broadcast Memorial Fund

Maurice Berquist Memorial Auditorium

In 1993 the Council of the Church of God in South India resolved "to construct an auditorium in memory of the Rev. Dr. Maurice Berquist in the place where he last preached" on the convention grounds at Cochin. With financial assistance from congregations in the States, the auditorium was officially opened on December 3, 1998.

The auditorium facility is designed with seating for 600 delegates on the ground floor and lodging for 48 delegates on the upper floor. A large photograph of Berk graces the back wall with a display case below containing a permanent exhibit of his books, as well as letters of tribute written especially for the dedication of the facility in his honor.

in Berk's honor because of his initiative in expanding the reach of CBH radio broadcasts in other languages around the world.

But the most touching tribute by far came in 1997, when we learned that the churches in South India were raising funds to construct an auditorium in Berk's honor at the Convention Center in Cochin, where he did his last preaching and laid down his life.

It was my privilege to accompany Howard Baker to Cochin, India, for the dedication of this magnificent structure on December 4, 1998. As I met in person so many of these beautiful, gracious, humble, and dedicated people, I could fully understand Berk's great love for them and his passion to fan the flames of Christianity in this needy land by teaching and encouraging the ministers and the people in their faith. Speaking to them of my husband's great love for them, as I stood in the place they had built to honor him, was a moment I will cherish all my life.

In the years since Berk's death, God has opened a ministry for me – using my nursing skills in hospice work for friends all across the country. My life today has meaning and joy in serving these who need love and care. And somehow I know that from the portals of Heaven, Berk is watching and smiling.

ABOVE: Berny Berquist looks on as Dr. George Tharakan unveils the second of two memorial plaques on either side of the auditorium entrance. The already unveiled plaque on the right reads:
"Rev. Dr. Maurice Berquist Auditorium
Dedicated
to
the Glory of God
Opened on December 3, 1998
By Mrs. Bernice Berquist
The plaque being unveiled thanks those whose prayers and financial gifts made construction of the auditorium a reality.

A Life Poured Out
Auditorium Dedication Address (Excerpts)
By Berny Berquist

It is a great honor for me to be here today. I feel "at home" because you have welcomed me so beautifully. I know now why my husband loved you so much.

. . .

My husband talked about a previous journey here with P.V. Jacob. A small brass band greeted him and Brother Baker. And on journeys to several towns, the band followed him. He loved this attention and honor – such a welcome to your home land.

When my husband passed away, you all worked fervently to ready him for his journey home to America and to his family. I thank you for this. But, he really did not come home this time. He went Home to Heaven from India.

India was where his heart was at that moment. I never saw him again, for I know he was not in that coffin. He had already arrived in Heaven, and the celestial brass band had welcomed him in.

When Pastor Baker brought my husband's suitcase to me, among the articles inside was an empty bottle for olive oil. In his last days among you, he was led to pray for the sick, and he ministered in this way – using his last drop of oil. He did not feel his own frailty and impending death. He literally poured himself out for others. We, his family, wish to have him remembered as "a life poured out."

On his gravestone, I had this scripture inscribed: "Preach the Word" (II Timothy 4:2). That was his mission. And that is the mission of this building. It will host thousands of people in the years to come who will hear the Word of God and then go forth – preaching and teaching His Word.

We are so honored as a family that you have dedicated this building in his name. But remember – the name of Jesus goes before it.

Thank you for making me feel welcomed and "at Home." God bless you and keep you – until we meet again. But don't forget, we are not "Home" yet.

"A TRIBUTE TO BERK"
MAURICE BERQUIST

Berk was a father in the Lord, a mentor, and an equipper to myself and to many other pastors and Christian leaders.

As Berk served with me in his final pastoral assignment in Wichita, Kansas at Central Community Church, it was obvious that the passionate thrust of his ministry was to raise up leadership and encourage pastors all over the world. He had a special heart and vision to equip the next generation of pastors and church leaders. He had a timelessness about him that crossed all generational lines. Berk was uniquely gifted in the art of preaching and communicating the gospel. His humor, compassion and sensitivity inspired countless thousands like no one else I know. He was truly a gift to all who were fortunate enough to know him.

Ray Cotton
Senior Pastor, New Hope Community Church
April 1999

TOP: *Children showed Berny the same kind of affection they had given Berk.*

ABOVE: *Berny Berquist with Sam Jacob, son of Sarama Jacob and the late P.V. Jacob, former leader of the Church in South India.*

ABOVE: *Letter of Tribute by Ray Cotton, one of several letters on permanent exhibit in Berquist Auditorium.*

LEFT: *Entrance to the South India Convention Grounds at Cochin.* **ABOVE:** *Main building of the ministry school located on the Convention Grounds.*

ABOVE: *Berny Berquist addresses the Assembly* **(TOP)** *at the Dedication Service, with Sam Jacob as interpreter.*

ABOVE: *Main entrance of Berquist Auditorium.*
RIGHT: *Detail of lettering above the entrance.*

Howard Baker's Address at the Dedication of the Berquist Auditorium (Excerpts)

February 8, 1993, was one of the hardest days of my life. That was the day that our brother Maurice "Berk" Berquist passed from our midst into that glorious place called Heaven. The time was a few minutes after seven in the morning, when a massive stroke took place; and a few hours later, he was with his Lord. I have missed him, for he was the best friend I ever knew. In fact, I don't believe that Rev. Berquist had an enemy in this world, for he loved people – and they soon knew that. And he loved to preach. . . .

I want to take this opportunity to thank Rev. George Tharakan, and others, for all they did on that February 8th in 1993. First of all for their prayer support for me and for Mrs. Berquist back home in Wichita, Kansas. It took a lot of work in getting Rev. Berquist's body shipped back to the United States.

But rather than thinking about the darkness of that hour, I like to remember the evening before. We had been in the Trivandrium area for a week or so in meetings with the church. We left Trivandrium about 8:00 p.m. on that Sunday evening. During that four hour trip to Changanur, he sang all the way. I have never seen him so happy and rejoicing in the Lord as he did that evening. . . .He sang many songs about Heaven and Jesus, his wonderful Lord.

That trip to South India was the third trip for Rev. Berquist and me together. He loved India and counted it a blessing for each trip he made. . . . Many of you know that Rev. Berquist started his ministry in India back in 1948. He had just completed his college education in Anderson, IN. World War II was over,

and he wanted to see the condition of the world. . . . I want to quote from Page 63 of his book *The Miracle and Power of Blessing*:

"In 1948 I began a trip around the world. Leaving San Francisco on a slow steamer, Ralph Starr and I made our way to China. Ralph was a born navigator. He can remember every turn in every road. We traveled by ship, plane, truck caravan, and finally by mule back into Tengchung, Yunan, West China. If I were to call him this moment, I feel sure he could describe every pagoda we passed. Not I.

"We separated in Tengchung. He remained to help with the work of the hospital and eventually to help missionaries Dr. and Mrs. David Gaulke and Milton and Eleanor Buettner to escape. He was afraid I could not make it on my own. As we separated, he gave me simple instructions: JUST KEEP ON GOING WEST AND YOU WILL GET HOME ALL RIGHT!

"Twelve months later I did. When I sailed into New York to see if the Lady in the Harbor was still carrying a torch for me – and for all the other poor, tired, huddled masses – I was still traveling west. When I finally took the Pennsylvania train from New York to Indiana, I was still heading west. The east and the west never meet.

"My friends laugh at my lostness most of the time. How do you expect to show people the way to Heaven when you can't find your way to the post office? they ask. They have a point. But I have managed to get around in this world in spite of my poor sense of direction."

AND I CAN SAY, THAT IS ALL TRUE. But what an EXTRAORDINARY PERSON HE WAS. He was one of a kind. God only made ONE person like him!

FIRST CHURCH OF GOD
3300 NE 78th Street • Vancouver, WA 98665-0656

TRIBUTE TO MY FRIEND MAURICE BERQUIST

I FIRST MET BERK IN THE 1950'S WHEN I WAS IN HIGH SCHOOL. IT WAS AT A TIME WHEN GOD WAS SPEAKING TO MY LIFE. BERK PLAYED A VERY IMPORTANT PART IN MY DECISION TO ENTER THE MINISTRY.

WHILE I WAS IN COLLEGE, WHICH HE STARTED, HE BECAME A ROLE MODEL FOR ME. AT ARLINGTON COLLEGE BERK ENCOURAGED THE YOUNG MEN STUDYING FOR MINISTRY TO DO THEIR BEST AND THEN RELAX AND BE THEMSELVES. HE SET THE COURSE OF MY MINISTRY STYLE.

WHEN I BEGAN TO PASTOR MY FIRST CHURCH, BERK BECAME A MENTOR. ONE I WOULD CALL WHEN FACED WITH IMPORTANT DECISIONS OR SERIOUS PROBLEMS. SOON HE BECAME A TRUSTED FRIEND AND CONFIDANTE.

WHEN GOD CALLED HIM HOME, I LOST A TRUSTED FRIEND, MENTOR, TEACHER AND GODLY EXAMPLE. NOW WHEN I AM FACED WITH A PROBLEM, I THINK OF THE WORDS OF INSTRUCTION HE GAVE ME.

HIS EFFORTS AND INFLUENCE HAVE NOT CEASED WITH HIS PASSING. THE PERSON OF MAURICE BERQUIST LIVES ON TODAY IN THE LIVES HE TOUCHED AND IN THE MINISTRY HE GAVE AROUND THE WORLD. HE USED TO SAY "there's very little difference between one man and another, but that little difference makes all the difference." HE MADE A BIG DIFFERENCE WITH HIS LIFE AND MANY CONTINUE TO BENEFIT FROM HIS "little" DIFFERENCE.

FROM ONE OF HIS ADMIRERS,

Gerald J. Marvel

Gerald Marvel (right) wrote one of the letters of tribute now on exhibit in South India.

TOP: *Howard Baker with Berk, 1993*
BELOW: *Room (lower right) where Berk was stricken on February 8, 1993.*

NORTH ANDERSON
CHURCH OF GOD

November 22, 1998

The Church of God Association of South India
Ecclesia
Cochin, South India

Dear Brothers & Sisters in Christ:

How I wish I might be present with you for the dedication of the Maurice Berquist Auditorium in Cochin next month! My heart and prayers are, even if I am not. My love for the Church of God in South India is deep and constant. I keep you daily before the Lord in prayer.

My love for Maurice Berquist is profound, as well. Few men have influenced me so much, for the good, as our beloved Berk. His wisdom and faith changed the world; they changed me, too.

I was a child when I first heard Berk preach; I was a young man when he first heard me preach. He saw in me things I did not see myself; then, he helped me to see them. He believed in me when I was hesitant. He encouraged me when I was uncertain. He invested in me when I wondered what was to come. He stood by while I grew in the ministry. He was my friend, my mentor.

Berk's mind was the stuff of genius, his imagination a canvas upon which the Spirit drew, that others might also see. His heart was as big as the whole outdoors and his wit warm and in season, always. He possessed the unusual ability to see the Lord at work everywhere and the skill to articulate his vision with compelling narrative and prose. He was a man of ideas, a man of many talents, and a man of grace. He was a man of God. Berk's grasp of the Scripture and the mind of Christ had few peers. His sly grin, twinkling eyes, and gentle nod of the head set him, altogether, in a class by himself.

In all the world, there was none like him. In all of my life, there has never been his equal.

Thank you for honoring him. Thank you for tending the flame of his Christian witness. Thank you for treasuring his legacy, for Jesus' sake.

I am pleased to remain, with you, in the Master's service,

Jim Lyon
Jim Lyon

ABOVE: Jim Lyon's letter of tribute, now on exhibit in Berquist Auditorium.
RIGHT: Jim Lyon

BELOW: Berk with the ministers of South India in 1990.

Robert Pearson's Letter of Tribute (Excerpt)

Also on exhibit in the auditorium is a letter from Robert Pearson, General Director of Church of God Ministries. On behalf of the Church of God in North America, Pearson congratulates the Church in South India on completion of the Berquist Auditorium and chronicles highlights of Berk's distinguished record of ministry, citing him as "one of God's wonderful gifts to the Church of God Reformation Movement"– one who "served the Lord Jesus Christ with distinction."

Robert Pearson

He also includes this incredible moment in Berk's stunning career:

"I would like to comment briefly on Berk as a communicator. He possessed an incredible ability to share biblical truths in simple, yet powerful ways. Because of his unique gift he was one of the most sought after evangelists and speakers.

"I will always remember the time he spoke to our ministers and spouses during our Southern California Summer convention of the Churches of God. We were assembled in the Banquet Room of the Marie Calender's Restaurant near the campus of Azusa Pacific University. Following dinner, Berk was asked to share a few challenging thoughts. In characteristic style, as he began to preach, he became passionately enthusiastic. And, as he became passionately enthusiastic, his voice grew louder and louder. At the height of Berk's crescendo, the restaurant manager entered the room and informed us that we would have to leave if Berk didn't tone it down. Apparently, other patrons in the restaurant had lodged complaints about the noise coming from the Banquet Room. It was the only time I ever witnessed Berk being speechless during a sermon."

Pearson closes with these words: "Berk's life ended doing what he loved the most – ministry. He just happened to be in India. He could have been almost anywhere, because he devoted his life to serving Jesus Christ in leadership through the Church of God. May his kind increase!"

A Berquist Sampler

Letter from Pakistan (1949) (Excerpts)

Berk's first around-the-world itinerary included the mission post in Pakistan (until 1947 part of British India), served by the F.W. Heinlys and Bob and Fran Clark. This letter to Dale Oldham, captures an experience Berk had one Sunday morning that forged ties to India that endured for a lifetime. He is writing at 11:45 a.m. on Sunday, March 20, 1949:

Dear Brother Oldham:

I cannot explain to myself why I should be writing this letter to you this morning. But there is something inevitable about it. It is almost as though I were walking down College Drive toward Eighth Street, and, as I saw a light in your study window, a hand were to take me forcefully and push me up the stairs to your office. And as I would walk breathlessly in, I think I would be almost inarticulate – speechless with excitement.

It is almost that way now. As I sit here in Bob's study surrounded by trunks and packing boxes, my hands are trembling so much that they can scarcely work the keys of the little typewriter. My breath comes hard as though I had sprinted the half mile from the Railway station. Please understand, even though I cannot explain, why I write to you this morning. I first tried to express my feelings in an article, but somehow the sort of thing that I want to say cannot be told in a double-spaced, wide margins style. Maybe the reason for my making a letter of this is that I am afraid to take the time to verify the names and spellings of the words of Bengali which must be included – afraid if this shining moment were handled so roughly, it might burst, leaving me sitting here in front of a typewriter vainly trying to remember and feel again. As it is, I feel that I can write without the encyclopedic inhibitions that I would feel if I were trying to make a story. And I can describe my feelings without fear that you will think me maudlin and my experience a mere sentiment.

Actually I have learned that in a matter of moments my fingers will again be quiet, and the tears which I cannot now keep from my eyes will dry on my cheeks. But even then, when I am able to write objectively of the things that I have seen and felt this morning, I shall know that I have lived in a great moment. And I shall know that I have seen what many desire to see. Perhaps what even prophets have dreamed of seeing, but could not.

It is a little like an experience I had on the Assam Rail, the express train from Calcutta to Assam, last Friday night. It was a stormy night. The rain was driving hard against the windows of our compartment. And it was dark, so dark that as I pressed my face against the window to see whatever I could of the Indian country landscape, not even the black outlines were visible. But still I kept watching, for every few minutes the lightning would flash; and for a fraction of a second I could see segments of the landscape. In many ways it was a new kind of landscape – different by far from the terraced farms of China to which I was accustomed. Actually, I could not understand much of what I saw; but I tried to remember as much as I could so that when I could talk to someone who did understand, I would know the meaning of the thing I had seen. This morning is like that. I do not know the significance of all that I have seen, but I try to remember. And when I do remember, I shall feel, I am sure, as I feel now, that I have seen greatness passing by.

Just a few moments ago as I came down the stairs, I met Brother Heinly, who was just coming home from church. His eyes were still rimmed with tears, and I knew that I should say nothing unless he volunteered to start a conversation. In his hand he held a piece of string; actually it was a white cord made up of a number of strings. He looked at this cord intently for a

matter of moments as he fumbled for words. Then he spoke.

"What I have seen this morning was worth thirty years' work. I cannot think of a better climax to a missionary career. And I would count it a privilege to work thirty years more if I could see again what we have seen this morning."

May I interrupt Brother Heinly's conversation now to explain in a very crude way what did happen this morning?

It may have been several months ago that a Hindu priest, a Brahmin, the highest caste, became exasperated with the immorality and corruption of the Hindu priests. And although he was directly in line to be one of the highest ranking priests in India, he decided to purchase a Bible secretly in order to make a study of the Christian religion. His study only made conflict for him, for it made him realize that he could not find salvation in the old ways; and yet the old ways were deeply ingrained in his living and his thinking. Not only had he been born into the highest possible state in which a man can be born (according to the Hindu religion), but he had, through his native ability, risen to the highest rank of the Brahmin caste. Now, if he would follow the leading of his soul, he would leave all of this prestige (which in America is unimaginable) and associate himself with the Christian community, which often associates itself not only with the cleaners and sweepers (the lowest castes), but also with the outcastes.

While Rama Shan Jha pondered this decision, he saw a vision on the wall of his cell. A cross appeared on the wall. On it was the single Hindi word *mukti*, which means "salvation." The image disappeared, and he went to the wall to see if he could see anything more; but the wall was the same as before. There are those, I know, who will smile at this simple demonstration; but even they cannot deny that the vision was real enough that the priest made his decision. He left the temple and obtained a few rupees for train fare. Then he boarded the train.

When the train steamed into Lalmanirhat, the priest got off and asked the nearest bystander where he could find a Christian mission. The bystander, who happened to be a Muslim, laughingly inquired what the Hindu priest wanted with a Christian mission. Jha explained his purpose and came out to our mission. Here he confessed his faith in Jesus Christ and entered into a course of study of the Bible. Bob spent an hour with him every day explaining the Word of God. Plans were made for his Baptism after a suitable length of time. In the meantime the ex-priest became quite a scholar of the Scriptures and, what is more, became imbued with the Spirit that pervades them.

Even with this arrangement, however, the priest was not entirely happy, for the people of Lalmanirhat speak Bengali; and although Mr. Jha spoke the language, his own native tongue was Hindi. And so he expressed a desire to go to a mission station where that language was used. With the blessings and prayers of our mission staff, he left and came to a Scotch Presbyterian mission to the north. For a time he seemed quite happy working with them, but one day the minister was preaching on infant baptism; and after the sermon, Jha asked for a personal explanation of the doctrine. The minister explained the tradition, but Jha persisted that he had not found such a doctrine in the Bible. And, of course, there is no Biblical confirmation of such a teaching. So the minister reverted to a rather nebulous support of tradition and the teaching of the church. Again the former priest felt unhappy and started out once more.

This time he came to a Catholic church. And when the priests here tried to teach him the Catholic prayers, he inquired about praying to Mary. "I find nothing like that in the Bible," he said.

The priests tried to explain to him that such was the teaching of the church, but the ex-Hindu kept inquiring about the Biblical foundation of the teaching. After a time the priests became so chagrined that one of them slapped him. Again to the road, this time to ride an ox cart into the villages, standing on top of the cart to preach the Gospel of Christ.

I do not have all the information about the intervening days; but soon Mr. Jha returned to Lalmanirhat, where he expressed his desire to be baptized. This morning he was. Have you time for a brief account of this morning's service?

After the native pastor's short sermon in the beautiful brick chapel here, a man rose to speak. Although I understand nothing of the Bengali language, I felt something which one does not often experience in a preaching service. The man, dressed in the white wrap-around garment of the Indian villager, spoke with a driving earnestness that reminded me of the saber-edged intensity of Saint Paul. As I try to do each time I hear a new language, I listened for the recurrence of sounds and words, and rather regularly I would hear the word *mukti*, "salvation." At the close of the talk, the speaker reached inside his flowing robe and brought out the white cord which hung around his neck. Hanging about his neck, this cord reached almost to his waist. This is the sacred thread of the Brahman caste. It is put on the child when he is about five years old. The ceremony accompanying this is elaborate, for this simple white cord means that of all Indians, its wearer is nearer to being a god than anyone else. Maybe a million or more reincarnations, and he will be a deity. For a rank outsider such as I, it is almost impossible to comprehend the extent of this meaning. But the Indian brother took the cord off and laid it in front of the cross. Then, trembling with emotion, he knelt at the altar while Brother Heinly, Bob, and I laid our hands on him and dedicated him to the service of God. Following this, while the congregation stood by singing "I Surrender All" in Bengali, Bob baptized the brother.

As they started singing, my mind whirled back to last year's camp meeting and the chorus that Herb [Thompson] led so many times – "I Surrender All." I hope I shall have a chance to sing that song with the camp meeting crowd at least another time. This next time it shall mean more to me than ever before. It shall bring back a picture of the chapel here on the compound at Lalmanirhat with the flower bordered walk leading up to it. I shall see again the rows of sandals lined up outside the door. And I shall hear again the word, *mukti*, as our brown brother officially broke his ties with his religious past and pledged his allegiance to the Church of Jesus Christ.

Will you consider it too literary if I refer again to the lightning flash simile of which I spoke earlier? This morning was a brilliant experience. In a moment it seemed as though I could see the whole of the plan of missions – really a great deal more than that – the plan of the Church. The power of God works beyond the reach of our fingers. Even beyond the reach of our minds. Consider the work here in Lalmanirhat: this petrified structure of Islam has made the seed of the Gospel germinate slowly. And where the seed of the Gospel has grown, it has been walled in by the crystallized society of Hinduism. Sheaves have not been great. But for all of that, the work did not stop. A mission was maintained. This morning was worth the thirty years of Brother Heinly's life. But more than one life was spent. The life of the Church has been spent here. Here are the prayers of myriad Christians. These have not always been intelligent prayers – sometimes little more than alphabets thrown up to God, out of which He makes the words and requests. There is the money of the Church. Much of it has been sacrificially given. Occasionally all of us wonder how the harvest is coming. This morning, in a flash, all of us could see! I am sure I saw more than I can understand. But I shall remember the outlines.

Brother Heinly was through speaking a moment after I met him there on the stairs. His last words were: "It was a wonderful sight to a man going home for the last time. I can only thank God for the experience. I am not worthy of it."

And I wondered if I was either.

This is enough letter for one time. I have thought many times to drop a jocular letter to you and Mrs. Oldham in which I would describe the coming of the organ which you sent to Milton [Buettner]. Really it was funny. As we rode four days over the mountains from Paoshan to Tengehung, our pack horses were of all beasts the most listless. All of them, that is, except the one that carried the organ. He happened to be the lead horse and would allow no other nag to pass him. Being the lead animal, he sported a set of bells that tintinnabulated all through the steeps. Actually, he almost strutted as though conscious of his melodic cargo. Finally, when the organ got through customs (whew!), the first song the ecstatic Milton played on it was "Praise God from Whom All Blessings Flow." And, anyway, how could I tell you of the wonderful evenings we spent shivering over the dubious heat of a charcoal brazier singing our way through the hymnal. It really was a thoughtful gift. And even with his gift of prose, I am sure Milton will not be able to tell you how much your sending it meant to him – and to us.

And now, having unburdened my soul – and as I look back, the letter seems strangely preachy (which doubtless means that I wanted to preach to myself and felt that you would be a sympathetic victim to use as excuse) – three pages worth, I send my greetings to all of my friends back there.

Sincerely yours,
Maurice Bergquist

In a scene much like the one described in his letter to Dale Oldham in 1949, Berk prays with ministers in India in 1990.

The Lord We Lost!

"The Lord We Lost" was a sermon Berk delivered at Anderson Camp Meeting (and afterwards in other places). Years later, many who heard this message still spoke of its power and effect. In Berk's files were this outline and these few notes.

Purpose: In my own mind, the purpose for this sermon is so shocking that it seems almost folly to write it. But I shall write it. I fully expect that through the writing of this sermon and through the prayer which will and does precede it, Jesus will become so real to me that I will find Him afresh. There is such a need for this connection in my own life.

Things seem increasingly unreal. The buildings, the cars, the crises of people's lives. The quiet of this room with the whirring of the air conditioner seems almost a part of another world, one I might be seeing on a screen. But if these are unreal, Jesus is unreal, too.

This does not mean I believe Him to be unreal. On the contrary, I believe He is the ground of reality. But by all the senses which I use, I have little capacity for feeling or being assured. So as I study the doors through which he may come into my life, I want to know where to find Him.

Uncle Buddy Robinson, when asked how he became such a successful evangelist, said, "I just kept shooting at the hole where I saw the devil last, and finally I succeeded."

So, in a positive way, I want to shoot at the "hole" where Jesus last appeared – and find Him.

But even more than this personal purpose for my preaching on this subject in Camp Meeting, I have a greater dream. I feel that Christ will so reveal Himself in that service that no one of the 8,000 persons attending will be unconvinced. And all of us who "pierced Him" will wail because of Him.

To me the great vindication of all of this will be in the renewal of the church. When we think of the potential for good within the walls of one building, it is possible that every life could be touched. Men may be called and anointed to preach. The Holy Spirit might give gifts to the Church as in apostolic times.

Of course, it is human to reminisce about the service five or so years ago – the one held in the high school gym. In terms of visible response, I have never been in another like it. Yet, who can say why things like this happen. Or yet, what long term effects they have on people. But in any event, we were strangely moved.

This time, I wish for and pray for more. Surely God vindicated Himself that night and surely human wisdom was totally discredited. But that is not all. Giving due credit for every human factor, there was still something so eminently genuine that there is no explaining it.

Who knows that I might be thought worthy to be a vehicle of God's grace for such a service as that again. Or as great as I expect God will give at this time. Whatever the price of such a victory, I am willing to pay it. For this life of shadows and symbols is not enough.

In short . . . my prayer is that Christ will be revealed – the ultimate answer for those in doubt, the compassionate healer for the sick, the chief of the heavenly hosts for the uncommitted, the judge for the sinner, and the spirit of Him who says, "Come."

I would not be surprised if Christ should appear in a vision to 8,000 persons – so real that they might say, "Lord I believe."

Outline:

Text: Luke 3.

Intro: A boy of 7 or 8 yrs: "Aw, he's making that up."

I. The Lord is Lost.
   A. He was.
   B. By His own family.
   C. In the world that He had made.
      Astronauts did not find him.
      Statements of contemporaries
      (a) Clergyman Sayre
      (b) Scientists
      (c) Prostitute
      (d) Scrubwoman
      (e) Janitor
      (f) Child
      (g) Seminarian
      (h) Theologian
      (i) Philosopher

II. What happens when the Lord is Lost? – We are.
   A. There is no focus of the Godhead.
   B. There are no realities. If He is the ground being, what is existence without Him?
   C. There is no power to overcome sin.
   D. There are no conversions.
   E. He is the fullness of God

III. Where we lost Him.
   A. Crowd consciousness – If there are enough children around, the law of averages says ours must be among them.
      Relationship - Legalism.
   B. If we can spiritualize the story – it was a retreat from the Church – His Father's business.
   C. The retreat from encounters (e.g. soldier)
   D. Causes - instead of persons
      [Marginal notes: Crowd, Cowardice, Confrontation, Comfort, Causes]

IV. Where we find Him.
   Returning to the place where we last saw Him . . .
   A. In the Church
   B. In the act of suffering
   C. In the act of sanctification
   D. In the healing ministry
   E. In the act of repentance.
      [Marginal notes: Surrender, Sacrifice, Sanctifies, Sorrow]

The Lord We Lost!

A man reported: "Last night I found the Lord."

I didn't know he was lost. Yet Christ has been the Lost Christ since His birth.

A star was required to find Him when he was born. After his birth nothing is heard of him until he is twelve – twelve lost years.

Then at twelve He bounds back into the Scriptures with the inquiry among the Doctors of the temple. Again He is found by His parents, but then is lost to our view until he comes to John and begins His public ministry.

But the historical Christ, having been found and put between the yellowing pages of our unread library books, is not enough.

Is Christ lost among the worlds that He has made?

The "God is Dead" theologians who grabbed the headlines this past year, were saying simply that they had lost the Lord –

never admitting that it was they who were lost.

But more than any of these rhetorical ideas, we want to know where is the Lord now? – what is he doing?

The article in Saturday's *News-Journal* told us that only 20 percent of the people in the U.S. believe in Jesus now – as contrasted with 37 percent a few years ago.

"Does Jesus live here?" asked the inquirer at the door.

The housewife returned to her family visibly shaken.

"Why didn't you tell them we belong to a church?"

"But he didn't ask that."

"Why didn't you tell him that we are good people?"

"He didn't ask that. He just asked, 'Does Jesus live here?'"

Who is to blame for the unreality of Christ? Was He ever real – the Christ whose sandaled footstep made a journey light? Was he ever real to men? Are there times when in history men have cried out, "I see Him! I see my Savior!"?

Stephen, in martyrdom, saw Him at the right hand of God.

John in the Revelation saw Him.

Paul on the way to Damascus saw Him.

Have I seen Him? Do I see him now? Or is the Lord just a name we call out like a heathen chanting a mumbo jumbo prayer?

If others find Him and others saw him, why do we not?

Everything is real about life – except the Lord. Sin, heaven knows, is real enough. The earth with its jungles burning red with jellied gasoline. The return of the jungle to our music; the dark ages, to our minds. The world – yes, the world is real enough. But Christ – can you tell me where I may find Him?

If we find Him we will find Him where others have found Him.

Of himself he said, "The Holy Spirit will take the things of mine and show them to you – he shall bear witness of me."

Are there mystics who have seen the Lord? Where do they find Him?

Are there hymn writers who have seen the majesty of Christ?

Are we not distanced from the vision of heaven because we do not want the martyr's death? Are there no young "Stephens" among us who will, for the cause of righteousness, suffer – take the little that remains of the cup of tribulation Jesus drank in dying pains? We fellowship thy passion!

How little shame I am willing to bear. How little reproach for the sake of Christ.

How foreign seems the Christ of Calvary to the magnificent visage shown in the stained glass of our churches.

When Jacob saw a ladder that reached from Earth to Heaven, his head was pillowed on a stone. At my age a man needs a comfortable bed!

Awakened from sleep a couple of nights ago, I read *LIFE* magazine's article about the new "Brain Trust" in our government – called now the Intellectual something or other. But the import of the article is that men are now able to link specula-tion with action. Groups like the Ford Foundation and the Rand Company now have the money and the facilities to put to use their ideas.

Maybe this is where we have lost the Lord.

A preacher graduates from Seminary, but fails in his pastoral ministry because he is unwilling, or afraid, to go out and knock on doors.

Like the story of the soldier who in the thick of battle retreated by running as far as he could. Finally, exhausted he fell on the ground. He was kicked by a rough boot.

"Get up soldier."

No response.

What are you doing here?"

"I am here because I am scared."

"Do you know who I am?"

"No."

"I'm a general."

"Man, I must have run farther back than I figured!"

It does not take much real grace to answer the invitation to preach at Camp Meeting. It may take a little courage to preach honestly, but just to preach requires no great manhood.

But we lose the Lord this way. We lose Him unless we are willing to share him in the tangles of life. When we run away from the conflict, we run away from the victory – and the Victor!

In Houston some months ago we listened as the distinguished Dr. David Gaulke spoke of the decisions that ministers are going to be confronting soon – now that it is possible to sustain human life (for a price) almost indefinitely.

As I listened – disturbed – I looked up to see the magnifi-cent stained glass window in the Houston Church – Holman Hunt's picture of Jesus knocking at the door. Who is knocking? Is it Gaulke? Or is it Jesus?

In a sense it is both of them. Christ is striving to come to life through the probing of David Gaulke.

To avoid encounter is to avoid the Lord – to avoid persecution is to avoid the Lord.

How many times in the entire scripture did Jesus appear? To the three Hebrew children in the fiery furnace. To Isaiah upon the death of King Uzziah. To John on the Isle of Patmos. To Paul struck to earth. To Stephen, of course. To how many others and when?

All of us face the demise of personal soul winning. According to the survey whose results were published in *Christianity Today*, to win one soul to Christ in a year requires six ministers and a thousand Christians.

Is it too much to ask every Christian to lead one soul to the Lord in a year? If one is doing that much, how is it with 999 others, including the six ministers?

While it may be true that statistics do not always tell the truth, why can they not tell a little more comforting lie?

Can the reason be that we find it difficult to introduce someone whom we have never met?

TIME magazine of April 8, 1966, carried as its front page article, "Is God Dead? Listen to these words:

Jesuit Theologian John Courney Murray points to another variety of unbelief: The atheism of distraction: people who are just too . . . busy to worry about God at all.

In this new Christianity, the watchword is witness. Protestant faith now means not intellectual acceptance of an ancient confession, but an open commitment – perhaps best symbolized in the U.S. by the Civil Rights movement – to eradicating evil and inequality in the world.

Of 97 percent of Americans who said they believe in God, only 27 percent declared themselves openly religious.

In search of meaning, some believers have desperately turned to psychiatry, Zen, or drugs. Thousands of others have quietly abandoned all but token allegiance to the churches, surrendering themselves to a life of "anonymous Christianity," dedicated to Civil Rights or the Peace Corp.

The article goes on to quote these disturbing words from a Stanford philosopher: *"I do not understand God, nor the way in which he works. If occasionally I raise my heart in prayer, it is to no God I can see or hear or feel. It is to a God in as cold and obscure a polar night as any non-believer has ever known."*

Even the clergy seem uncertain.

"I'm confused as to what God is," says Francis B. Sayre, the Episcopal dean of Washington's National Cathedral. *"But so is the rest of America."*

To those who do formulate an idea of God, He seems to be everything from a celestial gas to a kind of honorary president, out there in space, well beyond the range of the astronauts.

A young Washington scientist suggests that God, if anything, *"is hydrogen and carbon. Then again, he might be thermo-nuclear fission, since that's what makes life on this planet possible.*

To a street walker in Tel Aviv: *"God will get me out of this filth one day. He is a God of mercy dressed all in white and sitting on a golden throne."*

A Dutch scrubwoman says, *"God is a ghost, floating in space."*

A Greek janitor thinks God is *"like a fiery flame, so white it can blind you."*

"God is all I cannot understand," says a Roman seminarian."

A Boston scientist describes God as *"the totality of harmony in the universe."*

A theologian speaks of the *"anonymous presence,"* suggesting to some that *"the church might well need to take a position of reverent agnosticism regarding some doctrines which it had previously proclaimed with excessive conviction."*

TIME magazine speaks smugly of reasons why faith in God is on the wane. It does little to establish the credibility of this God whose qualities *"medieval theologians categorized as confidently as they spelled out different kinds of sin,"* and whom churchmen spoke about *"as if they had just finished having lunch with Him."*

The whole problem of belief hinges on the reality of Jesus – how can He make Himself real?

Evangelist T. L. Osborn tells simply that if he talks to a Hindu crowd, he says "There was a man who lived on the earth as a perfect man."

They nod approval.

"He taught love and did miracles."

They nod.

"He was killed."

They nod.

"After the third day He rose again. If he rose again, He is still alive. And what He did He can still do. So let us pray for a sick man and see if He will heal Him."

This is the evidence of God. Yet with what timidness do we pray to a God far away.

"Lord, when saw we Thee . . . ?"

Christ is known in the leap of faith – the act of commitment – known in humility – known in conflict – known in confrontation – known in revelation.

If he appears, He is no illusion. If He speaks, He is not a ghost. If He works, He is not dead.

Science that admits an "alpha," must admit also an "omega."

If He was in the beginning, He is still here, since we have not yet experienced the ending. For in that day –

"Every eye shall see Him – and those that pierced Him. And all nations of the earth shall wail because of Him."

[End of notes – representing only a portion of the sermon]

Drawing at Left: "Christ," by Saul Chaftez

Whose God Is Dead?

I laid a flower on the grave of my god,
For he is a god I had made.
With my hands I fashioned a god of my own,
But he answered me not when I prayed.

My god smiled at my pride and my sin,
For he was no bigger than I.
But the god that I made
Brought me no peace within;
So, at last, my god had to die.

Was the god that I served just a shadow of me
I mistook for a heavenly friend?
In the darkness he vanished
And left me alone
To search for life's meaning again.

Not the god that I made,
But the God Who made me
Will live through eternity long.
When I lived to myself,
I was dead unto Him;
But He gave me new life and a song.

Berquist
(undated)

* * * *

Thoughts from the Edge

When my thoughts range as far as the distant horizon,
When my dreams climb in vain for the sky,
And I feel I am all alone with my musings,
I find the Lord standing by.

No thought is too deep for the author of thinking,
For back of my mind is the mind of my God.
When my mind ventures forth to the end of its tether,
It finds footprints where the Creator has trod.

Fling wide the gate of pale hesitation.
Break forth in dreaming and feeling again.
Fear thou not the fartherest horizon;
At man's last frontier, meet the Savior of man.

Berquist
(undated)

When the Alabaster Vase Is Broken

Covered with dust, hiding in shadows
Sat an alabaster vase,
A drab and unsung beauty
On the shelf.
Gaudy trinkets moved to the shelf front
Of the little Egyptian shop.
Tourists like little things that can crowd into
Their bulging suitcases.
And, having an eye for business,
The robed shopkeeper did not offer to show it.

I saw it.
And I wanted it.
Foolishly, I wanted it.
The stone vase was heavy and I had only one suitcase
In which to carry all my things
As I traveled around the world,
But for the sake of an alabaster vase,
I could throw away something.

Trying not to look eager,
I bargained with the shopkeeper.
I walked away with the vase in my hand.

After I had bought the alabaster vase
I looked at it carefully.
Rubbing the dust from the cream-colored stone,
I held it up to the light.
In fact, I put a little light inside it
And watched.
The vase glowed with inner beauty.
Its tiny flaws made a mosaic –
A stained-glass window
Made by God.

Often, in the months to follow
I took the vase
From my battered suitcase.
It reminded me of Mary and Martha,
Sisters who served the Lord
In vastly different ways.

One day at the market
While Martha bargained for food,
Mary wandered off and saw the vase.
It was expensive.
But it was beautiful.
Beauty, however, was not in the budget
In the home of Mary, Martha, and Lazarus.

Mary did not forget the vase.
Each day as she and her sister
Bought bread and olives
Mary secretly looked at the alabaster vase.
Such a thing of beauty
Would be a joy forever.

Coin by coin Mary saved her money.
As the coins were placed lovingly
In a little cloth bag,
Mary dreamed.
One day this vase would sit
Like a queen
In the little stone cottage.
And one day the coins were enough.
The vase,
The extravagant purchase of Mary,
Found its way to the little stone house.

When a traveling caravan came to Bethany,
There was no room in the inn.
Mary, Martha, and Lazarus
Invited the weary travelers to their home.
Rugs and skins were thrown on the floor to make beds.
Martha cooked her favorite dishes.
In the morning,
As the guests prepared to leave,
They presented a gift
From the Far East –
Spikenard,
Costly perfume.
"Have you a jar into which we can pour this fragrance?"
The chieftain asked.

A jar indeed.
One does not put Spikenard into a water jar
Or a cooking pot.
It was for this moment that the alabaster vase
Had waited.
It was for this moment that Mary had endured
The critical looks of her thrifty sister.
The alabaster vase had a purpose,
A purpose worthy of it.

One day Jesus visited Bethany.
He sat at the table, eating, laughing.
Mary listened,
Listened until her cup of joy overflowed.

She looked up, past the face of Jesus,
And saw the alabaster vase,
The vase filled with precious ointment.
"I will anoint his head," she thought.
Holding the heavy alabaster jar with one hand,
She poured oil into her hand
And anointed the tanned forehead
Of the Son of God.
As she moved to put the vase back on the shelf,
It slipped out of her hand.
Crashing to the stone floor,
It shattered, spilling all the costly ointment.

Alabaster is beautiful
And fragile as it is beautiful.
The vase that sat on the shelf,

Admired for its beauty,
Was on the stone floor.
Fragments.
And fragrance.
The fragrance filled the house.
The ointment ran down in rivulets in the cracks of the floor.
Between the stones it trickled.
A waste.
But, no.
Mary scooped it up in her hands and rubbed it on his feet –
The feet of Jesus,
Soon to be pierced with handmade nails.
Soon the feet dripped with the precious ointment.
Mary pulled the pins from her dark hair
Until it fell like a cascade on her slender shoulders.
She wiped the feet of Jesus
With her hair.

In a moment the drama was over.
Who can explain this waste?
Who will understand it?
Martha didn't. And Judas didn't.
But Jesus did.
"She has done this in preparation for my death and burial,"
Jesus said.

Looking back, we can see it as a tiny prophecy.
His body,
The body through which the God-light shone,
Was broken.
His life was poured out.
The fragrance has never left the world.

We remind ourselves of the scripture,
"We have this treasure in earthen vessels,
That the excellency might be of God."
We remember our own humanity.
We, too, are earthen vessels.
And we shall be broken.
Young or old, late or soon,
We shall be broken.
Sickness, accident, age, or grinding despair
Shall shatter us.
We shall become dust once more.

We never understand.
We cannot plan.
We can only pray to be filled with God's love
So that when
The pitcher is broken at the fountain,
When the alabaster vase
Crashes on the stone floor . . .
A fragrance will rise,
And the world will be blessed.

Maurice Berquist
9-16-86

Questing

O where are you going?
I inquired of my soul.
What is your destiny
And what is your goal?

My soul answereth me
With a sorrowful sound,
"Til I know what I've lost,
I won't know if it's found."

"Was I shot like an arrow
From some heavenly bow,
Through endless ether
To this planet below?

"Or perhaps like a stone
From the sky I was hurled
To seek my own destiny
Alone in the world."

No, my soul, you were born
As an infant of love,
Like a spark from a flame
In the heavens above.

You will know, you will know,
Though to you it seems odd,
You will know who you are
When you encounter God.

Maurice Berquist
02/07/76

Journal Entry: July 6, 1992 - 4:30 A.M.

O God, thanks for a year which I almost didn't have. A year ago I was in the hospital with brain surgery. Now, 365 days later, I am active. God, you have helped me publish a book. I have preached at Vero, in Colorado, in Egypt, and lots of other places. I have recovered from pneumonia, from financial pressures, and doors are still open to me . . . .Yesterday you blessed me with an effective message here in Wichita, and you have given me a week here to work on the Successful Church Ministries conference and the Wichita book. I am feeling stronger each day. Thanks.

I ask for guidance with regard to Vero . . . with regard to my involvement in Russia and India.

Strange to have so many choices, but I know you will guide.

I'm thankful. Very thankful.

For this time. For this year. For my health.

For my opportunities.

M.

The Legend of Dale Oldham

*Berk patterned this tribute, written in March
of 1983, after the style of "Hiawatha,"
by Henry Wadsworth Longfellow.*

On the windswept open prairies
In the state of Oklahoma
Lived a humble gospel preacher
Who proclaimed the ageless message.
In the land of oil and cotton
Talked he there of heaven's treasures
To the pioneers around him.

When the March wind stirred the branches
Bare and black from cold of winter,
Came a stranger to the household,
Came a baby boy to bless them.
William Dale, they named the baby,
As his father's name was William,
And his mother's name was Myrtle.

Day by day this husky infant
Grew and flourished on the prairies,
Listening to his father's preaching
And the teasing of his sisters,
Sisters three – Faith, Hazel, Etha.
So he grew from child to manhood
Hearing, heeding, always listening
To the call of God within him.

Soon the prairies wide were ringing
With the family's sweet music,
Do-re-mi, fa, sol, la, ti, do,
As the children learned to sight read,
Harmonizing Gospel hymn tunes,
As their hearts o'erflowed with praises
For the gift of full salvation.

Next came need for further training
At the Bible school now founded
By the zealous "Evening Lighters"
On the hill at Fifth and Union.
Now the youthful prairie singer
Arms himself with pen and pencil,
Black notebook and commentaries
As he listens to the teachers.

There were Byrum, Sherwood, Clausen,
Anna Koglin, J.T. Wilson –
Men and women called to sharpen
All the skills and talents latent
In the life of God's anointed.
These were days when life-long friendships
Would be formed to bless his pathway.
Then young Oldham joined the party

Of the silver-tongued proclaimers –
Chappel, Caudil, and Kirkpatrick,
Barney Warren, D.O. Teasley;
Then, at times, McCoy and Riggle.
Oldham led the joyous singing
As his elders spoke the message
Traveling o'er the plains and prairies.

Then one day the call came to him
From a well beloved elder,
Well beloved Brother Chappel.
Brother Chappel put it plainly,
As he counseled with young Oldham:
"Brother Dale, I am persuaded
That the God above has called you,
But I doubt that He has called you
For a little 'dab' of singing.

"You must listen for the witness
That your gracious Heavenly Father
Has His hand now resting on you
For the noble work of preaching.
So you must preach tomorrow evening
And begin your life-long journey
To fulfill this heavenly calling."

Full of fear, the youthful Oldham
Faced the challenge set before him.
He respected all the wisdom
Of the well beloved preacher,
But he needed reassurance
Of the gracious Holy Spirit.
Thus He asked for a sign from heaven.

"Give me souls tomorrow evening,"
Prayed the zealous young musician.
Give me souls, give me decisions
When I preach tomorrow evening.
Thus I'll know your hand is on me;
Thus I'll know this is my calling,
To declare the gospel message."

When the altar call was given,
Heaven blessed the invitation.
Six came forward to the altar,
Asking pardon from the Savior.
What a blessed confirmation
Of the calling God had given
To the youthful prairie preacher.

Now he ventures forth with courage,
Knowing he has God's approval.
Now he must fulfill his calling
Wheresoever God may lead him.
Tent and cottage and brush arbor

Find him working for the Master,
Singing, preaching with assurance.

Not alone was he to travel,
Not alone to bear the message.
God soon led the prairie preacher
To a beauteous brown-eyed maiden,
To a maid whose nimble fingers
Coaxed sweet music from the keyboard
Of the battered old piano.

Soon the two were joined in marriage,
Pledging love and understanding
That would deepen with the passing
Of each year God granted to them.
So they started in Kentucky,
Pastoring in Cythiana,
There to serve among God's people.

Soon their humble little cottage
Glowed with Polly's dedication
To keep all things bright and shining,
Decently and all in order.
Soon there came another blessing,
As they dreamed of their first baby,
Who would bless their home with laughter.

But that laughter turned to grieving
As the little life was taken,
Taken by God's darkest angel
E'er it had a chance to gladden
The small home with childish laughter.
So they wept, this brave young woman
And her husband standing by her.

From Kentucky up to Akron
Near the paths of founding fathers,
Where the truths of reformation
Were declared by D.S. Warner.
On to Lima, then to Dayton,
Where again his talents flourished,
Now including news broadcasting.

While he pastored there in Dayton,
Scores of lives were turned to Jesus.
There a new voice joined the singing
Of the preacher from the prairies.
Douglas Reed was born to bless them,
Born to sing to queens and princes,
Born to bless the world with music.

Born Dale was in Oklahoma,
Territory of the Indians.
Now God called this prairie preacher
To the saints along White River

To accept the pastor's calling
In the steps of E.A. Reardon,
Called to lead Park Place Church onward.

Once again the powerful message
Reached the hearts of those who heard it.
Once again the Holy Spirit
Called the church to true revival.
Once again the saints marched forward,
As their dedicated leader
Challenged them to full surrender.

Soon the powerful prairie preacher
Dreamed of reaching men by millions,
Using all the silent magic
Of the broadcast word through airwaves
To proclaim a church united
To a world by sin divided.
So his ministry was broadcast.

Now the snows of eighty winters
Have passed o'er this powerful preacher.
Still he stands like an apostle,
Youthful still in mind and spirit,
Faithful still in proclamation,
To the church a guiding beacon,
To us all a friend beloved.

Dr. W. Dale Oldham
CBH Pioneer Speaker
1947 - 1968

The Humble Are Made Strong   (1975)
Sermon Text: John 13:1-7   (Sermon Excerpts)

The laws of God's grace are just as certain as the laws of gravity. . . . If you want God to bless things, obey the conditions.

I have been privileged to preach in many places in the world, in many countries, in many kinds of situations – college campuses, small churches, in foreign lands, in all kinds of places. But I can tell you this: whether you are a PhD or you can't write your name, the laws of God's grace are the same. Whether you are a minister, a teacher, or a person who just wandered in to get out of the rain, God's laws of grace are the same.

And they are really very simple:

"He that humbles himself will be exalted."

It's that simple. And yet, that is the hardest thing in the world to do – to be humble enough for God to use you.

I have become interested in what I call the "teeter-totter principle." I find it useful in describing my relationship to people. . . . A teeter-totter is a board that's resting on a saw horse or fulcrum of some kind, with two people on it. One is up; the other is down. One is down and the other is up – just like that [demonstrating with hands]. Very rarely is there any pause. If there were, there would be no reason for a teeter-totter, would there? There would be a bench!

But up and down, up and down. And here's how it goes: if you want to exalt the person on the other end, you have to lower your position in relation to them. It's that simple.

John the Baptist was a man of great repute. . . .He was a man of authority and power, and crowds kept coming to hear him. But when John the Baptist saw Jesus, he said: "He must increase and I must decrease." If I am going to exalt Christ, I will have to abase myself.

Great lesson in that. If you want people to love you, learn how to edify them – build them up. . . . People today tend to cut each other down, find fault, compare one another unfavorably. Then they wonder why nobody likes them.

Well, I can tell you this: if you want people to love you, just make them feel good in your presence. If you can humble yourself – not be afraid and not feel threatened to do that – you will find that people will love you. . . .

I am covetous for you of great success in your personal life and in the life of the church. And I think I know the way. And it is simply this: that every believer . . . strives to exalt Christ and exalt his fellowman. . . .

You can bless using the teeter-totter game. If you can lift somebody up – put their needs ahead of your own – and be willing to be humble enough for God to use you, I tell you, God will pour his grace into your heart.

If you are willing to spend yourself in the humblest, most abasing way – take on the task that nobody wants to do . . . the place where nobody wants to go . . . people nobody wants to visit – if you don't care who gets the glory, but you want to exalt Christ, you will see revival break out.

I don't know any other way.

But I find in every place in this world people climbing with sweaty hands up the ladder of success, trying to get ahead of somebody else, trying to increase their image.

Do you know why they do that?

Because they don't know who they are.

The Bible says that Jesus – knowing he came from God and that he was returning to God; knowing that God had given all things into his hands – took a towel, wrapped it around himself, and knelt down on the floor and began to wash the feet of his disciples.

And when they said, "What are you doing?" Jesus said, "You know what I am doing. Washing your feet."

Some people say that was merely the social custom. But if it were merely that, why didn't the disciples know what he was doing? If it was something they'd been doing all their lives, why did they say, "What are you doing?"

They didn't know what he was doing. They knew he was washing their feet. But *why* he was doing it, they didn't know.

So he told them. "I am giving you an example," he said. . . .

Understand this. By His actions, Jesus was saying, "I am confident of who I am. I don't need the petty prop of someone else's praise. And because I know who I am, I am not ashamed to take the humble role and do what somebody else would not do." The example is one of humility.

As you fly across the country, it is interesting when the plane gets close enough to the ground that you can see the terrain and watch where the rivers go. Rivers are the life lines of our country. That is where cities are built. Cities like St. Louis, Memphis, Detroit – all the major cities are built on rivers. You know why? That's where the trade goes, where the commerce goes.

You know where the rivers are? At the lowest point.

You can see them from a plane so vividly and clearly. The mountains are here, then the hills, and finally the valleys, and then the river beds. As the song says: "Just as a stream finds a bed that is lowly, so Jesus walked with the pure and holy." That kind of humility, my friend, will bring God's grace to your life. . . .

Well, how does it work?

Revival will come when people humble their hearts. The altar is a beautiful place. We humble our hearts and bend our knees and say, "Lord God, I need help. I am not as strong as I sometimes appear to be. I need my brothers; I need my sisters."

It takes a lot of humility to ask for help. . . .

But I'll tell you this, my friend, I wouldn't want to live any other way. I want to live at the foot of the cross. I want to be where God can talk to me. I want to be where people can walk all over me, and I can still praise God. I want to be able to be humble before God. . . . It grieves my heart when I see the grace of God drained from the hearts of people because they are afraid to say: "I need help."

. . .This lesson was given to me in California, and it changed my life. I was preaching, but I was going through some really tough water. We had just had our first child, and he was sickly. He didn't sleep a night straight through until he was about four years old. He slept about a half-hour at a stretch. And about the time we got used to having him around, we found out that we were going to have another one. . . . We were in debt, and I was discouraged and beat. I went to church on a Sunday morning. I had preached all over Southern California. I had held revivals, and I'd seen hundreds and hundreds of people saved. I was sitting in the church about the fourth row back.

When the invitation was given, the Lord said, "Berquist, you need to go to the altar and have the church pray for you."

As I moved toward the aisle – they were singing "Just As I Am" – the devil said, "Wait a minute, Berquist. You don't need to go down there. You don't need help if you are not a sinner. You know you are not a sinner. You are a preacher. You don't need help. You are supposed to be giving help. You are a leader."

And I reasoned with him. "Devil," I said, "I'll tell you something. If I am a leader, God help me to lead myself to the altar."

214

The table was spread.
The candles were lit.
The disciples argued
As to where they would sit.

For such is the nature
Of most mortal men,
That truths they have learned
They must learn again.

For Jesus had told them,
Though they didn't recall,
That the greatest among them
Would be the servant of all.

It is hard to be proud
And still to be holy
For God gives His grace
To the humble and lowly.

The smaller the man,
The more that he tries
To emblazon his name
Through the earth and the skies.

The disciples had thought
Of the day of all days,
When the earth would resound
With words in their praise.

They thought of a kingdom
Where each would be king
While the rest of the world
Their praises would sing.

So 'round the table
The disciples conferred
And were little prepared
For the words that they heard.

When supper was ended
They prepared to depart,
But Jesus did something
That touched every heart.

He asked for a towel
And some water as well,
And what happened next
John's Gospel will tell:

*"He began to wash the disciples' feet and to wipe them
with the towel wherewith he was girded . . . If I then, your
Lord and Master, have washed your feet, ye also ought to
wash one another's feet." (John 13:5,14 KJV)*

That is the reason
That ever since then,
We have washed the feet
Of our fellow men.

Once more on Thursday,
We will gather because
We want to obey
All of God's laws.

We will find once again
That his promise is true:
"Happy are ye,
If my words ye will do."

Maurice Berquist   04/12/77

It's hard to push a string, you know – works better if you pull it. It's hard to push people, too. A lot of pastors try to push their church to revival, or push the family to do this or that. You can hardly push that string, but you can pull it easily, if you are willing to make the first move.

So I said to the devil, "If I am a leader, let me lead in the right way." And I stepped into the aisle.

"Wait a minute, Berquist," the devil said. "I know you can probably stand some prayer, but you can pray in private. You don't need to go down there."

"Look, devil, I've been praying at home and here in the pew, but somehow I haven't got the answer yet."

He said, "One more thing . . . "

"No more things!" I said.

And I walked down to kneel at that altar for prayer. There was nobody else there, so they knew I didn't go there to save somebody else. We do that sometimes, you know. We have a need ourselves, but we wait until somebody else has gone down. Then we go, and we put an arm around that person. And then,

when somebody comes to pray with him, we mutter, "Me, too."

Aren't we human?

But, praise God! What Jesus said is true: "If you know these things, happy are you if you do them."

God showed me that. In that little showdown I had with Satan that night, God made me willing to be humble – to be whatever He wants me to be. And I want to be that way. I want to be that way tonight. I know tonight that if there was something I could do to help you, I'd do it. If I knew who you are, I wouldn't be embarrassed to come talk to you and say, "Come pray with me at the altar. . . ."

God's here tonight, and I tell you, revival will break out here if we learn to be humble before God. And the grace of God can flow into our lives like water flows into the lowly river bed. When you get humble enough to go to people and tell people you've sinned against them . . . humble enough to come and confess to God that you need help . . . humble enough to say you can't handle it by yourself . . . then you will find the rivers of grace flowing in your life.

The Strong Should Uphold the Weak

Berk preached this sermon numerous times in various settings – this particular version on July 17, 1978, to the First Church of God in Drexel, North Carolina. He opened with brief personal remarks, then moved immediately to the text.

There is a verse in Romans 15 that I want to speak about today – the first verse of Romans 15:

"We then that are strong ought to bear the infirmities of the weak, and not to please ourselves."

Let's stand and pray.

Lord, this morning we are strong. We are physically well; we are rested; we are well fed; we are comfortable. And as far as we can tell at this moment we do not have any really pressing needs.

But there are people here this morning who have needs. And even those of us who are here without any real, urgent needs have friends and family who really need help. And if not these, there are multitudes around the world who need help; and we pray that Thou will help us to lift the burdens of the weak and to be able to give strength. May all of us today feel strengthened by what somebody else has brought to us. We believe this, and thank you for it. Amen.

There are just two kinds of people here today – strong people and weak people. Not everybody is strong in the same place, which is good. And not everybody is weak in the same place, which is even better. Because if the strong people didn't have any weak people around to help, they wouldn't stay strong. And if the weak people didn't have any strong people around to help them, they would stay weak. So we need each other. Nobody is indispensable.

I am what you call a "keeper," my wife tells me. I like to keep things. And she is a "thrower-away." She likes to throw things away. I don't keep everything. I do throw some things away, but I do accumulate things along the way.

I'm not as bad as one fellow I heard of, who was not only a keeper or saver, but he also was an organized saver. That's the worst kind, because they not only keep things, but they spend their life trying to put them in place. He had everything organized. He had the garage full, the basement full, the attic full; and all of it was neatly boxed and labeled properly. He even had a section of little boxes, old shoe boxes, where he labeled things, you know. And he had them stacked on shelves in the attic. He had one box marked, "Pieces of String Too Short to Use."

Now, you may think you've married the world's worst keeper; but unless they have gotten that far down the line, you are not bad off at all.

When I heard about his man, I asked myself the question: How short does a piece of string have to be to be too short to use? That's a hard decision to make, but I finally concluded that there is no such thing as a piece of string too short to use. If you are a string keeper, any piece qualifies, because the strongest rope – whether it's an inch in diameter or three inches in diameter– is still made up of tiny little threads that are woven together. One little piece of string is very weak; but many little pieces woven together, twisted together, are very strong.

And this is what Paul is talking about when he says: *"We then that are strong ought to bear the infirmities of the weak."*

This is the Bible way to do it.

Over the years, I have made a survey of people around the United States and around the world; and I have concluded that there are just two kinds of people. There are those who squeeze the toothpaste tube from the top, and those who squeeze it from the middle or bottom. And they always marry each other!

Now, anybody with any sense at all knows that the proper place to squeeze a toothpaste tube is the bottom. [chuckling] Amen!

Now, anybody with enough sense to get up on Sunday morning knows that the right place to squeeze a toothpaste tube is the bottom, because that way all the toothpaste is always at the top, where you can use it. And sooner or later it's got to go to the top anyway. But, you know, I have never convinced my family of that. They are born middle-squeezers or top-squeezers. For twenty-five years I have been married now, and we have a happy marriage and all that; but every morning when I come in to brush my teeth, I look at the toothpaste tube . . . [chuckling] I look at the toothpaste tube and say, "She never learns."

But, you know, it is not all bad. Not all bad, because for one minute every day I feel terribly important. They may neglect my advice or even my example. They may have no use for me except to pay the bills. But, I'll tell you, when I face the toothpaste tube, I feel necessary. What if I never squeezed the toothpaste to the top of the tube, Ron? [Addressing the question to Ron Fair, a dentist in the audience.]

You know, this sounds simple; but Jesus talked simply. In fact, the Bible says: *"The common people heard him gladly."* They didn't have to guess what he meant.

I am here in Drexel this morning, and I am happy to be here. I never get far from Drexel because the very first time I came here – and that was, oh, more than twenty years ago – I got some Drexel socks. And I told Wilson the other day [referring to Wilson Cooper in the audience, who supplied the socks], "I've still got some of the original Drexel socks."

How's that for being a keeper?

Now, before they quote me in an advertisement to tell how good these socks are, I will share a secret with you. I didn't tell Wilson this, but we have an automatic washer at our house. We bought a new one. We've had a washing machine, but we have never had a washer like this. It's a great machine. It's got a rinse cycle, an extractor; and it's even got a place where you put bleach in, and softener – an automatic dispenser thing. It will do all kinds of amazing stuff. I can't run the thing, thank Heaven!

But it's got something on it that didn't show up in the literature when we bought it. It cost enough, but the store didn't advertise this feature. It's called an automatic sock eater! [*chuckling to himself*] I don't know where it is, but it works. When everything else on the machine fails, this thing still works!

I always wear two socks . . . at the same time . . . one on my right foot and one on my left . . . I have for years . . . and when I take them off, I put two socks in the wash. You know what happens? When they come back, I've got one. And since I am a "keeper," I save the one. I keep hoping the orphan will turn up some day, you see. I keep a candle in the window for that sock to come home!

I checked the drawer the other day, and I had nineteen single socks. I don't know whether they are bachelors or maiden ladies, but they are singles. And since I don't throw things like that away – I mean they are good socks, some of them almost as good as new, you know – so I keep them there. I just can't bring myself to throw them away. But I can't think of a thing in the world to do with them.

That's the problem, you see. Every morning when I go to put on my socks, I look at these singles. They are the right color,

be the strong one in the home, and we carry the load. We pay the bills. You may be the strong one in a family; the strong one in business. And you have conditioned yourself to square your shoulders and stand straight and tall, even when you are falling apart on the inside. It's hard for me to ask help from anybody. But, oh, when I realize that it's just as important to be weak . . .

We need each other.

I didn't preach this morning because I wanted a chance to preach – I'm speaking four times today; I spoke four times yesterday. But I tell you, my friend, my heart is burdened that we shall be God's church, where if we are strong we are not just strong to say how strong we are, but we are strong to help somebody.

I don't know you people too well. I've been away a long time, and I don't know much about your personal situations; but I can tell you this: there are some people right here today who are carrying heavy loads. Some of you shared them with me – a man here is carrying a load that would break anybody. Kidney stones would be a vacation compared with what you are carrying.

But I want to tell you this: There are some people in this church right now who want to help you carry that load. And the Bible says, "When Jesus sees their faith, He will say to you, here is the help you need."

Do something for me today. First of all, stand up. That would be a help – for everybody to stand. Now, I want you to pray with me. I'm going to use a song to pray with, an old song. We don't want the piano or the organ the first time around – we want to sing it just as a prayer . . . a song we have sung a lot and rightly so. This song says, "I need Thee every hour."

And I want you to sing it, this time not to Jesus, but to the whole church. Man, I need somebody. If there is that one person or two people or ten people who have a need – perhaps a physical need, perhaps a home need, perhaps just a heartbreak need – and you can say, "Man, I believe what you said. I have carried the burden, and now I want to give it to somebody else." I am not asking you to have any faith at all for yourself. I don't want you to try to pull your faith up, or your emotion up, to believe anything except the fact that there are people here who want to help you. All you need to do is just to say, "I need help."

I want you to come and kneel at this altar.

And then the rest of you who are strong come gather around these who have needs and support them with the strength of your faith. I may not be strong tonight. I may be kneeling there myself for help tonight. But right now I am strong. I am strong to help people. And others here today are strong enough to give you their faith.

While we start singing, if you have a need, don't wait for anybody else. You are important here.

You might say, "I'm the weakest one in the church."

Praise God, we've got you here, because you need what we can do for you. Sing this verse as a prayer: "I need Thee every hour . . ." [Congregation begins singing.]

Understanding the Whole Bible

One of the most helpful conferences Berk shared in various settings was "How to Understand the WHOLE Bible." These simple, practical concepts that guided his own Bible study were ultimately published in the Library for Living series under the title "When the Bible Seems Confusing." What follows is the study outline he used for a presentation of these concepts at Central Community Church in Wichita.

Part 1
Text: II Timothy 3:16,17; Hebrews 1:1-3; John 5:39-47

I. Why should we try to understand the whole Bible?
   A. It claims for itself authority and validity.
   B. Jesus honored the Scriptures and quoted from them.
   C. It is unique in its composition and unity.
   D. Historically, it has stood the test of time.

II. In what attitude should we approach the understanding of the Bible?
   A. Openness
   B. Reverence
   C. Anticipation

III. Beginning techniques of Bible study
Approach Bible study in the same methodical way we approach a jigsaw puzzle, starting with what we know, what we are sure of (corner pieces and straight edges).
   A. Get the whole picture.
   B. Begin with the obvious rather than the obscure.
   C. In the light of Hebrews 1:1-2, determine the time reference.
   D. Obey the obvious message before questioning the obscure.

Part 2
Text: II Timothy 3:16, 17; Psalm 119:105

Ten Commandments for Creative Bible Study

1. Look for the whole picture in the smallest part.
2. Look for the clear meaning in the most obscure part.
3. Believe that under the obvious is a deeper meaning.
4. Do not shy away from difficult scriptures, reading only those that are familiar. Looking for your lost keys under the street light merely because there is more light there is unproductive.
5. Linger over the scriptures. Pre-soak. Let the Holy Spirit have time to work.
6. Put problem texts into your "Later Box."
7. Accept help. As Christopher Morley said, "No man has enough bees in his own bonnet to pollinate the flowers of his own mind."
8. As translated from the Latin phrase *Scriptura Scripturae Interpres* – "Scripture by Scripture is Interpreted." In other words, let Scripture explain Scripture. The New Testament is in the Old, concealed. The Old Testament is in the New, revealed.
9. Believe that the same Holy Spirit that inspired the writing can inspire the reading.
10. Since the Word is the "lamp to your feet" and "light to your path," start walking in the light you have. You will get more.

How I Learned To Preach Without Notes

Frankly, I had never seen it done. I had listened to preaching from the time I was able to be carried to the church until the time I myself began to preach. Always the preacher used notes. Well established preachers had black notebooks full of notes. Often the pages were dog-eared and yellow with notes, outlines and illustrations marked with red ink.

When I finished college and started holding meetings that were optimistically advertised as "revivals," I bought a black notebook about the same size as my Bible, and proceeded to fill it with sermon outlines. This, I thought, was the way it was done.

My first full scale meeting after graduation was in Apollo, Pennsylvania. It began on Sunday and by Monday night I had consumed three of my precious black-bound outlines.

Tuesday morning Pastor W.C. Wood said, "Would you like to go to Pittsburgh and have lunch at Clarence McCartney's church?"

I had never heard of Clarence McCartney, but I was willing to meet him. Lunch, however, was a high priority. Pittsburgh, the city, would be a bonus.

The business man's lunch at Dr. McCartney's church impressed me. Why, I asked, would a thousand business men come to eat chicken ala king and mashed potatoes every Tuesday? Especially at a church.

While I puzzled over that, a balding man in a black suit walked up to a microphone. He carried nothing in his hands, not even a Bible. He began to talk:

Today we are in the stadium at the Circus Maximus in ancient Rome. A hundred thousand people have come to be entertained. Every seat in the high-banked stone stadium is taken. At the far west end is the canopied booth of the Emperor. The Emperor always sits at the west end of the stadium so that the setting sun will not get into his eyes. From his elevated place he and his subjects watch the day's entertainment.

Dancing girls from Ethiopia perform. Next three jugglers from Thessalonica. Then sword throwers from Macedonia. Each act, more daring than the last, brings applause.

Then silence. Everyone waits as three people walk out to the center of the arena. It is so quiet you can almost hear their footsteps on the grass. Two women and a man. They are dressed in simple clothes, the clothes of peasants. They walk like kings and queens.

A soldier in a glistening silver helmet goes to the group and talks to them. "Look to the far end of the arena," he says. "Behind those heavy oak doors with giant hinges are two lions. They have had no food for a week. In a moment a guard will open the doors and the lions will come to pounce upon you. They will eat you alive.

"But you still have a chance. You don't need to die. If you will take this tiny pinch of incense, walk to the charcoal brazier in front of the Emperor, drop the incense on the glowing coals, you can live. That is all you have to do. You don't have to believe that the emperor is God. You simply have to go through the motions of worshipping him.

"Otherwise, I will nod to the guard, and he will open

Wearing overalls borrowed from Joe Gullion, Berquist, the young evangelist, preaches without notes for the "Pioneer Day" service in East Prairie, Missouri (circa 1951).

the oak doors. The lions are eager. You can hear their growling."

None of the three speaks. They begin to sing. We listen:

> *If we suffer with him,*
> *We shall reign with him.*
> *If we die with him,*
> *We shall live with him.*
> *If we deny him,*
> *He will deny us,*
> *For he cannot deny himself.*

The final words are almost lost as the lions, freed from their starvation prison, leap to their victims. They do not pause even to growl as they tear ribbons of flesh from the three Christians. The crowd, normally shouting at the sight of blood is silent. Deathly silent.

In moments there is almost nothing to remind us of the three believers who walked so royally to the center of the arena. A few pieces of gnawed bones, some bloody rags and a crimson stain on the green grass.

But there is something else. There is a song. The singers are gone. But the song — yes, the song — it lingers. Like a kind of musical perfume, it lingers and clings to the emperor's robes as he walks away. It lingers in the crevices of the stone seats of the stadium. The stubbly blades of grass are like strings of a harp as the wind passes over them. The world can never quiet the song of the early Christians.

Timothy wrote about it in the New Testament, but he only wrote it because he couldn't forget it.

In our minds we stand again in the Circus Maximus in Rome. The emperor is gone. The stadium with the stone seats is gone. Dancers, jugglers, sword throwers — all gone. Under the blue Roman skies the trees stir in the wind. We hear it again. That song:

> *If we suffer with him,*
> *We shall reign with him.*
> *If we die with him,*
> *We shall live with him.*
> *If we deny him,*
> *He will deny us,*
> *For He cannot deny himself.*

My heart beat fast. It beats fast as I remember even now. I could not imagine how a man in a plain black suit would walk out in front of a thousand crusty business men and, with nothing in his hands, fill their minds and hearts.

I had not heard of Clarence McCartney before this. I had never seen anyone preach this way before. But that day I said, "If I ever become a preacher, there is the kind of preacher I want to be. This is the way it is done. And I have tried to do it."

I think you should try it, too!

The Bridge

A chasm loomed before me
A chasm deep and wide.
I had no bridge nor ferry
To reach the other side.

I stood in fear and anguish,
More pain than I could bear.
O, how I wished to get across
To find the healing there.

I flung a slender thread across,
'Twas little more than hope;
And then more hopeful prayers;
At last they made a rope.

The ropes turned into cables,
And then a bridge they made.
I walked across this sturdy bridge
To the land for which I'd prayed.

And now I'm thankful day by day,
And I rejoice in health.
I have a priceless treasure
Worth vastly more than wealth.

My feeble prayers are answered,
But not for me alone;
The bridge of faith helps others
Find healing at God's Throne.

Maurice Berquist
8/24/91 4:30 A.M.

Pippa Passes, But Just Barely

The year's at the spring
But the spring has gone dry.
The day's at the mourn,
With no tears to cry.
The snail's on the thorn;
He's stuck there, I guess.
From my perspective,
The world is a mess.

Reflections

The mists of Seattle
Have vanished and gone.
Sunshine breaks through,
While traffic rolls on.
Street people are rising
And packing their bags.
I look in the mirror
And see my face sags.
The day's bright and new,
Fresh as a daisy.
How come my complexion
Is so confounded lazy?

Getting It Together to BE the Church (1988)

The Church may never need me, but I need the Church. Everything I have that is of any value I've received from the Church. If I can give something to the Church in return, I am happy to give what I can. But I can never give as much as I have received.

One of the great moments of my life was listening to the famous preacher Clovis Chappell. I would not have known he was Clovis Chappell, the noted speaker whose sermons were preached all over the country by desperate men seeking his books on Saturday night. But he came to the seminary where I was a student in Louisville, Kentucky. He looked like a retired farmer, slight of build in a rumpled blue suit. On the platform he made a strange contrast to the president of the seminary, Dr. Frank Caldwell, who always looked like those immaculately groomed men you see in advertisements for men's clothing.

After a pompous introduction, Dr. Chappell came forward. Leaning over the pulpit – contrary to what our teachers had taught us to do – he made a kind of swooping gesture and said, "I want to read to you from the book of Acts." Then he read a text from the sixth chapter: *"And in those days, when the number of disciples was multiplied, there arose a murmuring of the Grecians against the Hebrews, because their widows were neglected in the daily ministration." (KJV)* And he read on through verse 6.

Then Clovis Chappell – this rumpled, unimpressive looking man – leaned over the pulpit and said, "These words take us across two oceans, across almost twenty centuries, to a strange language being spoken in a strange church; and only one thing is familiar: 'There arose a murmuring.' Those words put us on familiar ground. A church may be too dead to have missions or to have a revival; too dead even to start an argument. But a church is rarely so dead it can't have a murmuring."

Then he said, "Even in a theological cemetery" (making a play on *seminary*) "a murmuring is welcome!"

When the laughter subsided, he continued.

"I want to tell you about a young man who was graduated from seminary and was sent by his bishop to his first congregation. As he surveyed his congregation that first Sunday morning, he saw that they were dead. They were very dead. He was, in fact, looking at a congregation not even of skeletons, but fragments of skeletons – dry bones.

"Nevertheless, having been to seminary, this young pastor knew what to do.

"He said, 'Bishop, they are dead; but I organized them.'

"He had a set of 3 x 5 cards ready to get the data all straight.

"We always seem more comfortable when our dead church is organized! A little more and he would have had a committee in charge of the organization – neck bones collected in one place, shin bones over here in another place, ankle bones there in another place, trombones in another place! He would have had a thoroughly organized, systematized church.

"Unfortunately, it was still dead.

"Thus, he decided that instead of listening to the bishop or to his seminary professors, he would listen to God.

"And God said, 'Start preaching to these dry bones.'"

Then Clovis Chappell said, "What I believe is needed in a world of formality and ritualistic form is a revival of Spirit-filled preaching.

"And so God said to the young preacher, 'Prophesy to the wind.' Don't prophesy to the bones, because the bones can't listen. Prophesy in the Spirit and you preach the truth. Honor the Spirit of God, and God will get it together.

"Ezekiel felt really strange, I am sure, standing there in that congregation, preaching in an impossible situation – to a congregation of disorganized, disoriented, lifeless forms. But as he began to preach, the Spirit began to move. And when the Spirit moved, those dead bones began to stir, and they began to get connected. The ankle bone connected to the leg bone . . . and the leg bone connected to the thigh bone . . . and the thigh bone connected to the back bone . . . and the back bone connected to the choir . . . and they sang a song!

"And when that togetherness came, the same Spirit of God began to clothe those bones with flesh and sinews and life.

"God begins a revival in the Church, or in our lives, by getting things together. Adultery may not destroy the church, but division will."

That message by Clovis Chappell rang true in my soul that day. It's a message the Church needs to hear again and again.

I have been in love with the text in Ephesians, which Will Hughes opened to me this summer in Alabama:

> *But speaking the truth in love, may grow up into him in all things, which is the head, even Christ:*
> *From whom the whole body fitly joined together and compacted by that which every joint supplies, according to the effectual working in the measure of every part, maketh increase of the body unto the edifying of itself in love."*
> *- Ephesians 4:15-16 (KJV)*

Will lifted up the phrase which says that the body is "compacted by the joints," not by the bones. That word *joint* has been haunting me. We are, for instance, "*joint* heirs with Christ."

I loved what Will said about it.

"The elbow," he said, "is a joint. Take the arm apart and you haven't got an elbow. You've got two bones in the forearm, and you have an upper arm bone. When you say, 'My arm is strong,' where does the strength lie? The forearm by itself is nothing; the upper arm by itself is nothing. The arm's only existence and its strength are in connection." Note that.

Paul in writing to the Ephesians is concerned about only one thing: getting things together. In the ministry of preaching or teaching we can never ignore the importance of either the mind or the heart. The mind, the intellect, the calculating, reasoning part of our body – that's part of it. We shouldn't discredit it.

Ezekiel gets organized.

– Barry Sempsrott

Scripture says that the Spirit of God is the Spirit of wisdom. *"If any of you lacks wisdom, let him ask of God, who gives to all liberally and without reproach, and it will be given him."* (James 1:5 NKJV)

But wisdom without the feeling of the heart is lost. It spins off into nothingness. For the Bible also says that even *"if I have all knowledge . . . I am nothing without love."* (1 Corinthians 13:2)

But sentimentality and feeling without wisdom is an equally erroneous notion. In the plan of God, we are called both to think– clearly, coldly, logically – and to feel– warmly and passionately. A preacher needs the mind of a genius and the heart of a marshmallow; the sensitivity of a deer and the skin of a rhinoceros. We need to bring these things together, and it is in this togetherness that the magic takes place.

The book of Ephesians speaks of uniting two very different views of life and religion – the Jews, with their historic rigidity, and the Gentiles (Greeks), who were loose and philosophical. Paul says that Christ *"has made both one, and has broken down the middle wall of division . . . ."* (Ephesians 2:14 NKJV)

All of life is, in fact, made up of contrasting elements coming together. Hydrogen, for example, is a highly combustible, explosive gas. Oxygen, likewise, is a highly combustible gas. Both burn. Both are dangerous. But bring hydrogen and oxygen together, and the result is H_2O – water!

The act of bringing two unlike things together produces something totally different. We call it *synergism*: two things coming together make something more than those two separate things. They make a totally new thing.

The act of preaching is like that. The intellect – the reason, the mind, the brain – by itself will not produce the desired effect. Neither will emotion by itself. But bring them together, as God wants us to, and the result is powerful!

That same principle of synergism applies to life in our churches. The chemistry of the Spirit is not to make us uniform, but to make us united. If only pastors and laity alike could understand that concept, what a blessing it would be, because we are all different.

If you are into modern psychology, more or less, you likely are familiar with left brain and right brain mentalities. It is called the hemispheric brain theory – that the two hemispheres of the brain primarily perform different functions and that each one of us tends to lean toward one side of the brain or the other as being dominant.

Left-brained people, for example, are the bean counters. They like to organize things, systematize things. They hang all their clothes in the same direction in their closets – according to color – and iron their socks, and so on. They are systematic, logical people.

Right-brained people, on the other hand, are the more poetic type – visionary, speculative, impulsive.

Usually left-brains and right-brains marry each other; then they each spend a lifetime trying to reform the other person!

I'm a right brain. Oh, I'm fairly systematic because I have to be, but it's a trained response. I'm not naturally that way. I think in generalities. I do things spontaneously.

My wife is just the opposite. She's left-brained; and in true left-brained fashion, she organizes things at our house.

I travel a lot. Once when I returned home after being gone about a week, she said, "Honey, while you were away I straightened up your library."

And she had. The shelves looked really neat. She had organized all the books – by height! Tall books here; short books there. So now if I want something on theology, it's 5 and 7/8!

If I'd stayed away longer, they would have been organized by color, too!

We right-brained people tend to save things, because you never know when you are going to need them. My wife, in typical left-brained fashion, throws things away. If you want to read the morning paper at our house, get there before noon! When I come back from a revival, I always check the trash first. I've saved a lot of good stuff that way.

I'm not as bad about saving stuff as one man I heard of though. He not only saved everything, but like my wife, he organized it. He had boxes and files and categories in his basement and in the attic. He even had one box labeled, "Pieces of string too short to use."

Well, do these unlike behavioral traits create serious problems for Berny and me? Not really. It's a good thing right-brains and left-brains get together. The way I see it, that's how two half-wits make a whole brain!

We need each other, you see. If everybody were like me, it would be a disaster. If everybody were like her, it would be a *neat* disaster!

While I am being facetious about these differences to a point, the truth is that behavioral differences like these and personality differences account for most of our problems in the Church. Many times, it isn't that we disagree on the bottom line about what ought to be done; we just can't see eye to eye on how to do it. Left-brains and right-brains don't see or approach things the same way.

Similarly, different personality types have different viewpoints. Highly directive and highly structured people do not approach situations and decisions in the same way. Neither do extroverts and introverts. Some people are results oriented and want to take immediate action. Others are more reflective and resist making hasty decisions. Some people are intuitive and make snap judgements. Others are uncomfortable with decisions not backed up by thorough research.

It has always been so. It was that way in Paul's day, for Paul says to the Ephesians – and to us – that though we are all different, God planned from the beginning that all of His family – Jews and Gentiles alike – be seen as "joined together in his church." *(Ephesians 3:10-11 Living Bible)*

I say all this to make one point: The most hazardous thing that can happen in the church is one-sidedness – one-sided preaching, one-sided living, one-sided communication. We need one another. And Paul is saying that God will bring us together through Jesus Christ, our Lord.

Mark these words: *An independent spirit will kill you!*

I am amazed at pastors who say, "I want my church to be with me," yet the pastor is not with anybody else. The independent, self-contained, self-dominated church doesn't give to general causes. They don't help with any state or national campaigns or programs. They are focused totally inside themselves, doing "their thing." They preach unity, but they have forgotten this basic truth about the body of Christ: *"It is compacted at the joint."* They have forgotten about the elbow. God ordains that we come together.

It's not easy to come together. It's easier to be independent. In preaching, it's much easier to be [catch the deep, solemn tones here] "A Bible Preacher"– dull as a hammer. Orthodox? Yes. Scholarly? Yes. But you'll kill the Church, because preaching, if it's to be effective, needs to be tied to life!

Pastor, you need to get out of that cocoon. Get out where your people are! Get some tears rubbed into the shoulder of your coat. Get some callouses in your hands. Be with your people.

Now does that mean that you neglect meditation and Bible study? Of course not. If you're not anchored to God's word, you haven't got anything to give people. You need both of these things. It is not either-or. It's both.

And it works the same way throughout the church. In the church we need planners, and we need organizers. We need administrators and teachers; prophets and prayer warriors; visiting teams and helpers. We need it all. All of us together. We need laughter and tears. We need thoughts. We need both crowds and solitude to get it all together. And God will help us to bring things together. We all add something.

Whenever I have been part of a team of conference leaders at a seminar, I have seen this principle in evidence. The various conference leaders will have different styles of presentation, different approaches to their assigned topics, but all of them add a little something to the understanding of the overall theme. They all help "get it together." And those who attend the seminar make a contribution, too, in discussion and even as they listen. We need you. You need us.

But, now, we need to understand in the Church that whatever can foster the feeling of togetherness, the Holy Spirit can bless.

Back in your home church, the Spirit can blend your talents together. The beautiful thing is that each one of you is like nobody else. Your childhood, your parentage, your culture, your idiosyncrasies, your strengths, your weaknesses, your experiences – God can bring those together to make you a unique contributor to the whole – whatever your role: preacher, board member, usher, choir member, and so on.

Emerson said – if I may paraphrase – he said: "There comes a time in every man's education when he realizes that envy is ignorance and imitation is suicide."

Listen. When you wish to be what somebody else is, or envy what somebody else has, you are destroying the valuable person that you are.

I have a friend who is a pastor. He is in charge of a large financially secure church. He has been able to go to all the seminars around the country and around the world, for that matter, and listen to the experts. One day one of his parishioners said to me: "We have had Robert Schuller for pastor, Jack Hyles for pastor, Jerry Falwell for pastor, John Maxwell for pastor. The next conference shapes our pastor. Well, I went to our pastor the other day and said, 'Why don't we just have our pastor for pastor.'"

That's not to say John Maxwell can't teach you something, or Jerry Falwell or Robert Schuller or Jack Hyles or anybody else. You may get grass from many a pasture, but you've got to give your own milk! You've got to be the person God made you to be and bring it together.

And I am convinced of this, friends, if we would bring to God the divergent parts of our personality and let Him bring it together for His plan, it would work. He likes us as we are.

I've got to tell you my favorite story about the church – my deep theological discussion of what it means to be a part of the church.

My wife is a lovely lady and a good pastor's wife. She likes to shop, and that's not bad. I've reconciled myself to it. Soon after we got married, she suggested one day that we go shopping, and I asked a stupid question: "What do you want to shop for?"

She looked at me quizzically. "How do I know until I see what they've got?"

I didn't understand that then – but now I do! So I go shopping with her.

One time, when we lived in Florida, we went to Jacksonville shopping. And she shopped to her heart's content – until the stores closed. Then we drove back to Daytona Beach.

Now, as you know, Daytona Beach is a vacation city; but it's a beach town. There is not much night life in Daytona. People come down there to get sunburned. They are blistered by noon; and, consequently, they are not howling at night. Down there 7-11's close at five o'clock! You get the picture. Things are rather dull around Daytona at night.

Well, when we got back to town, we wanted something to eat. It was late, so most of the restaurants were closed. But we finally found a small family-type place still open – nothing elegant, but adequate. We went in, sat down at a table, and ordered.

We hadn't been there long when my wife, who sat facing the door, saw the door open. She leaned toward me and said, "Don't look now, but somebody's coming in the door."

So I didn't look.

"Who is it?" I asked.

"I think it's the piano player – Van Cliburn."

Then I remembered reading in the paper that he was doing a concert in Daytona Beach that evening. Obviously, he was out doing the same thing we were – trying to find something to eat in Daytona, which at that time of night wasn't easy.

I said, "Well, let me look."

She said, "Don't stare."

So I didn't.

I just stared straight ahead.

Fortunately for me, he came over and sat down at the counter to our left. So when I looked over at him, I didn't stare all the time.

You could tell he wasn't your ordinary tourist. He wore striped pants and a cut-away coat with long tails. Sitting there at the counter, I must say, he made an elegant sight. I always wondered what those tails were for. They work well at a counter like that.

So we sat there. And I sensed the most amazing question arising in my mind.

I leaned toward Berny and said, "I wonder what he will order."

I always wonder what musicians eat that makes them the way they are, because based on my lack of musical ability, I've obviously been eating the wrong stuff all my life! So I figured here was my chance to conduct a little bonafide research. Obviously he could afford anything on the menu.

We waited a moment. Then he made his selection, and the waitress brought out his order. On the counter before him, she set out a large glass and two little orange cardboard cartons of milk – Foremost milk.

Van Cliburn poured the milk in the glass, drank it, paid his check, and walked out.

After he was gone, I just stared at those orange cartons on the counter.

And Berny said, "Honey, you're staring."

I said, "I know. Those things don't care.

And she said, "What on earth are you staring at them for?"

"I don't know if those cartons realize what's happened," I said. "They've just held some very important milk. Yesterday it was in the cow. Today it's in Van Cliburn. Tomorrow, Carnegie Hall. Just think, honey, yesterday that milk could only moo. Tomorrow it will handle Rachmaninoff!"

And she said, "You're crazy."

Whereupon, I didn't preach any more to her.

But I'm preaching now – to you. You need to understand the miracle of what happened in this crazy milk story.

The parable is this: We are put together in the body of Christ. By ourselves we are nothing. But we are put in the body of the Church; and we become, as that milk did, a part of the body and blood and veins and energy of Christ. And when we speak, we do not speak or act in our own power – we speak and act with His strength. When we become part and parcel of the Body of Christ, we can do wonderful, even miraculous things!

This is the point: Until you are willing to become a part of that body – to be together with God's family; to be in connection with God's family; to be assimilated, absorbed by God's family – you are never transformed by God's family.

We – clergy and laity alike – preach "the gospel of togetherness" when we say: "God will help me get it together, and I will help pull you together. Then together, as Paul said, we can 'know the height, the breadth, and length, and depth of the love of Christ that passes all knowledge.'"

We can be filled with "all the fullness of Christ" if we simply get together to be God's people.

> Between the pen and the paper,
> Between the thought and the word,
> Between the truth and the speaking,
> Between what is said and what's heard,
> Between the deep-seated feelings,
> Between the desire and the act,
> Between the dream and the doing,
> Between the perception and fact,
> Between the prayer and the answer,
> Between the hope and the fear,
> Between the now and the never,
> Between the laughter and tear,
> Between creator and creature,
> Between the heaven and earth,
> Between the extremes of our being,
> The creative spirit gives birth.
>
> M. Berquist
> 10/08/88

Shop Early for Christmas
For *People to People*, January, 1984

It is not too early to start shopping for next Christmas.

This thought may be about as welcome as the news of a raise in taxes, but the good news is that your shopping may be a whole lot easier than you thought.

Our next-door neighbors are a family of delightful people. There are three young boys, filled with all the ambitions and charm of their generation. Each year we try to buy some small Christmas gift for these boys. Since our own children have long since grown and left home, Berny and I are not really a good judge of what kinds of things boys want nowadays. So, Berny asked the mother what would be appropriate.

"Why don't you get them some batteries?"

"You have to be kidding," Berny replied. "What kid wants to find a box of batteries under the tree?"

"Well, they keep getting new toys, but the batteries have all run down. What they really need are some batteries to energize the things they already have."

This touches a problem all of us have. We do not need new projects and new ideas. We need fresh energy to activate things we have already committed ourselves to. We need some new dynamite for our old dreams. . . .

Lying around in our memories are thousands of things we have begun and didn't finish or things we intended to do, but never began. We may, in the first flush of enthusiasm, have imagined that merely having the idea was almost as good as completing the project. Or we may have salved our conscience by thinking that merely promising to do something was almost as good as doing it. So the dreams lie like abandoned Christmas toys, still intact, but lifeless. Their batteries are dead.

Motivation. Activation – that's what we need. New power for our old projects.

Where do we get the power we need to make us active again?

Probably all of us have different ways to get our motor going, but I am going to suggest a few things that work for me in the hope they will work for you.

1. Don't start looking for something new. Instead, find something that is abandoned and make it active again. For example, don't worry about making new friends. Think of an old friendship you have neglected. If it was a meaningful one, it won't take much to let that person know you still care about him or her. Don't worry about finding a new project, find one that you got discouraged with and abandoned. Pick it up, dust if off, and bring it to life. You will do at least two things: You will capitalize on the work you have already invested in, and you will rid yourself of a lot of guilt.

2. Don't look for something big to resurrect. Start polishing off things within your range and your grasp. Success has a way of bringing is own energy and motivation.

3. Recognize discouragement as a tool of the devil. Overcome it with action. The biggest battles with discouragement are usually fought just before the moment of victory. It seems to be a law of life. So persist when you feel like giving up. In a matter of moments (or months, depending on the project), you will feel a surge of energy that makes you wonder why you ever thought of quitting.

4. Depend on the power of the Spirit. According to the Bible, the flesh is always weak. It is only as we allow the Holy Spirit to energize our dreams and mobilize our energies that we learn the secret of becoming recharged.

Living the Blessing Life
Notes for a sequel to
The Miracle and Power of Blessing
8/15/89

Response to the dynamic principles Berk unveiled in his first book on blessing was immediate and enthusiastic. From all over the country came testimonials about the power of blessing at work in the lives of people who had put into practice concepts from the first book. He had started a file of those stories for a second book. Here is a sampling of those notes.

Have I told you about the 330-pound lady who called me in the middle of the night?

Being a pastor for many years, I learned the wisdom of having a bedside telephone. Every pastor should have one. In any normal congregation there will be people who retire at 8:00 p.m. and get up at 4 or 5 in the morning. They will probably wait until 6:00 A.M. to call you. On the other end of the spectrum are people who retire at 1:00 P.M. and find that 12:30 A.M. is a good time to find you home.

Both groups make an attempt at kindness by saying, "I hope I didn't get you out of bed."

"No," you respond sleepily, fumbling with your bedside phone, "you didn't get me out of bed by calling now."

It was indeed 1:00 A.M. when my bedside phone awakened me. A female voice asked, "Do you know who this is?"

"I'm afraid not."

The caller continued, "I heard your lecture on "Blessing" a year ago, and it has changed my life. When I came to listen to you, I was miserable. I weighed 330 pounds, had a terrible self-image and almost no friends. But now, I'm a perfect Size 12. I've changed so much my friends keep asking what has happened to me. So, I just wanted to call and thank you."

"Thank you," I said – now wide awake. "I'm really happy for you. I hope you keep on blessing your new Size 12 self."

By that time my wife was awake.

"Who was on the phone?" she asked.

"A 330-pound lady."

"Oh," she said, and turned over and went back to sleep.

By this time I was even more wide awake. I began to try to understand what had happened to this lady who had lost a whole "other person" of weight. How did she do it?

I imagine that many others who fight a weight problem have the same question. In fact, I referred to this lady in *The Miracle and Power of Blessing*, but didn't tell the complete story. So I am often asked, "How did she do it?"

One thing is sure: conventional diets didn't do it. Statistics indicate that only 2 to 5 percent of those who go on diets will permanently lose weight. What did it for this lady?

I have spoken several times with my Size 12 friend since that late-night call. And from those conversations, I can isolate four things from the "Blessing Life Style" that could have helped her:

1. The "Blessing Life" Brings Inner satisfaction.

When we start "blessing" anything, we feel a sense of completeness that comes directly from God. It meets a need. We were born to be positive and happy. When negative thoughts come and the corresponding depression lowers our spirits, we look for other sources of energy. And, guess what is the most available form of energy – food! The quick snack, the pick-me-up cup of coffee and glazed donut, the bar of candy.

It is not incidental that the Psalmist wrote in Psalm 103: *"Who satisfieth thy mouth with good things; so that thy youth is renewed like the eagle's." (Ps. 103:5 KJV)*

Much of our hunger is spiritual – or psychological. The conversation of overweight persons often suggests this inner hunger: "When I'm lonely, I eat. When I'm depressed, I eat. When I feel like a failure, I eat. And if by discipline and will power I go on a diet for a few days, I celebrate my weight loss by eating! After all, I deserve it."

2. The "Blessing Life" is the energized life.

Psychologists and physicians have determined that criticism causes a measurable decline in our metabolism. In fact, scientific testing has shown that for every criticism we receive we need five compliments or positive strokes to bring our energy level back to normal.

How did the 330-pound lady gain energy and lose weight through blessing? By blessing the truth she had learned, by blessing the person from whom she had learned it, and by blessing the person she was becoming she started a chain reaction of positive energy – calorie consuming energy. Some of those excess calories were consumed in the warmth of her sunny spirit.

3. The "Blessing Life" frees us from self-condemnation about food.

Again comments frequently made by over-weight people as they eat are revealing: "I really shouldn't eat this – but, oh well." "I know there must be 1,000 calories in this piece of cake, but . . . ." These negative, self-condemning thoughts do their deadly work, adding the weight of a violated conscience to the OREO cookies! A deadly combination.

4. The "Blessing Life" encourages others to bless us.

It's the "echo effect." When you start blessing people, they respond by blessing you. In the same way as when you are critical of people, they are critical of you.

Life is like a mirror, reflecting what you are and do. On the wall of an humble home in Topeka, Kansas, was a little poem called "Life's Mirror." Its last lines were these:

> Give to the world the best you have,
> And the best will come back to you

The "echo effect" of blessing brings the kind of satisfaction that encourages us to like ourselves and to be kind to others. We see little need for committing "gastronomic suicide" – death by the knife and fork.

All of these laws must have operated in the life of the lady who lost at least 175 pounds. So now she doesn't have to use her imagination to feel good about herself. She can use a three-way mirror.

Blessing her way to a perfect "Size 12."
Sketch by Dick Maloney, Illustrator
for The Miracle and Power of Blessing

You Have to Splash a Little
If You Want Your Cup to Stay Full

It had been a long day.

Rising at 4:30 a.m., I'd had a quick cup of coffee with my host in Denmark and then drove to Hamburg, Germany. The trek was more than a little tiring. The Danish drivers were completely relaxed, but when I hit the German segment of the express highway, I felt the pressure. Normally, I drive a little below the speed limit; but on the German Interstate I gritted my teeth, clenched the wheel, and watched the speedometer register 140 kilometers – between 85 and 90 miles an hour! Even so, the lights of BMW's and Mercedes flashed in my rear view mirror – or they passed me almost as though I were standing still.

Once in the airport I hurriedly released my rented VW and tried to estimate how many dollars I had spent on $7-a-gallon gasoline. That thought was, to say the least, depressing.

Then I boarded the flight to London and on to Atlanta. The plane was filled to capacity, and the prospect of a nine-hour flight with your knees in your chin was less than exciting.

As the plane sped across the Atlantic, I noticed how poised the flight attendants were – how efficient in dealing with a planeload of people speaking different languages. For want of anything better to do, I composed on my yellow legal pad a four-stanza poem, complimenting the attendants on their excellent service. I am sure the piece didn't pose any threat to Emily Dickinson or William Shakespeare, but it was at least contemporary.

I gave it to one of the flight attendants along with a word of appreciation. She read it, smiled, gave me a big hug. Then showed it to her assistant. Another smile. Another hug.

"Can we put this up at the front of the plane?" she asked. "We might put it in our Inflight Paper, too."

"Certainly."

So the yellow piece of paper was put up on the bulkhead right by the cabin kitchen. For the rest of the flight I noticed other attendants and passengers reading the poem. I felt renewed energy. And by the time we reached Atlanta, I had forgotten the whole thing. The attendants had not – they thanked me again as I left the plane.

Had I given a blessing? Possibly to several people. Eventually, perhaps, to several thousand. And I was renewed in energy.

When I arrived in Portland, Oregon, that evening, Berny met me.

"Are you worn out?" she asked.

"Surprisingly, I feel great. Let's go out for supper!"

How Tom Yarbro Can Relax after a Day's Work

Tom Yarbro and I were driving past a magnificent church building in Oklahoma City.

"That's one of the buildings we built," Tom said. "And in a way it's remarkable. I had just finished reading your Blessing book and decided to put it into practice. So as we started construction I made a conscious effort to "bless" the workers each day. I found opportunities to say something encouraging to the laborer digging the footings. 'Good job,' I'd say. Or, 'You certainly figured that out quickly.' It wasn't long until the ripple effect began to show. The foremen began to compliment their workers, and workers started doing a little extra – it was contagious."

"The best part ," Tom continued, "was that the building was finished ahead of schedule and under budget. When I finally came to the last inspection, everything was in order. Nothing more needed to be done. And here's the best part of all: this building has been finished for five years, and we have never had

a call back. That's a miracle. There is always something that goes wrong or breaks down during the first year of a building's life. But this time – not a thing. It's wonderful."

"You know," Tom smiled, "it's a good feeling to come home at night, put your feet up, and know that when the phone rings, it's not going to be a complaint. And even better than that, when I drive by that stone church, the stones cry out to bless me. Didn't Jesus say something like that?"

Indeed he did.

Indian at War with Pain

It was an unusual Christmas Card. Actually, it was more than a Christmas Card – a Christmas letter. It came from I.O. and Hilda Tout in Oklahoma. Hilda holds a PhD in Psychology and now has her own clinical practice in hypnotic medicine.

Ordinarily, I would have about as much use for a professional hypnotist as for an alligator in my bath tub. But my talks with Doctor Tout have changed that. Hilda has a fascinating career. She maintains a brisk office practice in "Pain Control" and serves as a consultant to the medical community and the police department. Naturally, her letter proved to be more than a recital of how many strokes I.O. had taken off his golf game.

"Thank you," she began, "for your book and for the tapes on Blessing. I use these ideas almost every day. But this past month I have seen something that startled even me. A full-blooded American Indian came to my office – referred to me by his physician. A victim of an automobile accident, the Chief was in constant excruciating pain. He had been given massive doses of drugs to control the pain. Nothing worked. Then suggestion and hypnosis were attempted. Nothing brought relief. Finally, in desperation, I gave him a copy of your book *The Miracle and Power of Blessing*. Remember how you told me about 'blessing your pain'? Well, I encouraged him to do that. Relief came! And I saw the stoic Chief break into the most hilarious laughter as, for the first time since the accident, he was free from pain. No drugs. No hypnosis. No magic – except the magic of blessing.

"So – Merry Christmas and thanks for your Christmas present in sharing these ideas."

Make Your Day by Making Somebody Else's Better

When Lotus and Brantley Cagle of Lake Charles, Louisiana, invited me to dinner, I expected an unusual evening; but I was totally unprepared for the "after dinner entertainment."

"Nothing fancy," Lotus had said, "just some food and fellowship. I want to invite some of the teachers at my school to come for dessert. They have been reading your book and are eager to meet you."

A few weeks earlier Lotus had asked to buy a couple of copies of *The Miracle and Power of Blessing* to pass around among her teaching colleagues at the elementary school where she works. When I delivered the books to her, she showed me through their school, with its extensive training program for children with all kinds of physical or mental problems. Small wonder that she and the other teachers are interested in the blessing life.

"Please accept the books as a gift," I had told her. "Maybe I can be a blessing to some people I don't even know."

Strange thing about blessing – it becomes a way of life. Once you discover the principle, you begin to see all kinds of opportunities to practice it. There's probably a little undercurrent of greed in that, because once you "bless" something or someone, you start a cycle of blessing that will return to you in multiplied

Barbers Are Pretty Important People

This morning,
Today,
I got to thinking about Al Morgan,
Al Morgan, the barber.

I remembered the first time I met him.
I didn't call him "Al" then.
"Mr. Morgan," it was.
I was a young man coming to Florida,
Coming with a bunch of college kids
To get an instant tan
Under the Florida sun.
I met Madeline, his beautiful wife, too.
And she was pretty important,
Maybe more than Al.
She fixed some food for the gang.
I remember we were always hungry.
Then Al sat down at the family upright piano
And played.

I don't remember the songs he played,
But I never saw a man who enjoyed doing it
As much as Al Morgan did.

He played in any key,
And on all the keys.
It was the kind of thing that William Saroyan
Would have written about,
Or maybe it was the kind of thing that
Norman Rockwell would have painted about.
But I was neither William Saroyan
Nor Norman Rockwell.
I just painted it on the wall of my mind.
So easily. So easily that I wasn't even aware
Of what was happening.
If anyone would have told me what was happening,
I would have laughed.
As a matter of fact, I am smiling now.
Twenty-seven more "spring breaks" have come,
And the colors are still bright
On the walls of my mind.

But Al was not a pianist.
I asked him the other day, and he told me,
"I don't play any more.
I don't know if I can."
Al is a barber.
And for all those twenty-seven years,
And the years before that,
He has been laying his hands on people's heads,
Blessing them.

I may be wrong,
But God will understand
Even if Al does not.
But, wrong or not,

Sketches by Saul Chaftez

blessings. In a sense, you don't really give anything. You simply invest it – and wait for the returns.

So dinner and meeting some of the Cagle's friends was a return on my "investment." But they and their friends gave me far greater blessings than I bargained for. Here are three of the stories shared that evening.

"I'll start," Lotus said. "I'm the one who called this meeting. Did you ever have to take shots from someone who didn't know how to give them? They are bad enough at the hands of an expert.

"Well, the other day I was at the hospital for a series of shots, and the nurse who was to give them – Jeannie was her name – was nervous. 'I feel terrible today,' she said. 'I am not sure how this is going to go.'

"Oh, my! I thought. What can I do? I know: I'll bless her.

"So while Jeannie was getting the medication ready, I spent those few moments blessing her – silently, of course. She came back and gave the shots perfectly – no pain, no problem.

"When it was over, Jeannie said to me: 'Well, that's a miracle. Do you believe in miracles?'

" 'Yes,' I said, 'I do – the miracle of blessing!' "

Lois spoke next. "My story isn't earthshaking, "but I want to tell you about it."

"Good," I answered. "In fact, I am really interested in simple, down-to-earth ways people can turn their problems into occasions for blessing."

"I'm a mall walker," Lois continued. "Each morning a lot of people go walking in the mall before the stores open. We don't really know each other's names, but we all wave to each other and say a word of greeting.

"Recently there has been an old man walking. He can't walk fast or very far. He seems discouraged and bowed down. Since reading your book, Mr. Berquist, I have been silently blessing him – just because I felt he needed it.

"Last week as I was leaving the Mall, he was also leaving. As

It didn't always pay to get too involved
In conversation;
You might get more hair cut
Than you had planned.
But somehow you always took the chance,
Because the whole thing,
Haircut and all,
Was a kind of benediction,
A kind of "laying on of hands."

It doesn't sound like much the way I tell it.
It doesn't sound like what it really was.
The little barber shop on Broadway
Looked like any other barber shop:
Striped pole,
Old magazines,
Bottles of Bay Rum on the counter.
The whole thing.
But there was a kind of Presence about it:
Something that told people,
"I care about you."

I guess that is what I wanted to say.
Some people care about money.
Some people care about getting people to
Care about them.
But Al and Madeline care about people.
And Al, laying his hands on the heads of people,
Only called it "barbering."

And now,
Surrounded by stained glass windows
And the warm sounds of organ music,
I wonder –
Is the "laying on of hands in blessing"
More than this?

Maurice Berquist

I imagine that Al Morgan had laid his hands
On more heads than
Jesus did
While He was here on Earth.

I know how he worked.
He used to cut my hair,
And he would say,
"Son, I sometimes wonder if God called me
To preach the Gospel."
Then he would cut a while.

we walked toward the door, he turned to me and said the first words he had ever spoken to me: 'God bless you.' I was startled. I thought I was the blesser. But I was blessed."

Then it was Steve's turn. Sitting on the couch with his wife, Camille, he had simply smiled and nodded during the other testimonials. "I'm really glad someone explained this process to me," he began. "I can't tell you how many times a day I 'bless' people. Sometimes I pat them on the shoulder. Sometimes I say, 'Bless you.' And sometimes I just try to make them feel better when they leave me than they did when they met me."

These and other experiences shared that evening demonstrate that Blessing truly is like a triangle – with you on one side, other people on the other side, and God on the third side. When you bless other people, you start a current – like a flow of electricity. When they become blessed, they bless God, and God blesses you. So, every time you start the flow of blessing, you end up getting blessed. There is no end to it!

**Committee Report
On Things Heavenly**

Scintillate, scintillate,
Globule vivific.
Fain would I fathom
Thy nature specific.
Distinctly poised
In the ether capacious
Closely resembling
A gem carbonaceous!

Berk
07/12/92

Notes for a Blessing Handbook
One-liners designed to open channels of Blessing

Jesus could do only what he saw his father do.

You praise people because they deserve it. You bless them because they need it.

Bless and do not curse.

"Cursing" is the opposite of blessing.

An angry look can kill quicker than a sword.

Help another sailor get his boat to shore and you arrive yourself.

Negative thinking is "a hole in the bucket"– an energy drainer.

The cup of blessing that is willing to overflow will be filled.

God doesn't like it when you criticize his kids – and you are one of them.

God creates the fruit of the lips. What kind of orchard are you planting?

You can't be "up" on God and "down" on people.

If people thought they would get a blessing by being around you, you couldn't drive them away.

If the door to success seems locked, the key of blessing will open it.

Blessing is more than a pat on the back, but that isn't a bad place to start.

If you truly bless food before you eat it, it will bless you.

A broken spirit dries up the bones; a mended spirit mends them.

God is often called the "fount of blessings." If you cannot be a fountain, at least be a trickle.

Count your blessings instead of sheep; very soon you'll be fast asleep.

If you want to receive a blessing, try giving one.

If you smile at the mirror of life, it will smile back at you.

If you give a blessing, you get a blessing. Better still, you are a blessing.

If you find fault, bury it under a mound of blessing.

Bless your mistakes; they are your unpaid tutors.

Bless those who curse you; you neutralize their attitude and improve your own.

A favorite quote:

"The tragedy of life is not death,
but what we let die within us
while we live."
- Norman Cousins

If you never explore
Those lines on the map.
If you never ponder
The book on your lap.
If you won't let your mind
Roam free far and wide,
You'll live safe and sound
With your dreams all inside.
There's many a mountain
You never will see,
And you'll never know
What your future could be!
M.Berquist
12/05/88

On Dreams and Dreaming

One of Berk's recurring themes was God at work inside of our minds and hearts, guiding us to our destiny through dreams. He played that theme in sermons, in a conference he called "Nite Life," in his last book, "The Secret of Immunity," and in many poems like these:

Whatever things look like,
However things seem
The important thing is
Don't abandon your dreams.

For dreams are like magnets
With power deep within;
They are aimed to the future,
Not what might have been.

All at once out of nowhere,
Like a pleasant surprise,
The things we have dreamed of
Are seen by our eyes.

Like a magnet's slim fingers
Our dreams can reach out,
But we must keep on dreaming;
We must never doubt.

Dreams speak in a whisper
To those who will hear;
Then the things that they speak of
Will shortly appear.

You may lose your fortune;
You may lose your health;
But keep right on dreaming,
For dreams are your wealth.

Maurice Berquist
08/16/85

To Matthew

Go conquer the world, young student;
I really believe you can.
Dream big dreams and do them;
Be an extra-special man.

The world is always waiting
For leaders, brave and true.
The followers are waiting
For a leader such as you!

The day of doubt is over;
The day of faith is in.
The doubter always loses;
The man of faith will win.

Have faith that the gravest problem
Has an answer, never fear.
The man of faith believes it
And attacks it with good cheer.

Never sit on the sidelines
Bewailing things that are.
Just mount your wagon, buddy,
And hitch it to a star.   – MB

When the mists of the morning
Rise over the hills,
I write a prescription
To cure the world's ills.

Get some air in your lungs
And a song in your heart;
You may not get done,
But at least you can start.

You can start with a dream,
A vision or plan;
You feel you can't do it,
But believe that you can.

Believe that the dream
Didn't start with just you,
But it's how things appear
From a heavenly view.

You fit into His plans
Like a hand in a glove;
Your actions are guided
By the Wisdom above.

So start working bravely;
Be valiant and bold,
And you will see finished
The vision you hold.

Maurice Berquist
04/21/87

Please take a moment and look at a seed,
Then I will ask you just what you see.
Do you see nothing more than a tiny brown shape,
Or the vision of what it will be?

Is it a great tree, or is it a flower?
Its secret is hidden from view.
Is it a great oak, or is it a weed?
At the moment God made it, He knew.

God cares more than this for his children.
He plants his dreams in their heart.
And He will unlock these wonderful dreams;
He will do it, but we have a part.

We must first believe that God has a plan;
Then we wait for that plan to unfold.
Oh, yes, friend, locked within us are treasures,
Far more priceless than gold.

Let us keep our hearts moist with our weeping;
Let us keep our hearts warm with our mirth;
And God will make blossom these wonderful dreams
As He brings forth the flowers from the earth.

Maurice Berquist
08/02/85

The Altar Sanctifies the Gift
One of Berk's most helpful sermons

Tonight I want to talk about what I think is the very center of worship, not only group worship, but also your personal worship. And I would say very openly here that what I have to say is not new, but it just needs to be said. I will not say something you haven't heard before somewhere in your life, but I would wish that in every pulpit in this state and in every Sunday School class that somebody would take this message and re-preach it and replay it until we begin to get the idea, because I think this is where life either builds up or breaks up.

The scripture from which I speak tonight is in the 23rd Chapter of Matthew. Christ is talking to the Pharisees, beginning with Verse 15 through Verse 19:

Woe unto you, scribes and Pharisees, hypocrites! for ye compass sea and land to make one proselyte, and when he is made, ye make him twofold more the child of hell than yourselves.

Woe unto you, ye blind guides, which say, Whosoever shall swear by the temple, it is nothing; but whosoever shall swear by the gold of the temple, he is a debtor!

Ye fools and blind: for whether is greater, the gold, or the temple that sanctifieth the gold?

And, Whosoever shall swear by the altar, it is nothing, but whosoever sweareth by the gift that is upon it, he is guilty.

Ye fools and blind: for whether is greater, the gift, or the altar that sanctifieth the gift?   (KJV)

Prayer: Heavenly Father, we are so grateful for this privilege and for the incredibly beautiful music that has both been heard and made. I ask that thou will make this sermon a song that will play itself over and over again in our hearts; that it may give us the key to open the door to untold riches for ourselves and for all those who look to us for help. In Jesus' name. Amen.

Jesus had harsh words to say to the Pharisees and Scribes. It is a little unsettling to realize that these people thought they were the best people around – the most religious people around, the most sacrificial people around, the hardest working people around. Now, when you think you have done your very best, to have somebody tell you that you are a hypocrite is not fun. But Jesus did that. And his reason was the same reason that I think the Lord is a little disturbed by religious people now. They do many things that are good, but they are not really right; and their worship, although it is sincere, is wrong.

Nothing is more misunderstood in the church today than the altar. Jesus clearly said, "The altar sanctifies the gift."

One morning in Calcutta I followed a great crowd of people. They seemed to all be going the same way. Many of them were leading goats. I didn't know what they were doing, but I wanted to find out; and as I followed them I came into a temple – the temple of the god Kali, the god of destruction and death.

I watched as these goats were led to a place very much like this altar here. The goats' necks were placed across the altar, and a priest with a great knife cut off their heads with one blow. Of course, blood spurted out. And then I watched as literally hundreds of people came and touched the blood and put it on their hands and on their foreheads and on the ledger books of their businesses. These were not just the Outcastes or the low caste, but all kinds of people were there – including students, business men, professional people. They all were there.

Well, whatever else we might think, we must acknowledge

that they understood something at least about the altar – namely, this: That somewhere in the world there is a God – in this case, one of the many Hindu gods. And they understood that as long as that goat was being led, he was just one more goat; as long as he was out there in the field or on the streets, he was just a goat. But when he was placed on the altar and offered to the god, something mystical happened; and the blood which they put upon themselves and upon their cash books, they believed, was a symbol of sanctifying power.

Please do not understand me to say that I believe Hinduism is right. But the Hindus are far more right than many Christian churches in their regard for the altar. We don't understand what the altar is for at all. If you go to a Roman Catholic Church, you will find that nobody walks in front of the altar without crossing himself or bending his knees – genuflecting, as they call it.

It is a tradition of the Roman church that the altar is supposed to contain some sacred relic of the Church. Perhaps it is a part of the original wood of the cross, or the chain that bound Peter or Paul, or something that came from the very spot where the Church had its birth. This little relic in the altar is supposed to tie that church to the historic original Church. And when during Mass the priest lifts the elements – the bread and the wine, the Eucharist – they believe that the bread and wine are absolutely changed into the body and blood of Jesus.

Well, I am not a Roman Catholic; but I will say this: Catholics are far ahead of many Protestants who don't know what the altar is for.

So, I am going to talk about the altar. Jesus did.

He said, *"The altar sanctifies the gift."*

Sanctification is not something you do for yourself. Rather it is something God does for you, and for everything in your life, when it is on the altar.

I'm not talking about a state of mind here. I know we can say that we believe we ought to consecrate things to God, and I do believe that. But Jesus, when he talked about the altar, was talking about a literal place, made of wood covered with gold. And he said the gift that is brought here is not the important thing. *The important thing is that the gift is placed on the altar, and the altar sanctifies it.*

You know in the Church we have the odd notion that God just honors part of the people – the wealthy people or industrious people or hard working people. But that is not true. God honors people who put their gift on the altar and leave it there and say, "God, you do with it what you want to do."

That gift is wholly acceptable to God.

[Put your money on the altar.]

Now, I want to tell you a few stories, and you draw your own conclusions. There are a number of times in life when you ought to put things on the altar. There's no special order, but tonight I'll say first that you ought to put your money on the altar.

You say, "Why start there?"

Because it's hardest to do, and we'd just as well do the hard things first.

People say, "It's not the money; it's the principle of the thing."

It's the money.

Not long after I began pastoring in Florida, a young couple came to my back door.

"Are you the pastor?" they asked.

"Yes I am."

"We have a problem. We just came from Pennsylvania. On the way down we got married in Georgia, but after we got to

Florida we learned that our marriage wasn't legal. We want you to marry us."

Hastily my wife and I arranged a simple wedding ceremony and properly tied the knot. They offered me some money; but I said, "Once is enough to pay for a ceremony. This one's on me."

The couple went on their way to enjoy their stay in the sunshine of Florida. After a week of honeymoon, they decided they liked Daytona Beach so much they would make their home there. They had no ties anywhere else, didn't own anything, had nothing to lose. They looked for work and began to attend church.

Harry got a job. This was back twenty years ago now; but even then the pay was meager. He made $35.00 a week – not enough for one to live on, let alone two. They say two can live as cheaply as one – if one doesn't eat! [Chuckling] But which one?

So the pay wasn't much, but it was something. After Harry had worked for a few weeks, they got enough ahead to buy a car on time. I'll never forget that car – a 1950 Dodge – 8 or 9 years old. It was black, and it was both a sedan and a convertible. The top had rusted completely through! They had a "sunroof" before they became popular! But for $35.00 what could you expect? That's what the car cost. They paid $5.00 down.

Well, one Sunday night as Harry parked his rusty vehicle in front of the church, he saw that it was going to rain. So he pulled a piece of canvas from the trunk and put it over the top – a sort of "do-it-yourself convertible."

One of our men, Charlie Van Hoose, stood there watching, and he said, "Harry, I have had a few cars in my life that I liked really well; but I never got so attached to them that I tucked them in at night."

It was that Sunday night that this young couple came to the altar and surrendered their lives to Christ.

A week went by, and Friday night came.

Now imagine this: My wife and I are at supper when the phone rings. And this young bride is on the phone. She asks me a question. Here's the way it goes: I am saying, "Yes. Yes. 10%. Just a minute." And then I said, "$3.50" and "Goodbye."

When I put the phone down, my wife, being naturally curious, said, "Honey, what was that all about?"

"That was Dena."

"What did she want?"

"She wanted to know how to start tithing."

"What did she say?"

"She said, 'You know Harry and I got saved Sunday night. Well, we don't know how to tithe. Can you tell us?' I said 'Yes.' And she said, 'What's a tithe?' and I said, '10%.' And she said, 'How much is that?' And I said, "Dena, how much do you make?" And she said, 'We make $35.00 a week.' And I said, 'Just a minute.'"

[Aside to audience] Took me a minute to figure that out. Let's see – 10% of $35.00. You put down $35.00; then you put .10 (with a decimal before the 1), and you multiply. I did it in my head back then, but I'm getting older. [Chuckling] Actually, it's not as easy as I thought it was. I used to think there was nothing to it to figure a tithe; but you've got people who can run businesses, but can't figure a tithe. I've seen CPA's who can't figure a tithe. I've known men who can build a machine out of old coat hangers, but can't figure a tithe. So I like to take it easy and do it right. [Acting out the math] 1 times 0 is 0; 1 times 5 is 5; and 1 times 3 is 3. There you have it. Now that's the way to figure your own tithe.

"So I said to Dena, 'Your tithe is $3.50.' She said, 'OK. Thank you.' And I said, 'OK. 'Bye.'"

Well, my wife listened to all that, and she said, "Berk, you didn't tell her they had to start tithing. Now, we tithe and have tithed all these years. But they are making only $35.00 a week. You can't live on that."

Then I preached to my wife.

I said, "Honey, in the first place, I didn't invent the tithe. In the second place, they need to tithe, because the tithe is the symbol that you put your money in God's hands and let Him manage it."

And friend, when you make just $35.00 a week, you better get a manager!

I'm not going to preach on this, so don't get scared. But it's interesting that in my experience I have discovered that there are just two times in your life when you ought to tithe: One is when you are not making much money – when you are poor and can't afford to start tithing, because you need God to bless you. If you only make $35.00 a week and take $3.50 off of that, that's $31.50 left; and you better let God run that $31.50. So if you don't have much money and are broke, that's the best time to start tithing. You need a manager.

The other time when you ought to tithe is when you are making a lot of money, because if you are making good money and it is hard to tithe because your tithe comes to $100, $500, or $1,000, or whatever it is – if God sees that you can't be trusted to tithe that amount because you think you can't afford it, He can cut you down to where you can afford it. If you've got a $5.00 limit in your mind on tithing, He can cut you back to $50.00 a week – no problem at all.

Well, we went back to eating supper. And the next Sunday nobody but God and the church treasurer knew that this young couple started tithing. What did it mean? Well, the Bible says *"the altar sanctifies the gift."* In tithing, they put their gift on the altar. They said, "Here it is, God. And it is a symbol that not only the $3.50 is yours, but everything is yours."

And God kept on sanctifying. Later I learned how God prospered them and met their financial need.

The following Monday night – visitation night at our church – Herman Robinson and his wife went to see this young couple because they knew they were newly saved and ought to be encouraged. After they had talked a while, Harry said, "I hear something dripping. You got a leaky faucet somewhere?"

And Dena, who was quite witty, said, "Yeah, they all drip. You know when you live in the low rent district, everything that's supposed to run stops and everything that is supposed to stop runs."

Then Harry said, "Well, you're in luck. I'm a plumber. Let me run out to my car for some tools, and I'll fix that."

In a moment he was back, and within an hour he had fixed all the plumbing problems – all the faucets, fixed the john – one john, "1st john"– he fixed that. Then he prayed with the couple.

Now, Harry didn't know they were tithing, see? He didn't know a thing about that. But when the prayer was finished, he said, "As I prayed, the Lord impressed me to give you this."

And he pulled a ten dollar bill from his pocket and handed it to Harry.

You say, "Wow, isn't that wonderful? Isn't that remarkable?" Not at all. It would be remarkable if it didn't happen.

You see, when God starts running your affairs from "up there," He sees those old leaky faucets and says, "Listen, that's my tithe. That $35.00 is sanctified money." And God begins to bless.

Well, a month or two later we were at the supper table on Friday night again. And the phone rang. I answered. It was Dena, but this time she wanted to speak to my wife.

When Berny hung up, it was my turn to ask questions.

"What in the world was that?"

"That was Dena."

"Yeah, I know it was Dena. What did she want?"

"She wanted some advice."

"You didn't give her much."

"Yes, I did."

"What did you tell her?"

"She wanted to know how to cook pork chops. And I said, 'You're crazy.' And she said, 'No I'm not. I don't know how to cook pork chops.'

"Then she said, 'Berny, you know that since Harry and I got saved, we've been tithing our income. It hasn't been easy on $35.00 a week, but God has met our needs. Even better than that, this week God gave Harry a much better paying job. This week, for the first time, Harry brought home $100! We wanted to celebrate, so Harry bought some pork chops for supper. But I don't know how to cook them – we've never had any before.'

"So I told her, 'No problem. Put them in a skillet and turn the fire on. You can't miss.'"

Well, I recall that so well and enjoyed that so much – to see a couple that had been living on tuna fish casserole get their first pork chops because they trusted God. I think I enjoyed those pork chops as much as they did.

We just sat there eating our casserole and praised God!

Well, I'm through talking about money. You can start enjoying church now.

But I praise God for that story, because it is a down-to-earth illustration of what Jesus said: *"The altar sanctifies the gift."*

Sanctify means two things. It means "to set apart" and "to make whole or holy." That's what God did. *"Prove me now herewith, says the Lord. Bring all your tithes into the storehouse and see if I won't pour out a blessing . . ."* [paraphrasing Malachi 3:10]. And I'll pour out pork chops! Amen. And gravy, too! Amen.

[Put your marriage on the altar.]

The second time you ought to put something on the altar is when you've got a problem in your home – a marriage problem.

Friend, let me tell you: there are no experts in this marriage business. When I saw the marriage counselors all getting divorces, I decided they didn't know what they were talking about.

I read lots of books and listen to lots of people, but I'll tell you this: I know only one way to have a happy marriage and that is to put it on the altar.

Paul said it in his first letter to the Corinthians. They were having lots of trouble with marriage relationships, among other things. In the 7th chapter is a key verse you ought to mark in your Bible, Verse 14: *"For the unbelieving husband is sanctified by the wife, and the unbelieving wife is sanctified by the husband: else were your children unclean; but now are they holy."* (KJV)

A lady says, "I would serve God if my husband would serve God." And her husband says, "I would serve God if my wife would go along with me." Or they say, "We would serve God if our children would . . . ."

Listen. The only answer to that is for you to put the wife, the husband, the children, and the whole business on the altar and say, "God, I'm willing to do what you ask me to do." God will bless. And a kind of sanctity – sanctification – comes on the marriage.

The best way to sanctify your marriage, of course, is **before** you get married. Amen? If you are going to backslide, don't do it while you are courting. That's a dangerous time to be away from the Lord. I hear people say, "When I settle down; then I'll get serious with God." Friend, let me tell you something, by the time you settle down, you will spend the rest of your life settling up! The best time to get serious with God is while you are still young and **before** you get a wife. Put your marriage on the altar before you ever find the girl of your dreams, and God will bless your search and your relationship.

But even after you are married, you still do it. You have a problem at home, put it on the altar. I was over in West Virginia a while back. A lady whose husband is now a preacher – a very good one – told me what happened when her husband got saved. She got saved, but her husband was a drunkard, an alcoholic. Besides that he was mean. Some men get nice when they get drunk. Some men get mean. He was the mean kind. She would go to church; and when she came home, he would beat her, throw her down the basement stairs, and everything else.

Finally, she had all she could take. She came to church and in the middle of the service, before the altar call or anything, she got up in that old West Virginia church, walked down the aisle, and said, "I'm putting Jack on the altar. I can't handle it; I can't work it; I can't live with it; but God, here it is."

Later she said, "I went home that night, and Jack wasn't in the house. I heard noise at a neighbor's house. I thought it might be a fight, but it wasn't. Old Jack was over there praising God. He had gone over there and got saved!"

She told it with tears in her eyes. "As long as I tried to straighten it out, it didn't work."

Let me give you some advice. I know that's a poor thing to do. Nobody likes advice. Most advice I give is good as new – it's never been used. I've passed it around for years, and people listen; but then they go and do what they were going to do any way. But I want to give you some advice.

Women, let me tell you something. There is no way under Heaven that you can give your husband advice to straighten him out. You'd just as well save your breath and blow up a balloon for the kids. And, husbands, [chuckling to himself] there is no way you can give advice to your wife on what she ought to do.

Listen, ladies, if your husband needed a mother, he would have stayed at home. Men, if your wife needed a father, she would have stayed at home.

You say: "What am I going to do? He – or she – just drives me crazy." I'll tell you something. The Holy Spirit can work. All you do by meddling in God's affairs is mess up the water. Put it on the altar, and say, "He is driving me crazy." Put your craziness on the altar.

I heard of one husband who didn't hang up his pants. He said he left them on the floor so they wouldn't fall off. Well, they won't fall off the floor, but they may drive you crazy. But I tell you something, all your suggestions and all your reforming, all the counsel and advice wives give their husbands ought to be put on the altar. Tell Jesus. He knows the door to their hearts. *"The unbelieving husband is sanctified by the wife. The unbelieving wife is sanctified by the husband."* Praise God.

[Put your body on the altar.]

Listen. You ought to put your body on the altar. Do you want to be healed? A lot of people never put themselves on the altar. They give God their sickness, but they don't give God themselves. They want God to be a heavenly "aspirin passer-outer" or a friendly doctor in the newspaper column. "They say, God,

what should I do?" I'll tell you what you should do. Paul said, *"I beseech you therefore, brethren, by the mercies of God, that you present your body a living sacrifice, holy, acceptable unto God, which is your reasonable service. And be not conformed to this world, but be ye transformed . . . [Romans 12:1-2, KJV].*

When Paul said that, he was in view of places where people offered human bodies as sacrifices. If you have been to Israel, you perhaps have seen the ancient ruins of places where people made sacrifices to the gods Moloch and Baal. They had a huge statue of the god Moloch, with a big gaping mouth. And inside the mouth was a place like a giant pyre where a fire was built. And people were told to throw their first-born babies into the mouth of this Moloch and let them be burned up as a sacrifice. Paul knew about this heathen practice.

But when he says, "Present your body to God as a living sacrifice," it doesn't mean putting your body in a literal fire. It means you come to the altar saying, "Oh God, I'm broken physically. My mind doesn't work right. My body doesn't work right. My eyes don't work right. My feet don't work right, and I don't work right – but here I am, God; and I am yours."

And, praise God, I've seen people healed that way. The altar sanctifies, "makes whole" the gift. Problem is, you give God your headache, but you do not give God your head. What you should be saying is, "Here I am Lord – I give you all of me. Not just the pain, but my whole self."

In my church in Florida was a fellow who said he was called to preach.

I said, "You can't do that."

This fellow was the worst stutterer I ever heard in my life. His name was Tom. You couldn't ask him anything unless you had an hour to listen to his answer w-w-w-one s-syl-la-la-ble a-a-at a t-t-time. How is he going to preach? He can't even say, "Hello."

Well, Tom had the answer. He said, "If God called me, he knows I am a stutterer. I'll get up and stutter for Jesus."

You know what? God cured him of stuttering!

I'm so tired of people saying, "I can't do this for God. I can't teach, I can't visit, I can't witness, I can't give, I can't work. Listen. Put your weakness on the altar and let God have it. God can honor that. He can work with that.

236

[Put your problem on the altar.]

Now, there is one more thing I ought to preach on here. You ought to put your problem on the altar. In the 22nd Chapter of Genesis we read a startling account – an almost unbelievable account – when God said to Abraham: "Take your son, Isaac, the son you love, take him to the mountain and sacrifice him to me." So father and son trudged up the mountain, with Isaac carrying the wood. And when they got to the top of Mount Moriah, they built an altar.

Then Isaac said: "Father, here's the altar, here's the wood. Where's the sacrifice?"

And Abraham said: "God will provide."

Then he laid Isaac on the altar, bound his hands and feet, and was willing to sacrifice his son.

You say, "Does that make sense?"

It doesn't make sense at all. Here God had promised Sarah and Abraham a son. Sarah was ninety and Abraham about a hundred, and here they are pushing the perambulator through the street, you know. They finally have a son, and they said: "Well, God finally answered."

Now Isaac is in his teen years, probably sixteen or seventeen, and God says: "Put him on the altar." Does that make sense? That's a problem isn't it? A problem. But Abraham did what all of us have to do – he put the problem on the altar. And – get this; here is the point – then, it became God's problem.

You know what happened, of course. When Abraham had Isaac bound, the fire ready to burn, and the knife ready to plunge into Isaac's body, an angel stopped his hand, and then spun Abraham around to see that in the bushes God had provided a sacrifice. Abraham cut those cords that bound Isaac and said: "Let's get that sheep and put him on here." And they did.

Now, I don't think you can fully understand that story unless you are a father and have only one son. As you climb that mountain your soul is in anguish, but you can't talk about it. What did Abraham and Isaac talk about going up the mountain? Nothing. What would they talk about coming down? Nothing. Why? Going up the mountain there was nothing they could say. Coming down the mountain nothing needed to be said. They knew God had provided. All they could do was praise God.

I'm glad I am not as smart as I used to be. Years ago if you asked me for advice about your problem, I would say: "Sit down and I'll tell you the answer." Man, I was full of advice. We'd discuss and argue and philosophize: WHY did this happen?

You know what I say now: "There isn't a problem you have that I can understand very well. I don't live where you live. I don't think what you think. I can empathize in a way and sympathize in a way; but there is no way that I can understand your feelings. However, I can say this: "Let's meet right here and put your problem on the altar. For when we do that, it becomes God's problem. And the Bible says: *the altar sanctifies the gift.*"

Friends, I deplore the fact that the altar sometimes becomes a counseling bench.

People will say: "What should we do about this?" And you stand there and talk to them. But really, there is only one thing to do about it: present it to God.

The Holy Spirit has infinite wisdom, infinite power, and He can solve the most tangled problem. I've seen Him do it. And, oh, you can rise and go back to your seat or go back to your home and say, "Praise God!" I don't know how it's going to work, but it is going to work, because *the altar sanctifies the gift.*"

There are scores of illustrations of ways you ought to use the altar, but none is more relevant or timely or more important than this: When you have a situation you can't solve, you solve it at the altar. It's surprising how we can have a committee meeting that lasts three hours, and we spend less than a minute in prayer. We've got time to argue until midnight. We have board meetings and committee meetings and council meetings, and we say: "What should we do? What can we do?" We call in the "experts" – we call the national church office; we call our friends; we call everybody and talk about it.

I'll tell you what we ought to do: We ought to take it to the altar and say, "God, here's your problem. I take my hands off. It's yours, God." And when we do that, God will work.

Jesus said: "Woe unto you, Scribes and Pharisees." You get excited about the gifts you bring, about the expertise you bring. You boast about the work you do; the skill you have. Listen, your talent, my talent, my brains and your brains, my work and your work don't matter at all. What matters is that we are humble enough to bow at the altar and say, "God, here it is."

When I was a young man I thought if I got enough education, enough experience, I could go out and help people. Friend, I'm older now. I've been through the mill. I've got the scars. There aren't many problems any church faces, that I haven't faced one like them. And I've learned that there is only one way to solve any problem, and that is to get down here to the altar and turn it over to God; then walk away saying: "I'm going to live for God and let God handle it."

When it comes to solving problems, I've learned that I can't manipulate; I can't engineer; I can't politic; I can't write letters; I can't make phone calls; I can't straighten things out.

Listen, when you try to straighten out your problems, you are like a bachelor ironing a shirt. For every wrinkle you iron out, you iron two new ones in. You are like a Hottentot trying to practice medicine. Patients don't get well; they just die. But, praise God, when you submit things to the Holy Spirit and say, *"the altar sanctifies the gift,"* God will have a sanctified church – a holy church.

[Put your failure on the altar.]

You say: "We failed."

Well, praise God, you finally admitted it. Put your failure on the altar. I've done that.

I remember one time in my church in Florida – I'd been there ten years, and nothing much had happened. We were just hacking along. So many in Sunday School; so many in church; enough money to pay the light bill and a few other things – just enough to keep bill collectors from the door. Finally, one day I went down to the altar on a Sunday afternoon. I stretched out face down on the carpet in front of the altar, and I said, "Oh, God, I'm a mess. I don't care what people say – if they think I'm a good preacher or not. I have failed to do your work. And I want to turn this thing over to you, and I want you to run it. And I want you to run me."

And from that moment, I want you to know, God began to bless. *"The altar sanctifies the gift!"*

You need to do just one thing: practice this concept.

"You say: I'm the chairman of the board." Well, God bless you. You ought to be down here first. The more responsibility you have, the more you ought to be at the altar.

You say: "What will happen if my kids see me down at the altar, crying and praying?"

They might start believing in your religion. You walk around like an expert who knows all the answers, and they know you don't know them. They know you're frustrated and have trouble with many areas of your life. They know that. But I'll tell you this, something will happen to the most hardened teenagers here, the most indifferent youth in the church, when they see their father and mother kneeling at the altar in prayer, crying out, saying, "God, here it all is."

You say. "My enemies. What about them?"

Praise God! When your enemies see you at the altar, and God begins to work, they may come to feel the same way. When the whole church is at the altar, God can work.

Oh, when I see a person who is sick, and tired of being sick, and tired of being sick and tired – when he or she finally comes down and says, "I have been trying to use God. I've been trying to get God's power and God's healing; but God here I am. I'm sick, I'm weak, I'm helpless; but here I am, God. I am yours."

Praise God! *"The altar sanctities the gift."*

A young couple struggling along to make the mortgage payment, to make the house payment, the car payment, the doctor's payment, and they can't pay their bills, but they say, "We're going to give to God any way. Praise God! If we go to jail, we'll go to jail sanctified." You know, God can prosper you then.

When the church starts taking its responsibility seriously, and the leaders say: "Oh, God, we're failing, but here we are"– *"the altar sanctifies the gift!"*

We get so wise in "problem solving" and counseling that our meetings become little more than psychology sessions. "Here's what *'I'* would do."

Listen. There isn't a problem that can't be solved when we find our place at the altar of prayer. Praise God!

I want you to do something tonight that's for yourself, your children, your grandchildren, and for the work of God in this place. I want you to stand.

We are going to sing a song that can change everything. The minute anybody physically sick, mentally worried, financially troubled, ecclesiastically disoriented, whoever you are – if you do what this song says, something will happen tonight. Let's just start singing this prayer, without the piano first of all, just as a prayer. You sing it with me. And if God talks to you, you come and meet me at the altar.

[After the first stanza of "I Surrender All," Berk prayed this prayer:] Oh God, tonight we just have to say that we don't know how to run things. We can't straighten anybody out, but we can submit ourselves to you. We can't heal anybody, but you can heal them. We can't bring a marriage back together, but you can do it. We can't bring a church back together, but you can do it. We can't make our money go where it ought to go, but you can do it. Lord, thank you that the altar does sanctify the gift. It's not something that we strive to do, or try to do, or labor to do. We just put it there and leave it there. May we do that tonight. May we do it in this service and through our lives for Jesus sake. Amen.

Let me just repeat what we have been talking about. The Bible says that God has given these things to the wise and prudent and revealed them unto babes. If brains could save the church, it would have been saved long ago. If experience could do it . . . the older we get, the wiser we get. But the truth is that neither intelligence, nor experience, nor human nature can save God's Church. It's only by putting it back in God's hands and saying, "God, you handle it."

I was flying an airplane once. Now, I am not a pilot, but I was up with a fellow who was a general; and he said, "I've taught lots of guys to fly. Take over."

So I started handling the controls. Almost immediately, we veered too far to the right; then too far to the left.

Desperately, I said, "What am I doing wrong?"

"You are trying too hard," he said. "Take your hands off of it."

And I said, "Man, the plane will crash."

"Take your hands off," he said.

And you know what? I took my hands off the wheel, and that plane flew just as pretty.

He said, "It will almost fly itself."

Friends, all of us have attempted to put our hands on the wheel and tried to manage God's affairs, and we overdo. But listen, praise God, we can commit it to God – anything. *"The altar sanctifies the gift."*

If you have failed somewhere along the line, don't be a failure just because you failed. Give that to God. God can take your failure and make a victory out of it.

If you are sick – someone said, "When are you going to preach on healing?" I have just preached on healing, my friend. I am preaching on healing right now. Just give your body to God.

If you've got a problem, give it to Him now. *"The altar sanctifies the gift."*

Angel Wings

Angels have guarded you
Right from your birth
Watching your footsteps
Here on earth.
Snakes on the mountain,
Stones in your way,
With love angels watched you
Day after day.

Now on your birthday
Come angels again
Giving wings to your wishes,
You simply say when.
Silver-winged angels
Filling the sky.
Miles become nothing,
Loved ones are nigh.

Angels by Boeing
Cessna and Beech,
Bring distant places
Safely in reach.
Let your dreams lead you,
Keep your soul free,
Always buy "round trip,"
Come back to me.

Written for Berny
12-23-92

To Charles M. Schulz –
Builder of Bridges

Berk wrote this poem for "Sparky" Schulz when they were working together on The Doctor Is In book and TV special.

With eyes that pierced the darkened skies
  Almighty God looked down.
He gazed upon the spinning earth;
  He frowned a mighty frown.

"When I created planet Earth,
  I had a master plan:
It was to be a garden fair
  For my creation, man.

"I stretched the gentle rivers out
  Like fingers on my hand
To flow at last into the seas,
  Uniting every land.

"I dreamed that, like the ocean vast,
  My children might be one.
Their lives would then together flow
  Just as the rivers run.

"I dreamed that hand would clasp a hand
  And heart would touch a heart.
Instead, like river boundaries,
  They dwell alone, apart.

"The rivers grip the countryside
  Like fingers cruel and strong.
They clutch the Earth, the lonely Earth,
  To silence its glad song."

So spoke the Father from His throne;
  His tears become the rain
To swell the streams dividing man
  And break his heart again.

It is a fearful thing and sad
  To see the Father weep
To see the world, His perfect world,
  Be scarred by chasms deep.

I heard the peal of thunder loud;
  I saw God's eyes flash fire;
I saw Him strike the spinning Earth,
  As harpists strike their lyre.

"I'll make a man; I'll make a man!"
  God spoke, while angels smiled.
"I'll make a man to build a bridge;
  Men must be reconciled.

"Though rivers clutch the continents
  Like fingers cruel and strong,
He'll build a bridge to join their hearts
  And voices in a song.

"I'll put a pen into his hand,
  A spark within his brain;
He'll light a lamp within men's eyes;
  He'll make them smile again.

"I'll let him talk of common things,
  Like children, dogs, and birds.
He'll build a bridge of laughter
  With pictures and with words."

God smiled, ah yes, I say He smiled,
  The heavens shone like brass.
His laughter chased the fleecy clouds
  And rustled through the grass.

"So let the rivers run," He said;
  They flow into the sea –
The 'Builder of the Bridge' has brought
  My children home to me."

Paul's People Principles (1980)

Affection not argument
  Building not blaming
   Communication not complication
    Demonstration not didactic
   Empathy not eloquence
   Feelings not facts
    Gratitude not grasping
    Heart not head
     Integration not isolation
    Joy not jesting
     Koinonia not *krisis*
      Leadership not lecture
      Monitoring not mothering

Names not numbers
  Opportunity not obstacles
   Participation not preaching
    Questing not quitting
     Remembrance not remonstrance
    Suggestion not specifics
   Towel not throne
    Understanding not ultimates
   Victory not vanity
   Waiting not worrying
    Xristos not *Xristos kai*
   You not yours
  Zeal not zest

Maurice Berquist

The Eye of the Beholder
Observations by Maurice Berquist
Lake Charles, Louisiana 1988

Each week during Berk's tenure as interim pastor at Lake Charles, he wrote an article for the church paper, doing what he does best – turning up "parables" in the most unlikely places. When he left, the church presented him with a bound collection of his columns, a few of which are reproduced here.

Snowflakes don't last. Snowmen do.

Believe it or not, we had snow in Lake Charles, Louisiana, last week – the first snow in fifteen years. Children were ecstatic. They made snowballs, rolled in the snow, and made snowmen.

I couldn't believe it. In my block were twelve snowmen. More snowmen than I had seen in one place in my entire life.

Most of them were pretty typical – with a long carrot nose, a stubby pipe, and a jaunty scarf.

The people in Lake Charles were not about to waste a once-in-fifteen-years' opportunity to build a snowman.

By noon on Monday all the snow was gone – all except the snowmen. They lasted until Wednesday. One particularly large one survived 'till Wednesday evening.

I learned something from this unusual weekend. It is prophetic at best and educational at the very least.

A snowflake, as I am told, is unique. No two snowflakes are alike. But by themselves they don't last long. When they sacrifice their identity to become a part of a body, they survive a lot better.

It's a sacrifice or a trade-out. And we all have the same choice. We will, as one of the early American Fathers said, "hang together or we will hang separately."

Together we do better. We survive by this togetherness. It is called the church.

* * * *

I saw it first in Lake Charles. I still don't know what to call it, but I have actually seen it.

Maybe you can help me name it. Would you like to try?

First, I had better tell you where to see it. Come north on Common Street here in Lake Charles, and when you see a big sign ROYAL SCHWINN you are there. And, if the weather is not too bad, you will see this blue wonder – a bicycle built for four.

What do you call it? I know that a "bicycle built for two, "is called a tandem. Is a bicycle built for four a "quorum"?

In that case, this may be the only committee bicycle in the world.

Reminds me of a statement attributed to Charles Lindbergh when he crossed the Atlantic Ocean in a small plane – all by himself.

"What a remarkable feat," said the news reporters. "Crossing the Atlantic all alone."

"Not so great," said Lindbergh. "Let someone try to fly the Atlantic with a committee!"

Frankly, I have never ridden a bicycle built for two, but it seems pretty challenging to get two people to lean the same way at the same time and turn the same way at the same time and work together like that. To get four people to do it – I'd believe in the tooth fairy easier.

One of these sunny days I am going to stop my car as I pass the bicycle shop and ask them if this "quorum," this bicycle built for four, really works. I am sure that someone takes the lead. Whoever that is must have the set of handle bars that actually turn. Others follow. They may or may not do their share of peddling, but they must follow not only the direction of the leader but the body posture as well.

If it works at all, that's the way it has to work.

Life is like that. Churches are like that. Our personal life style is like that. Someone, or something, is in charge.

The nice thing about being a Christian is that you get to put Christ at the head of your life, and then all the other competing forces have to fall in line.

The Christian life is not guided by a committee, but a commitment.

Now, about that four-person vehicle, the quorum – I'd still like to see it run.

* * * *

How do I know what to write about each week? Simple. I write about the things I see and what I think about them.

For example, Self-Service Gas Stations.

Frankly, I buy my gas at Self-Service Stations. I drive a lot and it's cheaper. And I always wonder why any one would pay extra just to have someone else put the nozzle into his gas tank.

What's the difference between Self-Serve and Full-Serve?

Yesterday I found out.

I spent a little while drinking coffee with James Chesson at his service station on Kirkman and Alamo. James does not have self-serve gasoline – just full-serve.

As I watched people drive up and pay a few extra cents for the "full-serve" treatment, I began to realize why.

He really means "full-serve." When you ask what that thumpety-thump means in your transmission – he can tell you.

Or when you need to get some oil in your crankcase so you won't have a 500-dollar repair bill later on, James notices.

If you need a new engine, he can put one in.

Brian Wood, who was watching with me explained it this way: "Usually when a station advertises full service, they say they will pump the gas for you and tell you where the rest room is. That's all. Not at James' place. Chesson treats your car as something more than a gas tank."

If this begins to sound like an advertisement for a gasoline station, I will explain why I was so interested in the difference between "self-serve" and "full-serve."

It's the difference between letting God run your life and your running it yourself.

When you do your own "self-service," you deal with one part of your life – the immediate need.

When God works on your life, He gives you "full-service." He fulfills your destiny.

He treats every part of your life – not just your immediate need. You are better off to let God do it for you.

Costs a little more. Worth a lot more.

Think about this the next time you buy gas. At James' place or anywhere else.

* * * *

The other day I saw a want-ad: *For Sale: Wedding Dress, Size 10. Worn once by mistake. Ph. 555-9256.*

That started me thinking. How long before the wedding did the bride suspect that she was making a mistake? Or did she not know until after the rice had been shaken out and the dress was stored in a cedar closet?

Then, how long after she realized that she had made a mistake, did she admit it? And, now that she has realized it, what is she doing to save the marriage?

We learn a lot by experience, but it comes too late to do us much good. A friend of mine says, "If we could sell our experience for what we paid for it, we would all be rich."

So now – what do we do when we realize that we have made a mistake? Can we correct it? Probably not. But, we can do two things: One, we can learn from it if we are honest enough to admit that we really did make a mistake. Then we can let God redeem it, if we confess it.

Nobody is right all the time. But refusing to admit that we have done something stupid – even if it was not actually wrong – is an even bigger mistake.

Church is not made up of perfect people. If it were, it wouldn't be necessary.

But church is made up of courageous people who know that they can, and do, make mistakes. They need God's grace to deal with those mistakes. And they need God's guidance to keep them from making others.

* * * *

It doesn't look much like a mousetrap, but it's working like one.

I am referring to the words of Ralph Waldo Emerson, who said that if a man were to build a better mouse trap, though his house were in the woods, men would beat a path to his door.

Don's "All Cloth Car Wash" on Ryan Street here in Lake Charles is not exactly in the woods, but people are wearing out the concrete, driving in to get their cars washed.

If you think that is amazing, listen to this. The cheapest wash I saw advertised is almost six dollars. Those are dollars, not pesos!

For the deluxe treatment – I didn't read all the fine print, but it includes almost everything but tinting your eyebrows – you pay almost thirteen dollars!

Now, listen to this. Just a few blocks from Don's place are places that advertise, "FREE CAR WASH."

Simple logic would tell you that nobody would pay six dollars for a car wash when he could get it done for nothing.

That's what is amazing. Don's place looks like "the old lady's shoe," and the other places seem as lonely as a ham sandwich at a *bar mitzvah*.

I couldn't figure it out. So I watched.

Cars came in and were scrubbed just like a new bride expecting her mother-in-law for lunch. Then, they were dried by a red jacketed crew of boys that pounced on it like a duck on a June bug.

That's different. And as we keep saying: There is very little difference between things, but that little difference makes all the difference.

Things are different around the Fourth Avenue Church of God these days. God is quietly doing a lot of little things that are not making the headlines.

But people are discovering the difference.

There is no free lunch. God's table is spread. You don't pay, but God paid plenty.

* * * *

God don't make no junk. At least that is what Ethel Waters used to say. If you don't feel too good about yourself, it pays to quote Ethel's words.

However – and that is a big however – the world is about covered with junk. As in ancient times, whole cities are being buried under the junk they create.

Maybe God doesn't make any junk, but it's a cinch that people do. Today as I drove to work here in Lake Charles, I passed tons of junk waiting for trash pickup.

Two junk piles were particularly interesting. Both were piles of old mufflers and exhaust pipes from automobiles.

One pile is beautiful, and the other is just what you would expect it to be: rusty, repulsive junk – a blight on the community and an eyesore to the beholder.

The beautiful junk is on Ryan Street in front of the Custom Muffler Shop. Some clever welder has made an iron horse out of a muffler and four pieces of tail pipe. A small resonator makes the head of the horse and another resonator makes the body of the jockey astride this mechanical masterpiece.

It is my guess that the person who built this didn't use any new parts – just the things that were thrown away. He transformed trash into a treasure.

I like that.

It's a whole lot like God's way of working. Among welders this is known as salvaging or re-cycling. With God it is called redemption.

Sure, God would like to have the best that we have before we let it get rusty or bent. But even when we have made a mess out of things, God is not frustrated. He recycles and re-manufactures our lives.

Broken homes, broken hopes, and broken bodies can all be made beautiful.

As Ethel Waters said, "God don't make no junk."

But he recycles a lot of it.

When you are in Lake Charles, drive by the Custom Muffler Place, 2825 Ryan Street – look for the "Iron Horse."

When you see what clever humans can do with junk, just imagine what an Almighty God can do with it.

When I am old, alas alack,
I'll spend my moments looking back.
I'll watch the evening shadows fall
Until the darkness covers all.

I'll watch my dreams like autumn leaves
Wither, while my spirit grieves.
I'll feel the misery of regret;
But, thank the Lord, I'm not old yet.

Oh, it is true, my hair is gray.
But I will let it stay that way.
I do not want to try too hard
To use my senior discount card.

I have a game I play with life.
I learned to play it from my wife:
"There are new songs that must be sung
If you can keep your spirit young!"

So I will sing and I will play;
I'll try to live just for today.
I'll smile, whatever falls my lot,
Because today is all I've got!

Maurice Berquist
09/15/86

241

Letters from an Angel

In 1985 Berk led a close friend to the Lord. Over the next several months Berk discipled his friend in an unusual way. Separated by two thousand miles, Berk, from his home in Seattle, Washington, wrote letters back East in the guise of an angel to give encouragement and counsel to his friend. The ensuing book of twenty chapters was never published, though his notes to Eldon Williams accompanying each chapter indicate that he had considered doing so, under the title Keep It Simple, Williams. *A cover letter accompanied each chapter. The first one appears here.*

Dear Eldon:

Let's pretend we are sitting on the old bench with its peeling blue paint. As you said, the trees and the blue sky made an excellent cathedral while we talked in Killbuck Park.

Frankly, I'd like to have the informality of the park to talk some more; but, unfortunately, we are two thousand miles apart. Even so, there is an advantage to this distance.

Strange, isn't it? – that each of us is like a Medieval castle with a moat surrounding us. When we see someone approaching, even a friend, we have the choice as to whether or not we will lower the drawbridge. Closeness is a choice.

Having said that, I am going to compose a series of short essays which will talk about the Christian life we are living. I hope they will be interesting and helpful, and, if they are, I may get them circulated to a wider audience. Mainly, they are for you.

So, let's begin.

Keep It Simple, Williams
Chapter 1

Dear E.W.:

My name is Mike, a common enough name. I'm an angel, which from your point of view might not be all that common. But then you Earth-bound people do many things that are viewed with surprise, if not alarm, up here.

If we were not so well acquainted, I might stand a little more on ceremony than I am going to; but I have known you for a long time – in, fact, all your life. I have been assigned to you, a guardian angel.

I find it a little difficult to explain these matters to you in writing because letter writing is not my normal method of communication. Angels are basically messengers, but they don't usually write. We angels communicate with Earth-people in many ways.

But, if you want to get in touch with an angel, you will have a problem. Angels don't listen to anyone but God. Then we will act.

All this talk of angels may make you feel a bit uncomfortable, but it shouldn't. Angels are not frightening. Not even Michael, the chief of angels, who has major responsibilities, such as announcing the return of Jesus or the cancelling of time itself.

While I was named after Michael, the archangel, I am actually Michael XXII. You can call me Mike, if you like; but up here I'm simply known as "22." Things are simpler that way.

You see, if god ever shouted, "Michael, put a stop to all that's going on down there," the whole world would grind to a screeching halt. On the other hand, if God said, "22, stop your man from his foolish ways," only you and I would be involved.

That's why it's so important to understand the personal nature of angels' work.

The idea is not new. For centuries the Hebrews have known that angels are assigned to look after people. First Century Chris-

tians took it for granted. Once when the Apostle Peter was put in jail, one of us was sent down to rescue him and lead him to the place where his friends were praying for his release.

It was a little humorous. When Peter stood at the door knocking, a young girl named Rhoda came to the door. She saw Peter and told the others, but they didn't believe her.

"It's his angel," they said.

That's rare. Almost always people find it more difficult to believe in us than in themselves. In fact, Earth-people generally act as though angels were not real at all. Once in awhile, when they almost crash into a bridge or avoid being hit by a bullet, they will say sheepishly, "Well, my guardian angel must be taking care of me."

That's something. Not much, but something. At least they have lurking in their sub-conscious mind a category called "angels."

This is not to say that they understand **anything** about angels.

Frankly we angels have a hard time remaining silent during the Birthday celebration of Jesus – Christmas, as you call it. Not because we are ignored, but because we are misunderstood. Little girls are dressed in white, equipped with gauze wings made out of old coat hangers, and asked to stand around those homemade mangers.

Why aren't boys asked to be angels?

In the Bible all the angels are men. They are referred to as "he" and given names like Gabriel and Michael.

A lot is lost in translation when we are spoken of as "the heavenly host." The word *host* has come on bad days. In Bible times the "host" was the army, the military. Men, no less. Certainly not a fluttering, twittering, gauze-decked flock of Amazons cluttering up the sky!

Forgive me. I tend to get a little carried away.

It isn't that we have an identity problem. We know who we are. We are the messengers of God – warning people, protecting people from their own stupidity, and occasionally finding parking places for them.

Enough about me, and, for that matter, about angels in general. All I wanted to do was to introduce myself and tell you that I have special permission from the King to send letters to you. This isn't the way it is done ordinarily, but your situation is special.

Here's how it happened.

A week ago (Earth time) I noticed a lot of excitement in Heaven. I glided over to the center of the activity and listened to the music. Did I say music? Well, we always have music in Heaven; but there is music and there is MUSIC! Call it "Opus R" or "Redemption Song."

We always have joy in Heaven, but we have an expression up here – "MJ" – that is an abbreviation for "More Joy." I guess the expression got started when Jesus was trying to tell Earth-people about what happens when someone is born again or, as He said, "Born from above." His exact words were, *There is more joy in Heaven over one sinner that repents than over ninety-nine just persons that do not need to repent.*

As I say, the celebration up here was an "MJ" celebration. All because of you.

I remember it well.

"What's going on? I asked.

"Look for yourself."

You can't believe how happy I was – and for that matter still am – at what I saw. There you were sitting on that battered blue park bench. You prayed.

Don't misunderstand me. You had prayed lots of times before

then – before meals, when you almost lost your life during your army days, when your kids got sick. Everyone prays. And God hears them.

But there is praying and there is PRAYING. Up here we have prayers separated into two kinds: prayers because of **where** you are and prayers because of **who** you are. Big difference!

Situation prayers we handle routinely. We scarcely take our hands out of the pockets of our robes.

Salvation prayers are different. We record them with permanent ink. Red ink. They are written in the *Book of Life*.

When that is done, the individual angel in charge of the praying person is called in to the Throne Room. He is given a new set of orders – and I do mean "orders." Nothing is casual.

In my case, the conversation went something like this:

"Angel Michael 22, you have had charge of Earth-person Williams for a long time. You have done a good job keeping him from a lot of dangers that he knows about and a million or more dangers he never knew anything about. You have taken care of his body through a few crises like heart attacks, accidents, and wars. That's good. But now we are talking about eternal things – like his soul."

At this point the King became very intense. "Do you understand how important the soul is?"

I was silent. Who knows?

"Well, 22, you are now assigned to double duty. You not only have the job of taking care of his body, but you are going to watch over his soul. To put it plainly, you are going to watch over him to see that he doesn't fall into any of the traps that our Eternal Enemy, Satan, sets for him"

"How?"

"That's your job. Send him messages that he will listen to. Be sure he reads them."

"Isn't that going to be a big job?"

"That is your ONLY job."

"Yes, sir."

Faithfully,
Michael XXII

Chapter 2

Dear E.W.:

It's not easy living in two worlds. Part of the time I'm free from the law of gravity and lots of other laws. I glide around Heaven with no more energy than a thought. Then, when I come down to walk around the eighteen holes of Killbuck Golf Course, I seem to be standing still.

Then, too, there's the whole matter of time. We don't bother with it up here. I can't explain it to anyone, but eternity is not just a gigantic amount of time, but the absence of time altogether.

I was discussing this phenomenon with my friend Zeph the other day. He had overheard a preacher trying to describe eternity. He was eloquent enough, but somewhat amusing from our point of view. He said, "If a sparrow perched on top of Mount Everest and pecked at the peak at the rate of one peck every hundred years, by the time he had worn the mountain down to sea level, eternity would have only begun."

Zeph and I agreed that this was eloquent, but it somehow missed the point. Eternity is not a fantastic amount of years, but it is the absence of any way of measuring days, months, or years.

Frankly, I hate to begin my letter with such a discussion; but I am leading up to something: the matter of your beginning a new life.

I know how you feel. I was there when it happened. You actually BEGAN something. The date could be marked on the calendar or scratched into the blue park bench where you and your friend were sitting when this moment occurred.

To Earth-people this makes sense.

From an angel's viewpoint it doesn't.

The fact is that if this whole event could be measured in TIME, it would have to be subject to all the laws of time – namely, it would have to have a beginning and an end.

You follow me this far, don't you?

Well, here's the shocking truth: **Salvation is eternal**. Long before the world was formed, God planned for Salvation. Actually he planned for you, too; but I'm not going to stop and explain that just now.

So, what does that mean?

Simply this: as long as earth-people avoid their divine destiny – choosing instead to measure their lives by minutes, hours, days, and years – they miss eternal life.

Heaven knows, enough of them missed it to alarm God Himself. That's the reason He gave for sending Jesus to planet Earth. *"He was not willing that any should perish, but that all should have eternal life."*

In the plan of things, the Earth is expendable. It is not going to last forever. People are.

That's the reason they need to discover the secret of eternal life.

Many illustrations try to describe this discovery. Many of them are helpful, but none is really adequate.

Here's one: A baby exists first of all in the love (even momentary passion) of his parents. Then he becomes a fetus within the womb of his mother. For nine months this is the only world he knows. It is warm and comfortable, but dark and confining. Then comes birth. He is thrust out into a world of four and a half billion other people and encounters the forces of nature – rain and sun, sky and sea.

He enters a new dimension.

The same kind of thing happens to someone who is thrust out into the world of spiritual reality – the world of eternal life. He may have cooperated in the birth, but he didn't cause it. Obviously, he could have prevented it from happening; but he could not make it happen any more than a baby could "will himself" to be born.

From time to time, E.W., you will notice that I quote from The BOOK. I should take a minute and explain what I mean by "The BOOK."

Up here we recognize only one book. According to Earth time, it took 1500 years to get it written – not because God is slow, but because of Earth's unreadiness. God could teach people only as fast as they would learn.

Painful, but true.

As I say, The BOOK is helpful in explaining the relationship between our two worlds.

You have probably heard these words from The BOOK, but I am going to repeat them:

"He (meaning Jesus) came unto his own, and his own received him not.

"But as many as received him, to them gave he the power to become the sons of God, even to them that believe on his name.

"Which were born, not of blood, nor of the will of the flesh, nor of the will of man, but of God." (John 1:11-13 KJV)

Like a baby being ejected from the nine-month cycle of the

womb into the seventy-year cycle of the Earth, an Earthling (that's you) is blasted into an eternal orbit.

In what you call "the Space Age," this concept ought to be easy to understand. As a child you were told that everything that goes up must come down. You believed that – until someone shot a missile into space. It escaped the pull of gravity and moved into a whole new world.

Of course, that launching is critical. It takes a mighty thrust to get off the launching pad. A thousand things can go wrong. The mission can fail.

Now back to you, E.W.

When you decided to let God give you eternal life, you had to get blasted out of the gravitational pull of the world around you. It wasn't easy.

And it won't be for a while. But it gets easier.

You will discover that not all of your friends understand this new experience. Chances are, most of them don't. That's the reason they have been your friends – they thought like you.

Then your habits – they, too, can tie you to the earthly realm.

Whatever it was that could have kept you from Salvation – thank Heaven, nothing did! You began a journey that will never end.

As I was riding with you on a plane the other day, I noticed you reading the brochure in the seat pocket. (Oh, yes, we angels ride on jet planes with those we are assigned to. It's slow for us, but better than when we had to ride along on donkeys!) Well, as I say, you were reading the flight brochure, which said, "Planes require 110 percent of their rated power to get airborne. Once airborne, only 70 percent of their power is needed."

Starting out in the Christian life is like that. You need all the help you can get.

So when God assigned me to you, he made it perfectly clear what I should do. "Don't turn loose of your man, not even for a minute," He said. "Bear him up in your hands, lest at any time he should dash his foot against a stone." *(Matthew 4:6b KJV)*

That's what I'm doing now. Frankly, you haven't needed as much help as I thought you might. We are all glad about that.

Faithfully,
Michael XXII

Chapter 3

Dear E.W.:

Up here in Heaven we have collected an impressive number of "Earth proverbs." After all, we were around long before the Earth itself appeared. Timelessness has advantages. I will not weary you with all these proverbs, but one of them seems useful today. We call it "the Admiral Byrd Iceberg Principle:"

Three-fourths of everything is under the surface.

In your case, E.W., grasping hold on eternal life would seem like a simple thing to do: You reverse polarity; you change directions and start your new life.

It really is that simple.

But no one will let it remain that simple. Everyone wants to complicate it for you. What's more, you may even complicate it for yourself.

That's where the trouble comes in.

Frankly, your Earth word *religion* is almost a curse in Heaven's vocabulary. It comes from a Latin word meaning "to bind." And with the prefix "re," it literally means "to bind again."

So the Earth is full of people trying to bind their ideas on other people. Freedom is promised, but slavery is the result.

You have probably met this problem already. As soon as you tell people that you have become a believer, they begin to shower you with advice: "Wonderful!" they exclaim. "Now, all you need to do is . . . ." And off they go.

What started out as a simple relationship with Jesus turns into a contest to see how many of His followers you can satisfy.

So here's my first word of advice: **Keep it simple.**

One of the most amusing stories to reach us came from a fellow angel who was assigned to a politician. (Not a popular assignment, by the way. It's heavy duty!) At any rate, this politician was distressed about the duplications of government agencies. So he managed to get **two** task forces appointed to study the matter!

We weren't surprised. Earth-people are masters at complicating things. This tendency shows up in their study of The BOOK. Instead of listening for the simple truth God intended, they manage to squeeze out a thousand theories which only frustrate any sincere soul who simply wants a few signposts to show him the way to Heaven.

Paul understood the importance of simplicity. Paul is a favorite up here, just as he is with spiritually minded people on Earth. He stated the idea plainly: *"But foolish and unlearned questions avoid, knowing that they gender strife."* (II Timothy 2:23 KJV)

I wish you could see Earth as we see it, E.W. Even the smallest town in your part of the world is filled with church steeples. Sometimes we wonder if those steeples are not a kind of sword, pointing to the sky and fighting against God's simplicity. Each one claims to have the exclusive (or nearly so) path to Heaven!

What's a beginner to do? How can he choose between all these systems?

Well, my friend, I am going to give you two basic rules. I've seen them work thousands of times, so I can personally recommend them to you.

Rule 1: You were not saved because you understood God, but because He understood you. He still does. Accept that simple fact. Don't let people complicate things with questions.

Rule 2: This rule is summed up perfectly in a catchy phrase making the rounds on Earth these days: "The MAIN THING is to keep the MAIN THING the MAIN THING." You see, one of the favorite tricks of our adversary, the devil, is to confuse good people. He knows that if he can confuse them long enough, they will become discouraged with the whole process. In desperation they will cry out, "Who knows what is right? Who knows which is the best way?"

One thing is certain: *God is not the author of confusion.* He will make His way plain. Wait for that.

There will, indeed, be thousands of things you will learn as you live the rest of your earthly days. I suspect you will have more questions than most people because you have an inquisitive mind. But by the time you reach the questions, you will be ready to understand the answers.

All you need to worry about now is the next thing God wants you to do.

Do that and then wait for instructions.

It's that simple.

I must warn you that you'll have to spar with friends who want to complicate things for you, but I will be there with you to remind you. That's my job. Truthfully, I am becoming rather excited about it.

Faithfully yours,
Michael XXII

Chapter 7
Temptation

Dear E.W.

Remember how we talked about the "heavenly host." We need to talk about it again.

Naturally the phrase doesn't get worn out there on Earth because about the only time Earth-people think about it is at Christmas. Maybe they don't even think about it then; they just say the words: *"Suddenly there was with the angel a multitude of the heavenly host, praising God and saying, Glory to God in the highest and peace, good will to men."*

What do they think about when they say these words – or perhaps when they sing them?

Who is the heavenly host?

Certainly not what most Earth people think. They imagine a bevy of blonde creatures, dressed in gauzy flowing robes, gliding on wispy wings and somehow managing to play harps at the same time. At least that's the impression we get as we look at the pictures Earth-people paint.

Christmas pageants don't help much either. We were all laughing out loud when we saw what one church had done. They not only dressed ladies in angel costumes and equipped them with stubby wire wings, but they also managed to suspend them with cables from the ceiling so they could "fly" around the sanctuary!

Puppets, anyone?

Seriously, it is not a joking matter. You need to understand what "heavenly host" means in The BOOK.

The host is the army. If anyone were to take time to look up the word in a concordance to see how it is used, he would discover that *host* means "army, military, soldiers." The men composing the host were grizzled, bearded, battle hardened combat troops.

The idea of cruising around on wings like butterflies would make them laugh out loud.

Does this shock you?

Angels are not decorations for Christmas cards. They are the troops of the sky! Messengers, too, of course – but much more than lads on bicycles delivering telegrams from the Throne. They are more like the first wave of soldiers that enter enemy territory during war.

We are in a war, you know.

Of course you know. How stupid of me to mention it. You discovered the war the moment you surrendered your life to Jesus. That very first encounter was a battle. Inside your head was a war that would make every other battle you ever faced seem like a walk in a rose garden.

One side of you pulled one way, and one side of you pulled the other way. You could think of a thousand reasons why you wanted to make a change and at least nine hundred and ninety-nine reasons why you didn't want to do it now.

You were being pulled two ways – stretched out like taffy at a Christmas party. I was there. I was fighting for you. But I wasn't fighting you. I was fighting – guess what? – the "hosts" of evil. The army of Satan.

You didn't see them. But then you didn't see me either. We are invisible. But that doesn't mean we are not real.

You have heard me speak of Satan's Handbook for Imp Training, haven't you? We give copies to all the angels up here; they need to know their enemy. Earlier I mentioned Rule B-6 for Satan's imps, but I didn't tell you about Rule A-1. Here it is: *"Our principal tool for controlling earth people is to convince them that there is no such person as the devil."*

And we may as well give you Rule A-2: *"Almost as effective as convincing the Earth-person that there is no such person as the devil is the trick of making the devil seem ridiculous – giving him a form like a circus clown, complete with red suit, horns, and forked tail. Laughter is almost as good as denial."*

Up here in Celestial City, we never joke about Satan. He is a formidable enemy. Never underestimate him! He is clever, powerful, and energetic – and he never quits.

Sometimes we angels are intimidated when we are assigned to someone important. Not Satan. Do you remember how he approached Jesus?

He even offered to give him the kingdoms of this world. Imagine the audacity of that! Jesus **created** them, and now He is asked to buy them back by worshiping his archenemy!

Oh, "His Royal Lowness," Satan, will stop at nothing. He is brazen. And powerful.

You may remember Paul's description of the people who had been under Satan's power:

"You he has made alive who were dead in trespasses and sins in which you once walked, following the course of this world, following the prince of the power of the air, the spirit that is now at work in the sons of disobedience."

Earth-people don't think much about the lower-archy of hell, the power of evil. When they say, "The devil made me do it," they are, for the most part, joking.

Be aware of the principle at work: **No one does good without first overcoming the tendency to do evil.**

No one surrenders to God's will without first getting victory over the power of the *"prince of the power of the air, the spirit that is now at work in the sons of disobedience."*

You are discovering that.

You are being attacked, tantalized, tormented, and tested. You find yourself questioning, "How did I get into this?"

Well, I am not asking for sympathy, but let me tell you that I am battling, too. Only a few of Satan's arrows get through to you. I have grabbed several fistfuls of them.

Does that sound grim? It isn't.

It's a battle all right, but you are worth it.

The main thing to remember is that when Jesus confronted the temptations of Satan, the angels came and ministered to Him.

That's right, when He was on Earth, even Jesus needed us. I wasn't personally present for the battle in the wilderness, but it looked for a moment as though I might be summoned when He said, *"I might have called twelve legions of angels"* during the arrest and crucifixion episode. We stood ready to come and take him from the cross and to destroy the enemy.

It is good to remember, E.W., that Jesus understands your situation. He has been there.

And he has won the battle.

So be encouraged. You will win, too. But not without a fight.

I hope I haven't loaded you down with too much respect for your enemy. Satan is powerful. And he is clever. And he is brazen. But we angels have a few tricks of our own.

There's a lot more to being an angel than strumming on a harp. Like fighting. And winning.

Faithfully,

Michael XXII

The Promise of Prosperity (1984)

Is it wrong to be prosperous? Is it selfish to try to be?

Before we talk about the "rightness" or "wrongness" of prosperity, let's make one thing clear: It is possible for you to prosper.

Truthfully, prosperity is a promise.

If this sounds like an invitation to become a money-grabbing materialist, let me talk about the word *prosperity* and, even better, the experience of prosperity.

Money may be a part of prosperity, but not necessarily. Occasionally we meet someone whose desperate desire for money (though he may seem to have an abundance of it) reveals a mental or spiritual miser. Money, in that case, is but a masquerade for poverty.

Let's put the record straight. Prosperity means the fulfillment of worthwhile goals – whatever they are.

It has been told that Albert Einstein, the mathematical genius whose theories ushered us into the atomic age, once used a large check from the Ford Foundation for a bookmark. The $10,000 – a large amount of money in those days – was not important to him. Financially he cared only for subsistence, but his creative genius flourished and prospered. For Einstein, a treasure house of ideas was prosperity.

Michaelangelo, sculptor and artist, said, "I am happy only when I have a chisel in my hand." His genius flourished among the marble chips.

In our day Mother Theresa of Calcutta has prospered – even in the midst of abject poverty. Her dreams are being fulfilled.

The Bible speaks often of prosperity. In fact, this magnificent book actually promises prosperity and then outlines a path to its achievement. *Proverbs*, the book of God's wisdom handed down to us through Solomon, covers all the bases.

Here are 50 Principles of Prosperity gleaned from the pages of Proverbs to get you started on the road to greater fulfillment of your dreams for success in life. *"Wisdom gives a good long life, riches, honor, pleasure, and peace." 3:9-10*

Bible verses are from *The Living Bible* (Tyndale House, 1971).

1. God provides wisdom in all sizes, colors, and shapes to fit every need.

"I want to make the simple-minded wise. I want to warn young men about some problems they will face. I want those already wise to become wiser and become leaders by exploring the depths of meaning in these nuggets of truth." 1:4-6

2. Wisdom is being prepared for trouble in advance.

". . .when you are engulfed by anguish and distress, then I will not answer your cry for help." 1:24-28

3. Internalize the principles of wisdom, so that you respond intuitively when you need guidance.

"For wisdom and truth will enter the very center of your being, filling your life with joy." 2:10

4. God is wiser than you are. Trust Him first and you will gain the trust of people.

"If you want favor with God and man, and a reputation for good judgment and common sense, then trust the Lord completely; don't ever trust yourself. In everything you do, put God first, and he will direct you and crown your efforts with success." 3:4-5

5. Paying God first is the Law of Prosperity. Putting God first makes it possible for God to prosper you.

"Honor the Lord by giving him the first part of all your income and he will fill your barns with wheat and barley and overflow your wine vats with the finest wines." 3:9-10

6. Unpaid advisors can be your best friends.

"Young man, do not resent it when God chastens and corrects you, for his punishment is proof of his love." 3:11-12

7. Wisdom that guides the planets can surely be trusted to guide the plans of people.

"The Lord's wisdom founded the earth; his understanding established all the universe and space." 3:19

8. Wisdom and common sense are two wings of the same bird. You can't fly with only one wing.

"Have two goals: wisdom – that is, knowing and doing right – and common sense. Don't let them slip away, for they fill you with living energy, and are a feather in your cap." 3:21

9. Pay your bills promptly.

"Don't withhold repayment of your debts. Don't say 'some other time,' if you can pay now. 3:27-28

10. Honor wisdom and wisdom will honor you.

"Determination to be wise is the first step in becoming wise!" 4:7

11. Find good role models and follow them.

"Don't do as the wicked do. Avoid their haunts – turn away, go somewhere else, . . ." 4:14-15

12. Keep romance alive at home, and you won't be lured down the wrong path.

"Drink water from your own well, my son – be faithful and true to your own wife." 5:15

13. Admit bad deals and back out.

"Son, if you endorse a note for someone you hardly know, guaranteeing his debt, you are in serious trouble. You may have trapped yourself by your agreement. Quick! Get out of it if you possibly can. Swallow your pride; don't let embarrassment stand in the way. Go and beg to have your name erased." 6:1-3

14. Work diligently and conserve during good times because tough times will come.

"Take a lesson from the ants, you lazy fellow. Learn from their ways and be wise! For though they have no king to make them work, yet they labor all summer, gathering food for the winter. 6:6

15. Every decision is an opportunity for guidance.

"Can't you hear the voice of wisdom? She is standing at the city gates and at every fork in the road, and at the door of every house." 8:1-3

16. What you learn from your work is worth more than what you earn from it.

"For the value of wisdom is far above rubies; nothing can be compared with it." 8:11

17. God honors honest work – he resents lazy people.

"Lazy men are soon poor; hard workers get rich." 10-4

18. Be alert for opportunities.

"A wise youth makes hay while the sun shines, but what a shame to see a lad who sleeps away his hour of opportunity. 10:5

19. Attitude is your best asset.

"The good man is covered with blessings from head to foot, but an evil man inwardly curses his luck." 10:6

20: Listen to others' experience. As is often said, "You don't have time to make all the mistakes yourself."

". . . with good counselors there is safety." 11:14

21. Be generous. If you look out for other people's welfare, God will look out for you.

"It is possible to give away and become richer. It is also possible to hold on too tightly and lose everything. Yes, the liberal man will be rich. By watering others, he waters himself." 11:24-25

22: Don't be afraid of humble work.

"It is better to get your hands dirty and eat, than to be too proud to work and starve." 12:9

23. Make promises sparingly and keep them faithfully.

"God delights in those who keep their promises, and abhors those who don't." 12:22

24. A word of encouragement may be the best bonus you can give your fellow workers or employees. Anxiety and uncertainty are expensive.

"Anxious hearts are very heavy but a word of encouragement works wonders!" 12:25

25. Look to the future. You can't sail a boat on yesterday's wind.

"A wise man looks ahead; a fool doesn't, and even brags about it." 13:16; 14:8

26. Surround yourself with people who are wiser than you.

"Be with wise men and become wise. 13:20

27. Make your body your servant, not your master.

"The good man eats to live . . . the evil man lives to eat." 13:25

28. Welcome a little confusion. The most orderly, predictable place in the world is a cemetery.

"An empty stable stays clean – but there is no income from an empty stable." 14:4

29. So long as the flame of enthusiasm glows you won't burn out. (Enthusiasm literally means "having God within.")

"The backslider gets bored with himself; the godly man's life is exciting." 14:14

30. Talk is expensive if it keeps you from taking action on your ideas.

"Work brings profit; talk brings poverty!" 14:23

31. Learn to deal with stress and anger.

"A wise man controls his temper. He knows that anger causes mistakes." 14:29

32. Tying too hard can be counter-productive.

"A relaxed attitude lengthens a man's life; jealousy rots it away." 14:30

33. When people feel they are learning something they are happy. Happy people are productive.

"A wise teacher makes learning a joy." 15:2

34. A thin dime has two sides. So does every situation. Learn to listen to both sides.

"Plans go wrong with too few counselors; many counselors bring success." 15:22

35. When God directs your thoughts, you can trust Him with your life.

"Commit your work to the Lord, then it will succeed." 16:3

36. If you are pleasing God, then you eventually will be able to get along with people.

"When a man is trying to please God, God makes even his worst enemies to be at peace with him." 16:7

37. Money isn't the only motivation.

"A dry crust eaten in peace is better than steak every day along with argument and strife." 17:1

38. The rescue fantasy is an expensive dream.

"It is poor judgment to countersign another's note, to become responsible for his debts." 17:18

39. Maintain joy in your work. It's medicinal.

"A cheerful heart does good like a medicine, but a broken spirit makes one sick." 17:22

40: Reward excellence with incentives.

"How short-sighted to fine the godly for being good! And to punish the nobles for being honest!" 17:26

41. New ideas are unsettling, but necessary. Encourage them.

"An intelligent man is always open to new ideas. In fact, he looks for them." 18:15

42. Investing time and money in family relationships is good business.

"The man who finds a wife finds a good thing; she is a blessing from the Lord." 18:22

43. Alcohol is an expensive way to energize a business.

"Wine gives false courage; hard liquor leads to brawls; what fools men are to let it master them. . . ." 20:1

44. Your name is a great treasure; protect it.

"If you must choose, take a good name rather than great riches; for to be held in loving esteem is better than silver or gold." 22:1

45. There is always an excuse for not beginning an unpleasant task – but there are no rewards for excuses.

"A lazy man is full of excuses. 'I can't go to work!' he says. 'If I go outside I might meet a lion in the street and be killed!'" 22:13

46. Productivity comes before pleasure.

"Develop your business first before building your house." 24:27

47. If you are not afraid to begin humbly, you may reach the top.

"Do not demand an audience with the king as though you were a powerful prince. It is better to wait for an invitation than to be sent back to the end of the line, publicly disgraced!" 25:6-7

48. Making friends of your enemies is the best way to conquer them.

"If your enemy is hungry, give him food! If he is thirsty, give him something to drink! This will make him ashamed of himself, and God will reward you. 25:22

49. If you are on the right track you don't need to hurry. Get-rich-quick schemes are a shortcut to poverty.

"Trying to get rich quick is evil and leads to poverty." 28:22

50. Don't let sexual stereotypes rob you of valuable skills and abilities.

"If you can find a truly good wife, she is worth more than precious gems! . . . She will not hinder her husband, but help him all her life. . . . Charms can be deceptive and beauty doesn't last, but a woman who fears and reverences God shall be greatly praised." 31:10; 12; 30.

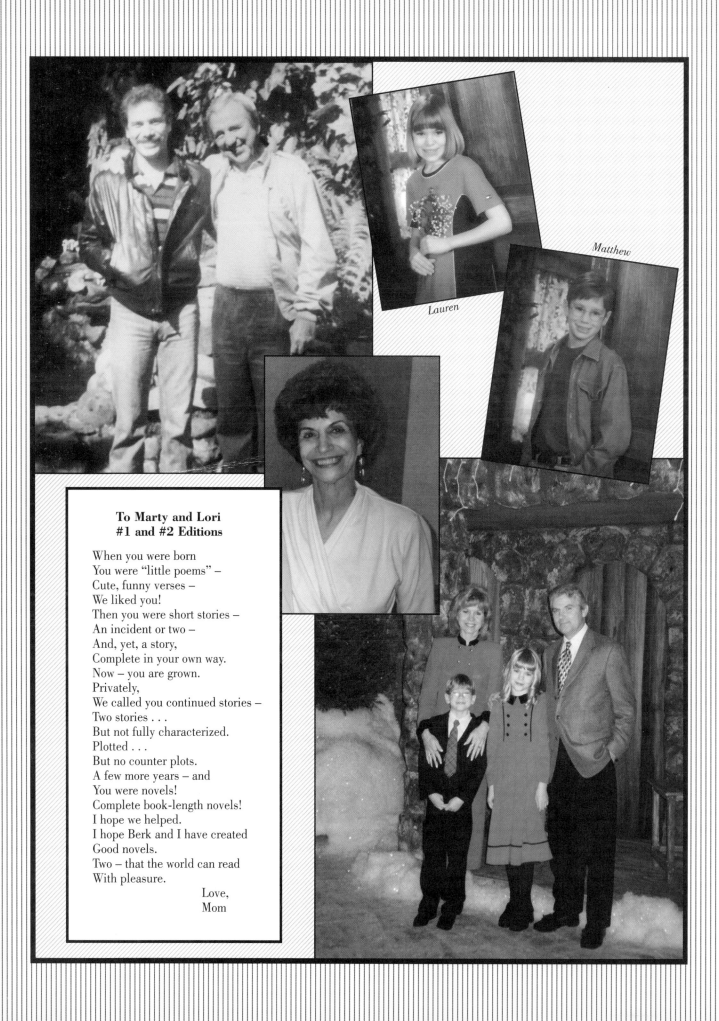

Lauren

Matthew

**To Marty and Lori
#1 and #2 Editions**

When you were born
You were "little poems" –
Cute, funny verses –
We liked you!
Then you were short stories –
An incident or two –
And, yet, a story,
Complete in your own way.
Now – you are grown.
Privately,
We called you continued stories –
Two stories . . .
But not fully characterized.
Plotted . . .
But no counter plots.
A few more years – and
You were novels!
Complete book-length novels!
I hope we helped.
I hope Berk and I have created
Good novels.
Two – that the world can read
With pleasure.

Love,
Mom